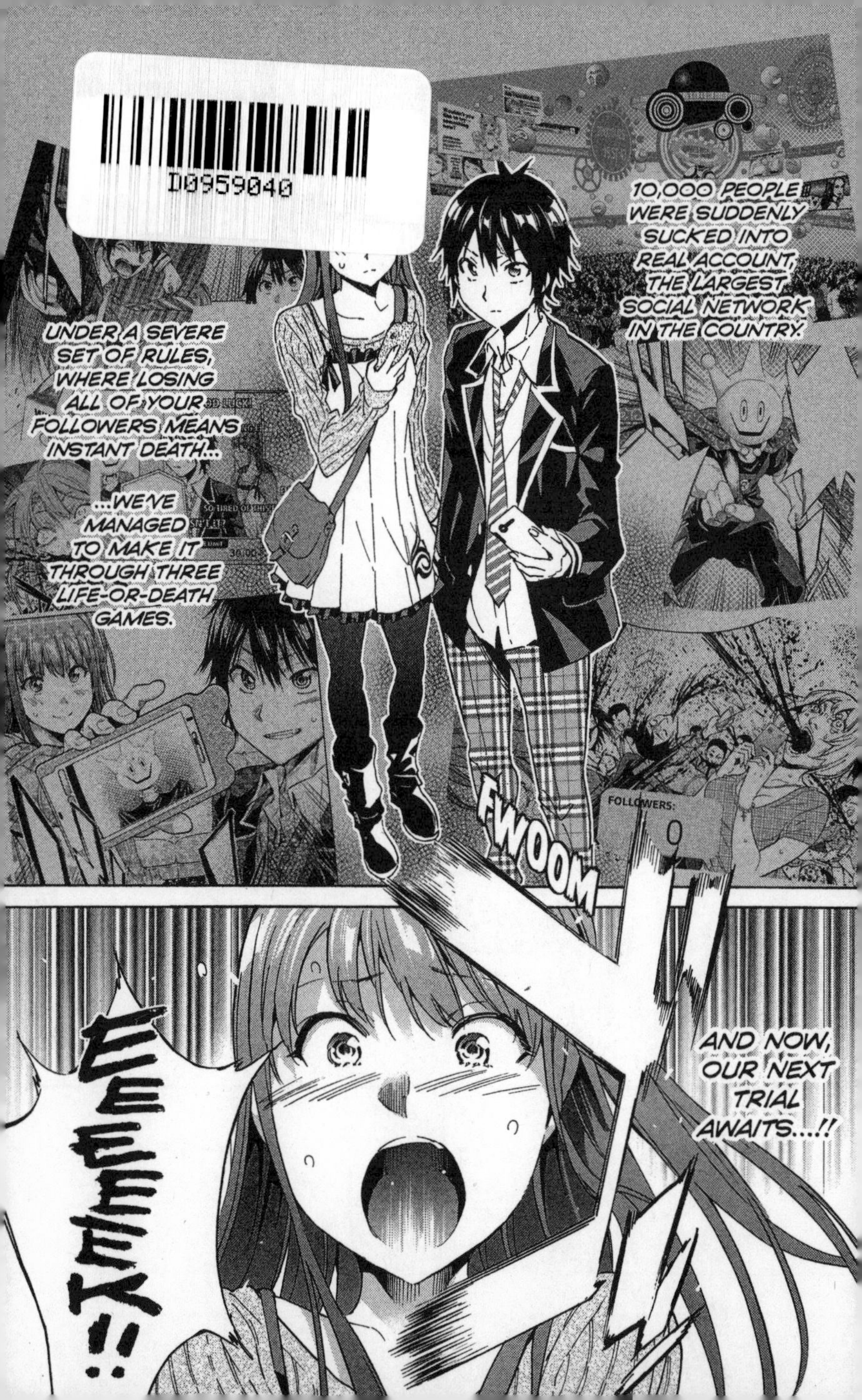
10,000 PEOPLE WERE SUDDENLY SUCKED INTO REAL ACCOUNT, THE LARGEST SOCIAL NETWORK IN THE COUNTRY.
UNDER A SEVERE SET OF RULES, WHERE LOSING ALL OF YOUR FOLLOWERS MEANS INSTANT DEATH...
...WE'VE MANAGED TO MAKE IT THROUGH THREE LIFE-OR-DEATH GAMES.
FOLLOWERS: 9
FWOOM
AND NOW, OUR NEXT TRIAL AWAITS...!!
EEEEEK!!

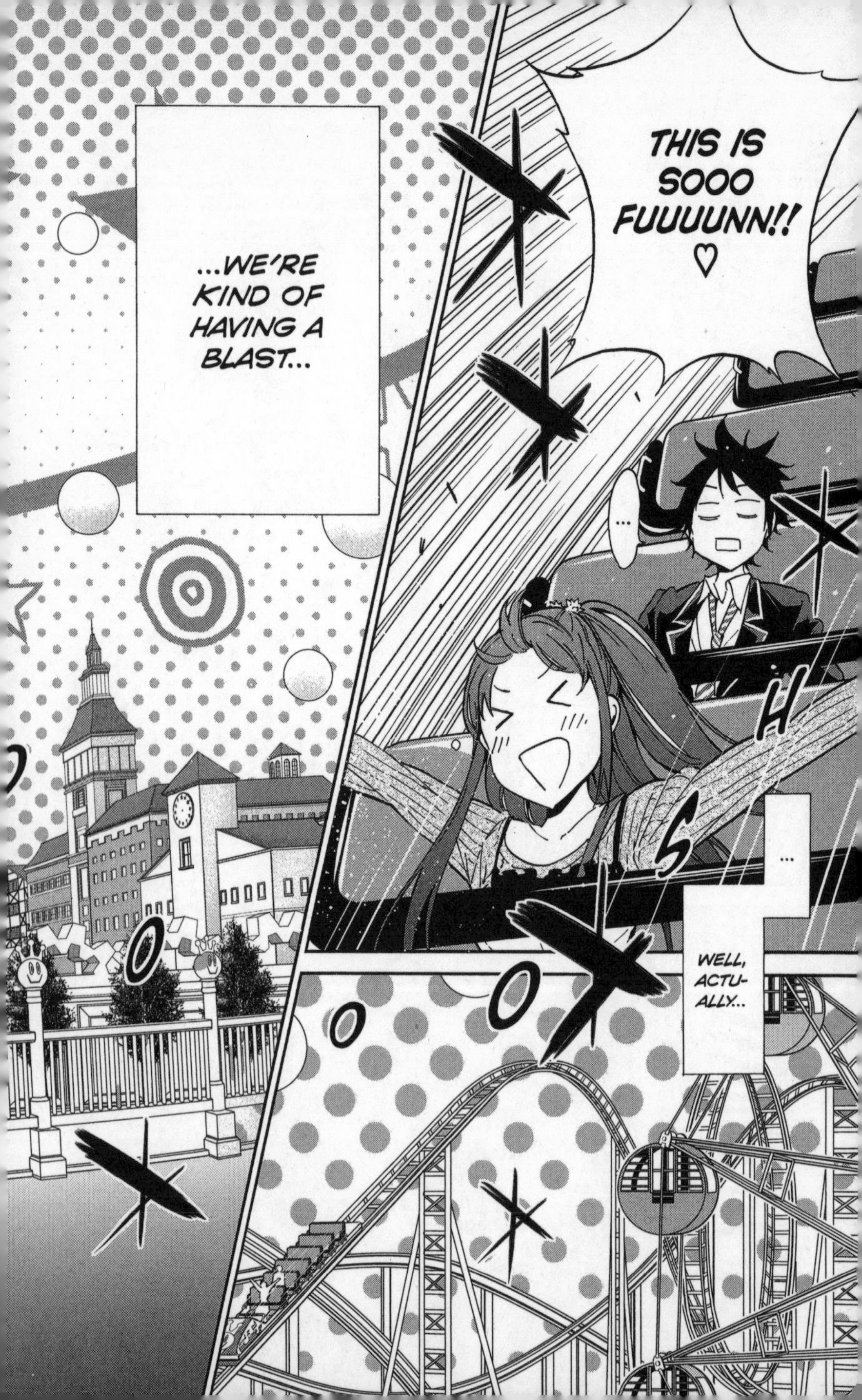
THIS IS SOOO FUUUUNN!! ♡
...
...
WELL, ACTU-ALLY...
...WE'RE KIND OF HAVING A BLAST...

ACCOUNT 7
The End of the Day

4/25
21:53

Great job!
great job!
Great job!

REAL ACCOUNT ® RESORT SEA

ACCOUNT 7   The End of the Day   001
ACCOUNT 8   Appease the Attention-Seeker   023
ACCOUNT 9   The Attention Spiral   043
ACCOUNT 10   Dealing with the Attention   063
ACCOUNT 11   The End of Love   089
ACCOUNT 12   Operation: Reply or Regret   109
ACCOUNT 13   Real and Virtual   132
ACCOUNT 14   The Reply Police   157
EXTRA   Live from Reality   177

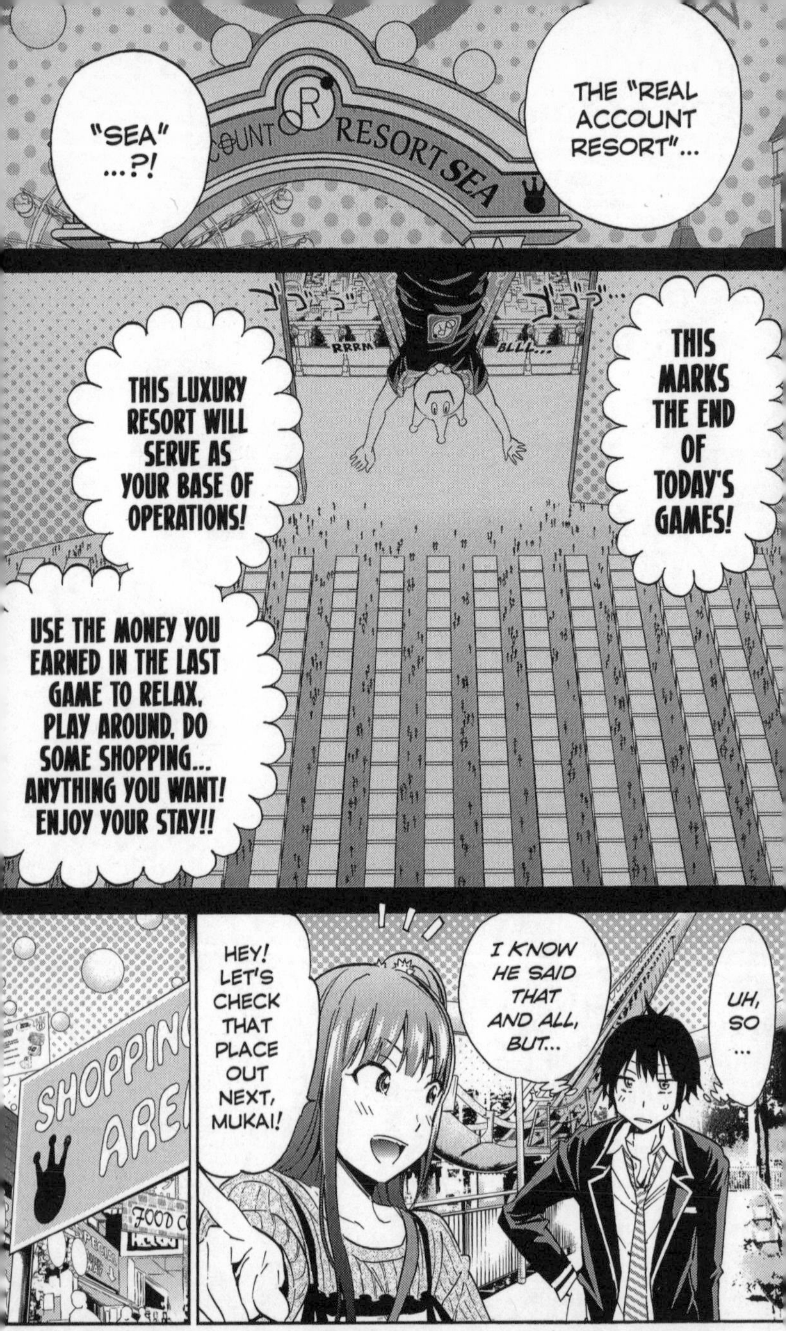
THE "REAL ACCOUNT RESORT"...
"SEA" ...?!
RESORT SEA
THIS MARKS THE END OF TODAY'S GAMES!
BLLL...
RRRM
THIS LUXURY RESORT WILL SERVE AS YOUR BASE OF OPERATIONS!
USE THE MONEY YOU EARNED IN THE LAST GAME TO RELAX, PLAY AROUND, DO SOME SHOPPING... ANYTHING YOU WANT! ENJOY YOUR STAY!!
UH, SO ...
I KNOW HE SAID THAT AND ALL, BUT...
HEY! LET'S CHECK THAT PLACE OUT NEXT, MUKAI!

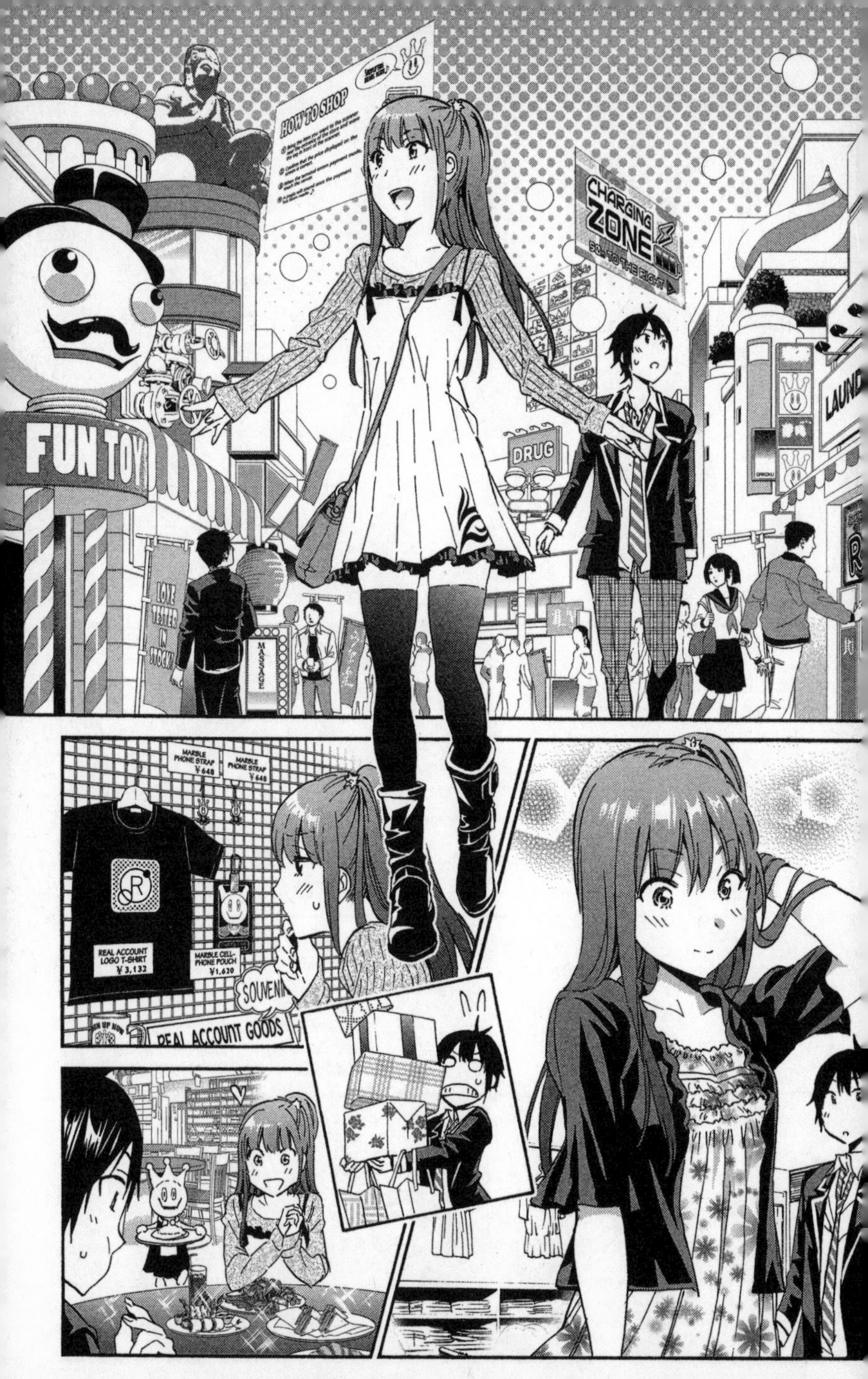
HOW TO SHOP
CHARGING ZONE
50m TO THE RIGHT
LAUND
DRUG
FUN TOY
LOVE TESTER IN STOCK!
MASSAGE
MARBLE PHONE STRAP ¥648
MARBLE PHONE STRAP ¥648
REAL ACCOUNT LOGO T-SHIRT ¥3,132
MARBLE CELL-PHONE POUCH ¥1,620
SOUVENI
REAL ACCOUNT GOODS

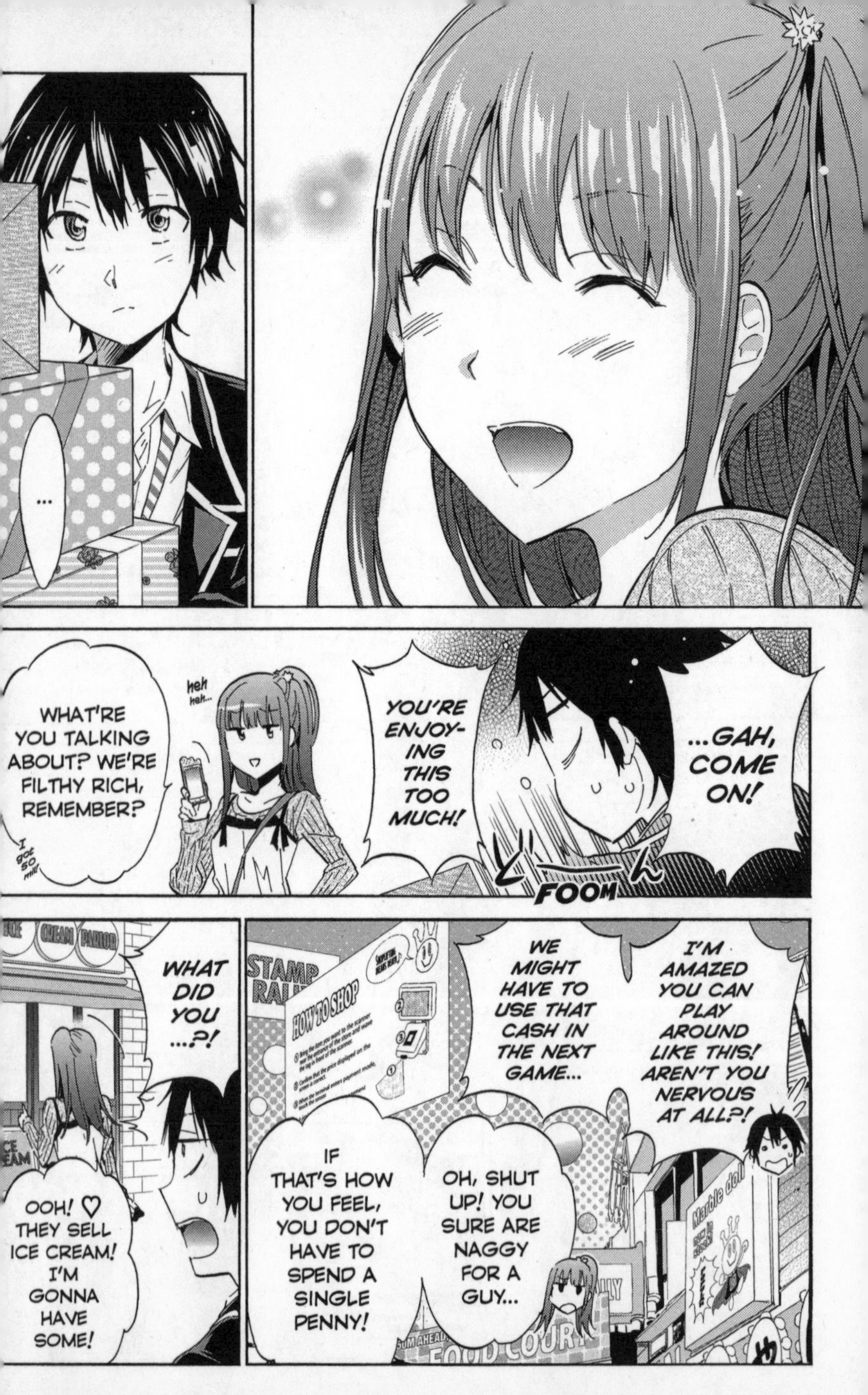
...
...GAH, COME ON!
FOOM
YOU'RE ENJOY-ING THIS TOO MUCH!
heh heh...
WHAT'RE YOU TALKING ABOUT? WE'RE FILTHY RICH, REMEMBER?
I got SO rich!
I'M AMAZED YOU CAN PLAY AROUND LIKE THIS! AREN'T YOU NERVOUS AT ALL?!
WE MIGHT HAVE TO USE THAT CASH IN THE NEXT GAME...
HOW TO SHOP
OH, SHUT UP! YOU SURE ARE NAGGY FOR A GUY...
IF THAT'S HOW YOU FEEL, YOU DON'T HAVE TO SPEND A SINGLE PENNY!
CREAM PARLOR
WHAT DID YOU ...?!
OOH! ♡ THEY SELL ICE CREAM! I'M GONNA HAVE SOME!

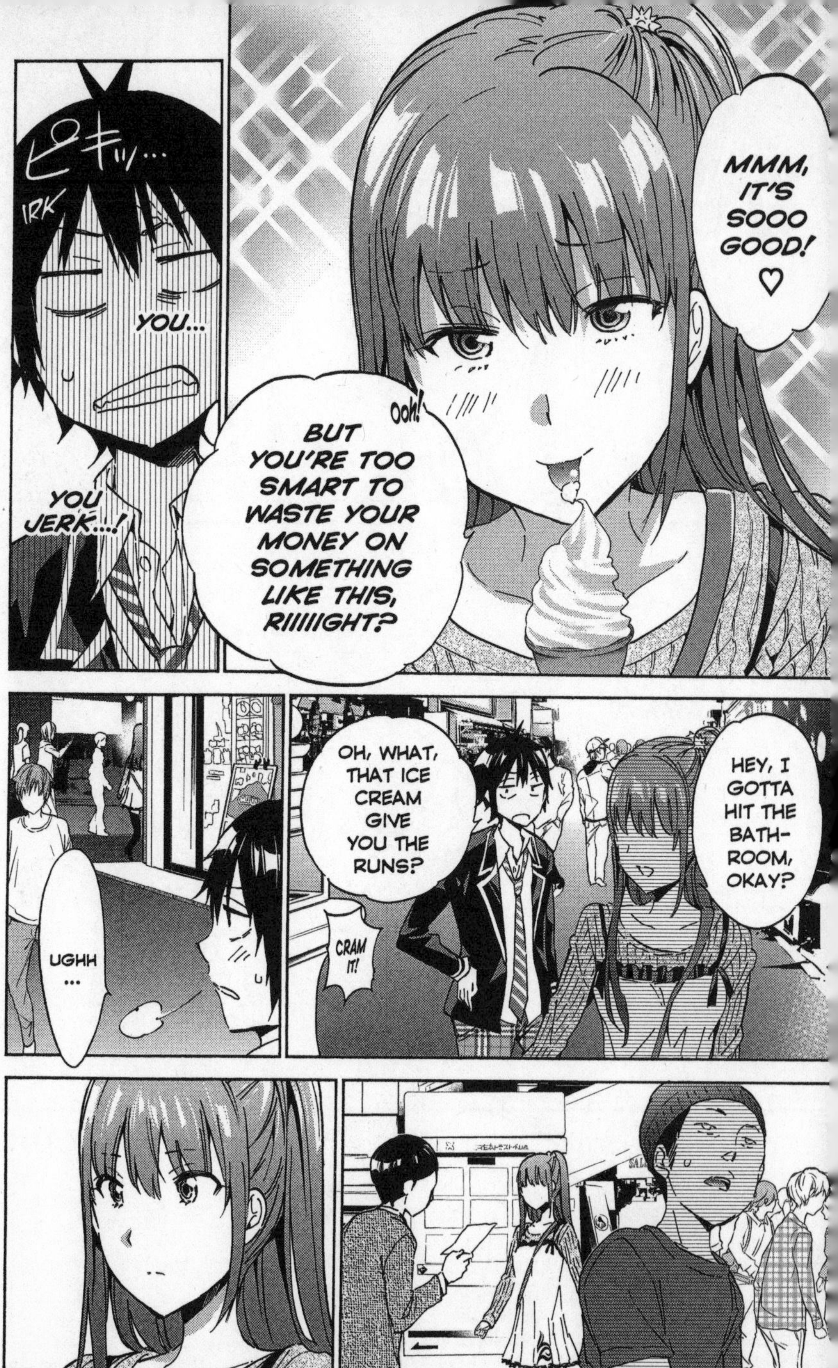
MMM, IT'S SOOO GOOD! ♡
Ooh!
BUT YOU'RE TOO SMART TO WASTE YOUR MONEY ON SOMETHING LIKE THIS, RIIIIIGHT?
ピキッ…
IRK
YOU...
YOU JERK...!
HEY, I GOTTA HIT THE BATH-ROOM, OKAY?
OH, WHAT, THAT ICE CREAM GIVE YOU THE RUNS?
CRAM IT!
UGHH ...

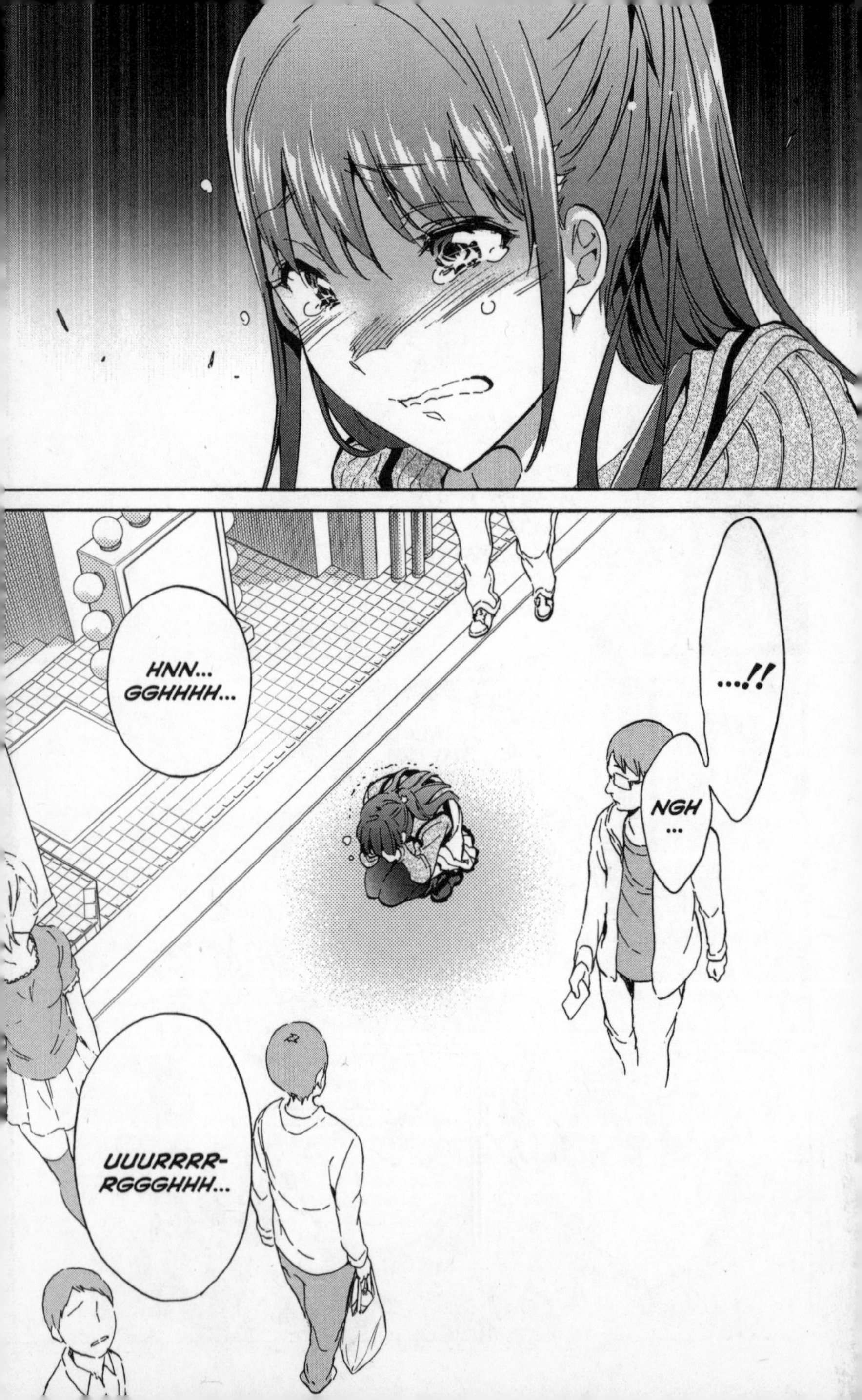
...!!
NGH ...
HNN... GGHHHH...
UUURRRR-RGGGHHH...

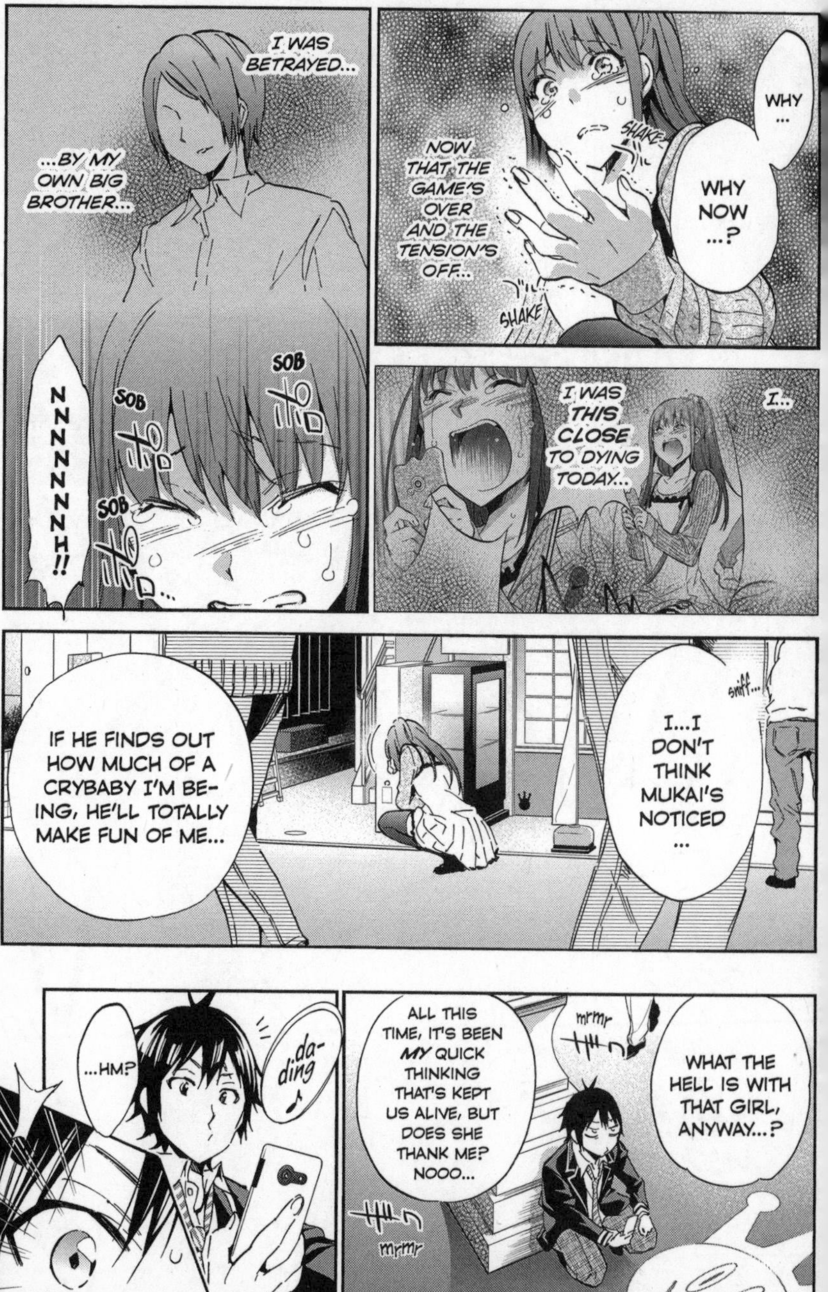
WHY ...
WHY NOW ...?
NOW THAT THE GAME'S OVER AND THE TENSION'S OFF...
SHAKE
SHAKE
I...
I WAS THIS CLOSE TO DYING TODAY...
I WAS BETRAYED...
...BY MY OWN BIG BROTHER...
SOB
SOB
SOB
NNNNNNNNH!!
sniff...
I...I DON'T THINK MUKAI'S NOTICED ...
IF HE FINDS OUT HOW MUCH OF A CRYBABY I'M BE-ING, HE'LL TOTALLY MAKE FUN OF ME...
WHAT THE HELL IS WITH THAT GIRL, ANYWAY...?
mrmr
ALL THIS TIME, IT'S BEEN MY QUICK THINKING THAT'S KEPT US ALIVE, BUT DOES SHE THANK ME? NOOO...
mrmr
da-ding ♪
...HM?

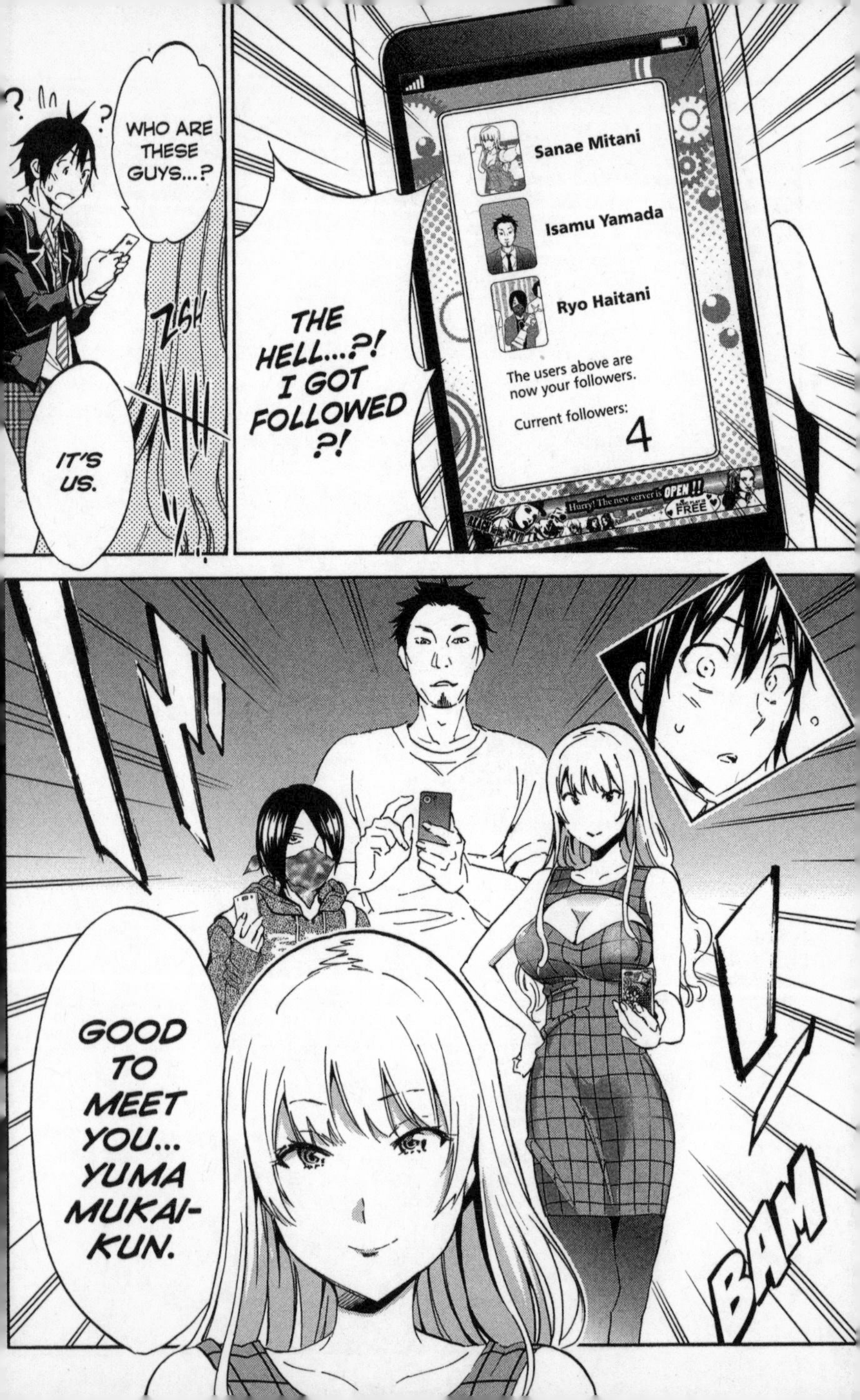
Sanae Mitani
Isamu Yamada
Ryo Haitani
The users above are now your followers.
Current followers:
4
Hurry! The new server is OPEN!!
FREE
THE HELL...?! I GOT FOLLOWED ?!
WHO ARE THESE GUYS...?
ZISH
IT'S US.
BAM
GOOD TO MEET YOU... YUMA MUKAI-KUN.

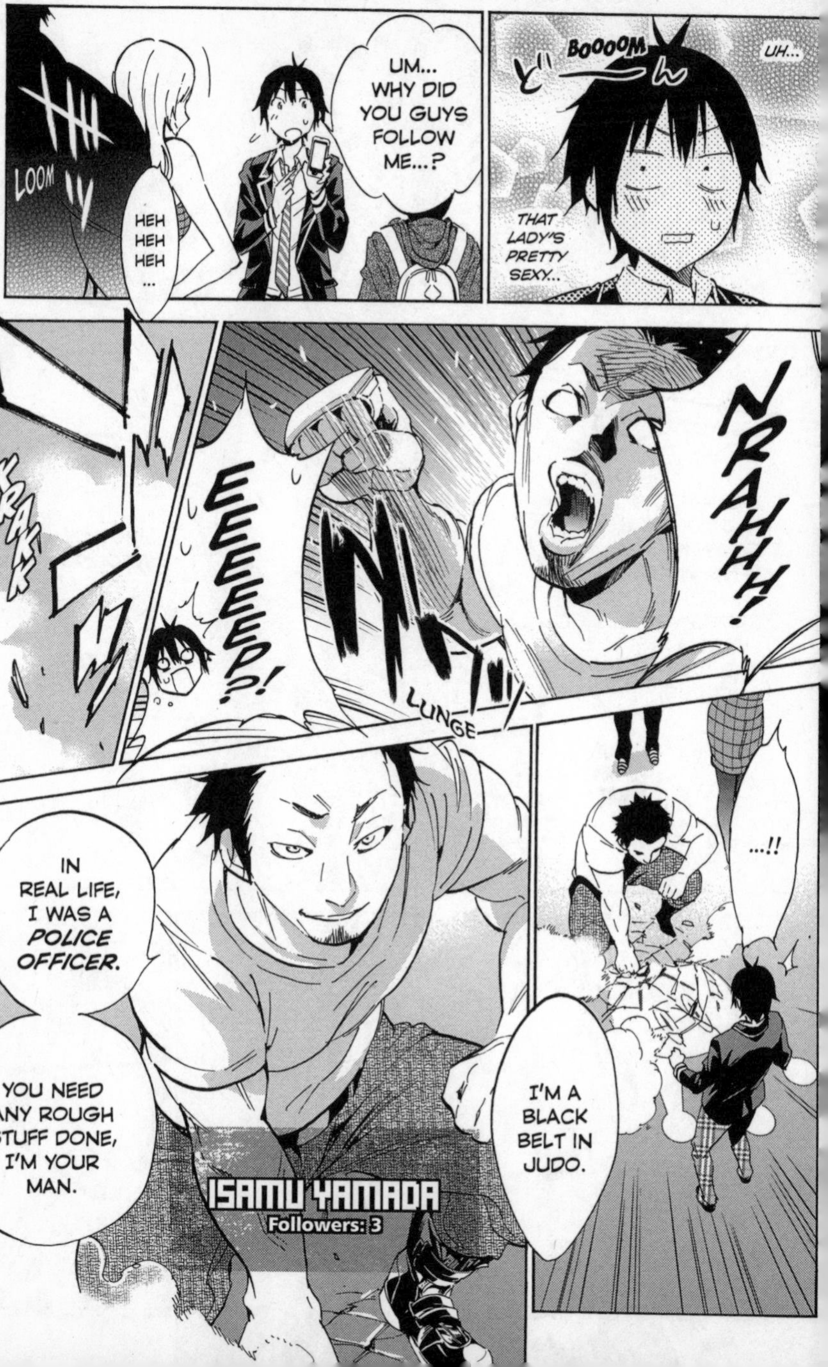
BOOOOM
UH...
THAT LADY'S PRETTY SEXY...
UM... WHY DID YOU GUYS FOLLOW ME...?
LOOM
HEH HEH HEH ...
NRAHHH!
LUNGE
EEEEEEP?!
KRAKK
...!!
I'M A BLACK BELT IN JUDO.
IN REAL LIFE, I WAS A *POLICE OFFICER*.
YOU NEED ANY ROUGH STUFF DONE, I'M YOUR MAN.
ISAMU YAMADA
Followers: 3

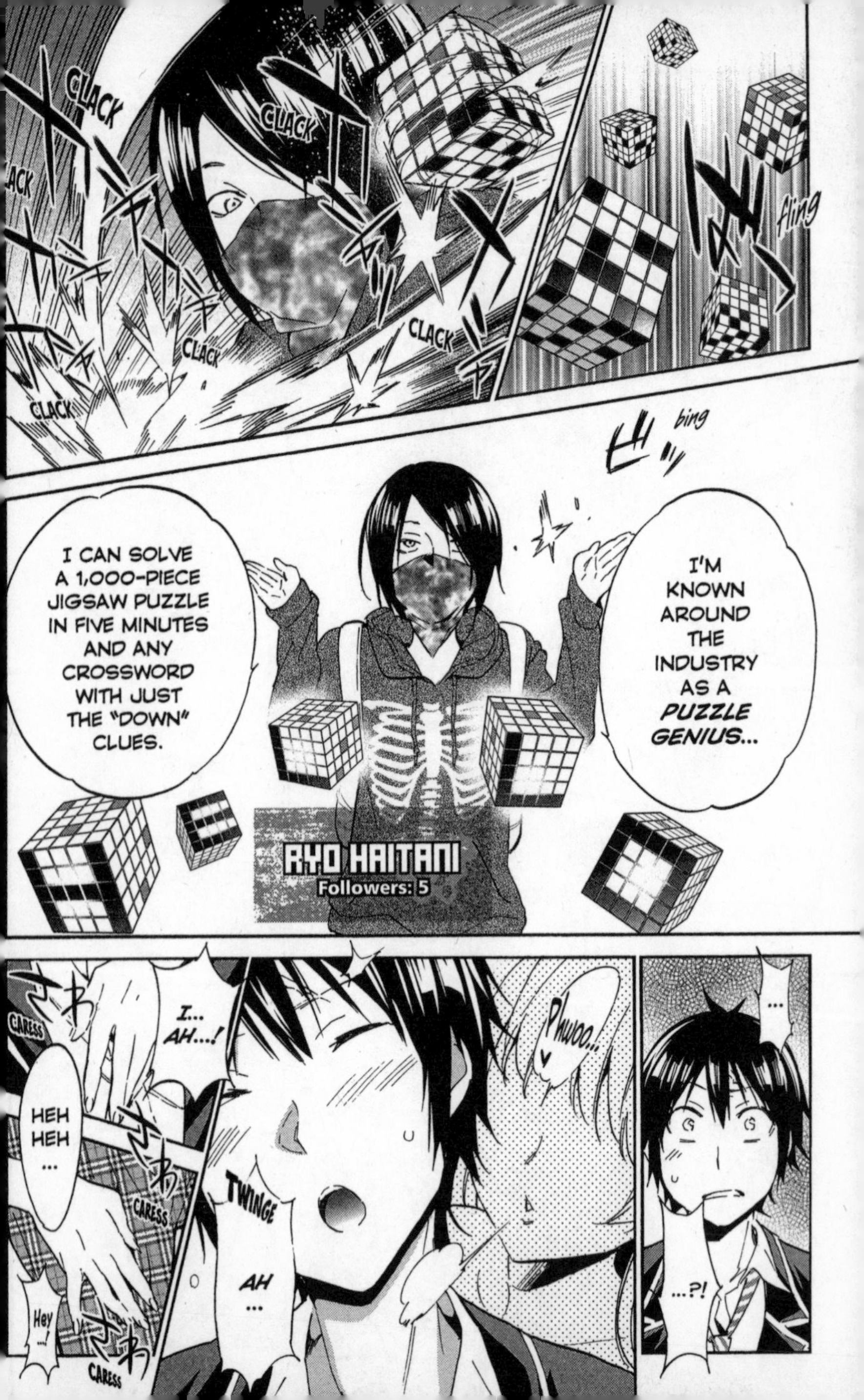
fling
CLACK
CLACK
ACK
CLACK
CLACK
CLACK
bing
I'M KNOWN AROUND THE INDUSTRY AS A *PUZZLE GENIUS*...
I CAN SOLVE A 1,000-PIECE JIGSAW PUZZLE IN FIVE MINUTES AND ANY CROSSWORD WITH JUST THE "DOWN" CLUES.
RYO HAITANI
Followers: 5
...
...?!
Phwoo...
I... AH...!
CARESS
HEH HEH ...
TWINGE
CARESS
AH ...
Hey ...!
CARESS

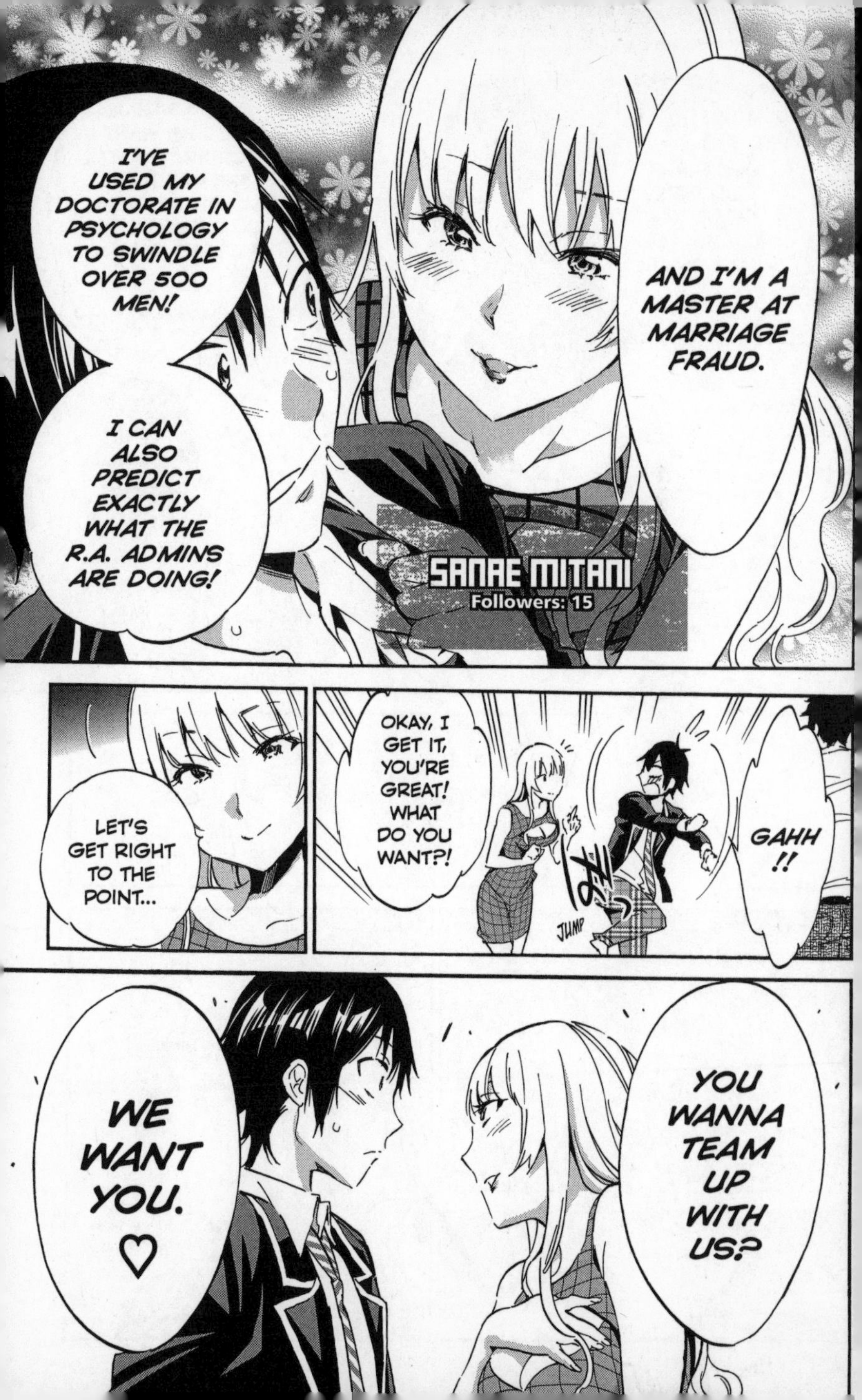
AND I'M A MASTER AT MARRIAGE FRAUD.
I'VE USED MY DOCTORATE IN PSYCHOLOGY TO SWINDLE OVER 500 MEN!
I CAN ALSO PREDICT EXACTLY WHAT THE R.A. ADMINS ARE DOING!
SANAE MITANI
Followers: 15
GAHH!!
OKAY, I GET IT, YOU'RE GREAT! WHAT DO YOU WANT?!
JUMP
LET'S GET RIGHT TO THE POINT...
YOU WANNA TEAM UP WITH US?
WE WANT YOU. ♡

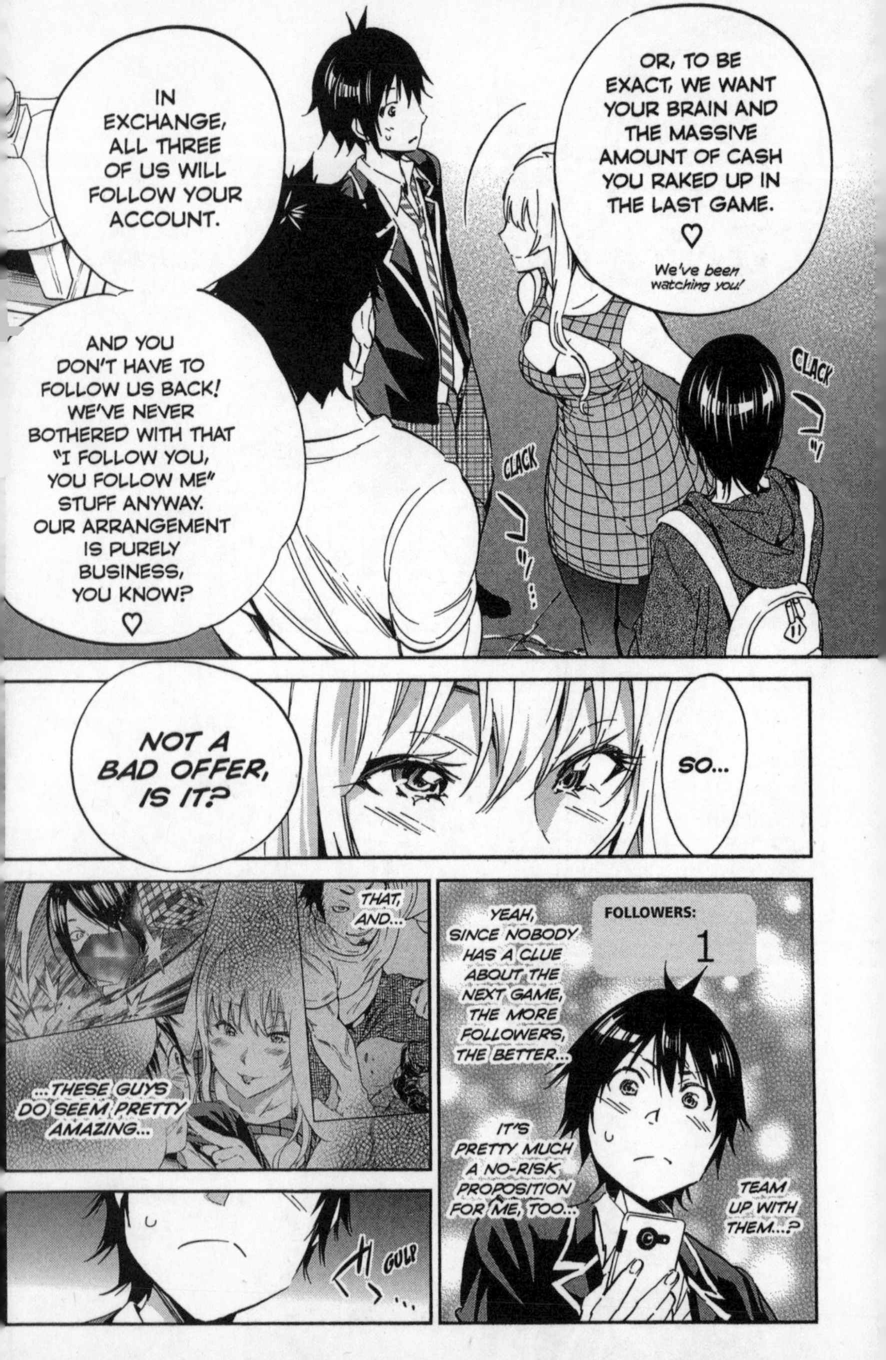
OR, TO BE EXACT, WE WANT YOUR BRAIN AND THE MASSIVE AMOUNT OF CASH YOU RAKED UP IN THE LAST GAME. ♡
We've been watching you!
IN EXCHANGE, ALL THREE OF US WILL FOLLOW YOUR ACCOUNT.
CLACK
CLACK
AND YOU DON'T HAVE TO FOLLOW US BACK! WE'VE NEVER BOTHERED WITH THAT "I FOLLOW YOU, YOU FOLLOW ME" STUFF ANYWAY. OUR ARRANGEMENT IS PURELY BUSINESS, YOU KNOW? ♡
SO...
NOT A BAD OFFER, IS IT?
FOLLOWERS: 1
YEAH, SINCE NOBODY HAS A CLUE ABOUT THE NEXT GAME, THE MORE FOLLOWERS, THE BETTER...
IT'S PRETTY MUCH A NO-RISK PROPOSITION FOR ME, TOO...
TEAM UP WITH THEM...?
THAT, AND...
...THESE GUYS DO SEEM PRETTY AMAZING...
GULP

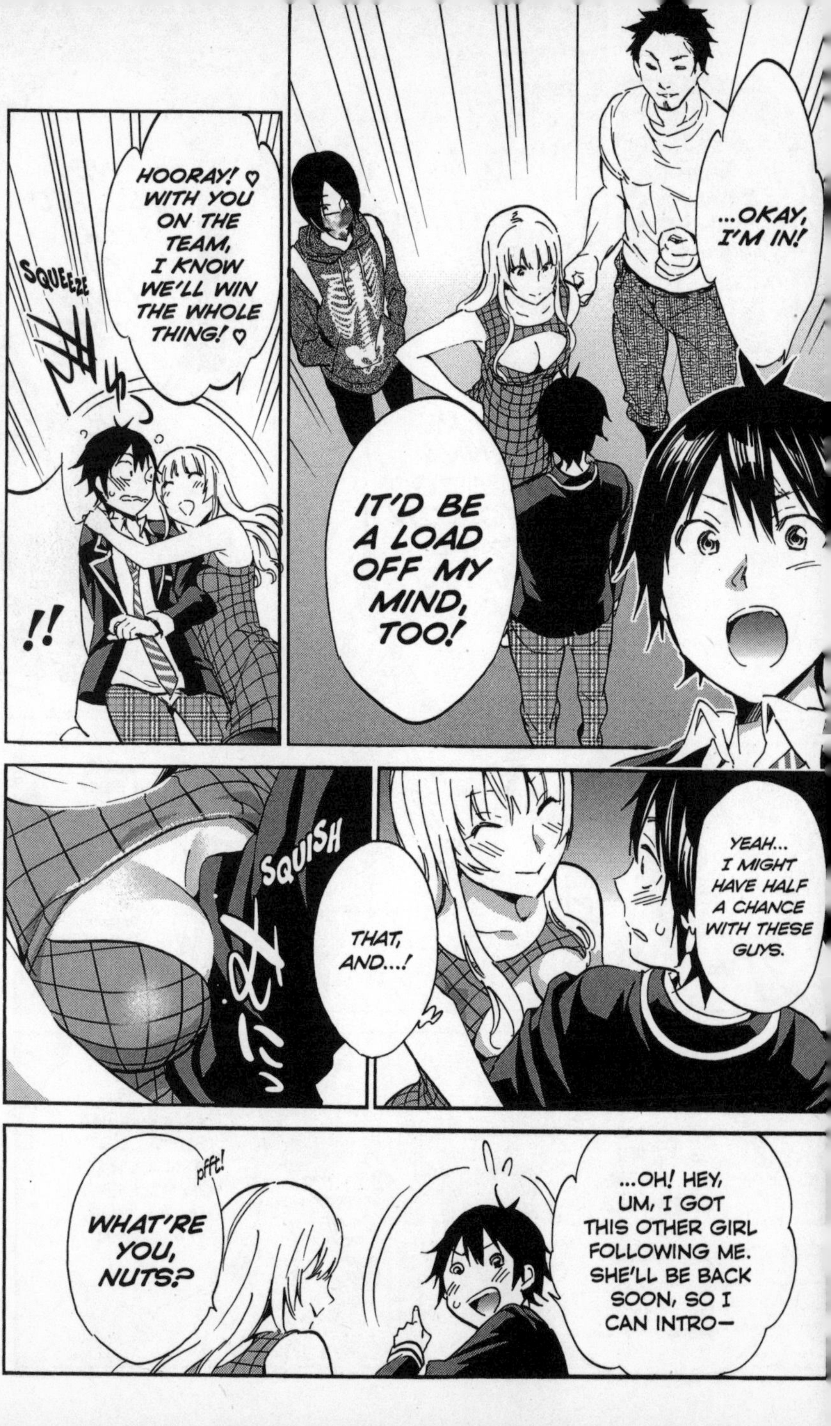
...OKAY, I'M IN!
IT'D BE A LOAD OFF MY MIND, TOO!
HOORAY! ♡ WITH YOU ON THE TEAM, I KNOW WE'LL WIN THE WHOLE THING! ♡
SQUEEZE
!!
YEAH... I MIGHT HAVE HALF A CHANCE WITH THESE GUYS.
THAT, AND...!
SQUISH
...OH! HEY, UM, I GOT THIS OTHER GIRL FOLLOWING ME. SHE'LL BE BACK SOON, SO I CAN INTRO—
pfft!
WHAT'RE YOU, NUTS?

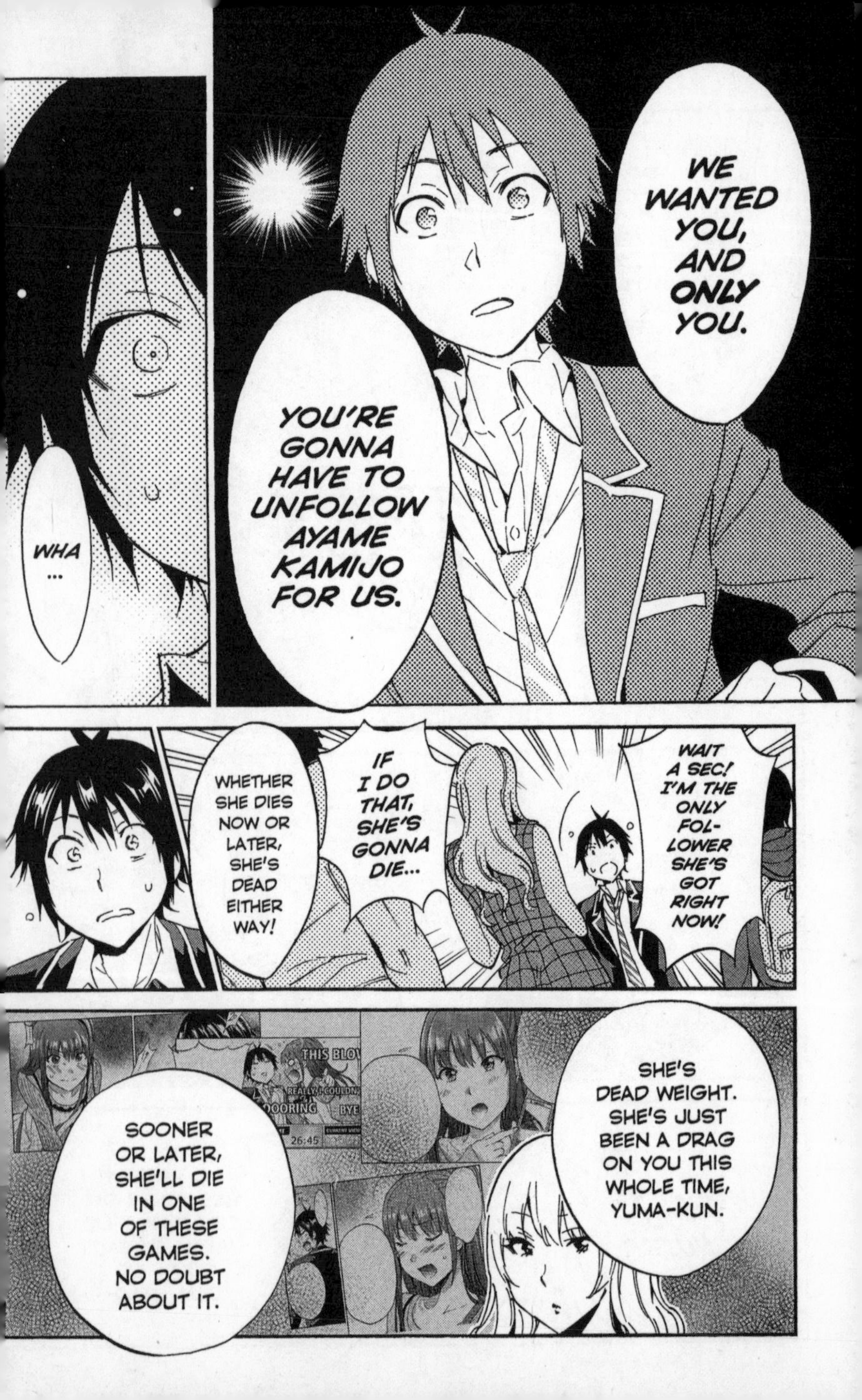
WE WANTED YOU, AND ONLY YOU.
YOU'RE GONNA HAVE TO UNFOLLOW AYAME KAMIJO FOR US.
WHA ...
WAIT A SEC! I'M THE ONLY FOL-LOWER SHE'S GOT RIGHT NOW!
IF I DO THAT, SHE'S GONNA DIE...
WHETHER SHE DIES NOW OR LATER, SHE'S DEAD EITHER WAY!
SHE'S DEAD WEIGHT. SHE'S JUST BEEN A DRAG ON YOU THIS WHOLE TIME, YUMA-KUN.
26:45
SOONER OR LATER, SHE'LL DIE IN ONE OF THESE GAMES. NO DOUBT ABOUT IT.

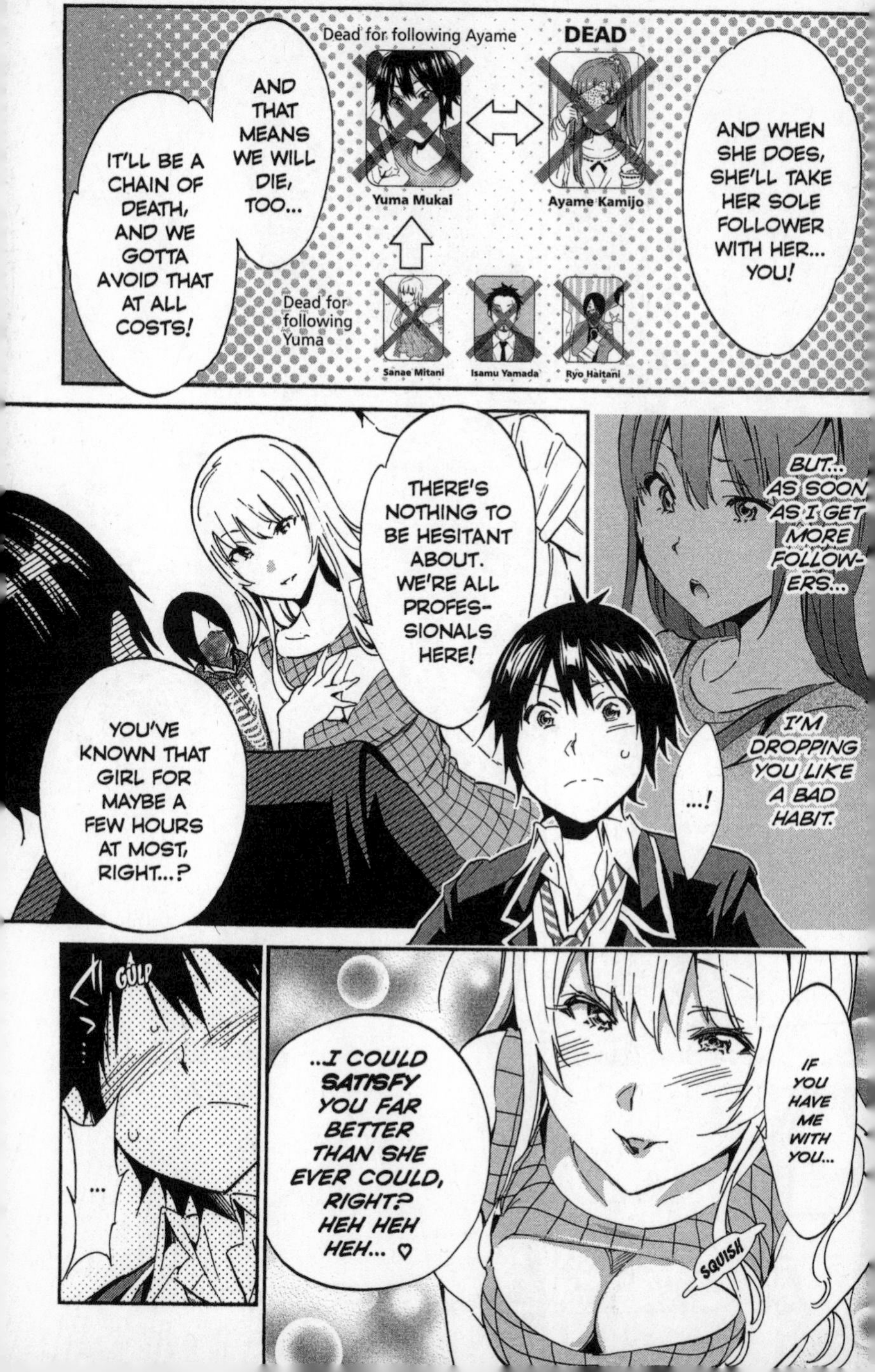
AND WHEN SHE DOES, SHE'LL TAKE HER SOLE FOLLOWER WITH HER... YOU!
DEAD
Dead for following Ayame
Ayame Kamijo
Yuma Mukai
Dead for following Yuma
Sanae Mitani
Isamu Yamada
Ryo Haitani
AND THAT MEANS WE WILL DIE, TOO...
IT'LL BE A CHAIN OF DEATH, AND WE GOTTA AVOID THAT AT ALL COSTS!
BUT... AS SOON AS I GET MORE FOLLOW-ERS...
I'M DROPPING YOU LIKE A BAD HABIT.
THERE'S NOTHING TO BE HESITANT ABOUT. WE'RE ALL PROFES-SIONALS HERE!
...!
YOU'VE KNOWN THAT GIRL FOR MAYBE A FEW HOURS AT MOST, RIGHT...?
IF YOU HAVE ME WITH YOU...
..I COULD SATISFY YOU FAR BETTER THAN SHE EVER COULD, RIGHT? HEH HEH HEH... ♡
SQUISH
GULP
...

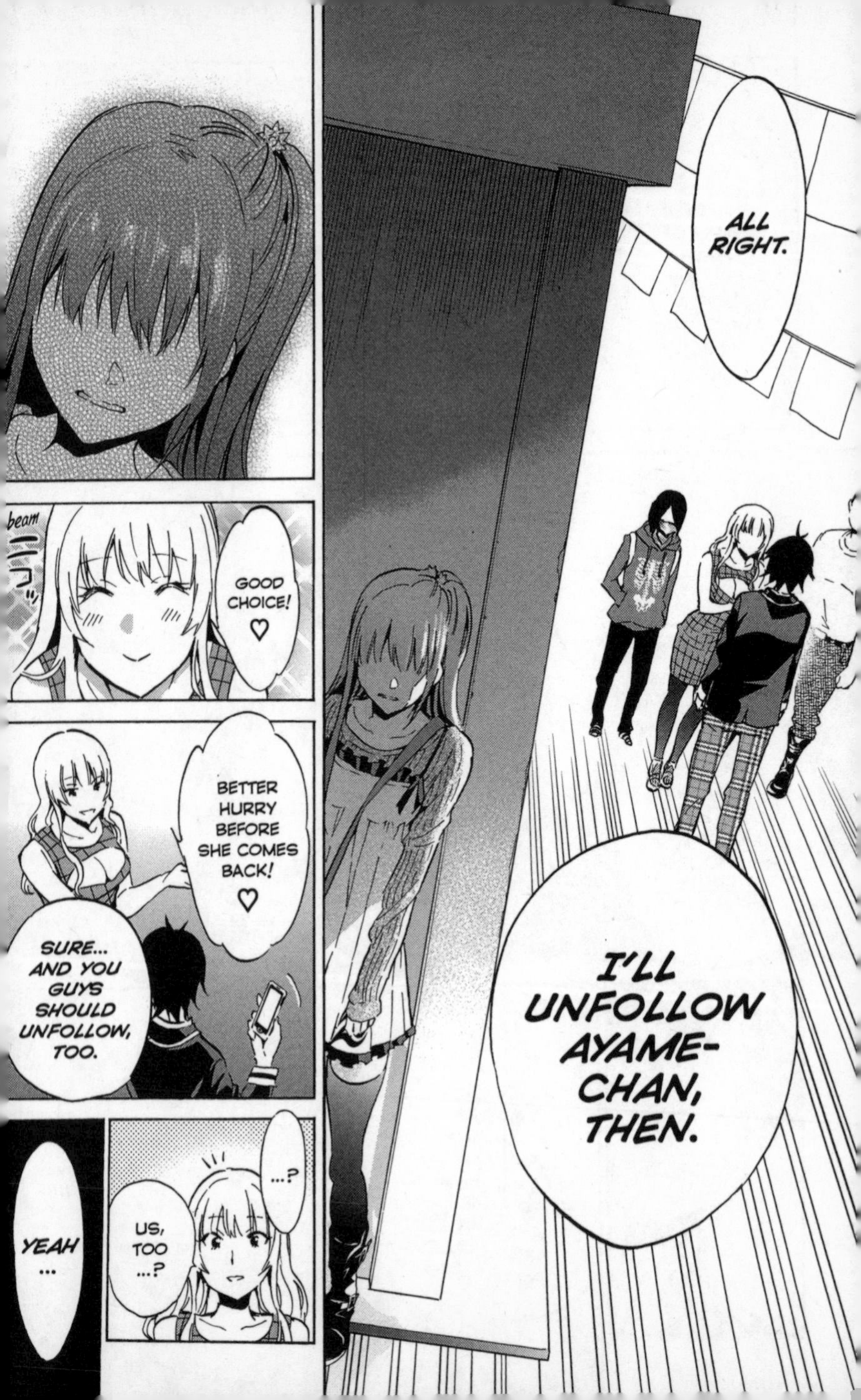
ALL RIGHT.
I'LL UNFOLLOW AYAME-CHAN, THEN.
beam
GOOD CHOICE! ♡
BETTER HURRY BEFORE SHE COMES BACK! ♡
SURE... AND YOU GUYS SHOULD UNFOLLOW, TOO.
...?
US, TOO ...?
YEAH ...

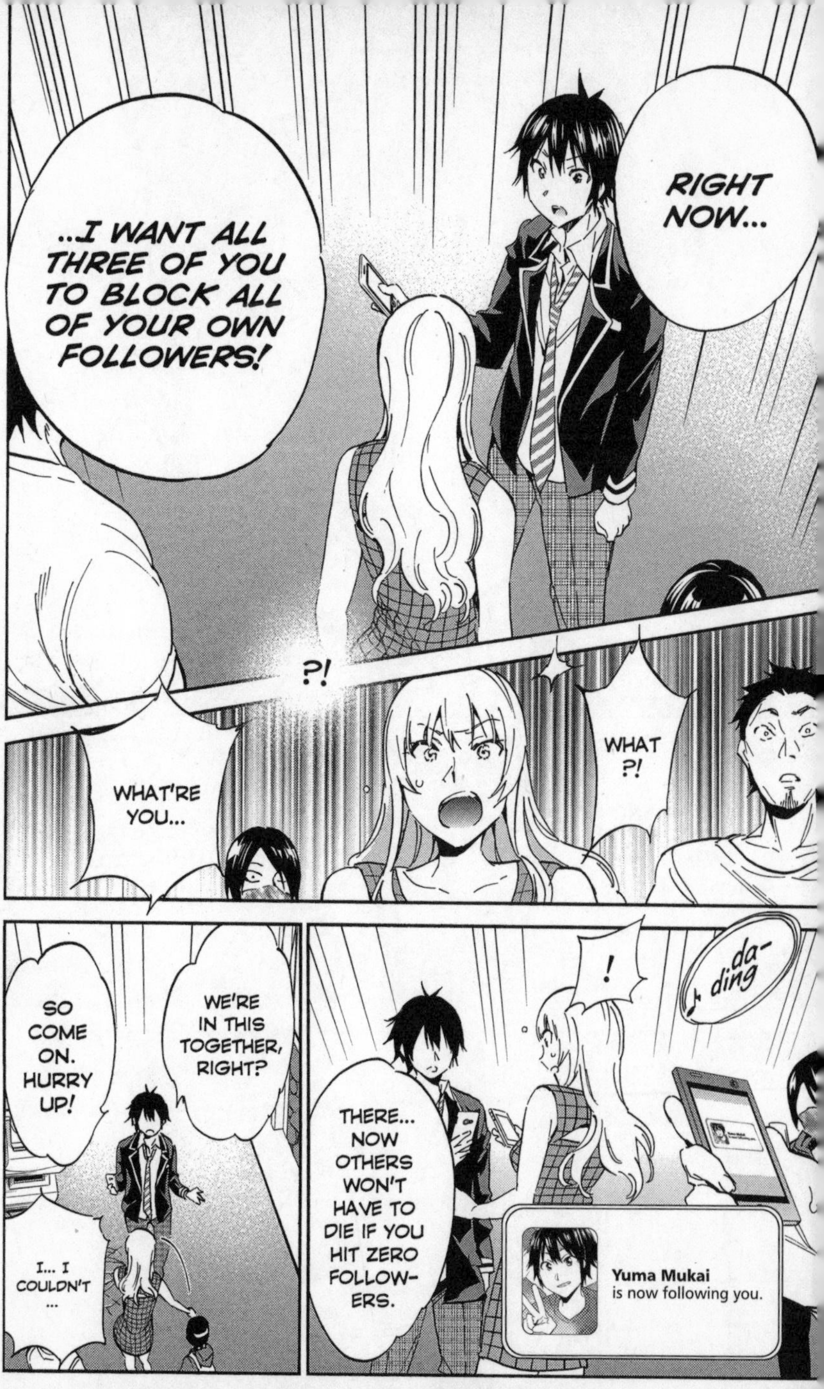
RIGHT NOW...
...I WANT ALL THREE OF YOU TO BLOCK ALL OF YOUR OWN FOLLOWERS!
WHAT ?!
?!
WHAT'RE YOU...
da-ding
!
THERE... NOW OTHERS WON'T HAVE TO DIE IF YOU HIT ZERO FOLLOW-ERS.
Yuma Mukai is now following you.
WE'RE IN THIS TOGETHER, RIGHT?
SO COME ON. HURRY UP!
I... I COULDN'T ...

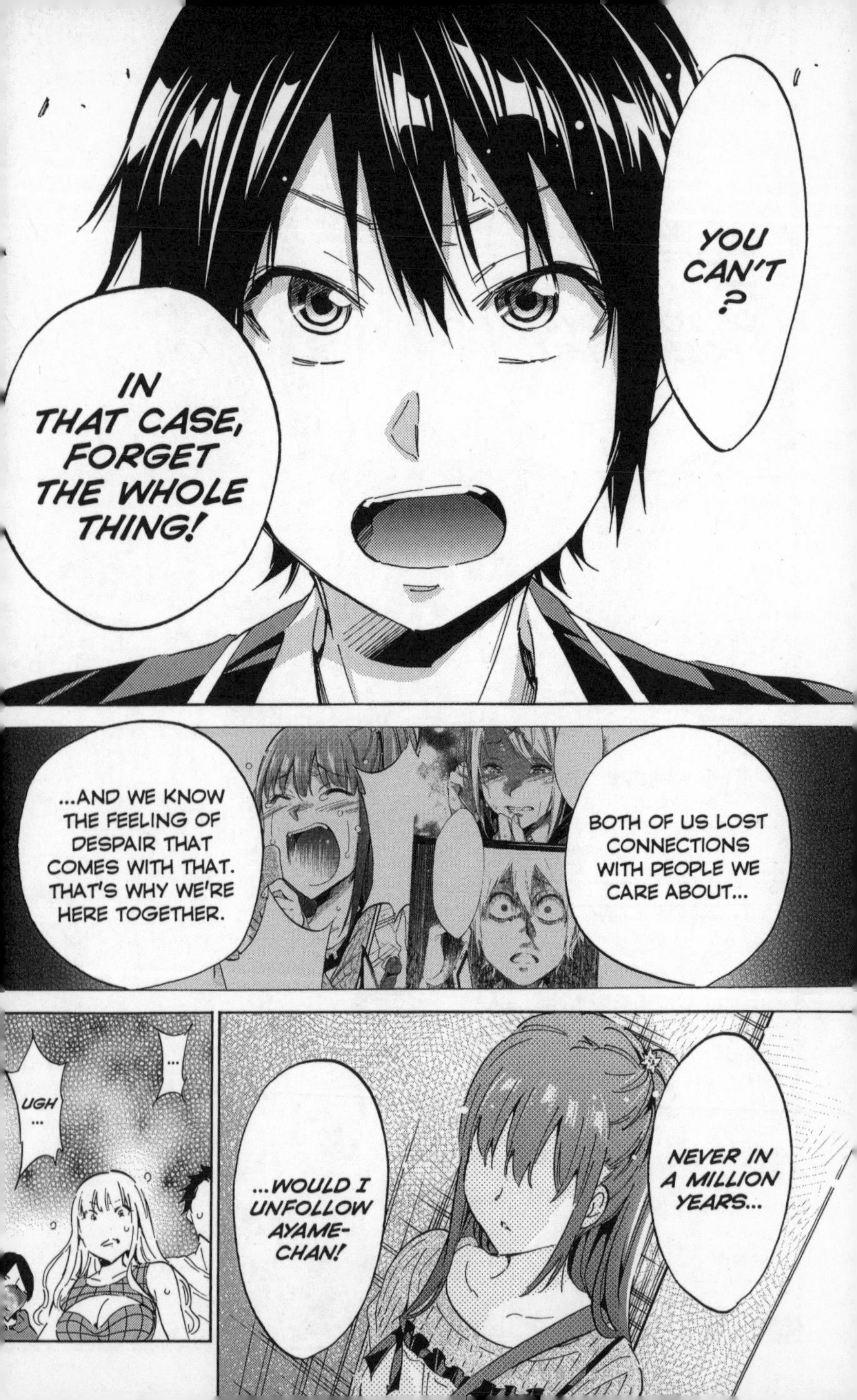
YOU CAN'T?
IN THAT CASE, FORGET THE WHOLE THING!
BOTH OF US LOST CONNECTIONS WITH PEOPLE WE CARE ABOUT...
...AND WE KNOW THE FEELING OF DESPAIR THAT COMES WITH THAT. THAT'S WHY WE'RE HERE TOGETHER.
NEVER IN A MILLION YEARS...
...WOULD I UNFOLLOW AYAME-CHAN!
...
UGH...

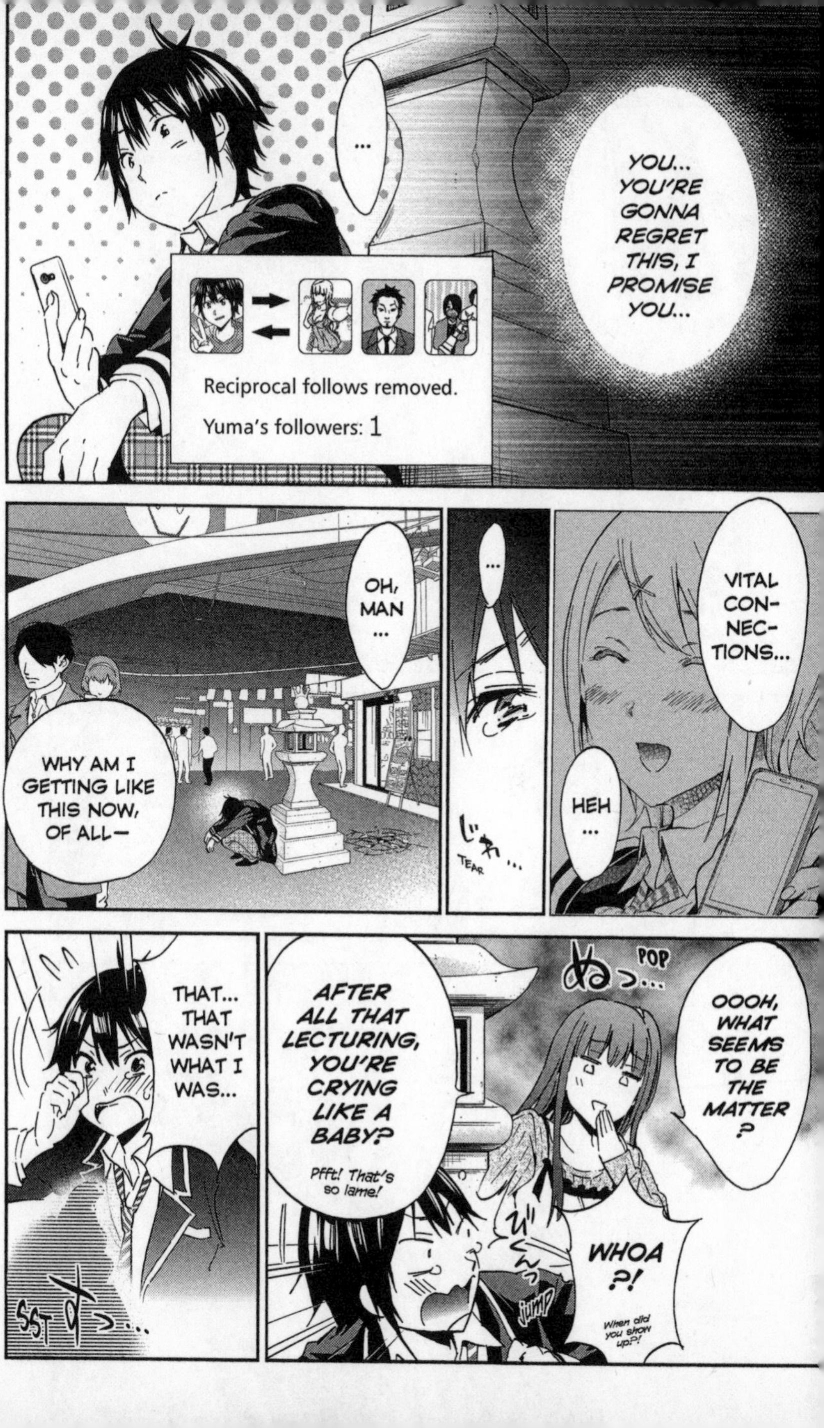
YOU... YOU'RE GONNA REGRET THIS, I PROMISE YOU...
...
Reciprocal follows removed.
Yuma's followers: 1
VITAL CON-NEC-TIONS...
HEH...
...
TEAR
OH, MAN...
WHY AM I GETTING LIKE THIS NOW, OF ALL—
POP
OOOH, WHAT SEEMS TO BE THE MATTER?
AFTER ALL THAT LECTURING, YOU'RE CRYING LIKE A BABY?
Pfft! That's so lame!
WHOA?!
When did you show up?!
JUMP
THAT... THAT WASN'T WHAT I WAS...
SST

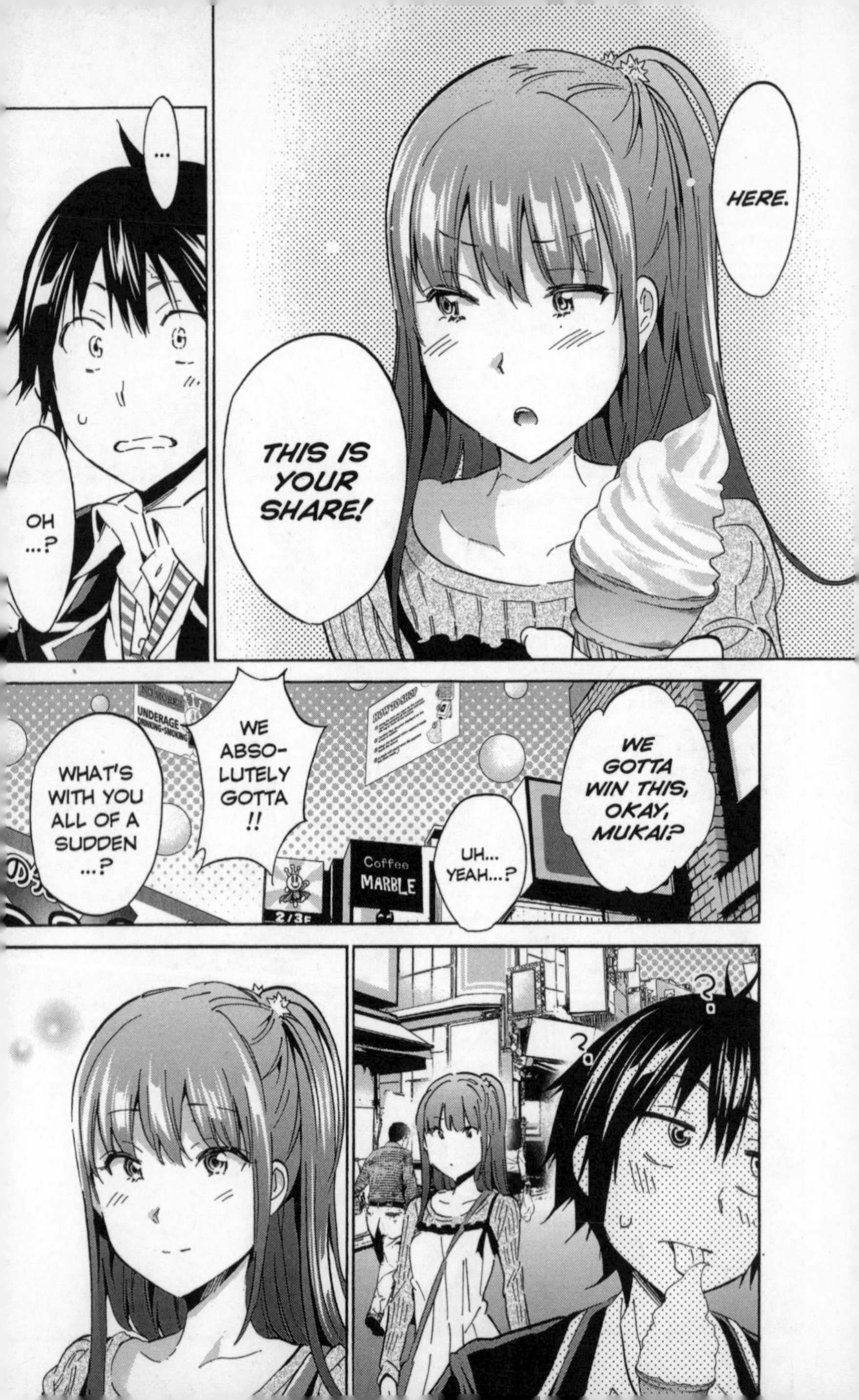
HERE.
THIS IS YOUR SHARE!
...
OH ...?
WE GOTTA WIN THIS, OKAY, MUKAI?
UH... YEAH...?
Coffee MARBLE
2/3F
WE ABSOLUTELY GOTTA !!
NO MORE!
UNDERAGE DRINKING • SMOKING
WHAT'S WITH YOU ALL OF A SUDDEN ...?

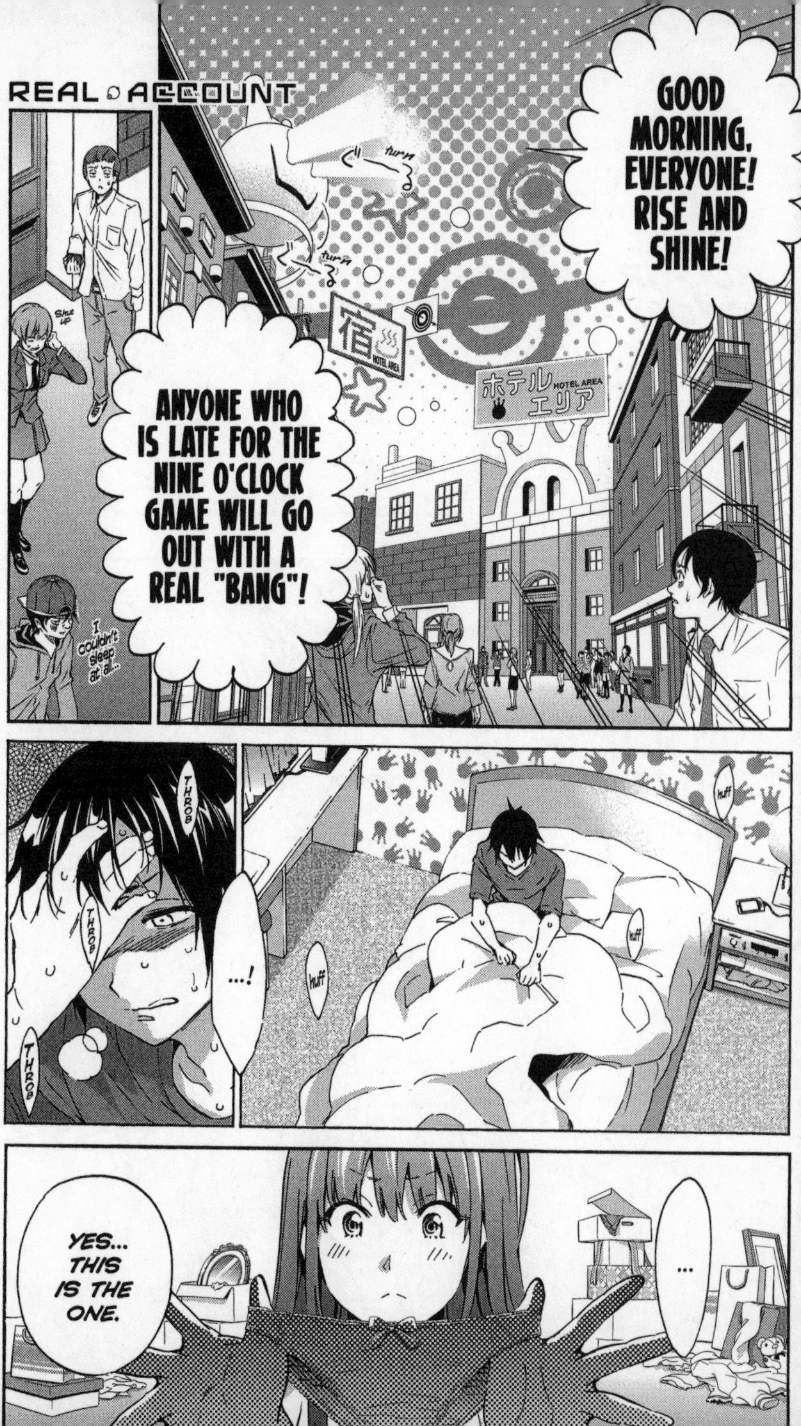
GOOD MORNING, EVERYONE! RISE AND SHINE!
turn
turn
宿 HOTEL AREA
ホテル エリア HOTEL AREA
ANYONE WHO IS LATE FOR THE NINE O'CLOCK GAME WILL GO OUT WITH A REAL "BANG"!
Shut up
I couldn't sleep at all...
huff
huff
huff
THROB
THROB
...!
THROB
...
YES... THIS IS THE ONE.

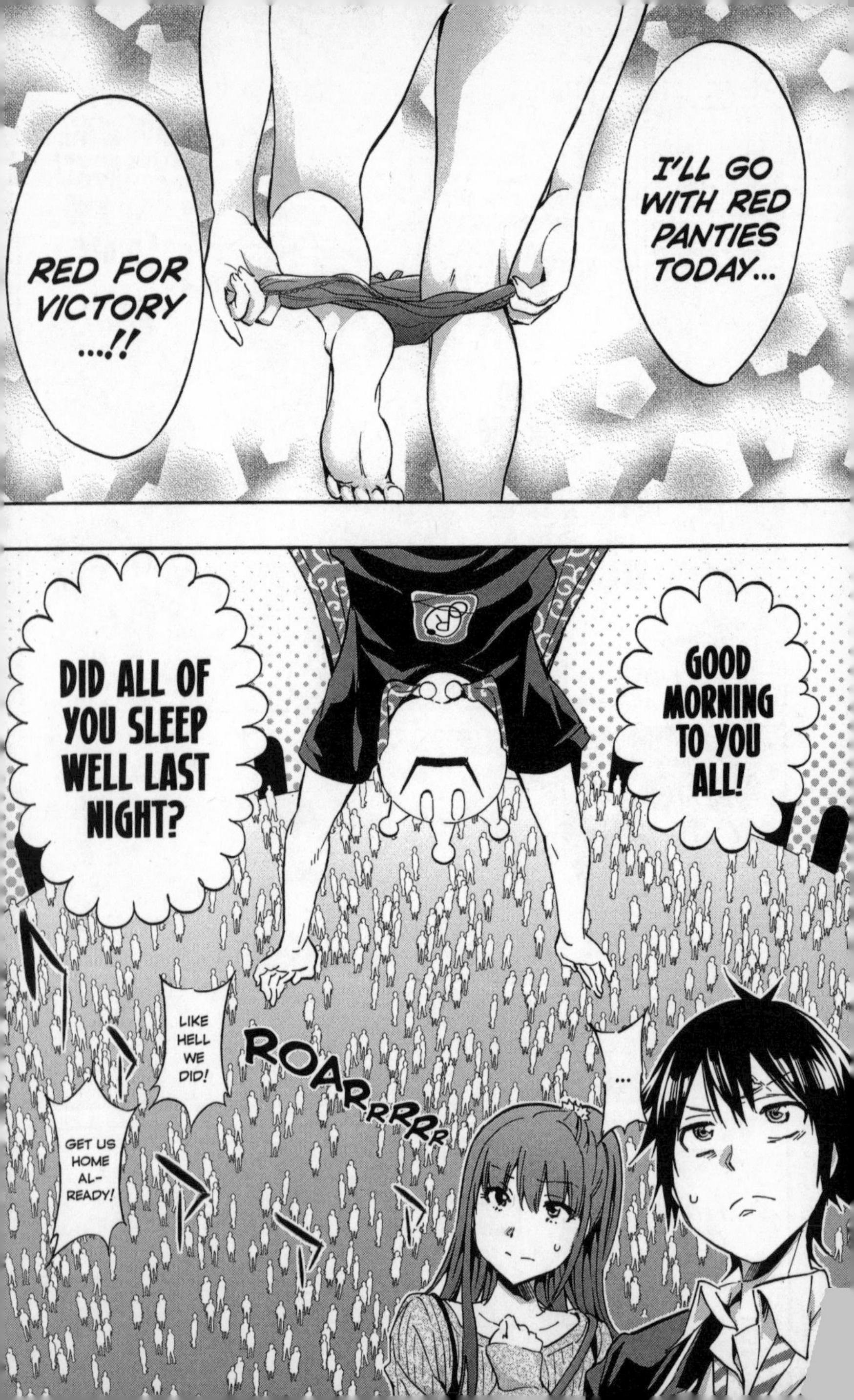
I'LL GO WITH RED PANTIES TODAY...
RED FOR VICTORY ...!!
GOOD MORNING TO YOU ALL!
DID ALL OF YOU SLEEP WELL LAST NIGHT?
...
ROARRRRRR
LIKE HELL WE DID!
GET US HOME AL-READY!

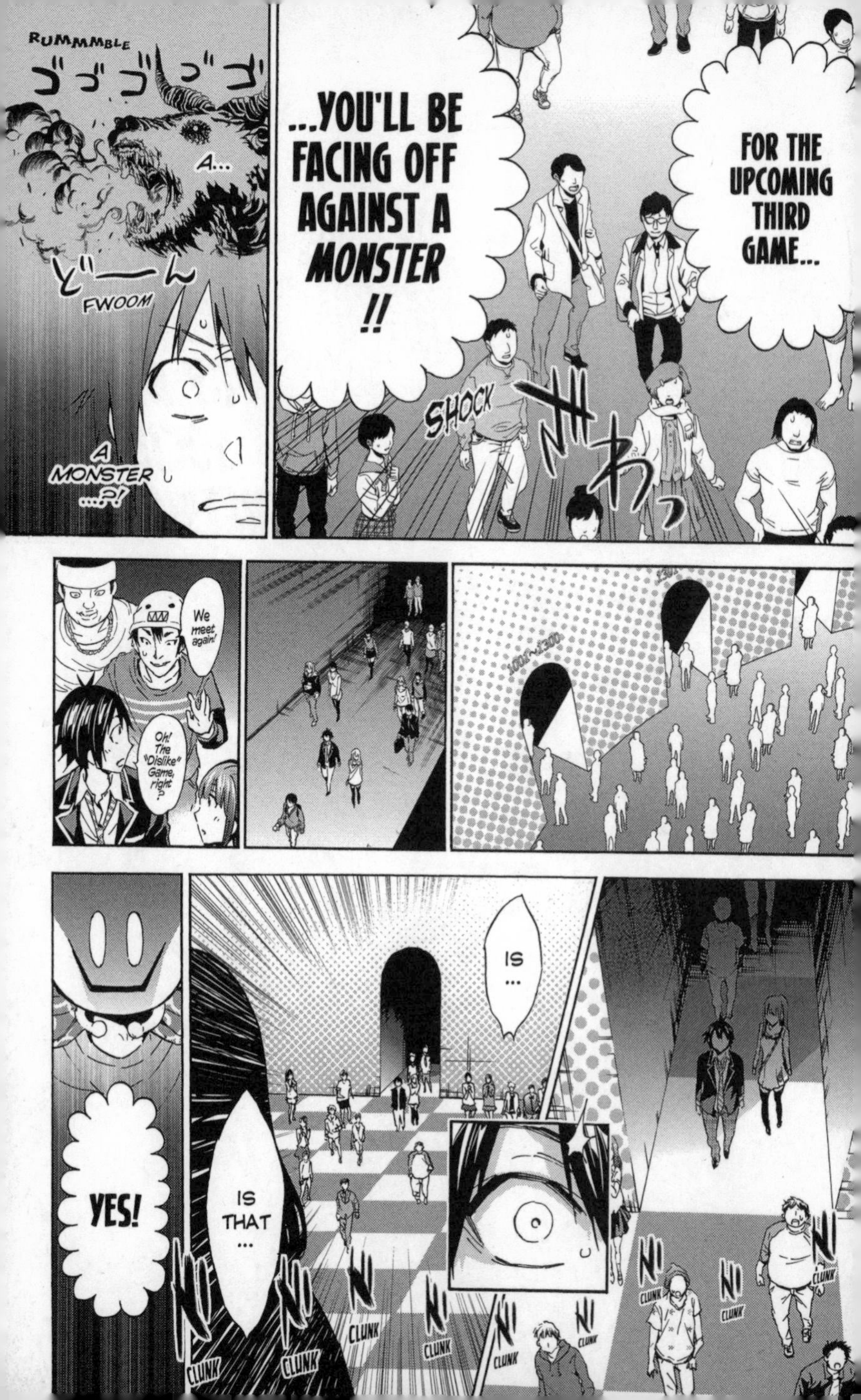
FOR THE UPCOMING THIRD GAME...
...YOU'LL BE FACING OFF AGAINST A MONSTER !!
SHOCK
ざわっ
RUMMMBLE
ゴゴゴゴゴ
A...
どーん
FWOOM
A MONSTER ...?!
1301
1001~1300
We meet again!
Oh! The "Dislike" Game, right?
NI
CLUNK
NI
CLUNK
NI
CLUNK
NI
CLUNK
IS ...
IS THAT ...
NI
CLUNK
NI
CLUNK
NI
CLUNK
YES!

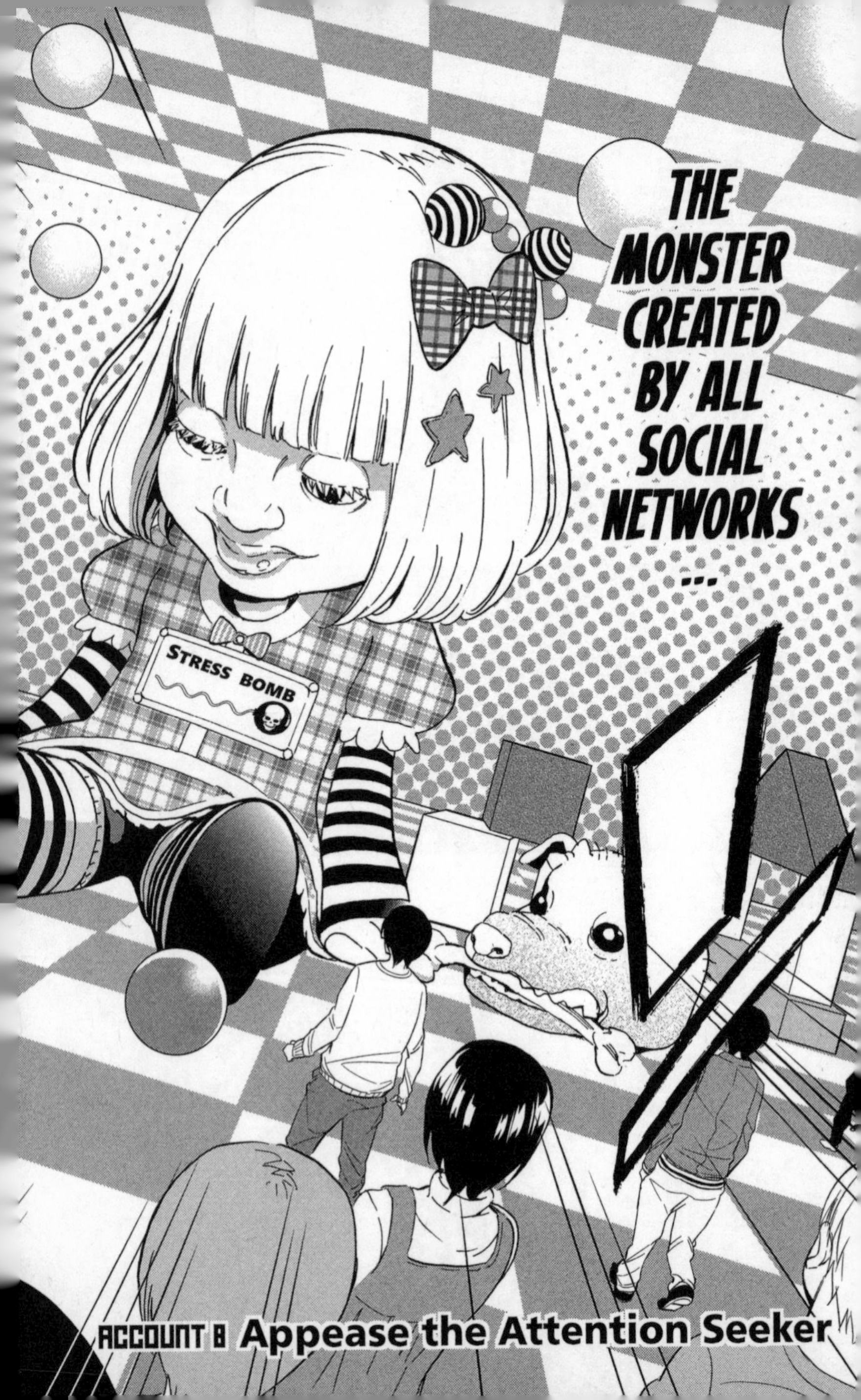
THE MONSTER CREATED BY ALL SOCIAL NETWORKS ...
STRESS BOMB
ACCOUNT 8 Appease the Attention Seeker

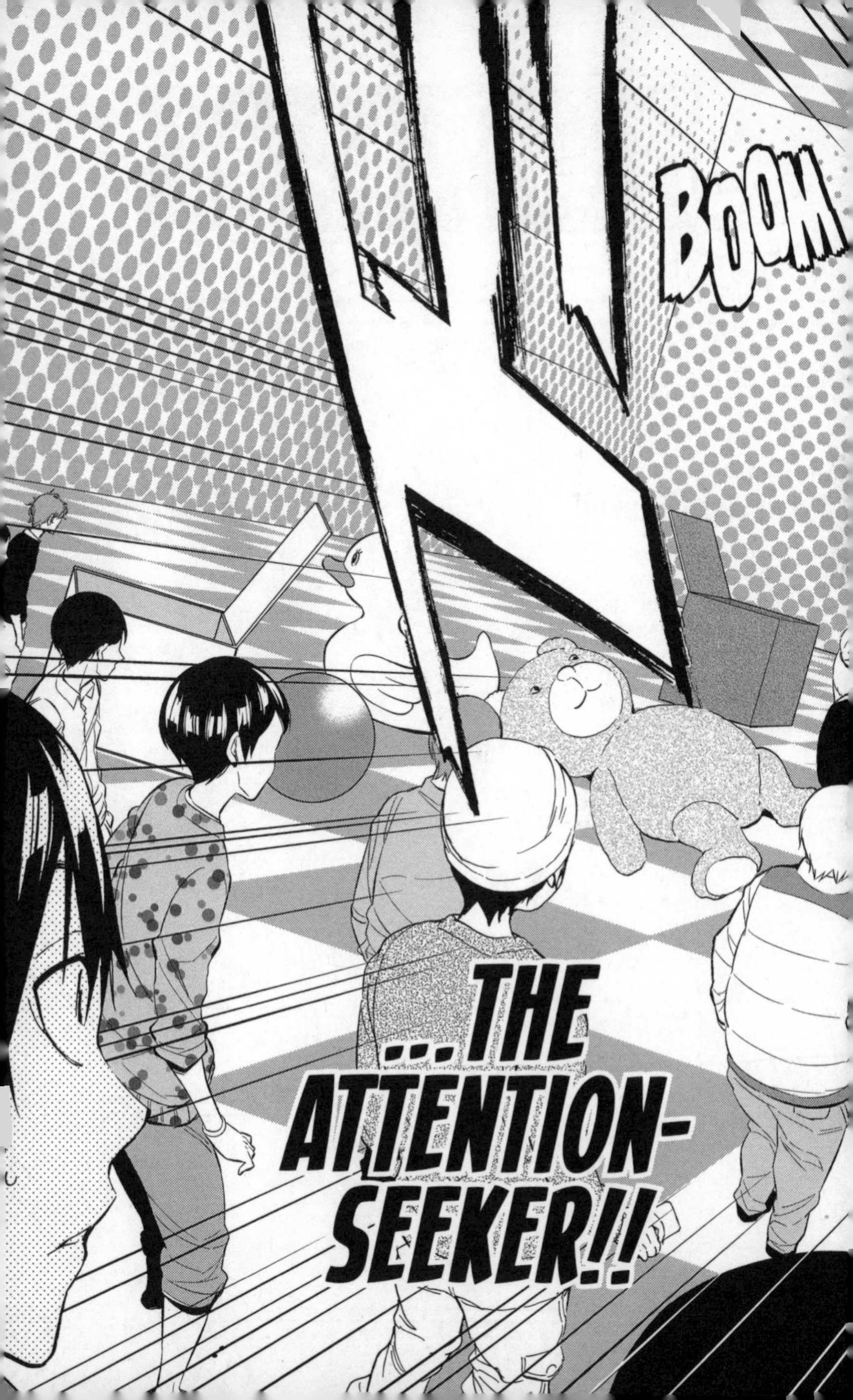
BOOM
...THE ATTENTION-SEEKER!!

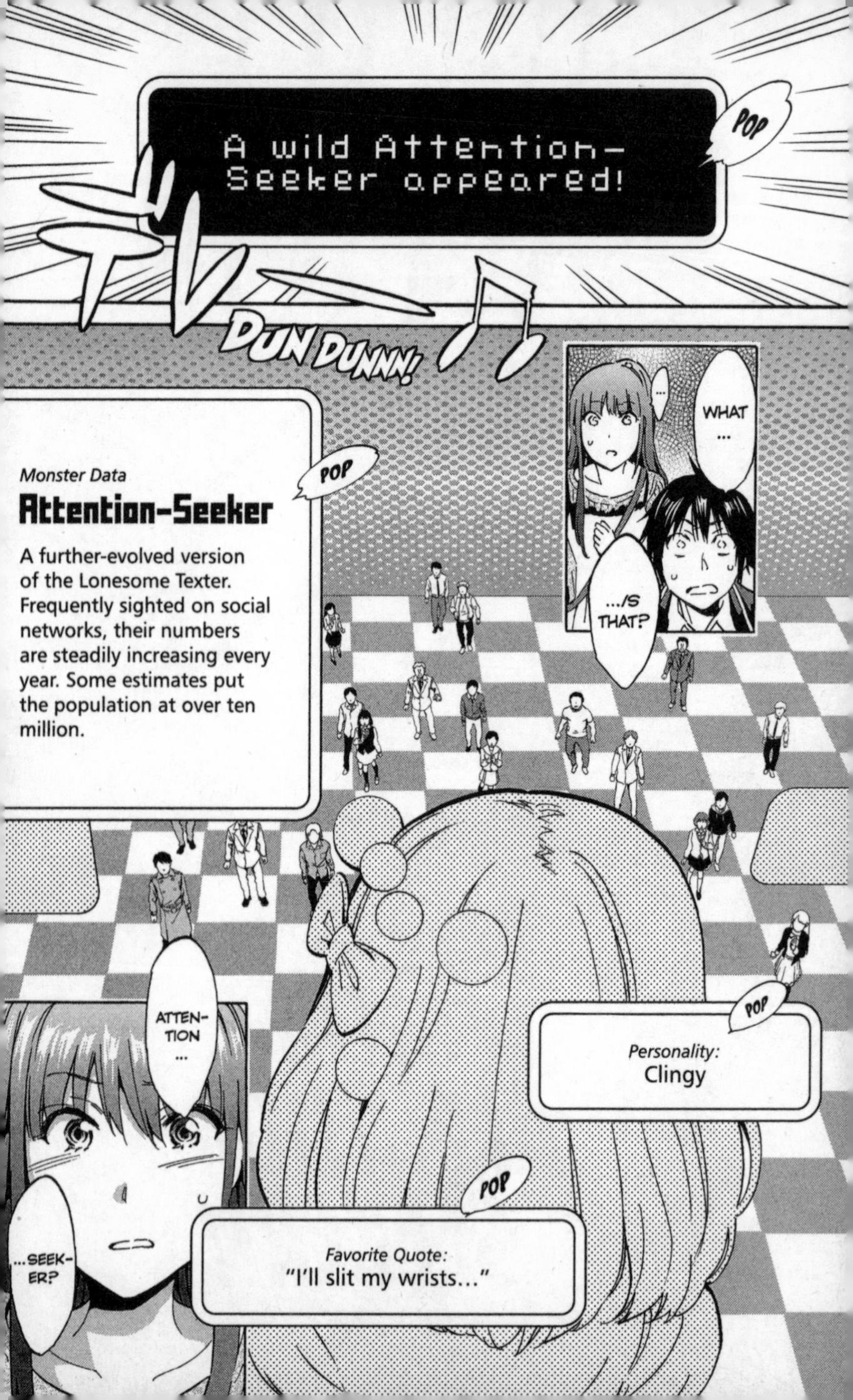
POP
A wild Attention-Seeker appeared!
DUN DUNNN!
WHAT ...
...
.../S THAT?
POP
Monster Data
Attention-Seeker
A further-evolved version of the Lonesome Texter. Frequently sighted on social networks, their numbers are steadily increasing every year. Some estimates put the population at over ten million.
POP
Personality:
Clingy
ATTENTION ...
POP
Favorite Quote:
"I'll slit my wrists..."
...SEEKER?

Traits: **Will do anything for attention**

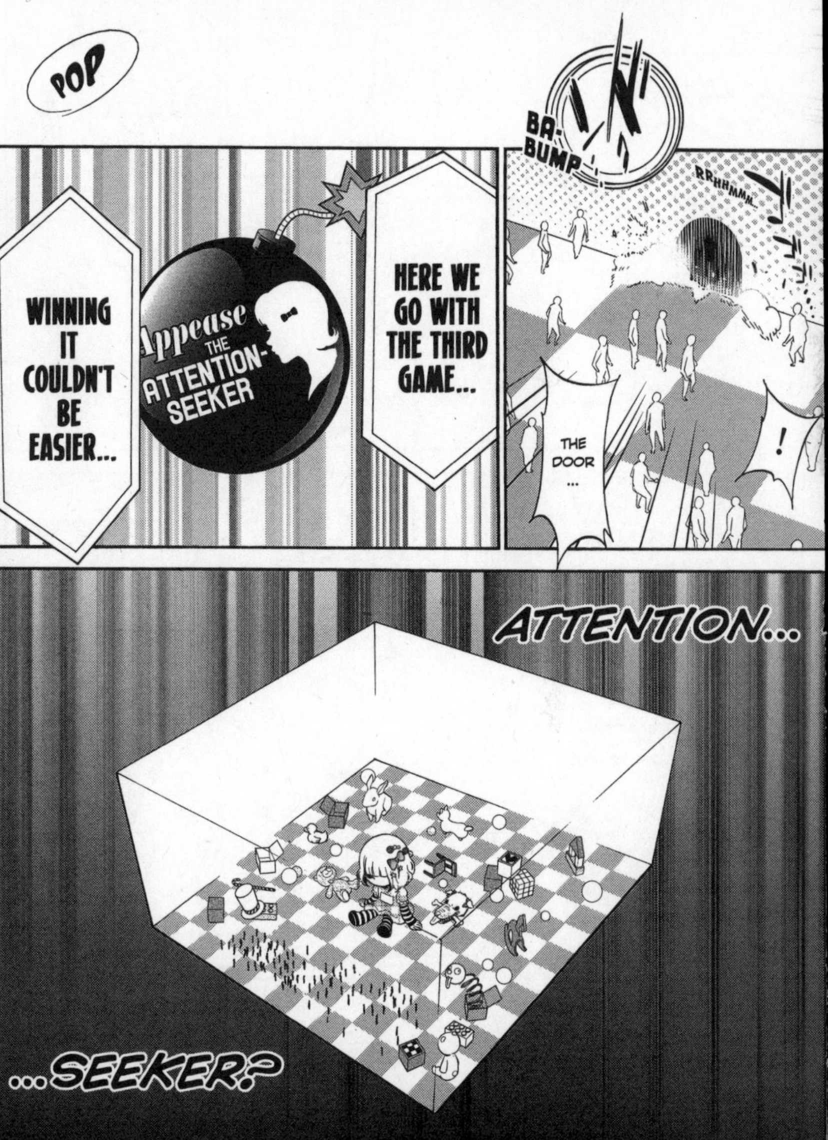
BA-BUMP
RRHHMMM
THE DOOR ...
!
POP
HERE WE GO WITH THE THIRD GAME...
Appease THE ATTENTION-SEEKER
WINNING IT COULDN'T BE EASIER...
ATTENTION...
...SEEKER?

3rd Game: **APPEASE THE ATTENTION-SEEKER**

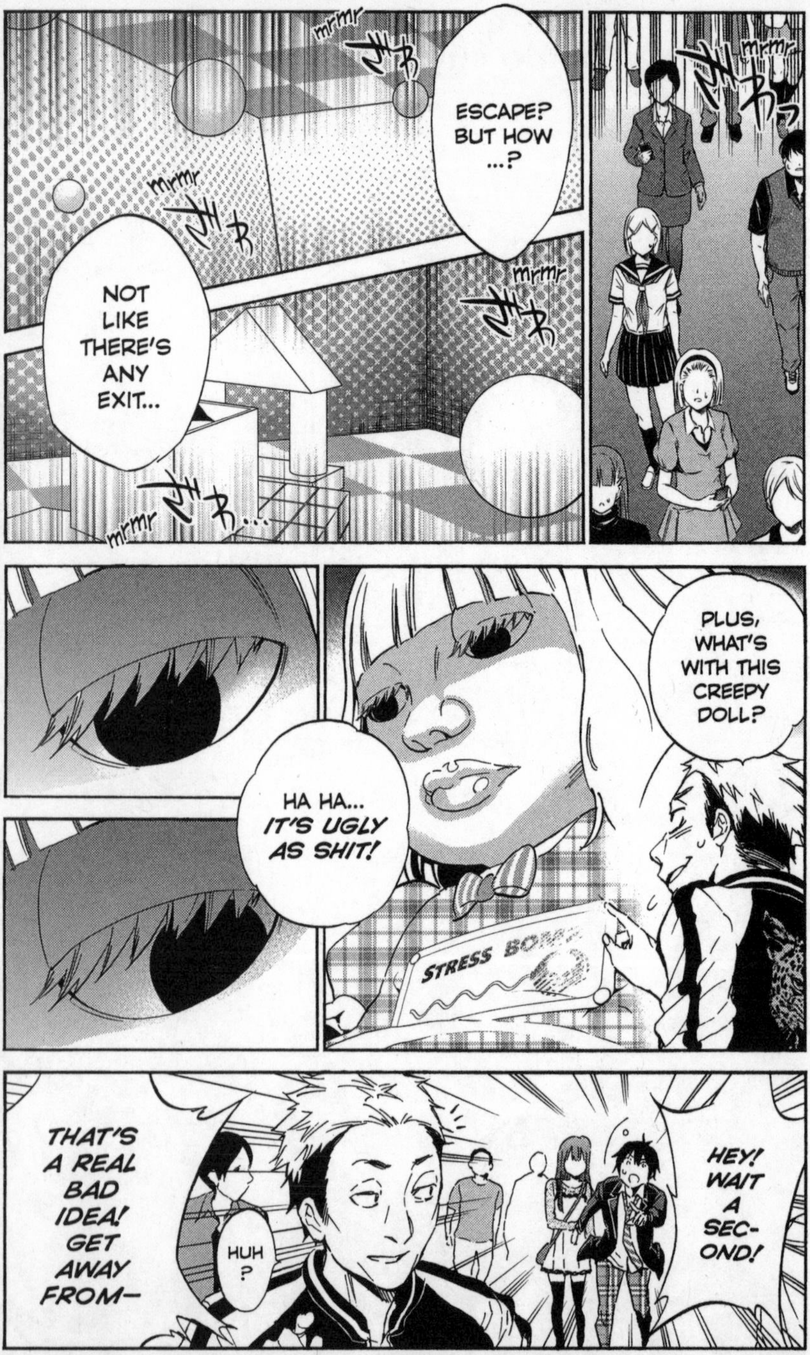
mrmr
ざわっ
mrmr
ざわ
ESCAPE? BUT HOW ...?
mrmr
ざわ
NOT LIKE THERE'S ANY EXIT...
mrmr
ざわ
mrmr
ざわ...
PLUS, WHAT'S WITH THIS CREEPY DOLL?
HA HA... *IT'S UGLY AS SHIT!*
STRESS
HEY! WAIT A SEC-OND!
HUH?
THAT'S A REAL BAD IDEA! GET AWAY FROM—

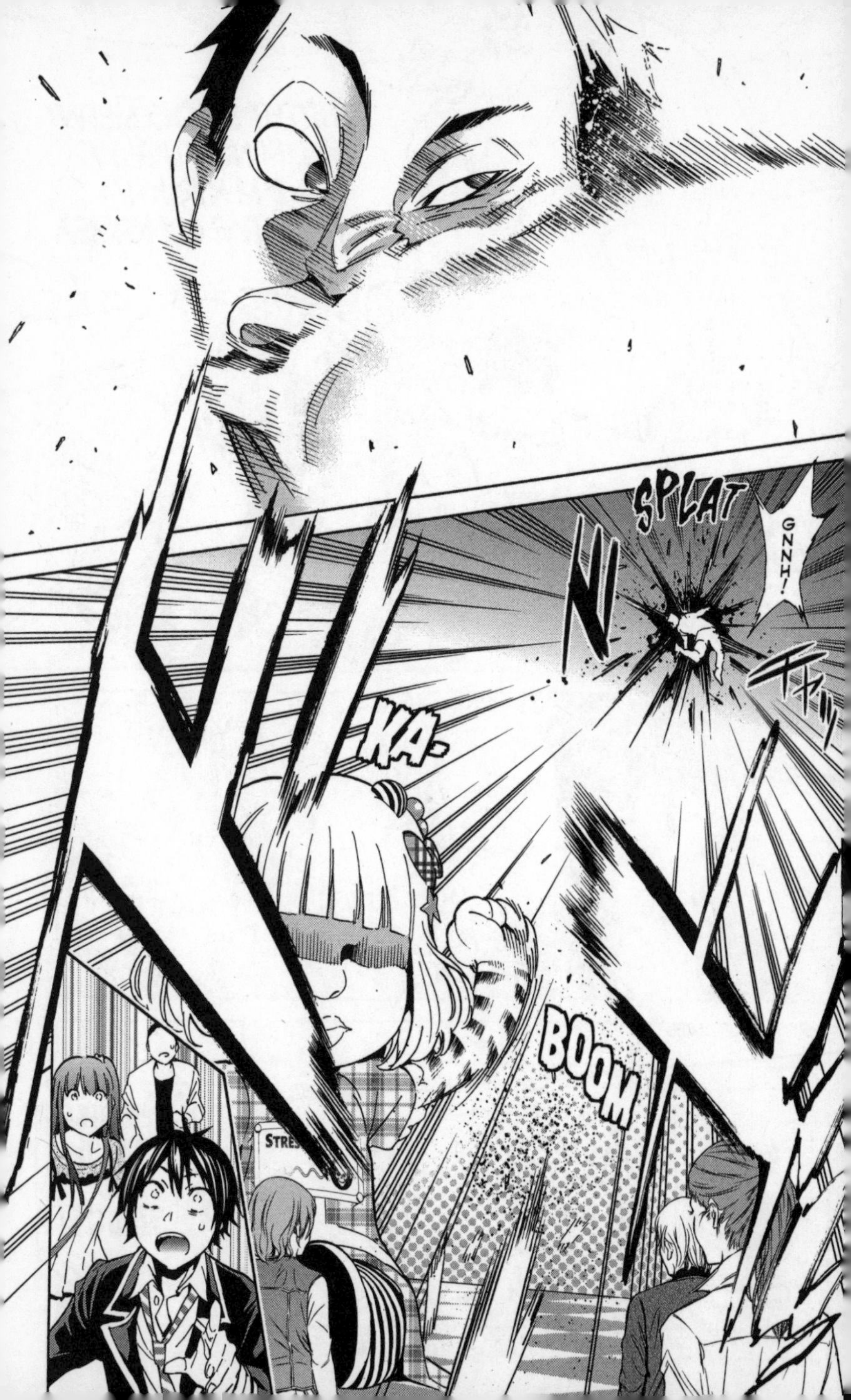
GNNH!
SPLAT
チャッ
KA-
BOOM
STRES

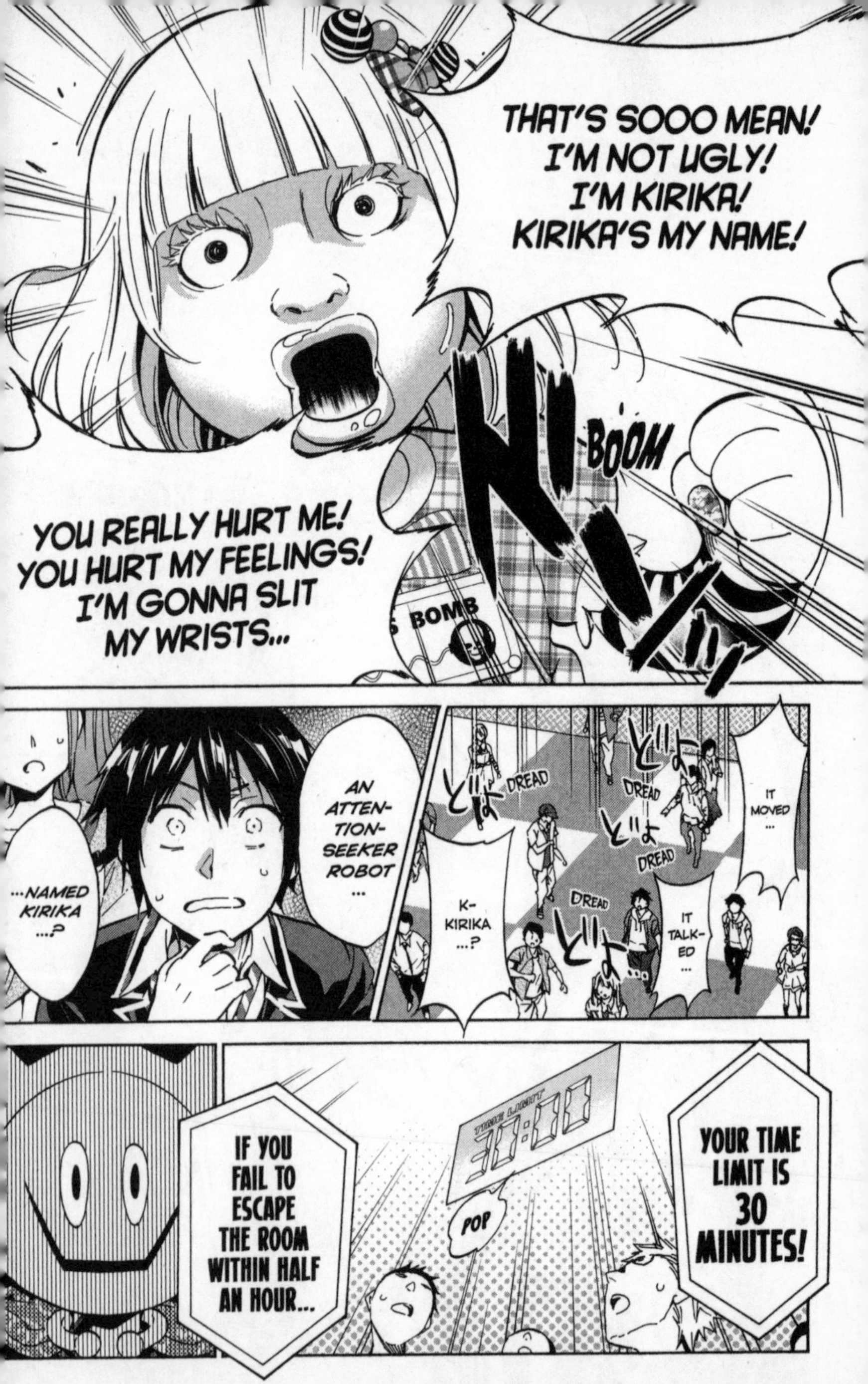
THAT'S SOOO MEAN! I'M NOT UGLY! I'M KIRIKA! KIRIKA'S MY NAME!
HI-
BOOM
BOMB
YOU REALLY HURT ME! YOU HURT MY FEELINGS! I'M GONNA SLIT MY WRISTS...
IT MOVED ...
DREAD
DREAD
DREAD
DREAD
IT TALK-ED ...
K-KIRIKA ...?
AN ATTEN-TION-SEEKER ROBOT ...
...NAMED KIRIKA ...?
YOUR TIME LIMIT IS 30 MINUTES!
TIME LIMIT
30:00
POP
IF YOU FAIL TO ESCAPE THE ROOM WITHIN HALF AN HOUR...

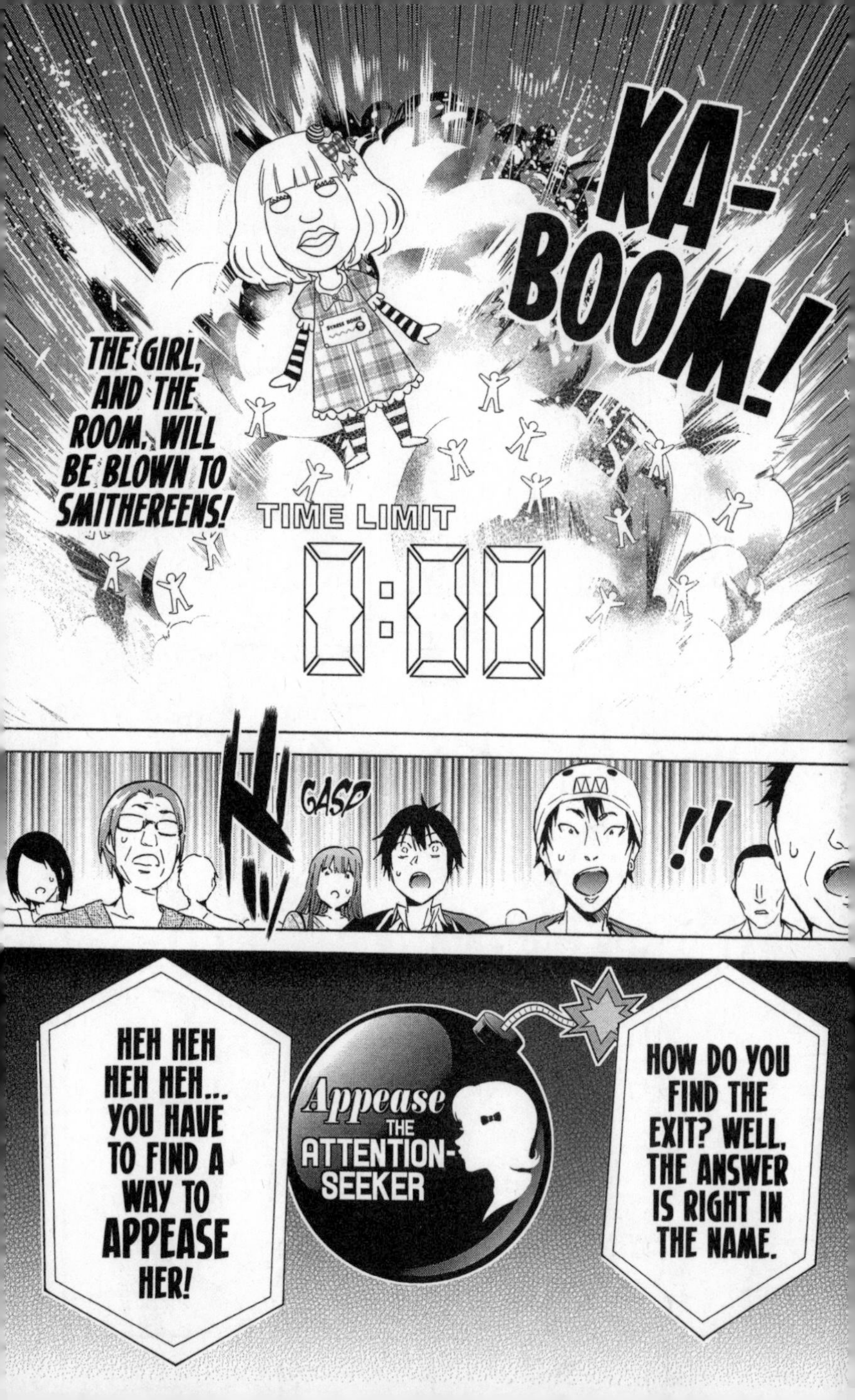
KA-BOOM!
THE GIRL, AND THE ROOM, WILL BE BLOWN TO SMITHEREENS!
TIME LIMIT
0:00
!!
GASP
HOW DO YOU FIND THE EXIT? WELL, THE ANSWER IS RIGHT IN THE NAME.
Appease THE ATTENTION-SEEKER
HEH HEH HEH HEH... YOU HAVE TO FIND A WAY TO APPEASE HER!

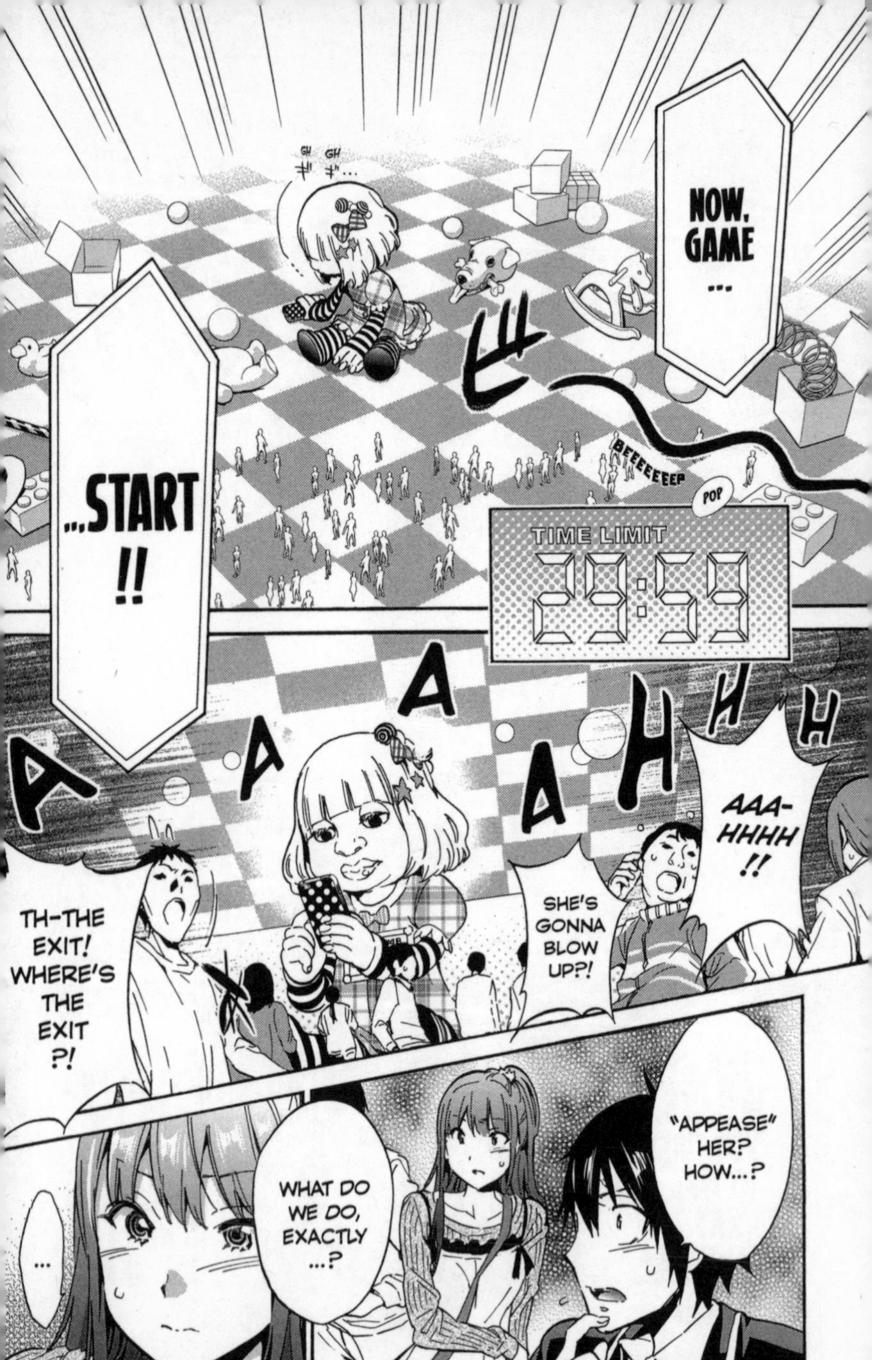
NOW, GAME ...
GH GH
BEEEEEEEP
POP
...START !!
TIME LIMIT
29:59
AAAAHHHH
AAA-HHHH !!
SHE'S GONNA BLOW UP?!
TH-THE EXIT! WHERE'S THE EXIT ?!
"APPEASE" HER? HOW...?
WHAT DO WE DO, EXACTLY ...?
...

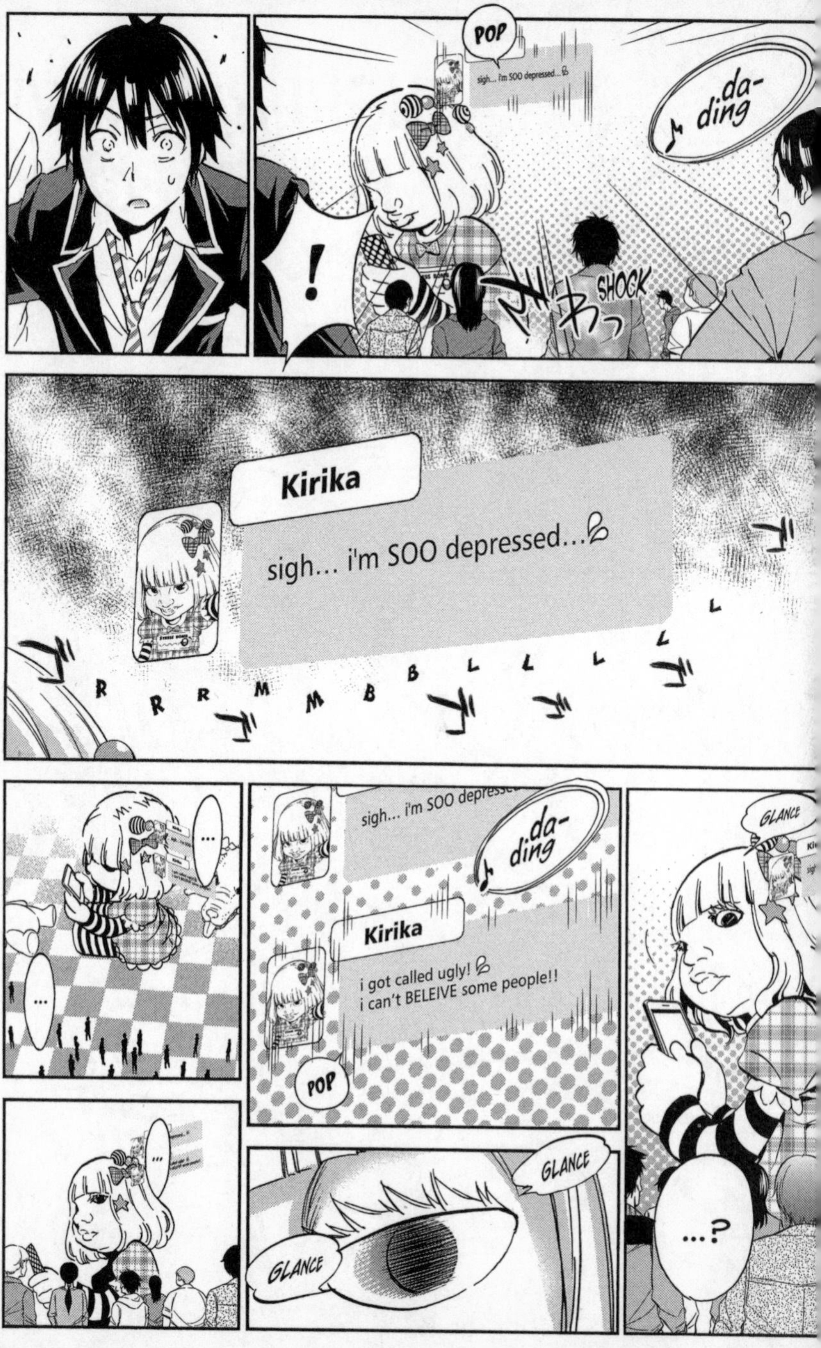

POP
sigh... i'm SOO depressed...
da-ding
!
SHOCK
Kirika
sigh... i'm SOO depressed...
RRRMMBBLLLLL
GLANCE
...?
sigh... i'm SOO depresse
da-ding
Kirika
i got called ugly!
i can't BELEIVE some people!!
POP
...
...
GLANCE
GLANCE
...

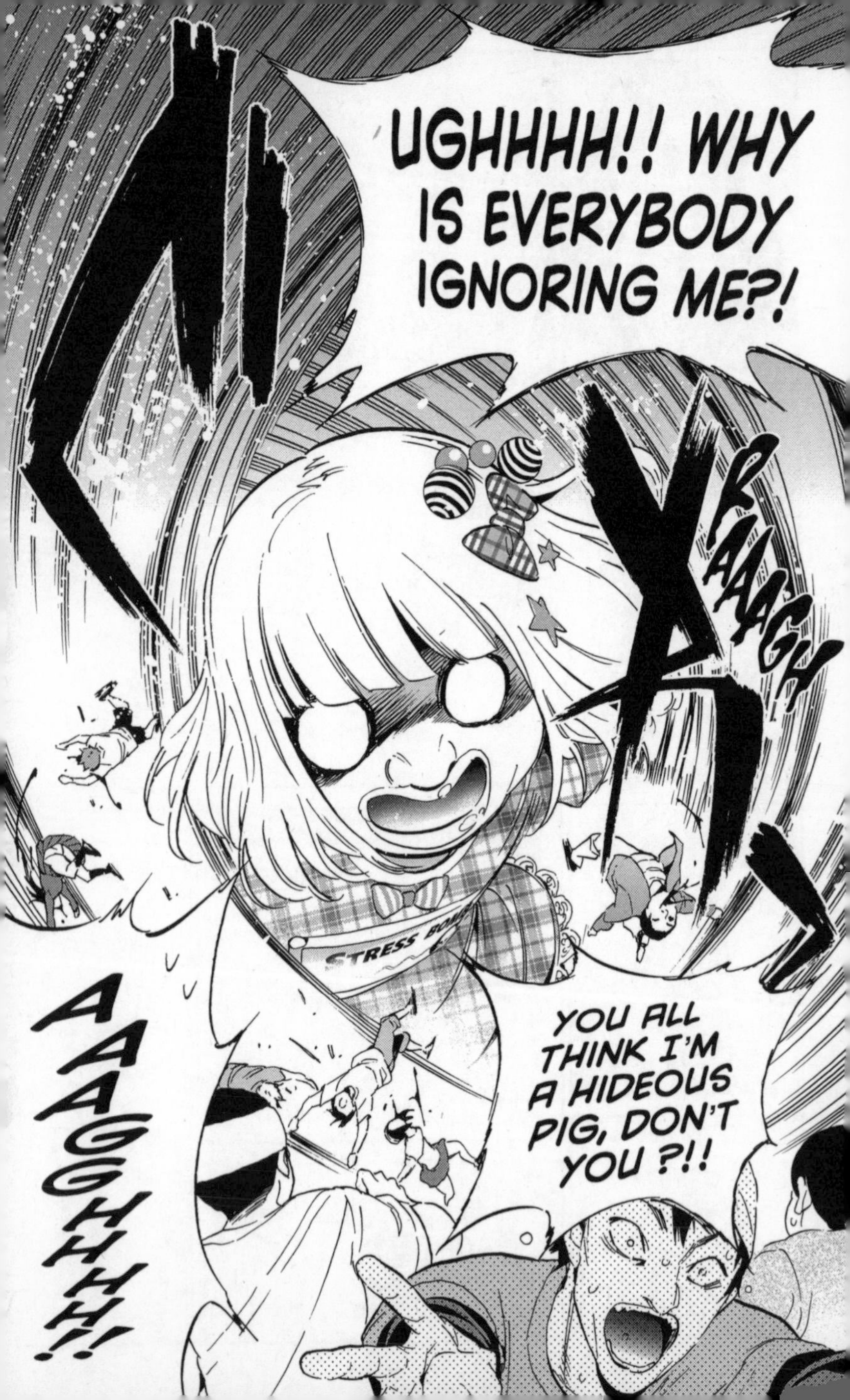
UGHHHH!! WHY IS EVERYBODY IGNORING ME?!
KRAAAGH
STRESS BOM
YOU ALL THINK I'M A HIDEOUS PIG, DON'T YOU ?!!
AAAGGHHHH!!

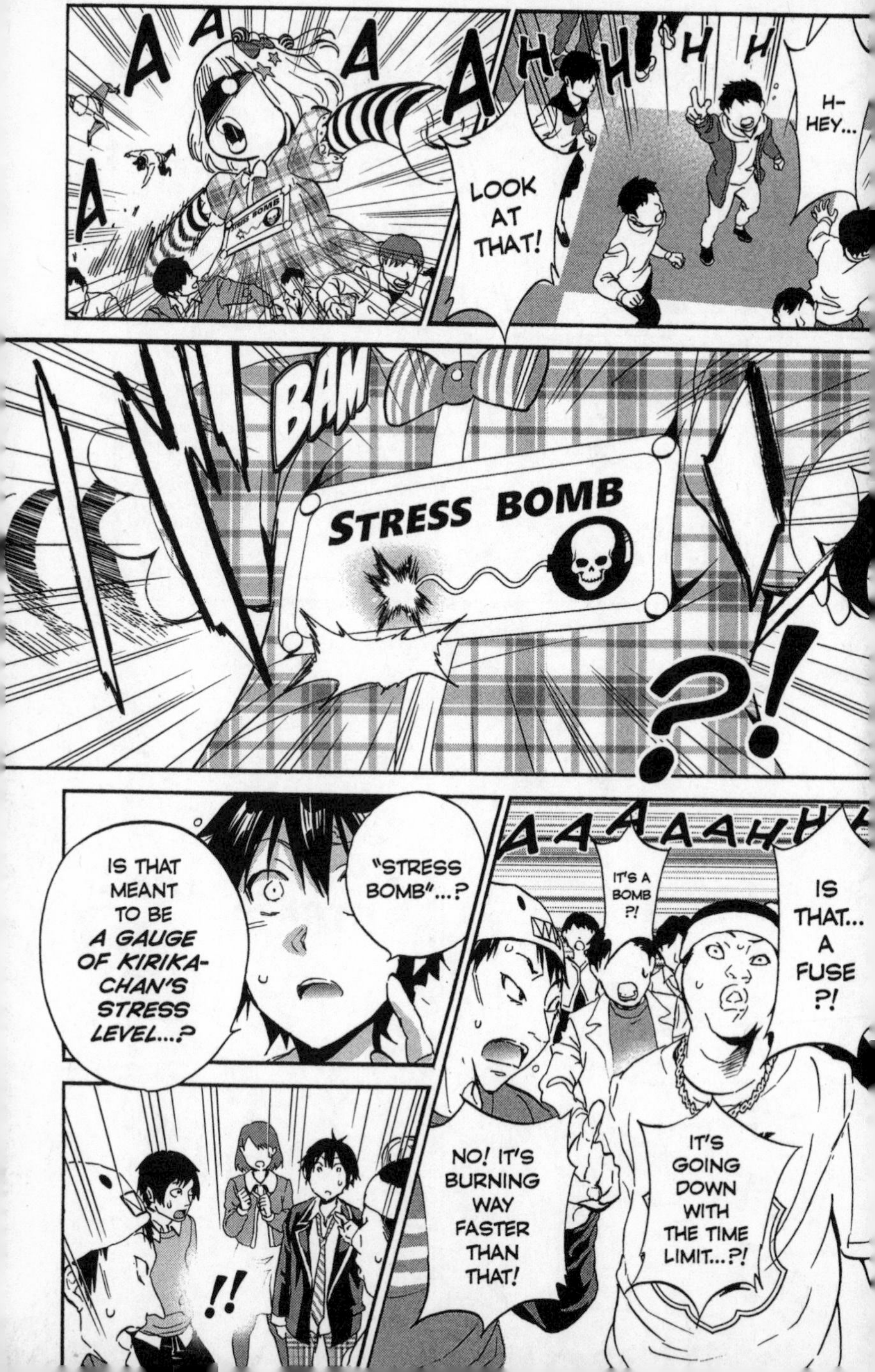

AAAAAAHHHHH
H-HEY...
LOOK AT THAT!
BAM
STRESS BOMB
?!
AAAAAHH
IS THAT... A FUSE?!
IT'S A BOMB?!
IT'S GOING DOWN WITH THE TIME LIMIT...?!
NO! IT'S BURNING WAY FASTER THAN THAT!
"STRESS BOMB"...?
IS THAT MEANT TO BE *A GAUGE OF KIRIKA-CHAN'S STRESS LEVEL...?*
!!

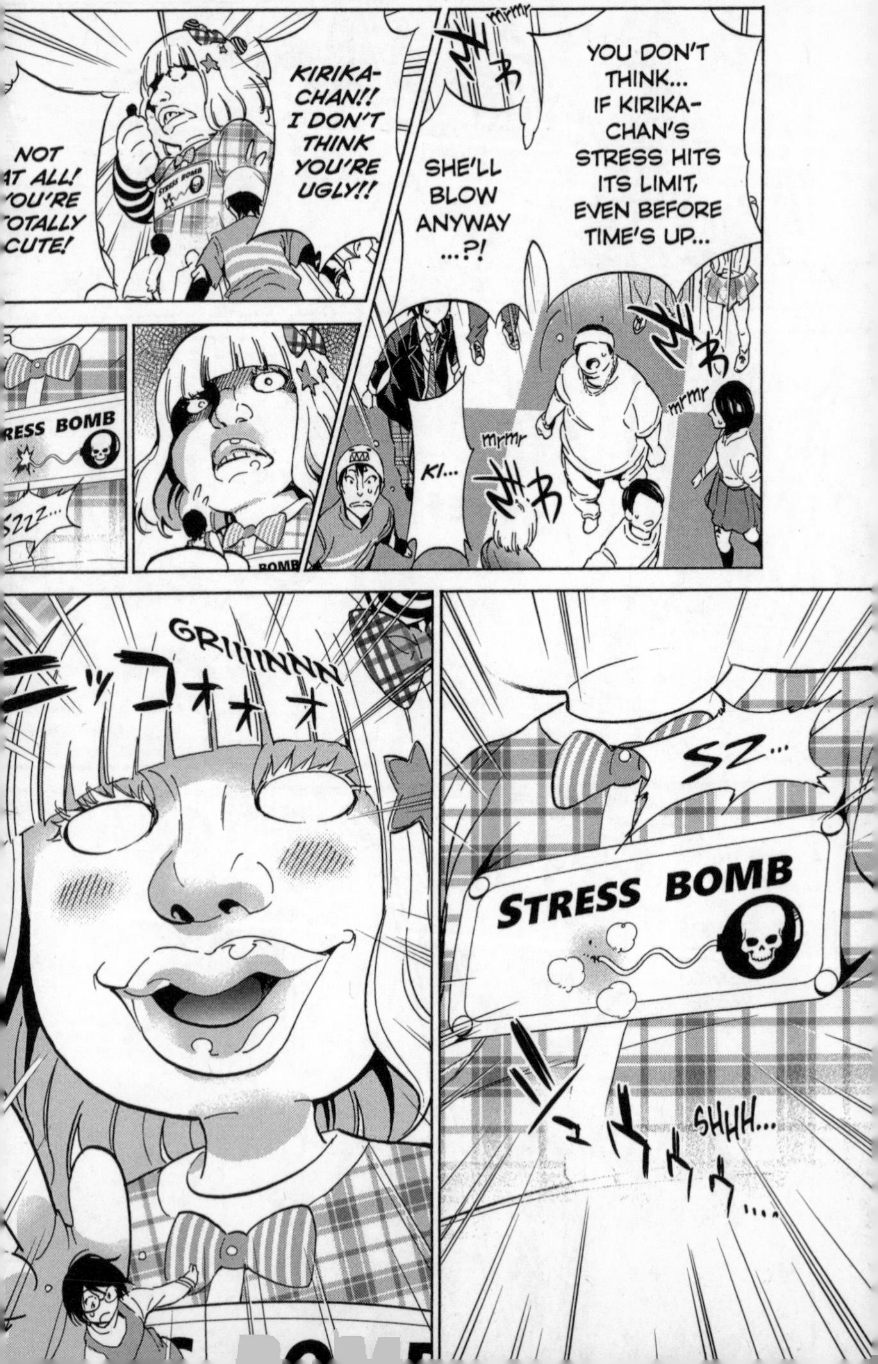
mrmr
YOU DON'T THINK... IF KIRIKA-CHAN'S STRESS HITS ITS LIMIT, EVEN BEFORE TIME'S UP...
SHE'LL BLOW ANYWAY ...?!
mrmr
mrmr
KI...
KIRIKA-CHAN!! I DON'T THINK YOU'RE UGLY!!
NOT AT ALL! YOU'RE TOTALLY CUTE!
STRESS BOMB
BOMB
RESS BOMB
SZZZ...
SZ...
STRESS BOMB
SHHH...
GRIIIINNN

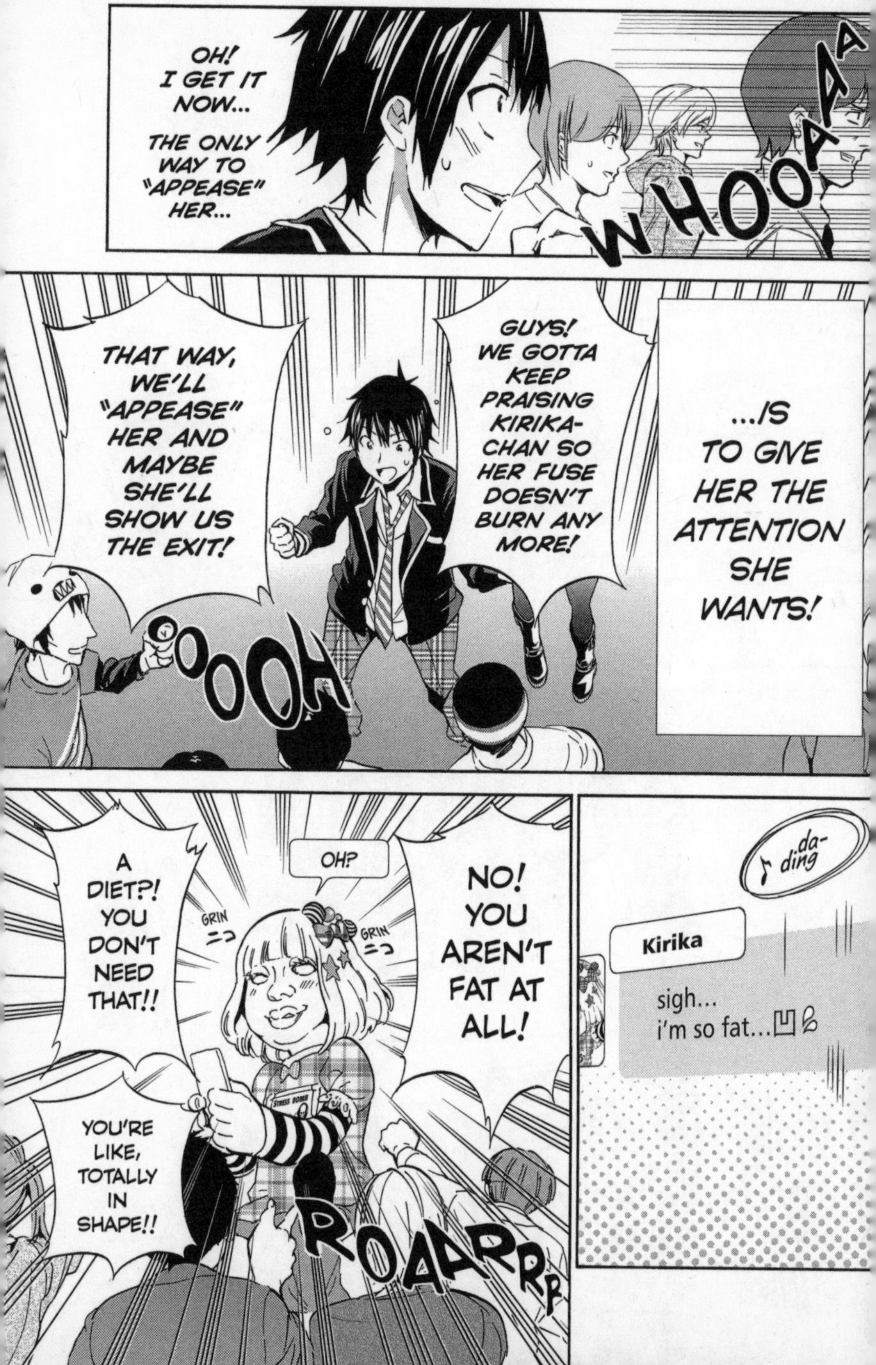
OH! I GET IT NOW...
THE ONLY WAY TO "APPEASE" HER...
WHOOAAA
...IS TO GIVE HER THE ATTENTION SHE WANTS!
GUYS! WE GOTTA KEEP PRAISING KIRIKA-CHAN SO HER FUSE DOESN'T BURN ANY MORE!
THAT WAY, WE'LL "APPEASE" HER AND MAYBE SHE'LL SHOW US THE EXIT!
OOOH
♪ da-ding
Kirika
sigh...
i'm so fat...
NO! YOU AREN'T FAT AT ALL!
OH?
GRIN
GRIN
A DIET?! YOU DON'T NEED THAT!!
YOU'RE LIKE, TOTALLY IN SHAPE!!
ROAARRR

Kirika
lol, i totes thought the name "Nicholas Cage" was cuz his fam worked in a jail or something. i'm such a dumass
da-ding
HAHAHA
YOU'RE SO FUNNY, KIRIKA-CHAN!
RIGHT?
I TOTALLY SEE HOW YOU COULD MAKE THAT MISTAKE!
HILARIOUS!
LOLLLL, DUDE!
OMFG LMFAO! SO FUNNY!

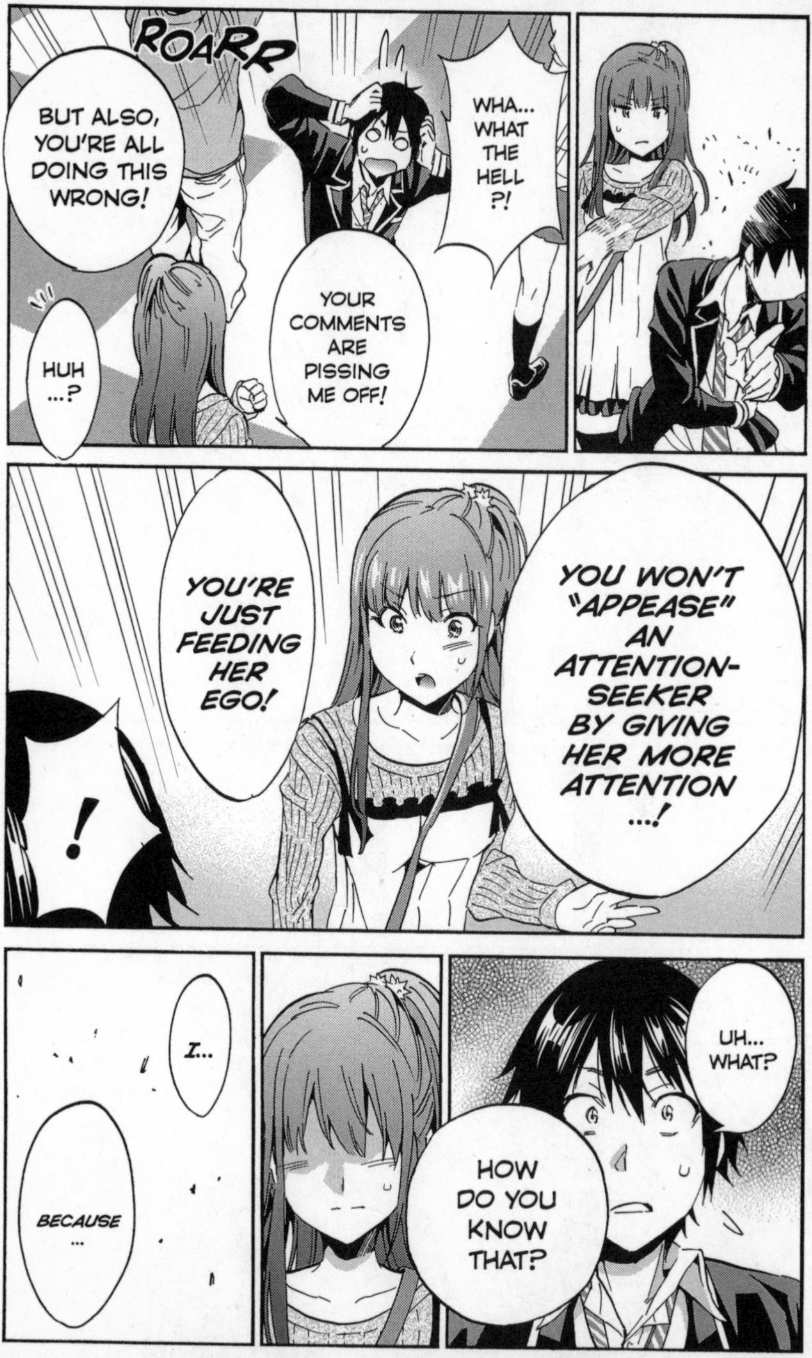
WHA... WHAT THE HELL?!
ROARR
BUT ALSO, YOU'RE ALL DOING THIS WRONG!
YOUR COMMENTS ARE PISSING ME OFF!
HUH...?
YOU WON'T "APPEASE" AN ATTENTION-SEEKER BY GIVING HER MORE ATTENTION...!
YOU'RE JUST FEEDING HER EGO!
!
UH... WHAT?
HOW DO YOU KNOW THAT?
I...
BECAUSE...

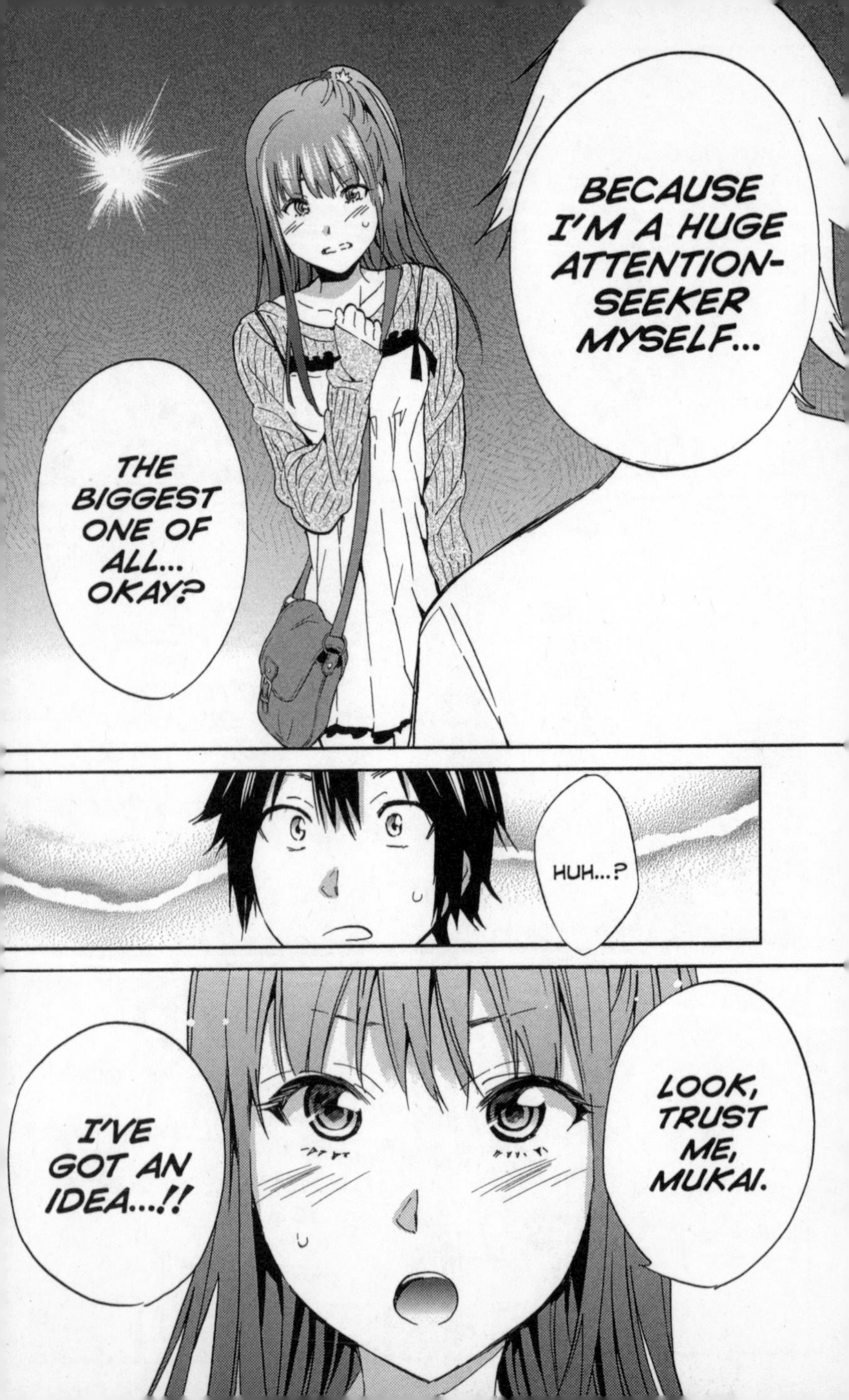
BECAUSE I'M A HUGE ATTENTION-SEEKER MYSELF...
THE BIGGEST ONE OF ALL... OKAY?
HUH...?
LOOK, TRUST ME, MUKAI.
I'VE GOT AN IDEA...!!

PROFILE

NAME:	Ayame Kamijo
SEX:	female
DATE OF BIRTH:	Aug. 27
AFFILIATION:	High School (1st year)
RELATIONSHIP STATUS:	Single

FOLLOWING:	FOLLOWERS:
64	1

ABOUT ME:

I don't like people too much. I like plants.
I'll only follow you back if you understand where I'm coming from.

Looking at flowers puts me at ease.
They don't lie to you the way people do, and they don't try to figure you out.
Plus, unlike pets, they're pretty easy to keep.
Kind of makes me wish I could live off sunlight, water, and air too…

I do have somebody I like.

ACCOUNT 9
The Attention Spiral

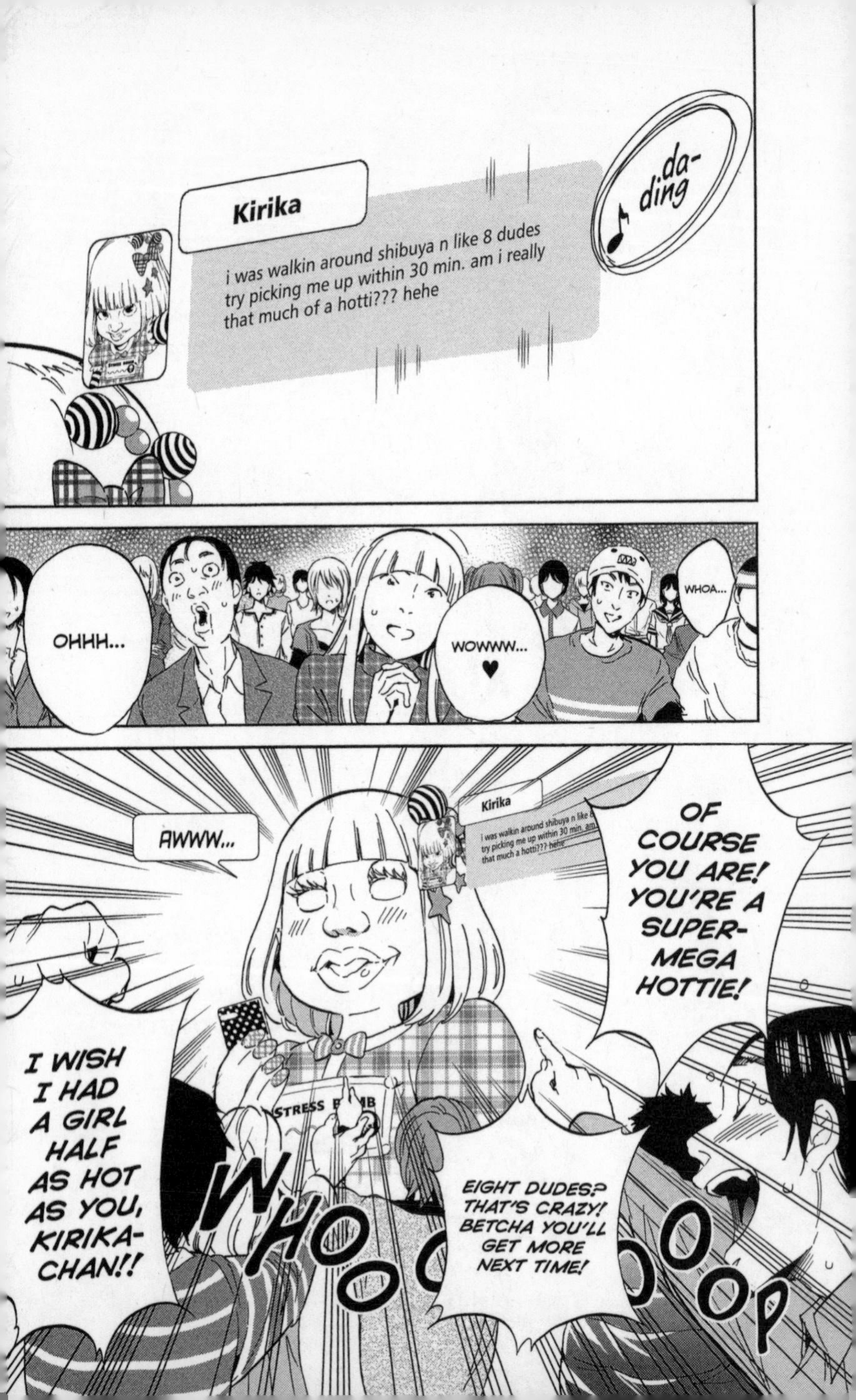
da-ding
Kirika
i was walkin around shibuya n like 8 dudes try picking me up within 30 min. am i really that much of a hotti??? hehe
WHOA...
WOWWW... ♥
OHHH...
Kirika
i was walkin around shibuya n like 8 dudes try picking me up within 30 min. am i really that much a hotti??? hehe
OF COURSE YOU ARE! YOU'RE A SUPER-MEGA HOTTIE!
AWWW...
STRESS BOMB
EIGHT DUDES? THAT'S CRAZY! BETCHA YOU'LL GET MORE NEXT TIME!
I WISH I HAD A GIRL HALF AS HOT AS YOU, KIRIKA-CHAN!!
WHOOOOOOP

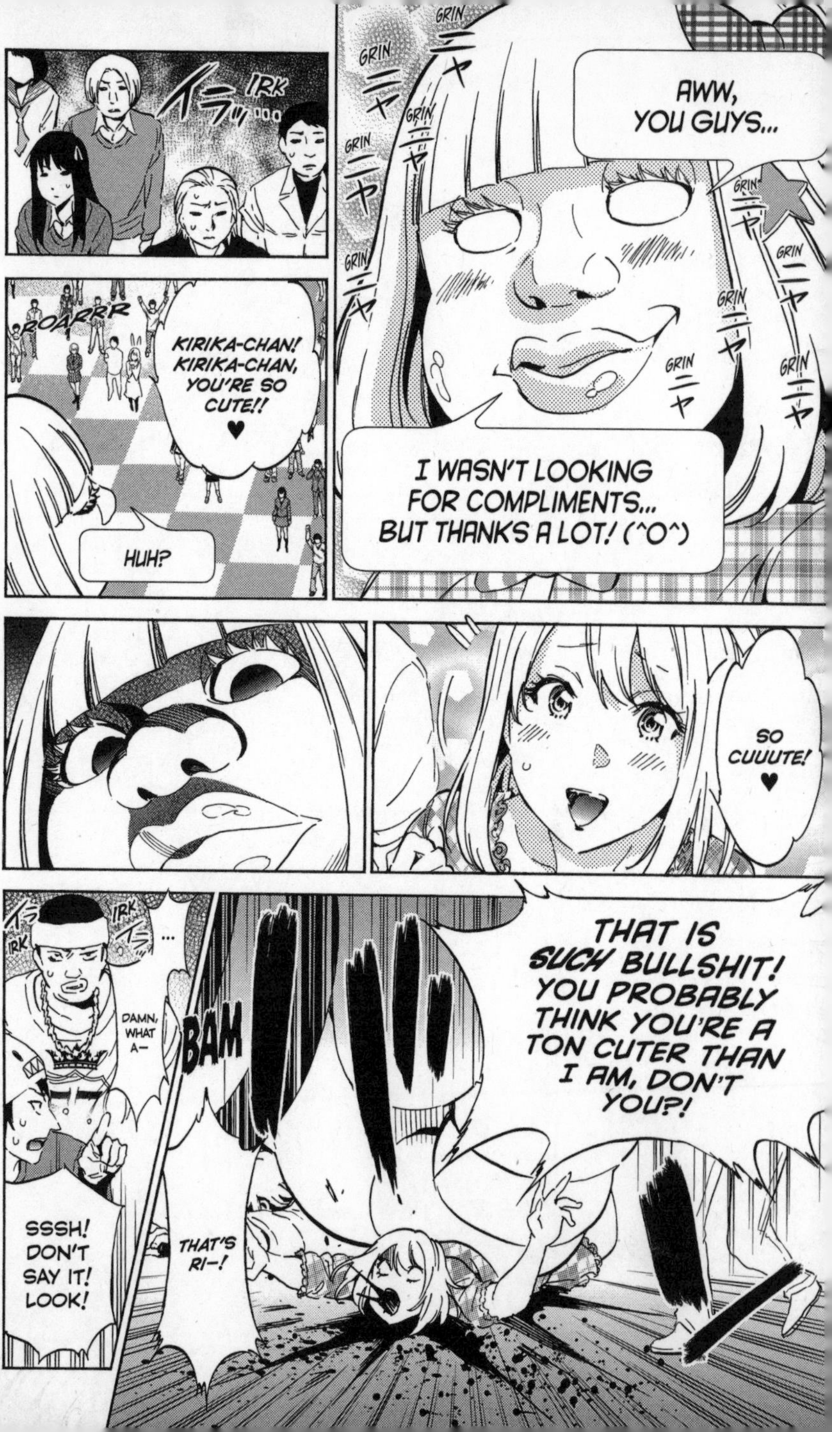
GRIN
GRIN
GRIN
GRIN
AWW, YOU GUYS...
GRIN
GRIN
GRIN
GRIN
GRIN
GRIN
I WASN'T LOOKING FOR COMPLIMENTS... BUT THANKS A LOT! (^O^)
IRK
ROARRR
KIRIKA-CHAN! KIRIKA-CHAN, YOU'RE SO CUTE!! ♥
HUH?
SO CUUUTE! ♥
THAT IS SUCH BULLSHIT! YOU PROBABLY THINK YOU'RE A TON CUTER THAN I AM, DON'T YOU?!
BAM
THAT'S RI–!
IRK
IRK
...
DAMN, WHAT A–
SSSH! DON'T SAY IT! LOOK!

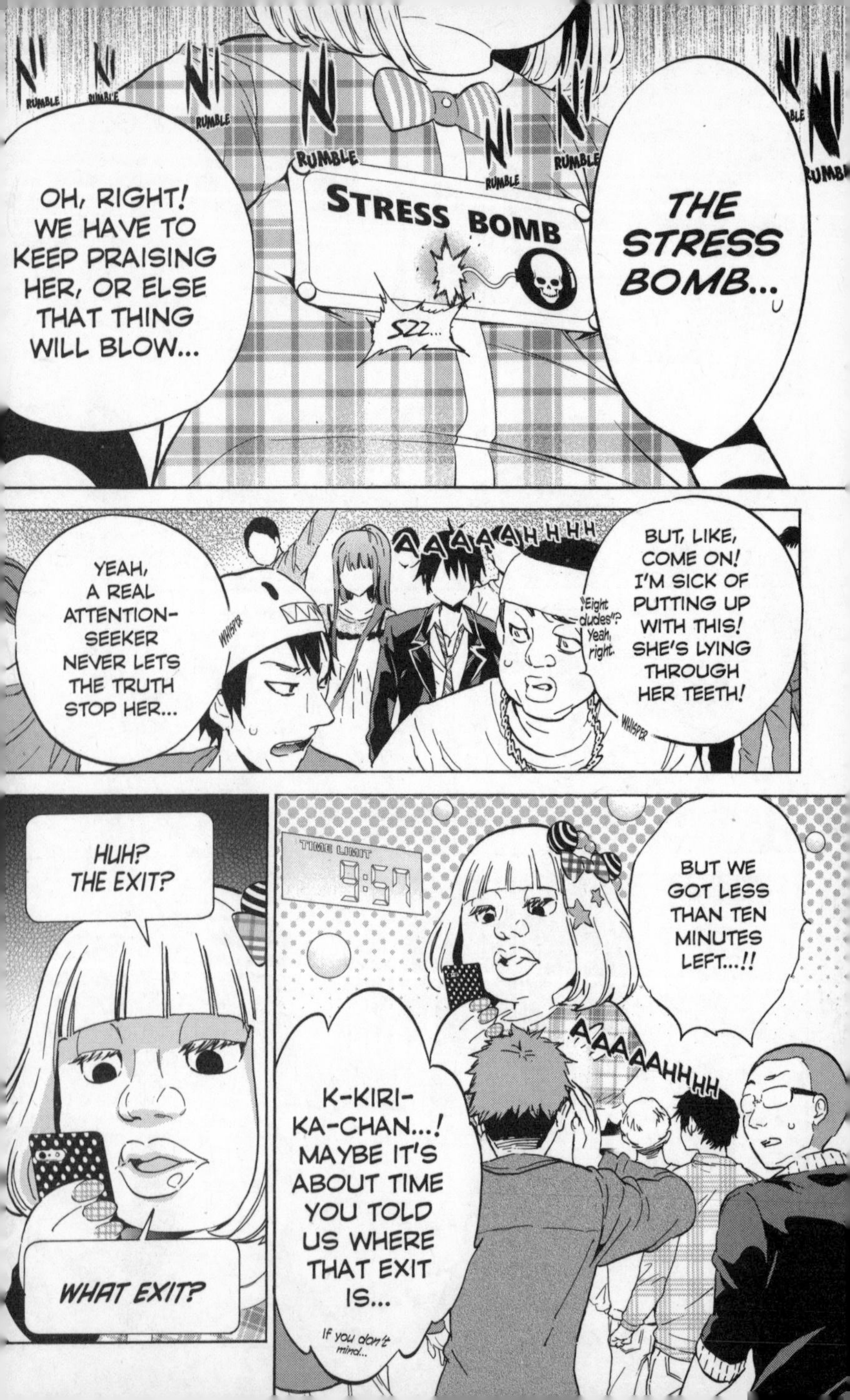

RUMBLE
RUMBLE
RUMBLE
RUMBLE
RUMBLE
THE STRESS BOMB...
STRESS BOMB
SZZ...
OH, RIGHT! WE HAVE TO KEEP PRAISING HER, OR ELSE THAT THING WILL BLOW...
BUT, LIKE, COME ON! I'M SICK OF PUTTING UP WITH THIS! SHE'S LYING THROUGH HER TEETH!
"Eight dudes"? Yeah, right.
WHISPER
AAAAAHHHH
YEAH, A REAL ATTENTION-SEEKER NEVER LETS THE TRUTH STOP HER...
WHISPER
BUT WE GOT LESS THAN TEN MINUTES LEFT...!!
TIME LIMIT
9:57
AAAAAHHHH
K-KIRIKA-CHAN...! MAYBE IT'S ABOUT TIME YOU TOLD US WHERE THAT EXIT IS...
If you don't mind...
HUH? THE EXIT?
WHAT EXIT?

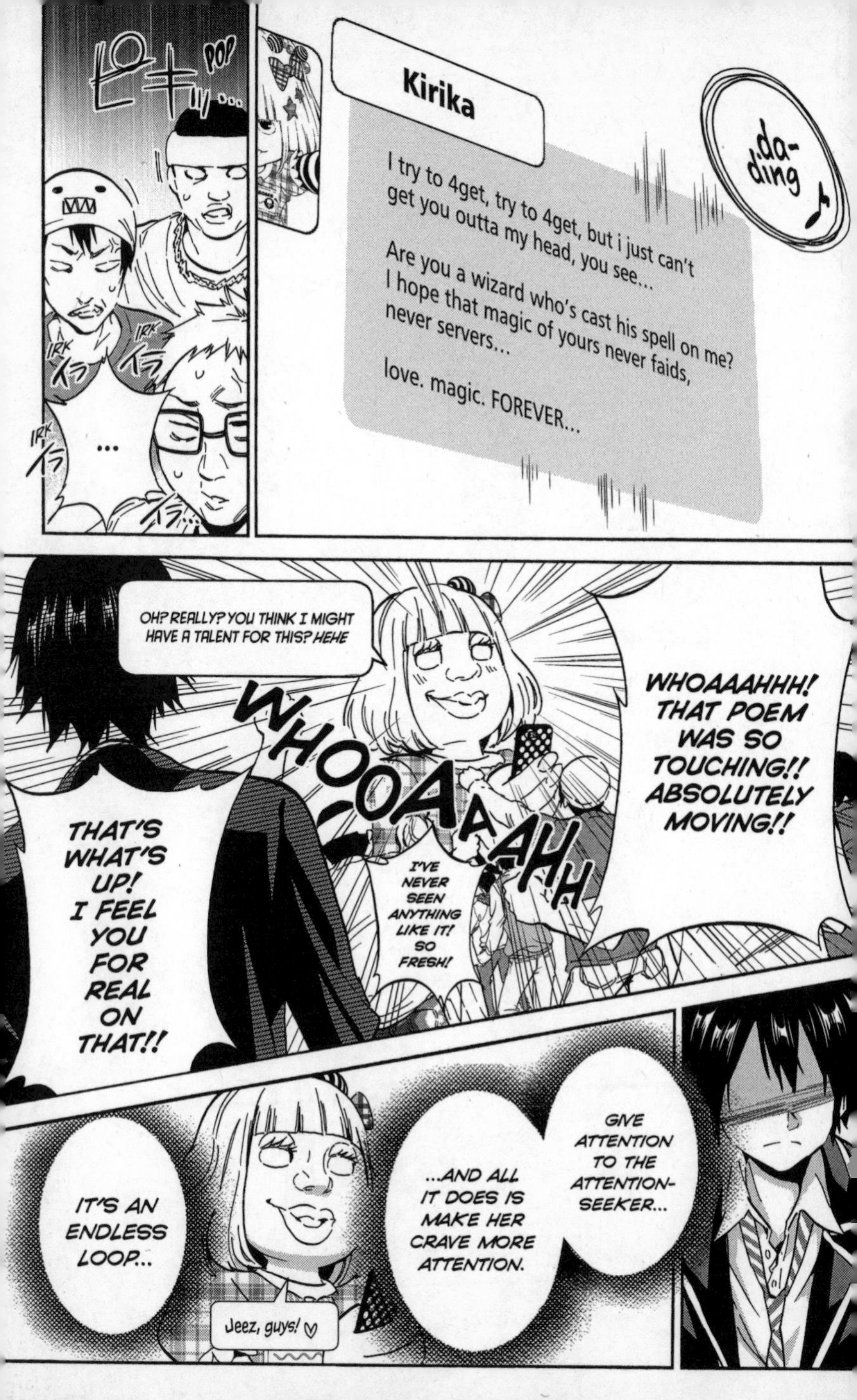
da-ding ♪
Kirika
I try to 4get, try to 4get, but i just can't get you outta my head, you see...
Are you a wizard who's cast his spell on me? I hope that magic of yours never faids, never servers...
love. magic. FOREVER...
POP
IRK
IRK
IRK
...
WHOAAAHHH! THAT POEM WAS SO TOUCHING!! ABSOLUTELY MOVING!!
I'VE NEVER SEEN ANYTHING LIKE IT! SO FRESH!
WHOOAAAHH
OH? REALLY? YOU THINK I MIGHT HAVE A TALENT FOR THIS? HEHE
THAT'S WHAT'S UP! I FEEL YOU FOR REAL ON THAT!!
GIVE ATTENTION TO THE ATTENTION-SEEKER...
...AND ALL IT DOES IS MAKE HER CRAVE MORE ATTENTION.
IT'S AN ENDLESS LOOP...
Jeez, guys! ♡

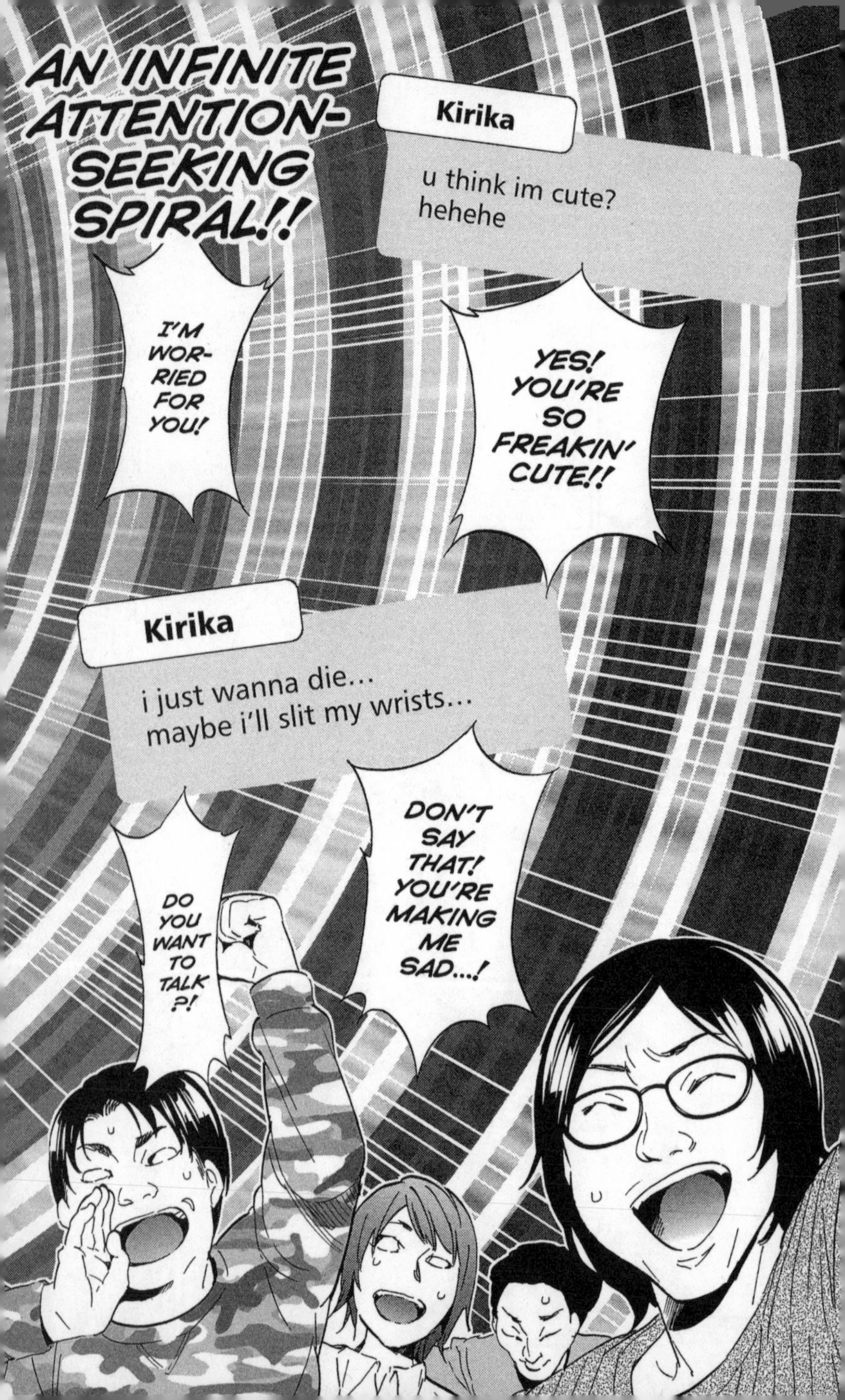

Kirika
u think im cute? hehehe
YES! YOU'RE SO FREAKIN' CUTE!!
I'M WORRIED FOR YOU!
AN INFINITE ATTENTION-SEEKING SPIRAL!!
Kirika
i just wanna die... maybe i'll slit my wrists...
DON'T SAY THAT! YOU'RE MAKING ME SAD...!
DO YOU WANT TO TALK?!

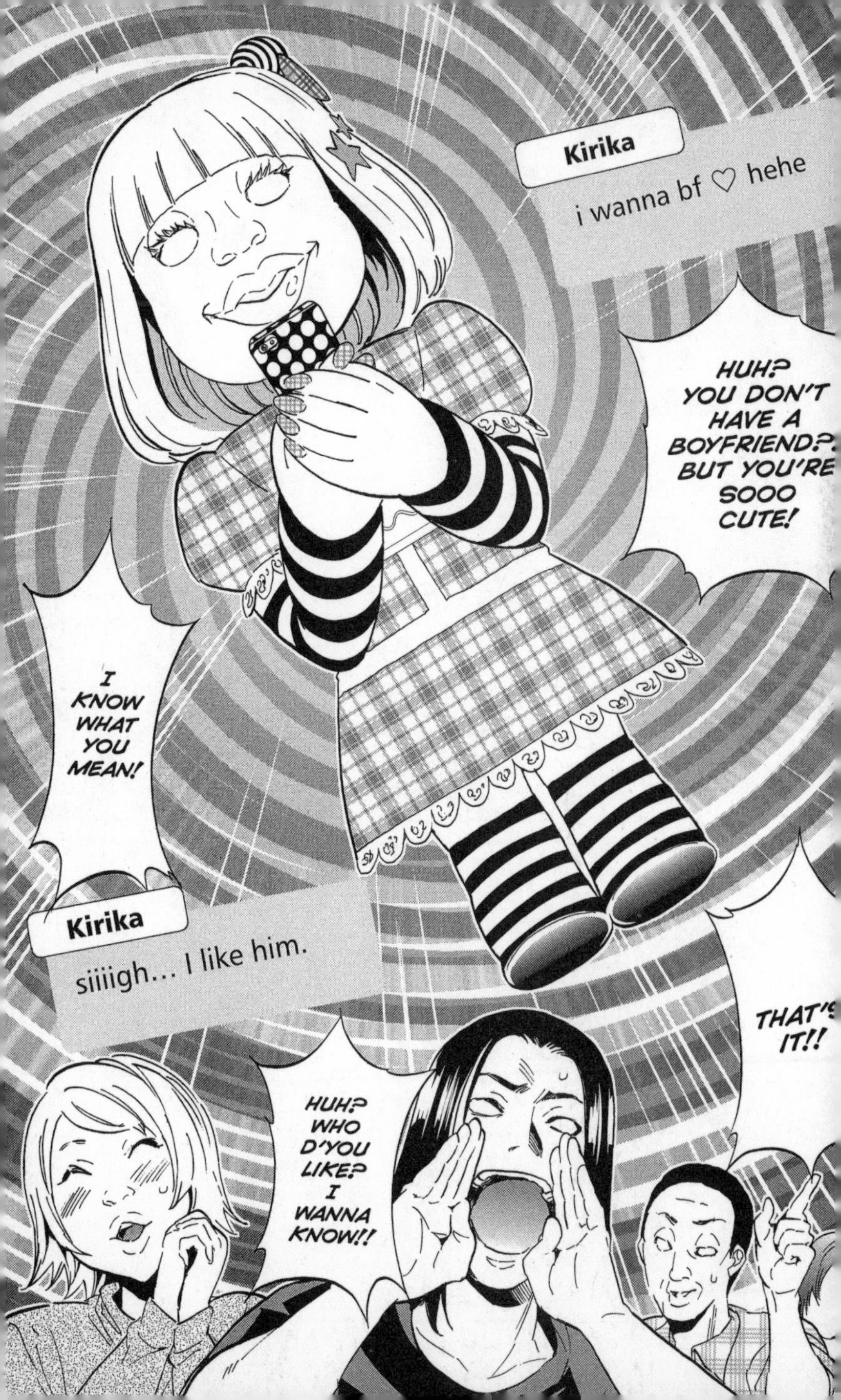
Kirika
i wanna bf ♡ hehe
HUH? YOU DON'T HAVE A BOYFRIEND?! BUT YOU'RE SOOO CUTE!
I KNOW WHAT YOU MEAN!
Kirika
siiiigh… I like him.
THAT'S IT!!
HUH? WHO D'YOU LIKE? I WANNA KNOW!!

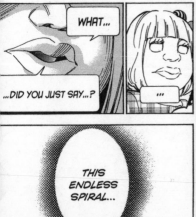

WHAT...

...DID YOU JUST SAY...?

...

THIS ENDLESS SPIRAL...

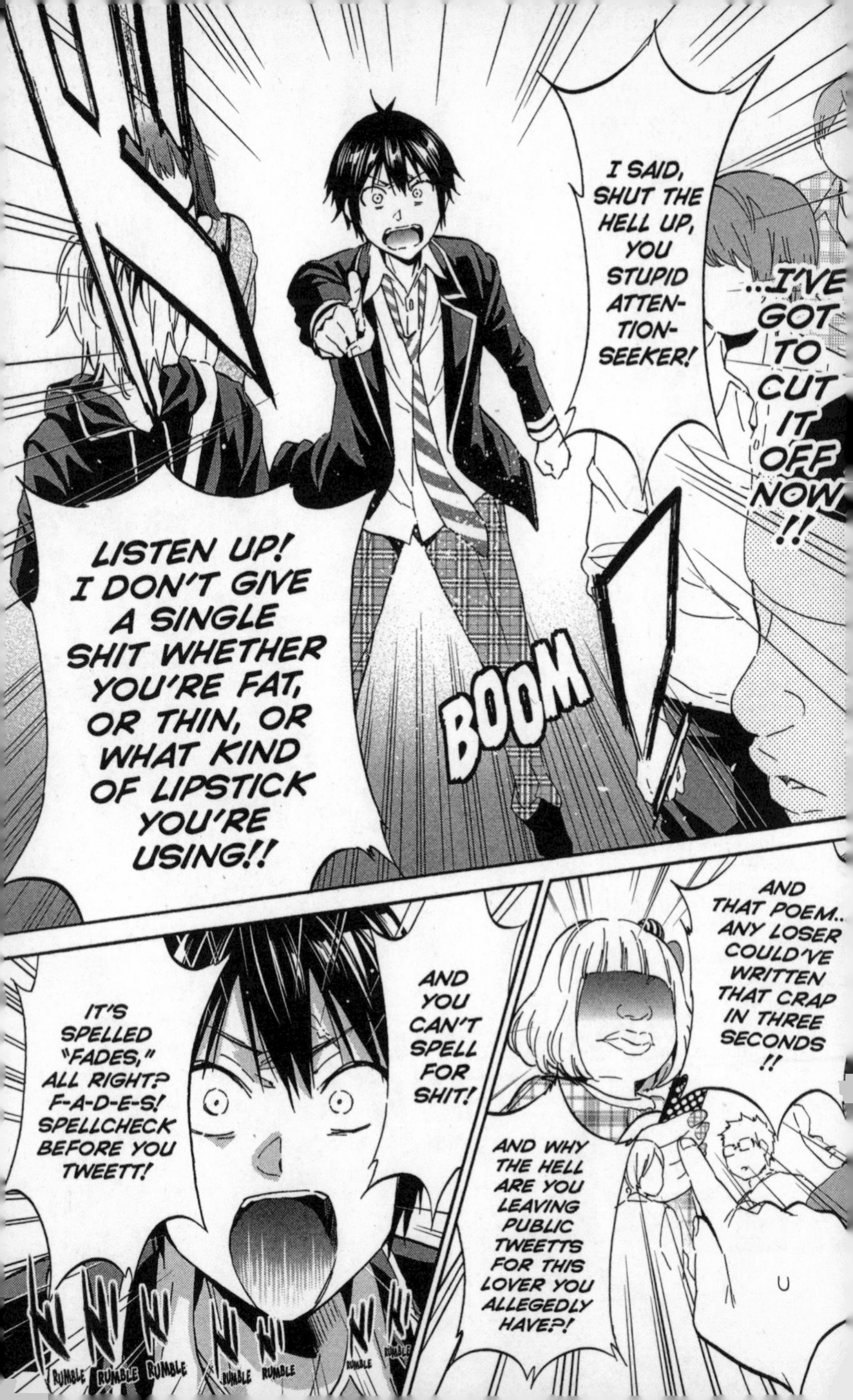
I SAID, SHUT THE HELL UP, YOU STUPID ATTEN-TION-SEEKER!
...I'VE GOT TO CUT IT OFF NOW!!
LISTEN UP! I DON'T GIVE A SINGLE SHIT WHETHER YOU'RE FAT, OR THIN, OR WHAT KIND OF LIPSTICK YOU'RE USING!!
BOOM
AND THAT POEM.. ANY LOSER COULD'VE WRITTEN THAT CRAP IN THREE SECONDS!!
AND WHY THE HELL ARE YOU LEAVING PUBLIC TWEETTS FOR THIS LOVER YOU ALLEGEDLY HAVE?!
AND YOU CAN'T SPELL FOR SHIT!
IT'S SPELLED "FADES," ALL RIGHT? F-A-D-E-S! SPELLCHECK BEFORE YOU TWEETT!
RUMBLE RUMBLE RUMBLE RUMBLE RUMBLE RUMBLE RUMBLE

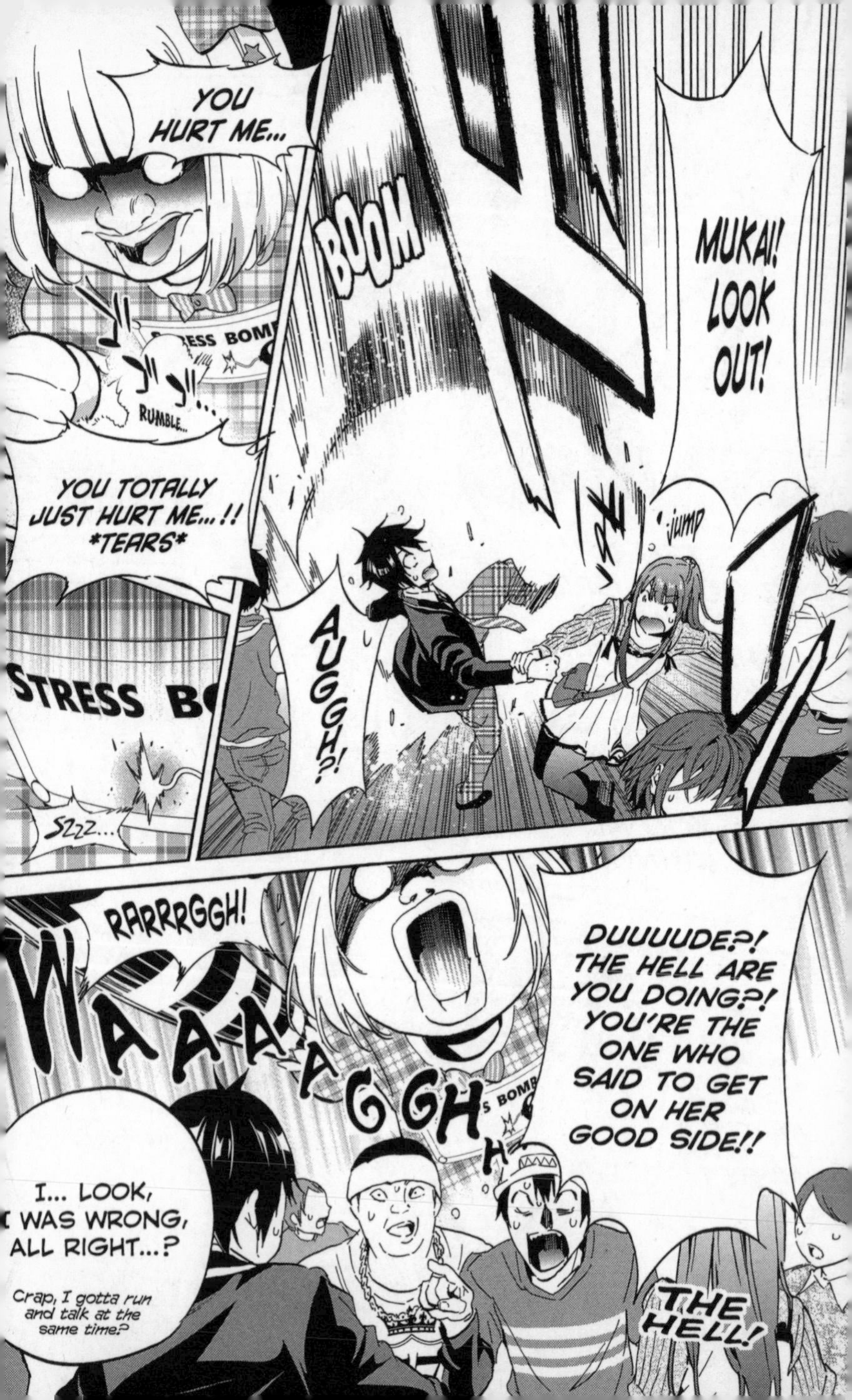
MUKAI! LOOK OUT!
BOOM
jump
AUGGH?!
YOU HURT ME...
RUMBLE...
YOU TOTALLY JUST HURT ME...!! *TEARS*
SZZZ...
DUUUUDE?! THE HELL ARE YOU DOING?! YOU'RE THE ONE WHO SAID TO GET ON HER GOOD SIDE!!
THE HELL!
RARRRGH!
WAAAAGGH
I... LOOK, I WAS WRONG, ALL RIGHT...?
Crap, I gotta run and talk at the same time?

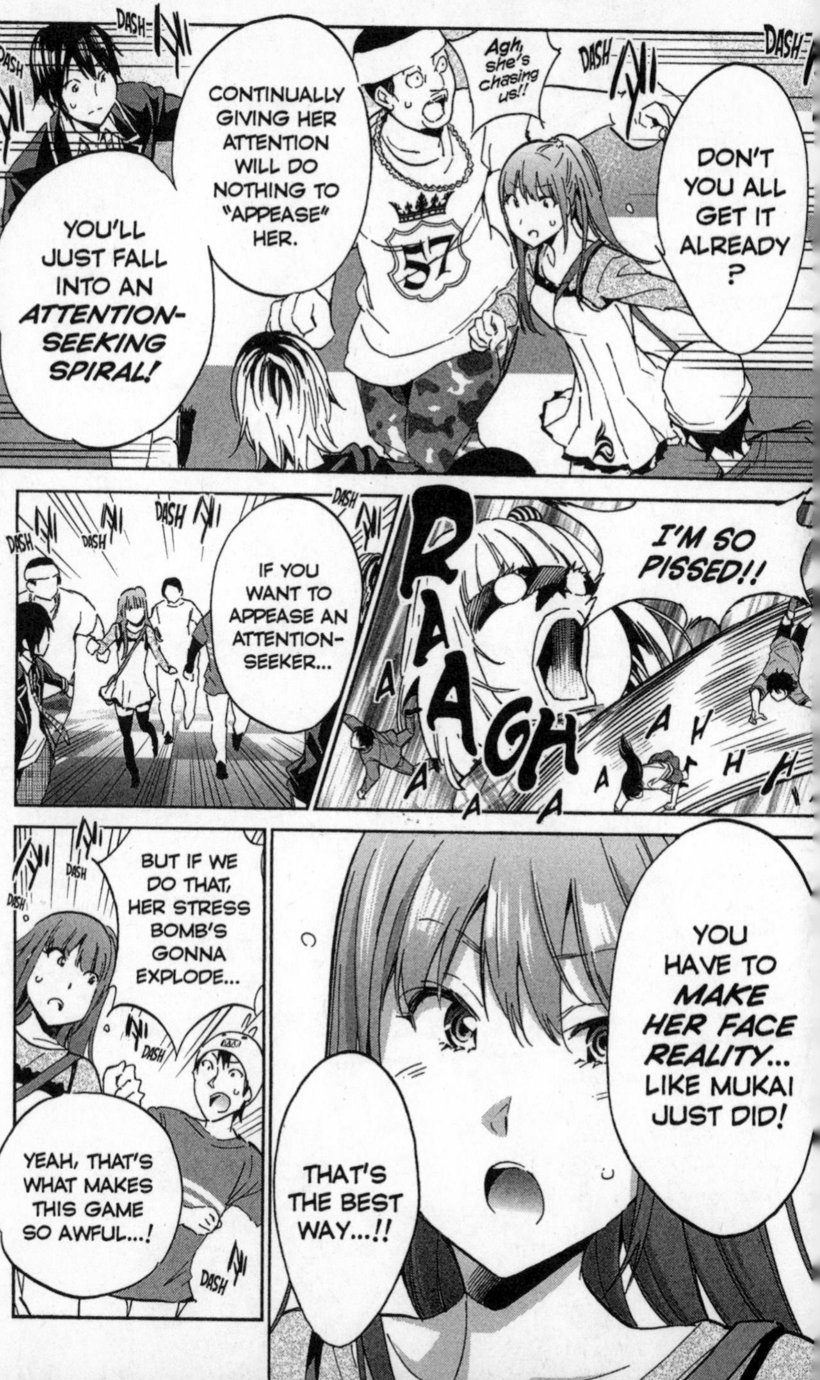
DASH
DON'T YOU ALL GET IT ALREADY?
Agh, she's chasing us!!
DASH
CONTINUALLY GIVING HER ATTENTION WILL DO NOTHING TO "APPEASE" HER.
DASH
DASH
YOU'LL JUST FALL INTO AN *ATTENTION-SEEKING SPIRAL!*
I'M SO PISSED!!
RAAAGH
AAAA
AHHH
DASH
IF YOU WANT TO APPEASE AN ATTENTION-SEEKER...
DASH
DASH
DASH
YOU HAVE TO *MAKE HER FACE REALITY...* LIKE MUKAI JUST DID!
THAT'S THE BEST WAY...!!
DASH
DASH
BUT IF WE DO THAT, HER STRESS BOMB'S GONNA EXPLODE...
DASH
YEAH, THAT'S WHAT MAKES THIS GAME SO AWFUL...!
DASH

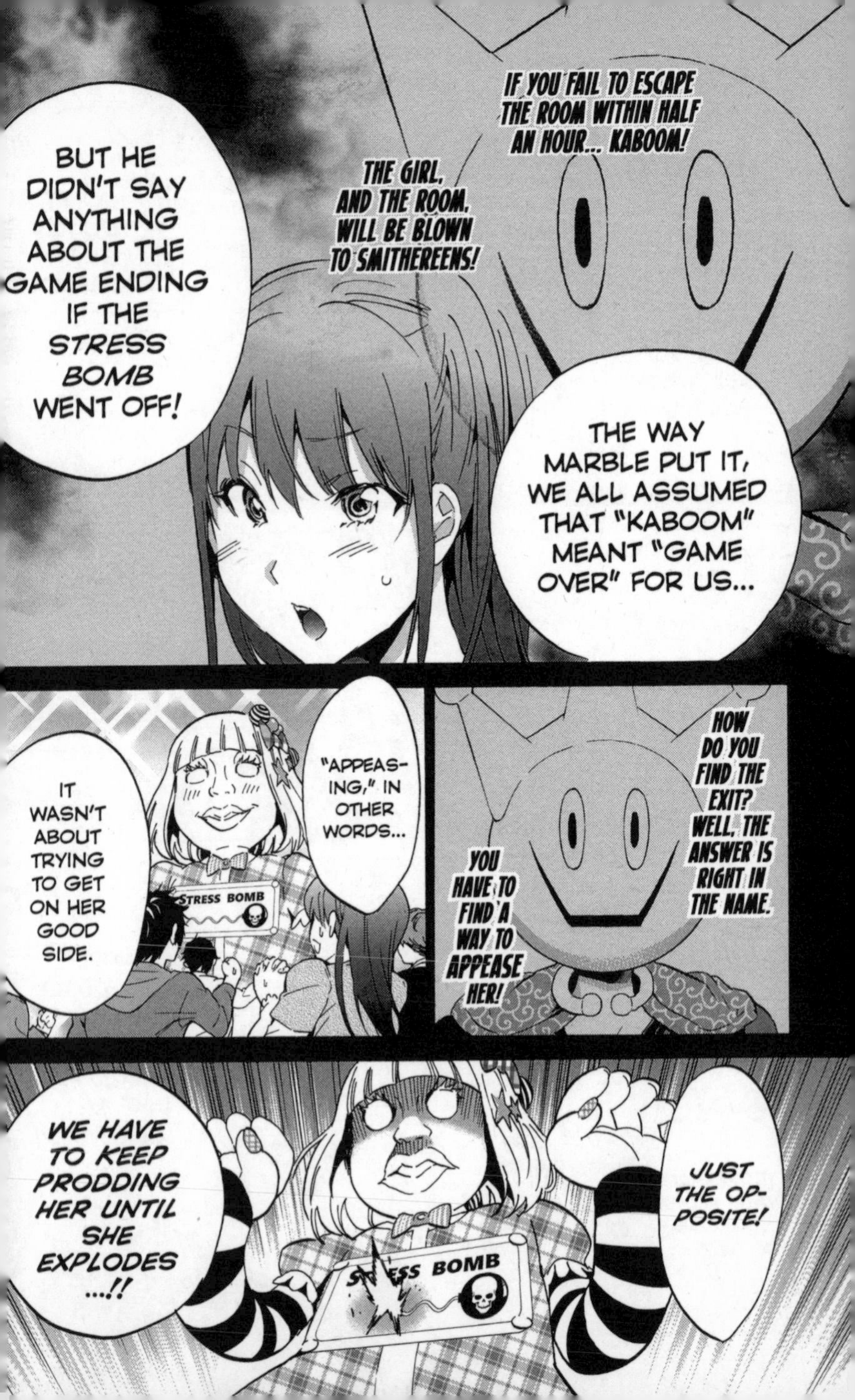
IF YOU FAIL TO ESCAPE THE ROOM WITHIN HALF AN HOUR... KABOOM!
THE GIRL, AND THE ROOM, WILL BE BLOWN TO SMITHEREENS!
THE WAY MARBLE PUT IT, WE ALL ASSUMED THAT "KABOOM" MEANT "GAME OVER" FOR US...
BUT HE DIDN'T SAY ANYTHING ABOUT THE GAME ENDING IF THE *STRESS BOMB* WENT OFF!
HOW DO YOU FIND THE EXIT? WELL, THE ANSWER IS RIGHT IN THE NAME.
YOU HAVE TO FIND A WAY TO APPEASE HER!
"APPEAS-ING," IN OTHER WORDS...
IT WASN'T ABOUT TRYING TO GET ON HER GOOD SIDE.
STRESS BOMB
JUST THE OP-POSITE!
WE HAVE TO KEEP PRODDING HER UNTIL SHE EXPLODES ...!!

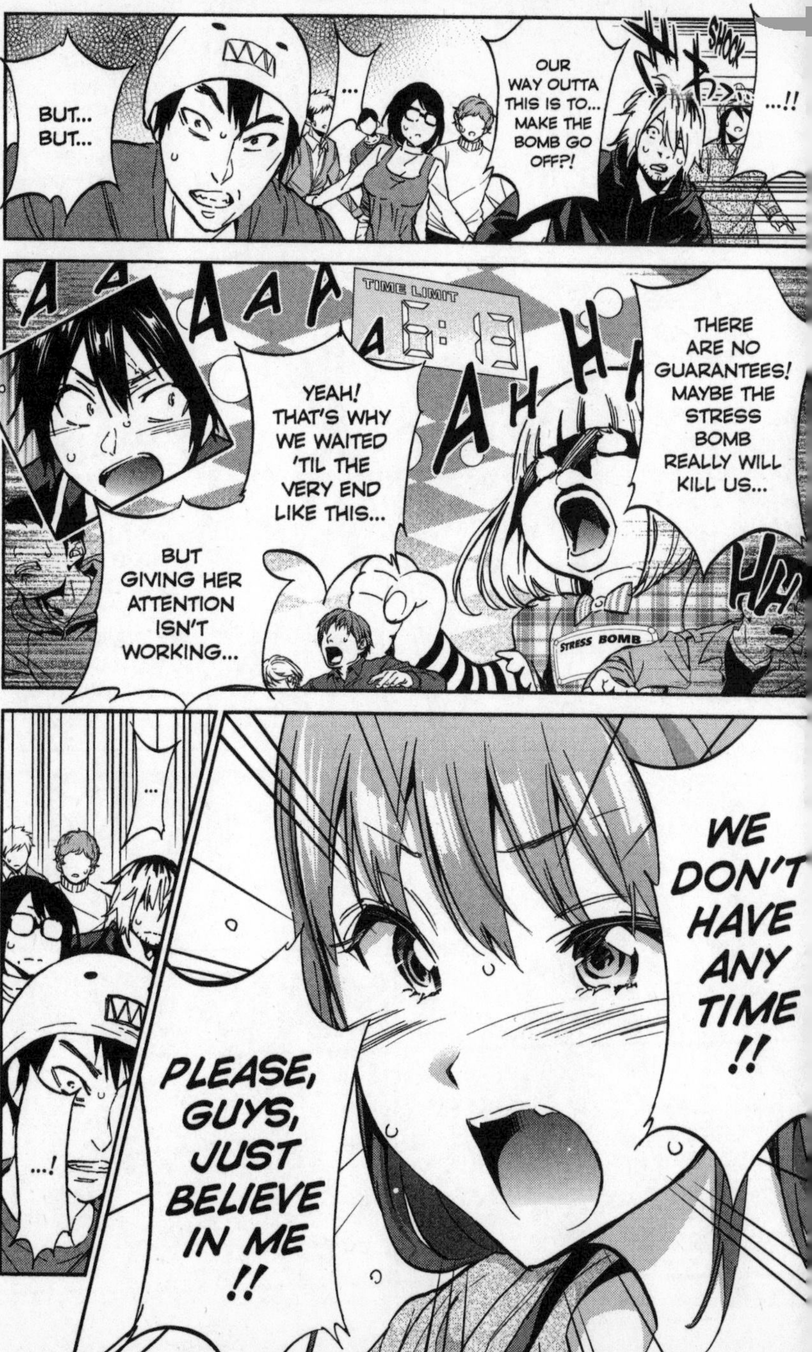
SHOCK
...!!
OUR WAY OUTTA THIS IS TO... MAKE THE BOMB GO OFF?!
...
BUT... BUT...
THERE ARE NO GUARANTEES! MAYBE THE STRESS BOMB REALLY WILL KILL US...
AAAAAAHHHH
TIME LIMIT
6:13
YEAH! THAT'S WHY WE WAITED 'TIL THE VERY END LIKE THIS...
BUT GIVING HER ATTENTION ISN'T WORKING...
STRESS BOMB
WE DON'T HAVE ANY TIME!!
...
PLEASE, GUYS, JUST BELIEVE IN ME!!
...!

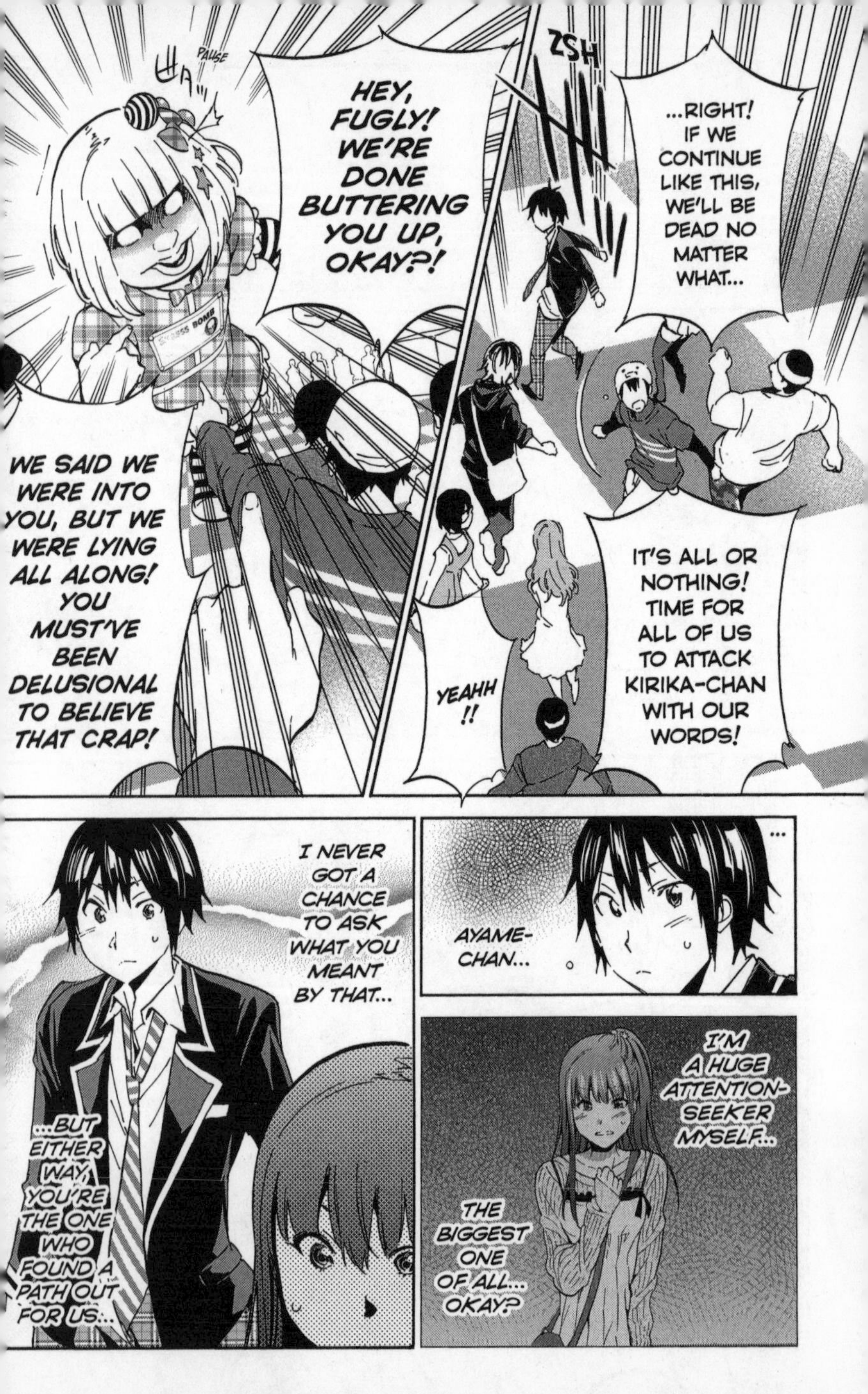
ZSH
...RIGHT! IF WE CONTINUE LIKE THIS, WE'LL BE DEAD NO MATTER WHAT...
IT'S ALL OR NOTHING! TIME FOR ALL OF US TO ATTACK KIRIKA-CHAN WITH OUR WORDS!
YEAHH !!
PAUSE
HEY, FUGLY! WE'RE DONE BUTTERING YOU UP, OKAY?!
WE SAID WE WERE INTO YOU, BUT WE WERE LYING ALL ALONG! YOU MUST'VE BEEN DELUSIONAL TO BELIEVE THAT CRAP!
...
AYAME-CHAN...
I'M A HUGE ATTENTION-SEEKER MYSELF...
THE BIGGEST ONE OF ALL... OKAY?
I NEVER GOT A CHANCE TO ASK WHAT YOU MEANT BY THAT...
...BUT EITHER WAY, YOU'RE THE ONE WHO FOUND A PATH OUT FOR US...

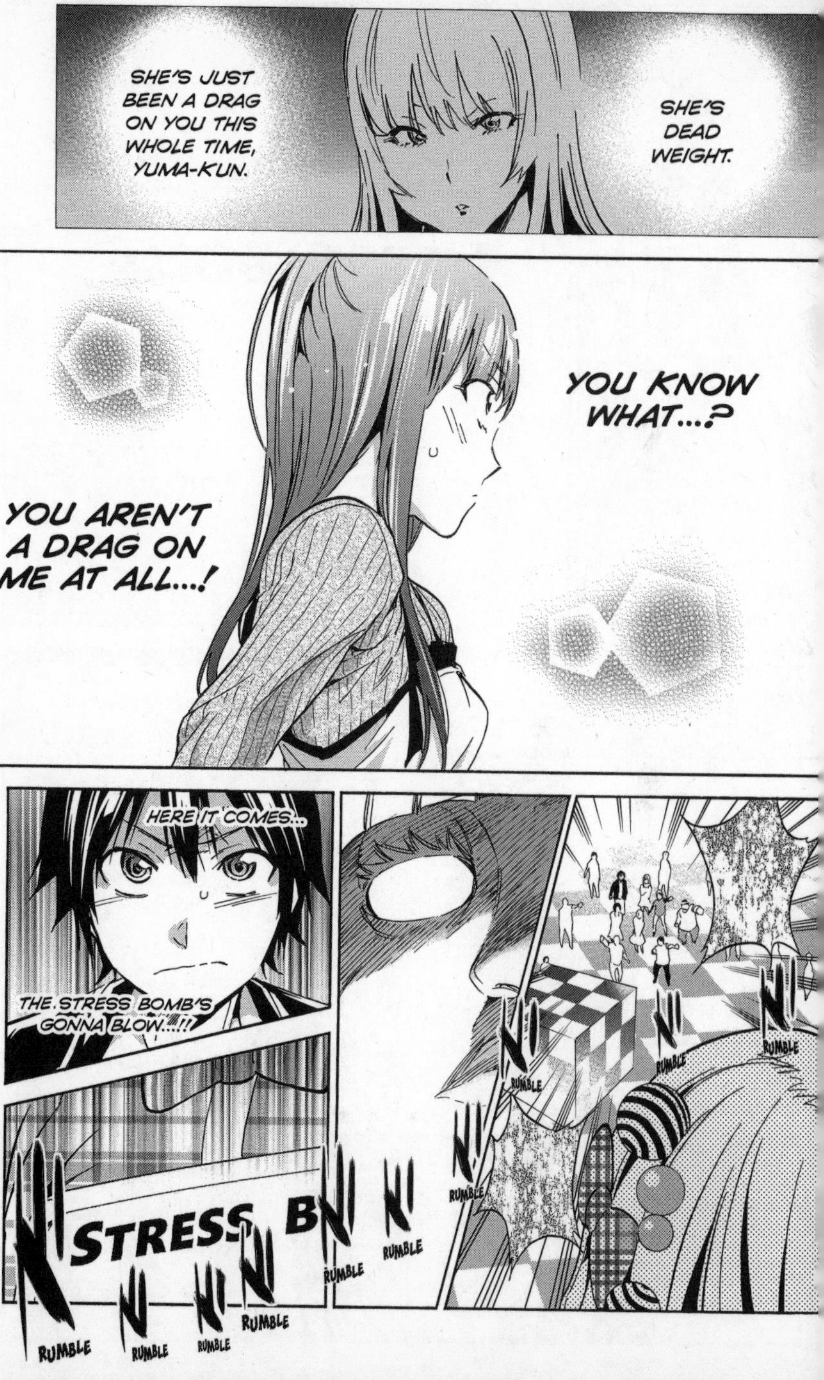
SHE'S DEAD WEIGHT.
SHE'S JUST BEEN A DRAG ON YOU THIS WHOLE TIME, YUMA-KUN.
YOU KNOW WHAT...?
YOU AREN'T A DRAG ON ME AT ALL...!
RUMBLE
RUMBLE
RUMBLE
RUMBLE
HERE IT COMES...
THE STRESS BOMB'S GONNA BLOW...!!
STRESS B
RUMBLE
RUMBLE
RUMBLE
RUMBLE
RUMBLE
RUMBLE
RUMBLE

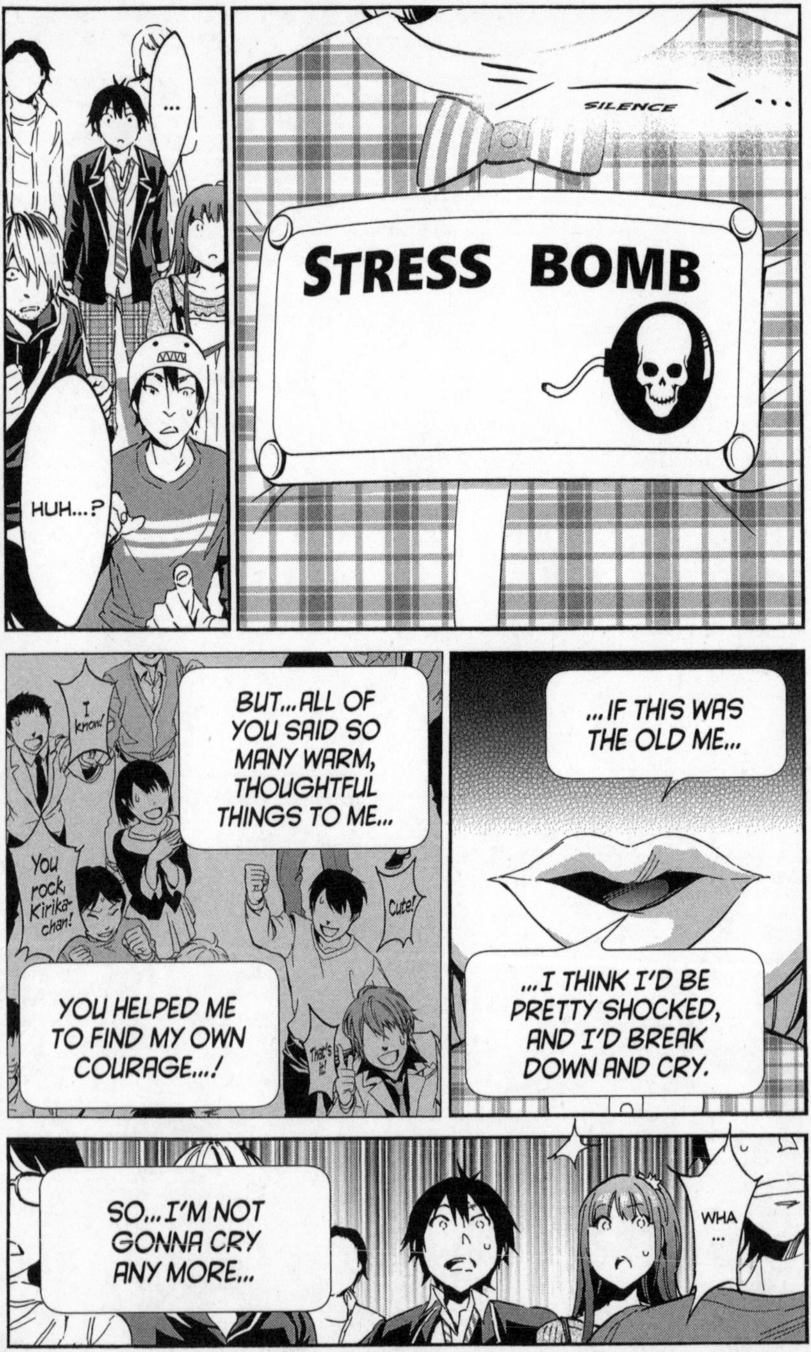
SILENCE
...
STRESS BOMB
...
HUH...?
...IF THIS WAS THE OLD ME...
...I THINK I'D BE PRETTY SHOCKED, AND I'D BREAK DOWN AND CRY.
BUT...ALL OF YOU SAID SO MANY WARM, THOUGHTFUL THINGS TO ME...
I know!
Cute!
You rock, Kirika-chan!
That's it!
YOU HELPED ME TO FIND MY OWN COURAGE...!
WHA ...
SO...I'M NOT GONNA CRY ANY MORE...

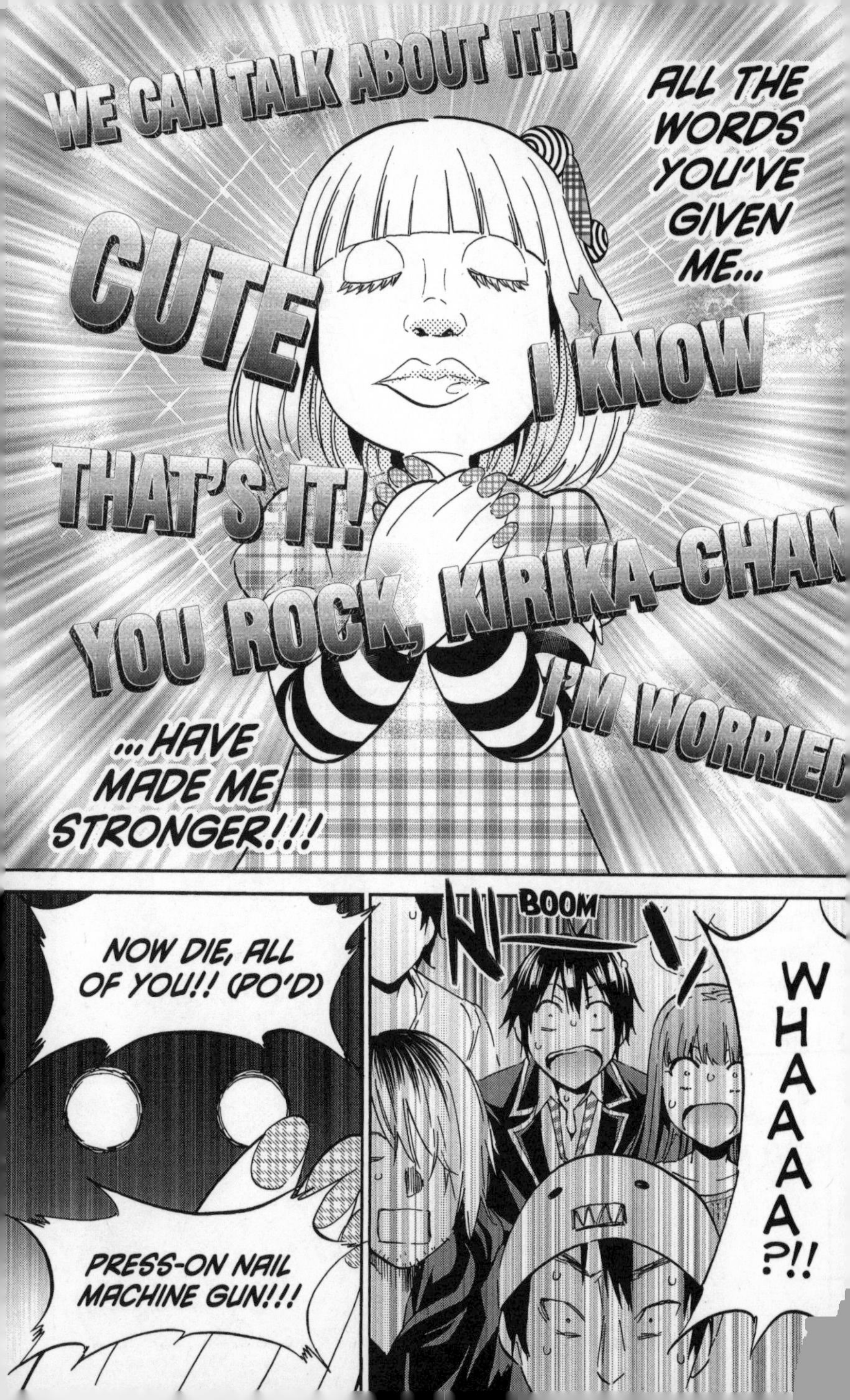
ALL THE WORDS YOU'VE GIVEN ME...
WE CAN TALK ABOUT IT!!
CUTE
I KNOW
THAT'S IT!
YOU ROCK, KIRIKA-CHAN
I'M WORRIED
...HAVE MADE ME STRONGER!!!
BOOM
WHAAAAA?!!
NOW DIE, ALL OF YOU!! (PO'D)
PRESS-ON NAIL MACHINE GUN!!!

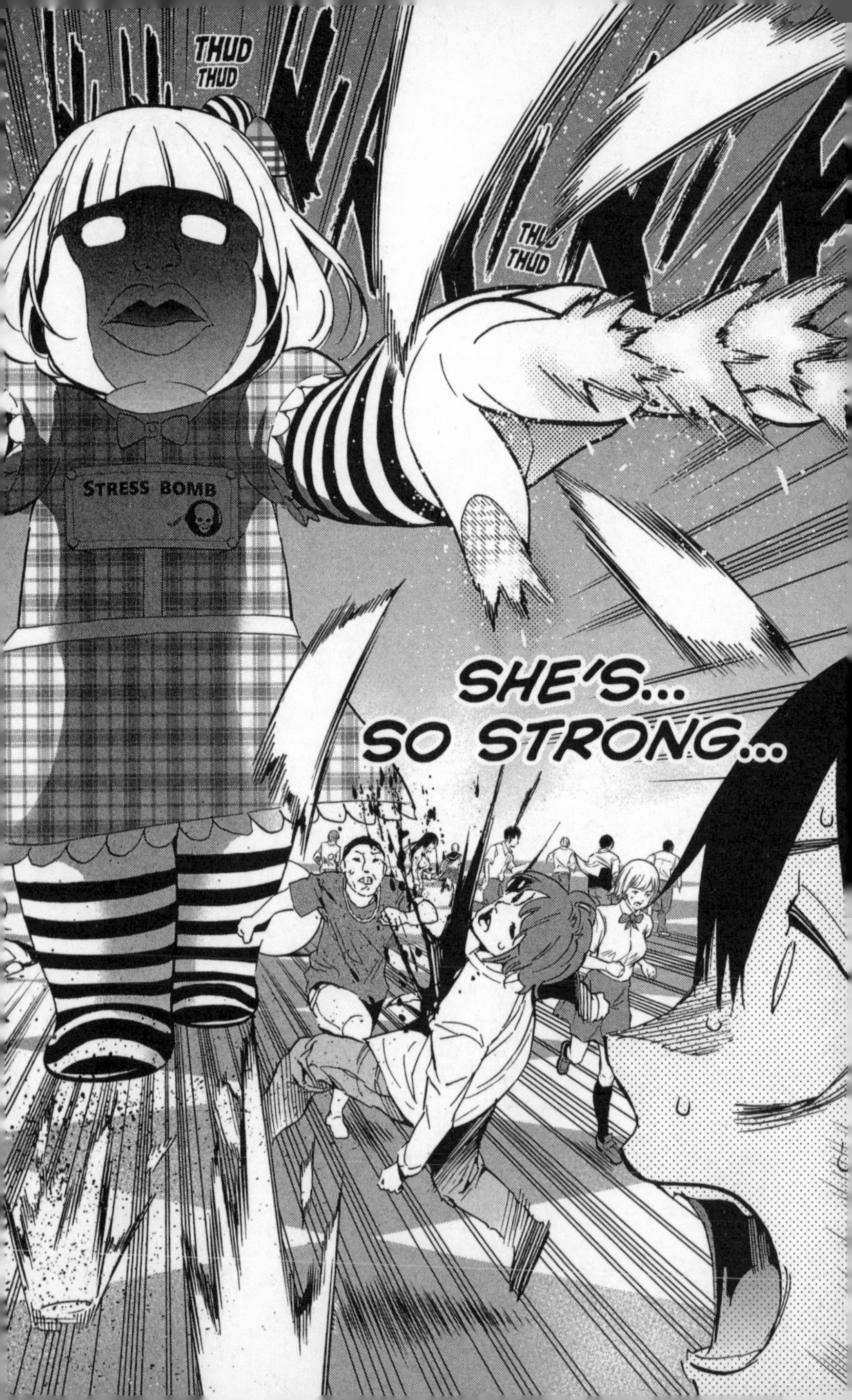
THUD
THUD
THUD
THUD
STRESS BOMB
SHE'S... SO STRONG...

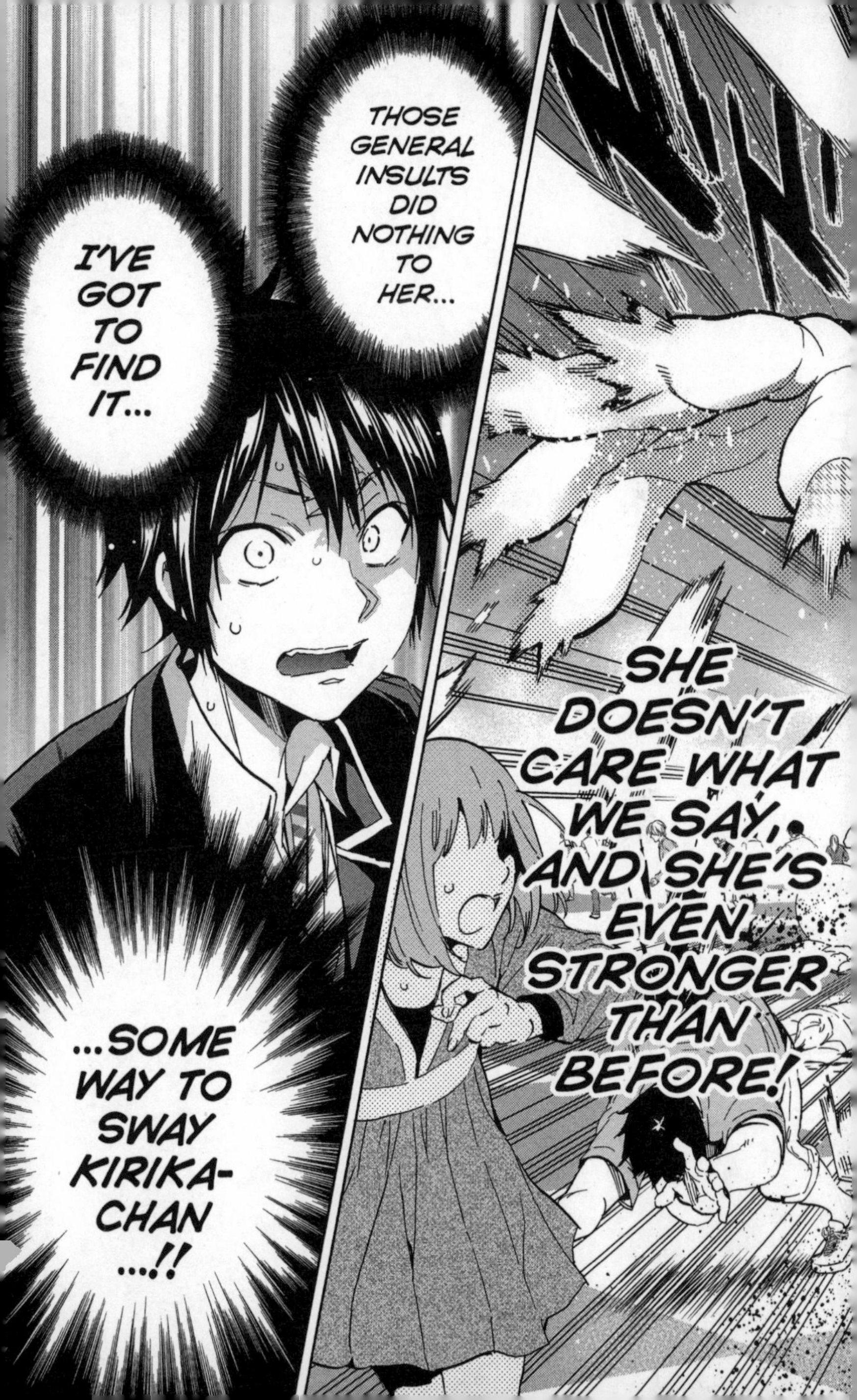
SHE DOESN'T CARE WHAT WE SAY, AND SHE'S EVEN STRONGER THAN BEFORE!
THOSE GENERAL INSULTS DID NOTHING TO HER...
I'VE GOT TO FIND IT...
...SOME WAY TO SWAY KIRIKA-CHAN ...!!

REAL ACCOUNT

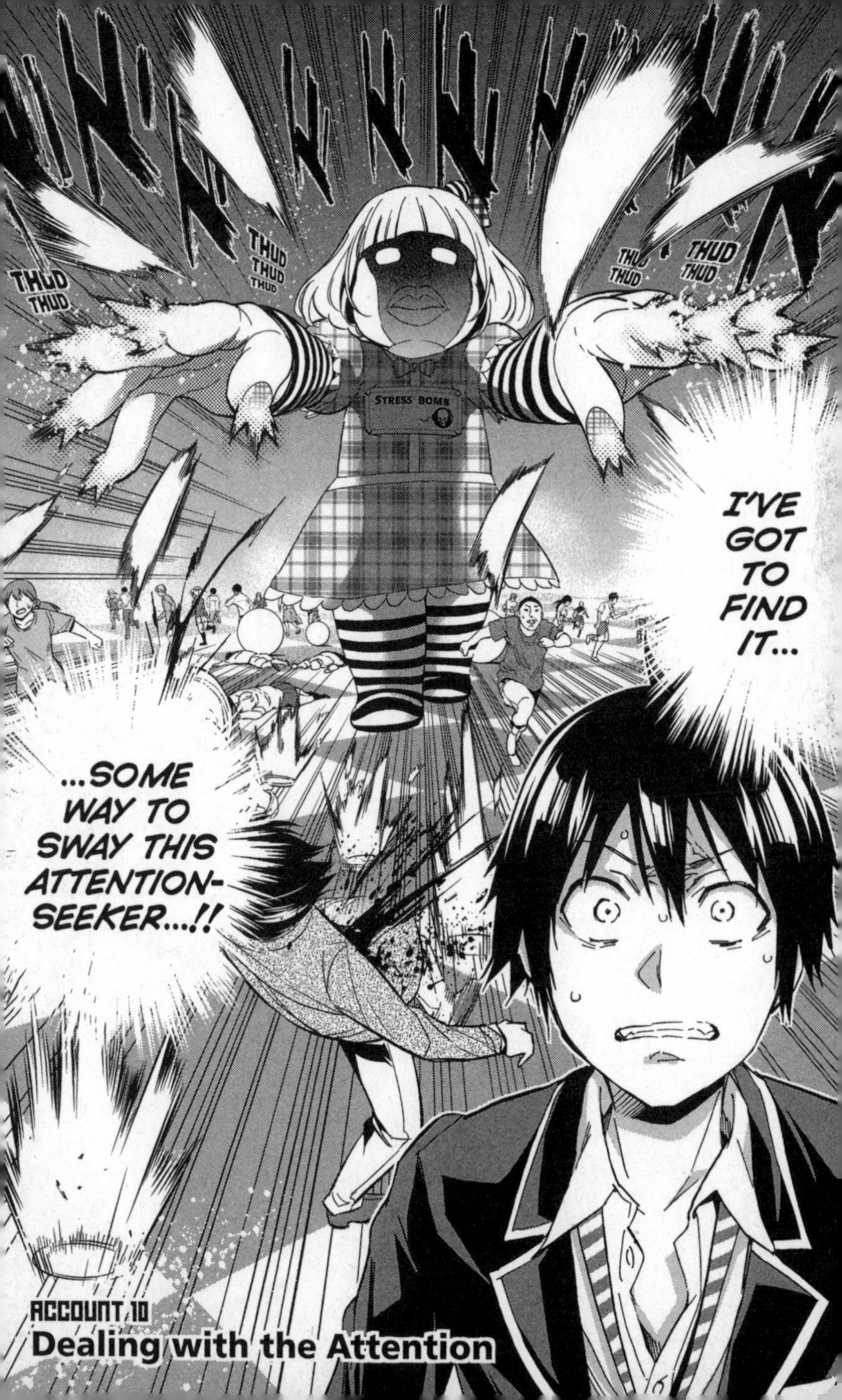
THUD THUD
THUD THUD
STRESS BOMB
THUD THUD THUD
THUD THUD
I'VE GOT TO FIND IT...
...SOME WAY TO SWAY THIS ATTENTION-SEEKER...!!

ACCOUNT 10
Dealing with the Attention

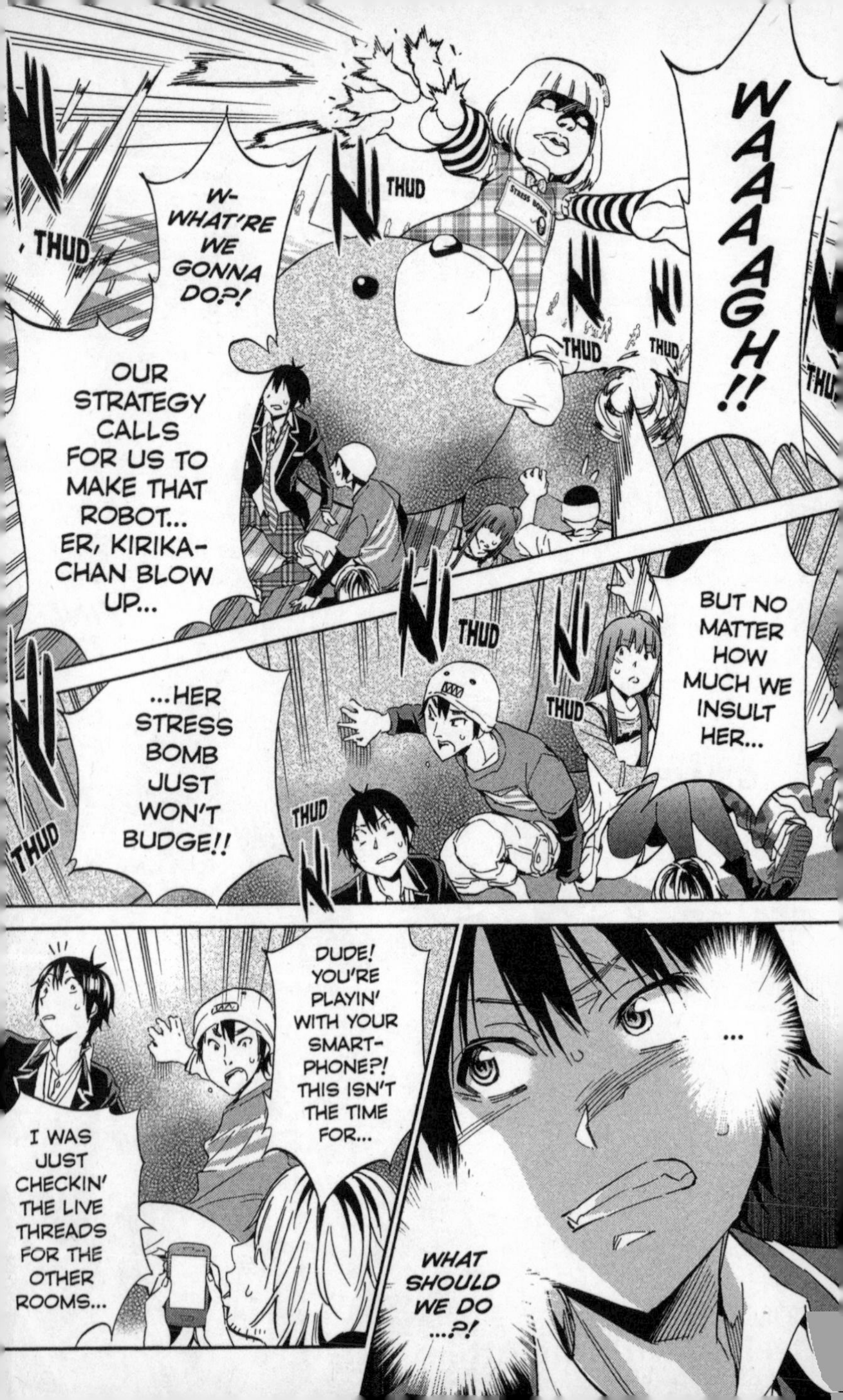
WAAAAAGH!!
THUD
THUD
THUD
THUD
W-WHAT'RE WE GONNA DO?!
THUD
OUR STRATEGY CALLS FOR US TO MAKE THAT ROBOT... ER, KIRIKA-CHAN BLOW UP...
BUT NO MATTER HOW MUCH WE INSULT HER...
THUD
THUD
...HER STRESS BOMB JUST WON'T BUDGE!!
THUD
THUD
...
WHAT SHOULD WE DO ...?!
DUDE! YOU'RE PLAYIN' WITH YOUR SMART-PHONE?! THIS ISN'T THE TIME FOR...
I WAS JUST CHECKIN' THE LIVE THREADS FOR THE OTHER ROOMS...

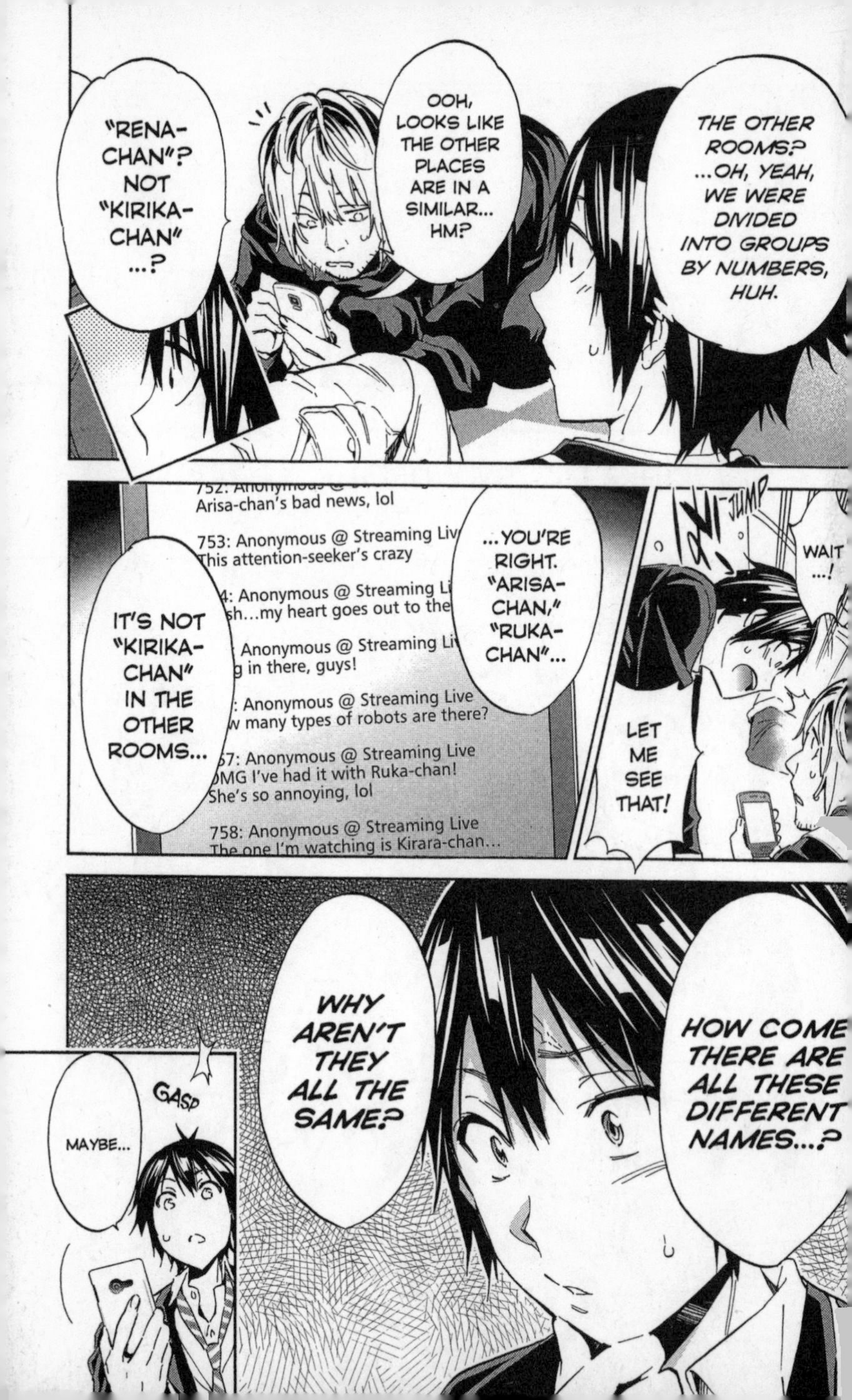
THE OTHER ROOMS? ...OH, YEAH, WE WERE DIVIDED INTO GROUPS BY NUMBERS, HUH.
OOH, LOOKS LIKE THE OTHER PLACES ARE IN A SIMILAR... HM?
"RENA-CHAN"? NOT "KIRIKA-CHAN" ...?
JUMP
WAIT ...!
LET ME SEE THAT!
...YOU'RE RIGHT. "ARISA-CHAN," "RUKA-CHAN"...
Arisa-chan's bad news, lol
753: Anonymous @ Streaming Live
This attention-seeker's crazy
Anonymous @ Streaming Live
my heart goes out to the
Anonymous @ Streaming Live
in there, guys!
Anonymous @ Streaming Live
many types of robots are there?
Anonymous @ Streaming Live
I've had it with Ruka-chan!
She's so annoying, lol
758: Anonymous @ Streaming Live
IT'S NOT "KIRIKA-CHAN" IN THE OTHER ROOMS...
HOW COME THERE ARE ALL THESE DIFFERENT NAMES...?
WHY AREN'T THEY ALL THE SAME?
GASP
MAYBE...

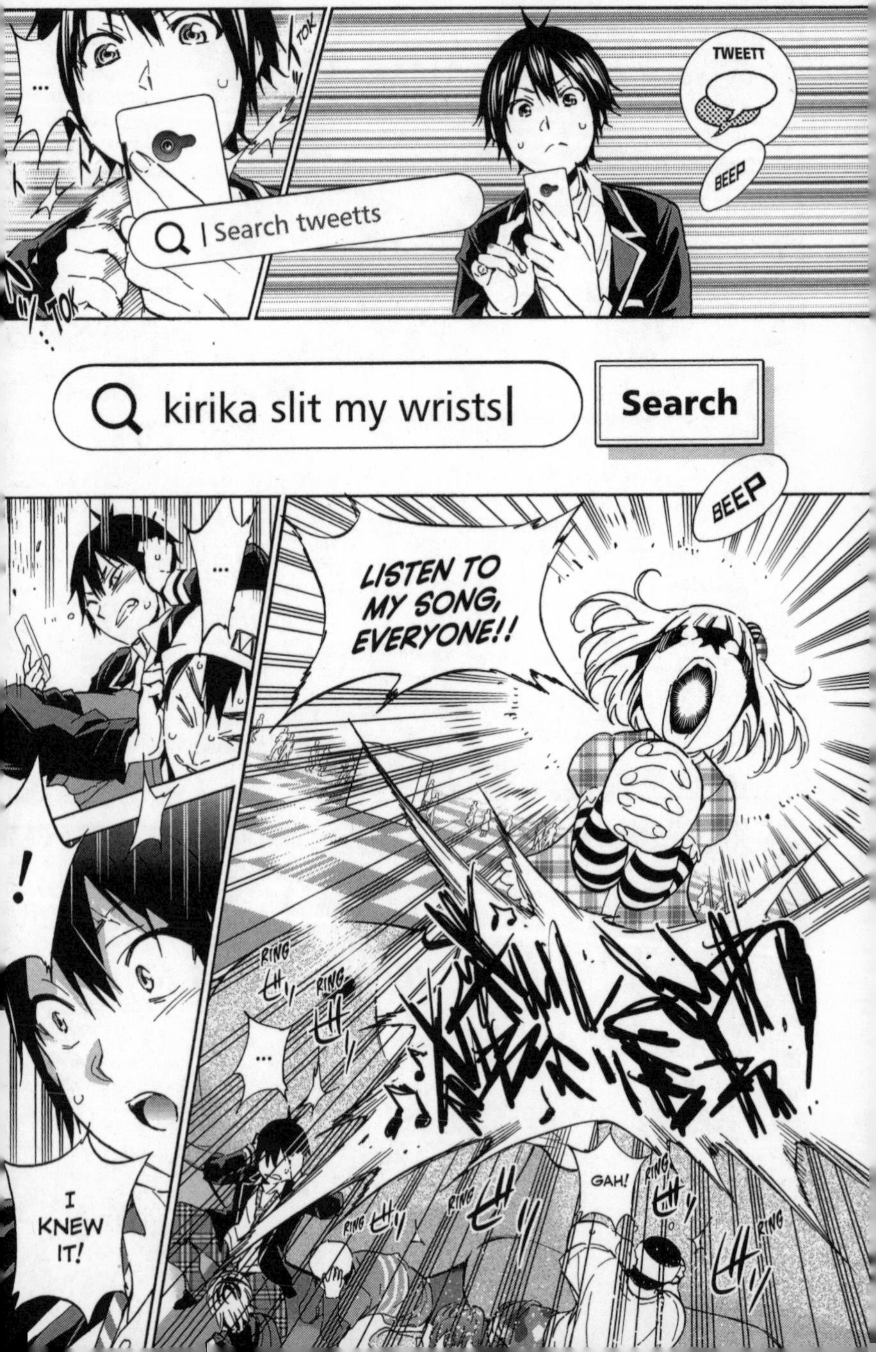
TWEETT
BEEP
...
TOK
TOK
Search tweetts
kirika slit my wrists
Search
BEEP
LISTEN TO MY SONG, EVERYONE!!
RING
RING
...
GAH!
RING
RING
RING
RING
...
!
I KNEW IT!

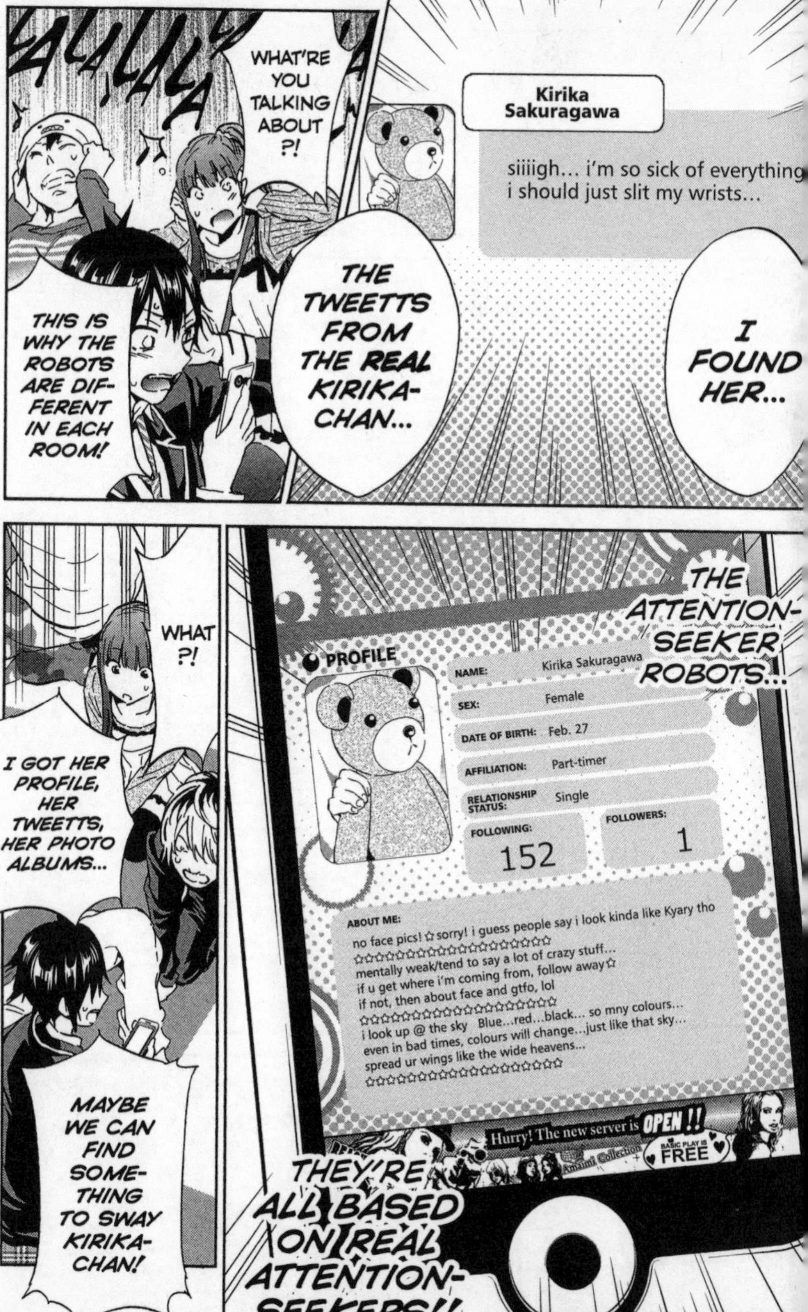

Kirika Sakuragawa
siiiigh... i'm so sick of everything
i should just slit my wrists...
I FOUND HER...
WHAT'RE YOU TALKING ABOUT?!
THE TWEETTS FROM THE REAL KIRIKA-CHAN...
THIS IS WHY THE ROBOTS ARE DIF-FERENT IN EACH ROOM!
THE ATTENTION-SEEKER ROBOTS...
PROFILE
NAME: Kirika Sakuragawa
SEX: Female
DATE OF BIRTH: Feb. 27
AFFILIATION: Part-timer
RELATIONSHIP STATUS: Single
FOLLOWING: 152
FOLLOWERS: 1
ABOUT ME:
no face pics! ✩ sorry! i guess people say i look kinda like Kyary tho
✩✩✩✩✩✩✩✩✩✩✩✩✩✩✩✩✩✩✩✩✩
mentally weak/tend to say a lot of crazy stuff...
if u get where i'm coming from, follow away✩
if not, then about face and gtfo, lol
✩✩✩✩✩✩✩✩✩✩✩✩✩✩✩✩✩✩✩✩✩
i look up @ the sky Blue...red...black... so mny colours...
even in bad times, colours will change...just like that sky...
spread ur wings like the wide heavens...
✩✩✩✩✩✩✩✩✩✩✩✩✩✩✩✩✩✩✩✩✩
Hurry! The new server is OPEN!!
BASIC PLAY IS FREE
THEY'RE ALL BASED ON REAL ATTENTION-SEEKERS!!
WHAT?!
I GOT HER PROFILE, HER TWEETTS, HER PHOTO ALBUMS...
MAYBE WE CAN FIND SOME-THING TO SWAY KIRIKA-CHAN!

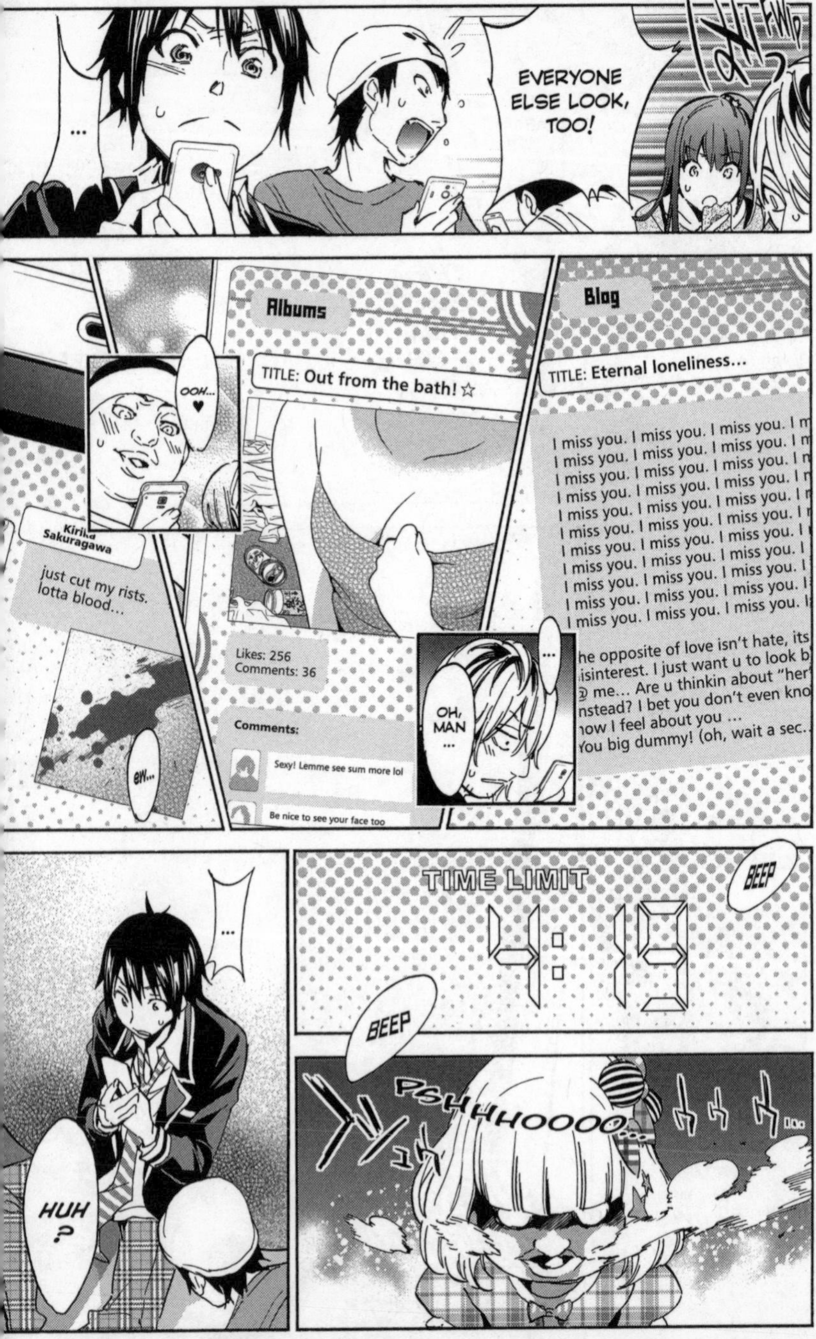
EVERYONE ELSE LOOK, TOO!
...
Blog
TITLE: Eternal loneliness...
I miss you. I miss you. I miss you. I m
I miss you. I miss you. I miss you. I m
I miss you. I miss you. I miss you. I m
I miss you. I miss you. I miss you. I m
I miss you. I miss you. I miss you. I m
I miss you. I miss you. I miss you. I
I miss you. I miss you. I miss you. I
I miss you. I miss you. I miss you. I
I miss you. I miss you. I miss you. I
I miss you. I miss you. I miss you. I
I miss you. I miss you. I miss you. I
he opposite of love isn't hate, its
isinterest. I just want u to look b
@ me... Are u thinkin about "her"
nstead? I bet you don't even kno
now I feel about you ...
You big dummy! (oh, wait a sec..
...
OH, MAN ...
Albums
TITLE: Out from the bath! ☆
Likes: 256
Comments: 36
Comments:
Sexy! Lemme see sum more lol
Be nice to see your face too
OOH... ♥
Kirika Sakuragawa
just cut my rists. lotta blood...
ew...
TIME LIMIT
4:19
BEEP
BEEP
PSHHHOOOO...
...
HUH?

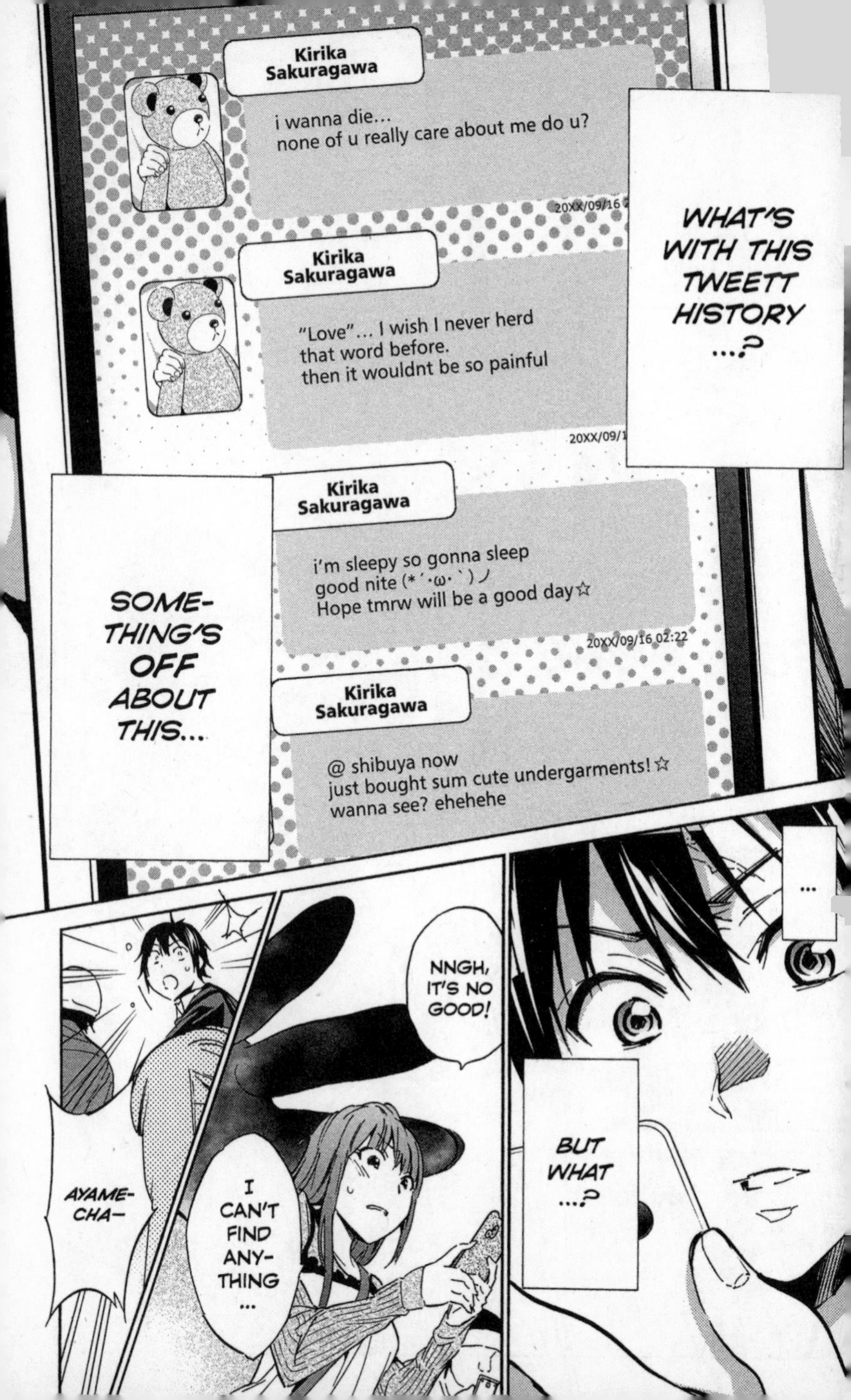
Kirika Sakuragawa
i wanna die...
none of u really care about me do u?
20XX/09/16 2
WHAT'S WITH THIS TWEETT HISTORY ...?
Kirika Sakuragawa
"Love"... I wish I never herd that word before.
then it wouldnt be so painful
20XX/09/1
Kirika Sakuragawa
i'm sleepy so gonna sleep
good nite (*´･ω･`)ノ
Hope tmrw will be a good day☆
20XX/09/16 02:22
SOME-THING'S OFF ABOUT THIS...
Kirika Sakuragawa
@ shibuya now
just bought sum cute undergarments! ☆
wanna see? ehehehe
...
BUT WHAT ...?
NNGH, IT'S NO GOOD!
I CAN'T FIND ANY-THING ...
AYAME-CHA-

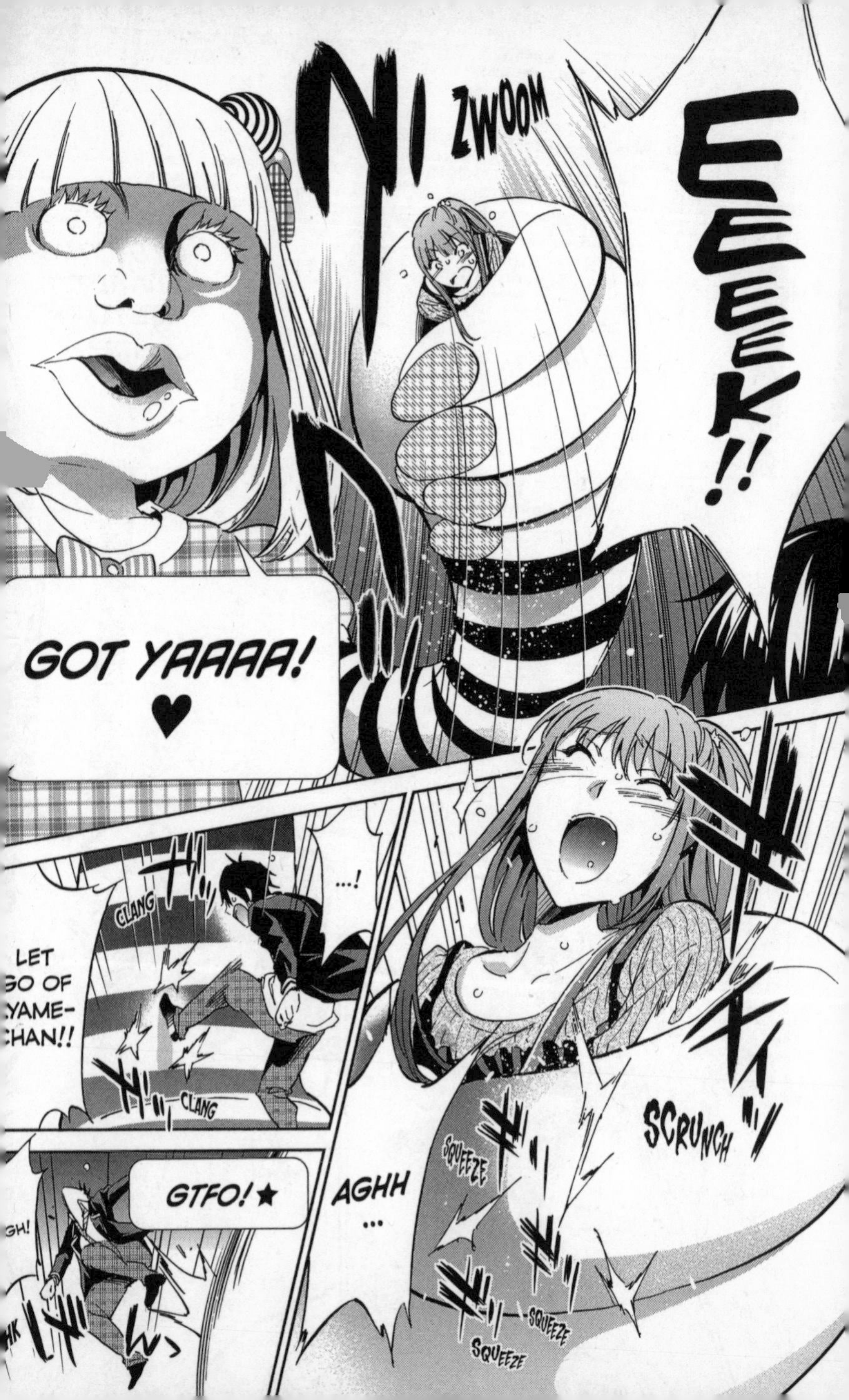
EEEEK!!
ZWOOM
GOT YAAAA! ♥
SCRUNCH
SQUEEZE
AGHH ...
SQUEEZE
SQUEEZE
...!
CLANG
LET GO OF YAME-HAN!!
CLANG
GTFO!★
GH!

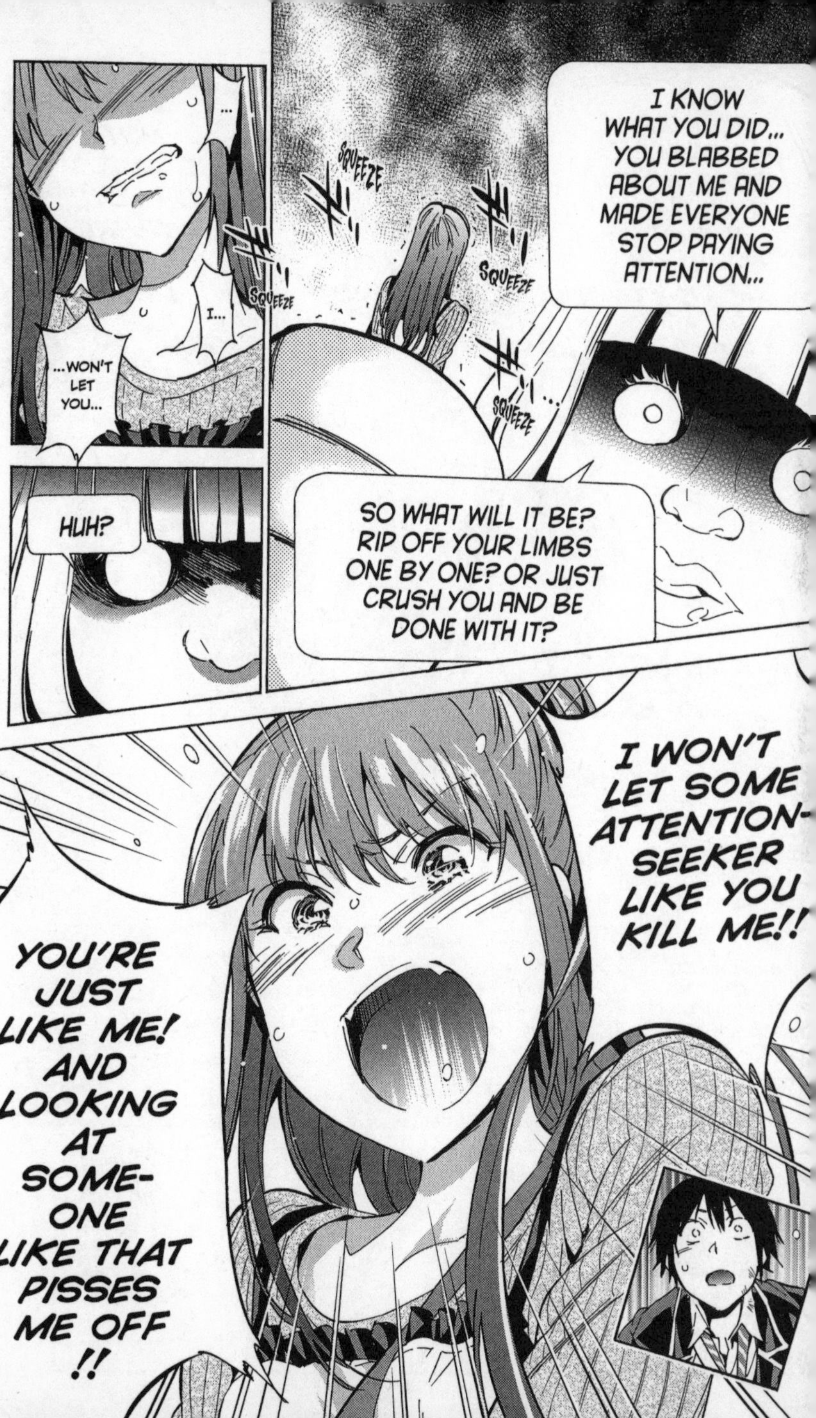

I KNOW WHAT YOU DID... YOU BLABBED ABOUT ME AND MADE EVERYONE STOP PAYING ATTENTION...
SQUEEZE
SQUEEZE
SQUEEZE
SQUEEZE
...
SO WHAT WILL IT BE? RIP OFF YOUR LIMBS ONE BY ONE? OR JUST CRUSH YOU AND BE DONE WITH IT?
...
I...
...WON'T LET YOU...
HUH?
I WON'T LET SOME ATTENTION-SEEKER LIKE YOU KILL ME!!
YOU'RE JUST LIKE ME! AND LOOKING AT SOME-ONE LIKE THAT PISSES ME OFF!!

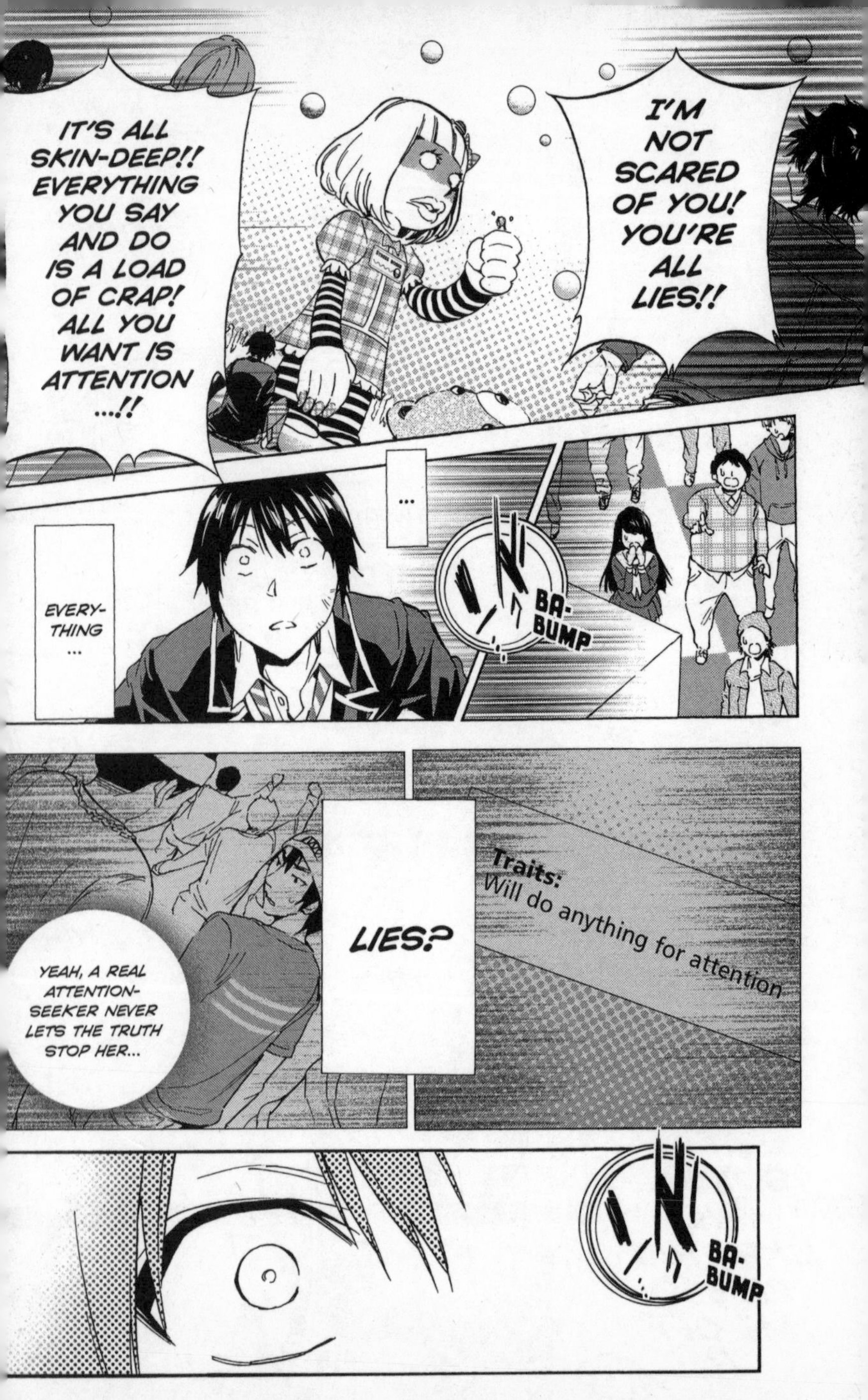
I'M NOT SCARED OF YOU! YOU'RE ALL LIES!!
IT'S ALL SKIN-DEEP!! EVERYTHING YOU SAY AND DO IS A LOAD OF CRAP! ALL YOU WANT IS ATTENTION ...!!
BA-BUMP
...
EVERY-THING ...
Traits:
Will do anything for attention
LIES?
YEAH, A REAL ATTENTION-SEEKER NEVER LETS THE TRUTH STOP HER...
BA-BUMP

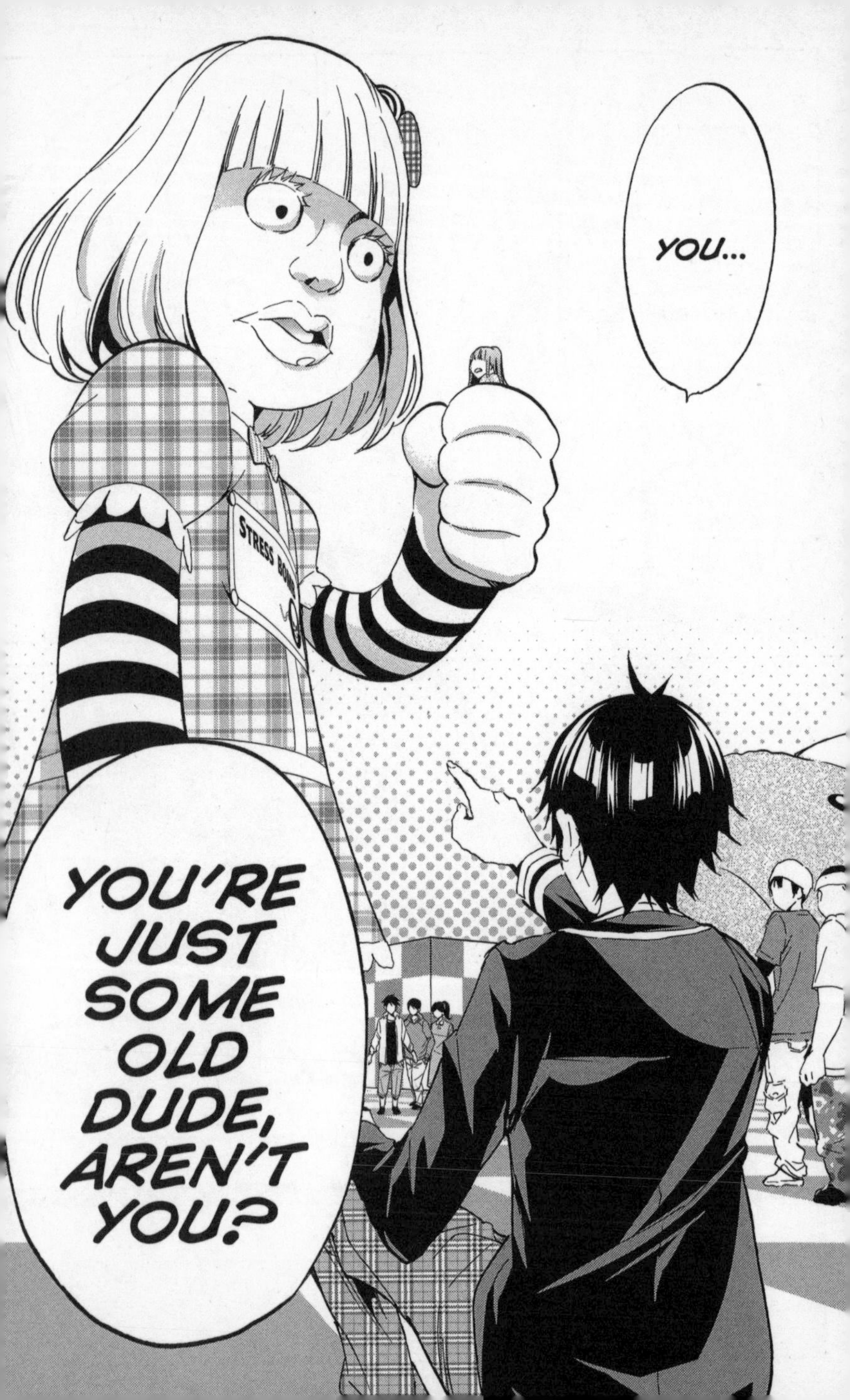
YOU...
YOU'RE JUST SOME OLD DUDE, AREN'T YOU?

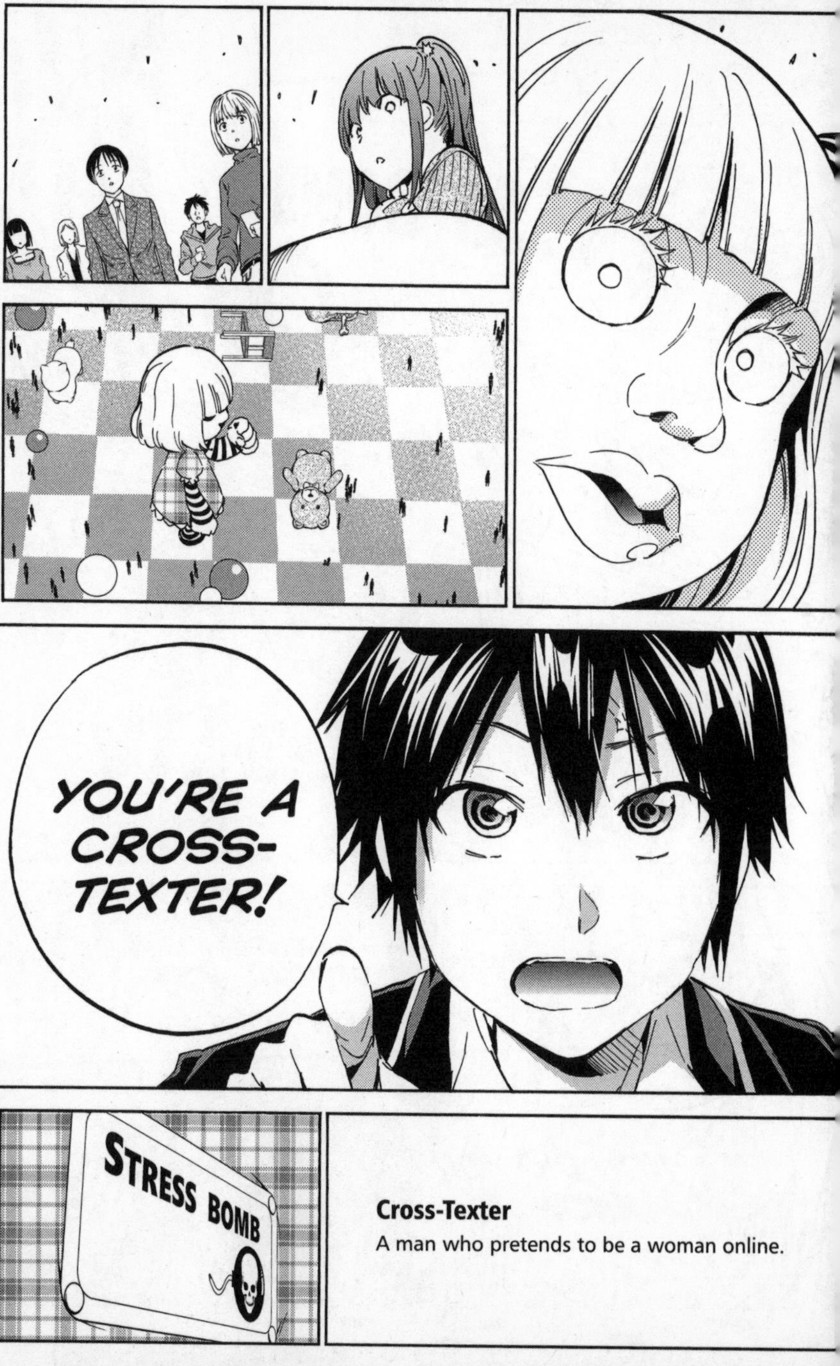
YOU'RE A CROSS-TEXTER!
Cross-Texter
A man who pretends to be a woman online.
STRESS BOMB

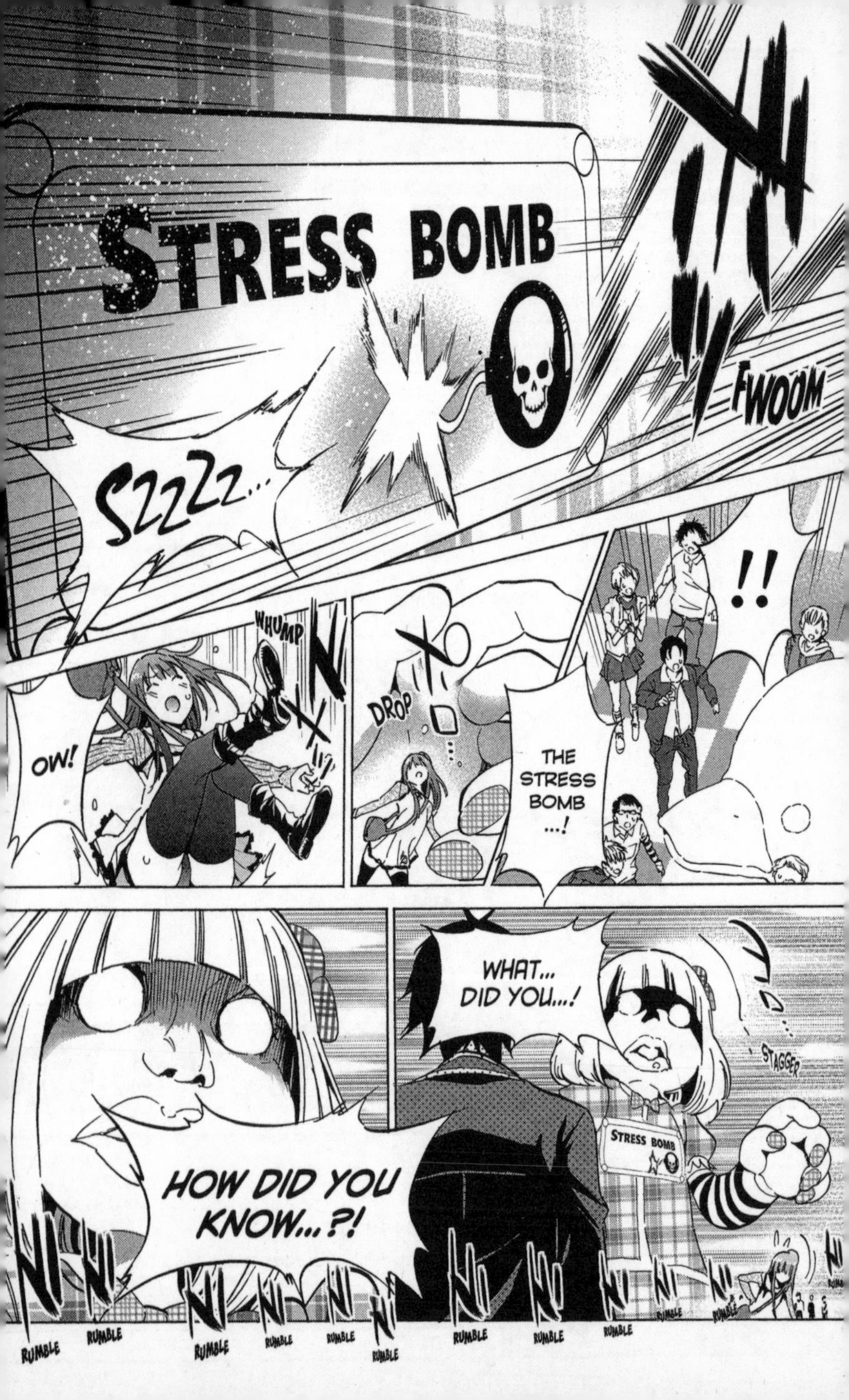
STRESS BOMB
FWOOM
SZZZz...
!!
THE STRESS BOMB ...!
DROP
WHUMP
OW!
WHAT... DID YOU...!
STAGGER
STRESS BOMB
HOW DID YOU KNOW...?!
RUMBLE

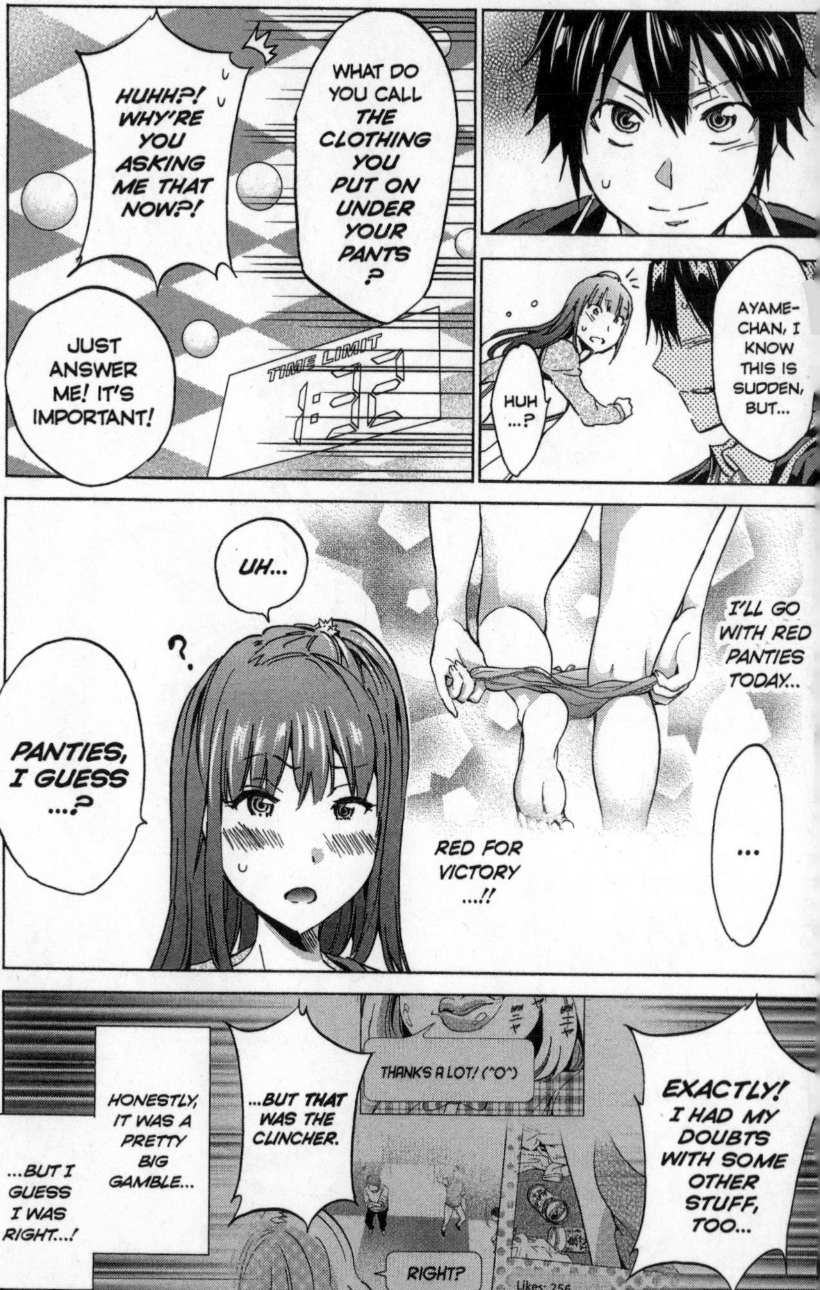
AYAME-CHAN, I KNOW THIS IS SUDDEN, BUT...
HUH ...?
WHAT DO YOU CALL THE CLOTHING YOU PUT ON UNDER YOUR PANTS?
HUHH?! WHY'RE YOU ASKING ME THAT NOW?!
JUST ANSWER ME! IT'S IMPORTANT!
TIME LIMIT
I'LL GO WITH RED PANTIES TODAY...
RED FOR VICTORY ...!!
...
UH...
PANTIES, I GUESS ...?
EXACTLY! I HAD MY DOUBTS WITH SOME OTHER STUFF, TOO...
THANKS A LOT! (^O^)
RIGHT?
Likes: 256
Comments: 36
...BUT THAT WAS THE CLINCHER.
HONESTLY, IT WAS A PRETTY BIG GAMBLE...
...BUT I GUESS I WAS RIGHT...!

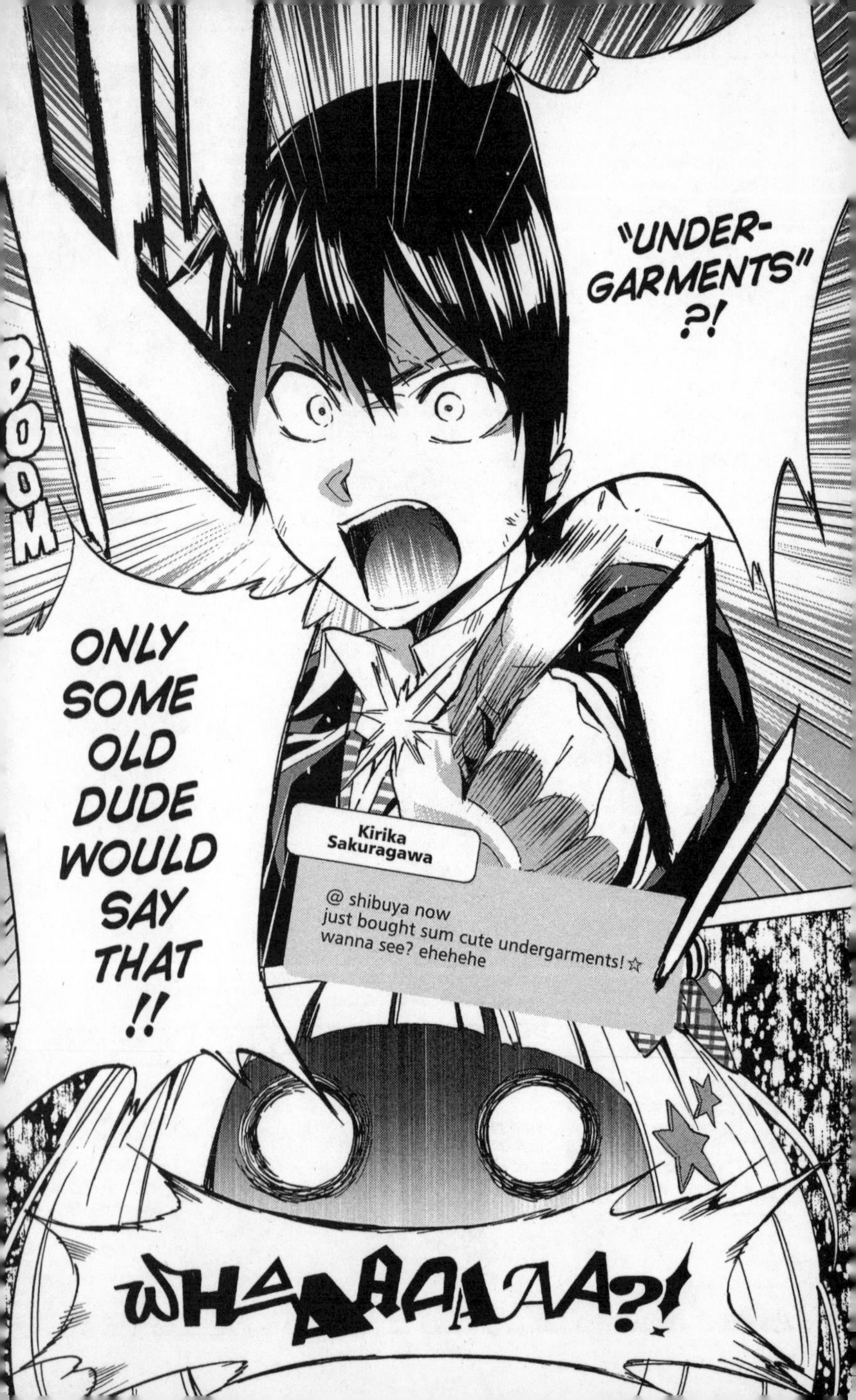
"UNDER-GARMENTS"?!
BOOM
Kirika Sakuragawa
@ shibuya now
just bought sum cute undergarments! ☆
wanna see? ehehehe
ONLY SOME OLD DUDE WOULD SAY THAT!!
WHAAAAAAAA?!

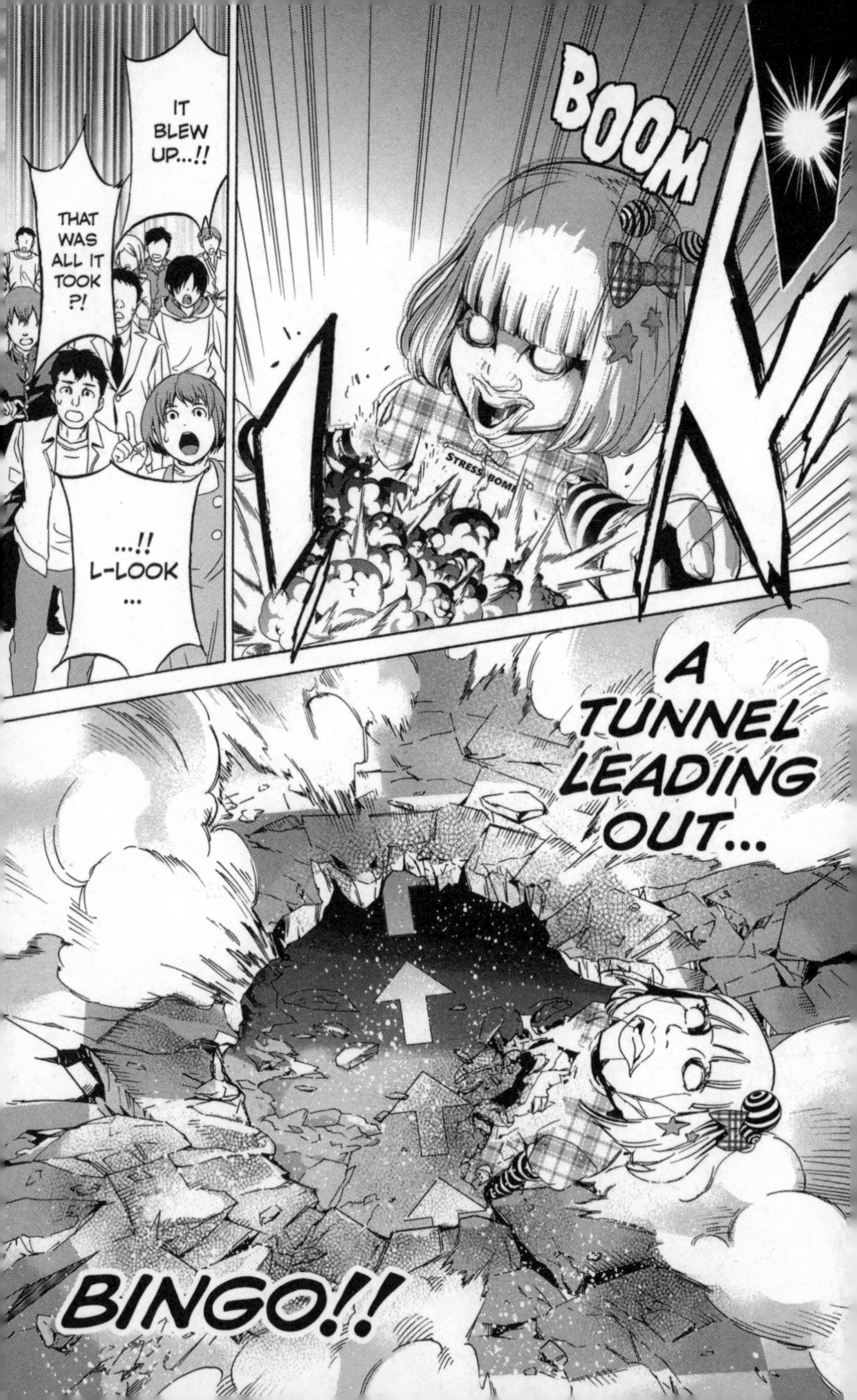
BOOM
STRESS BOMB
IT BLEW UP...!!
THAT WAS ALL IT TOOK?!
...!! L-LOOK...
A TUNNEL LEADING OUT...
BINGO!!

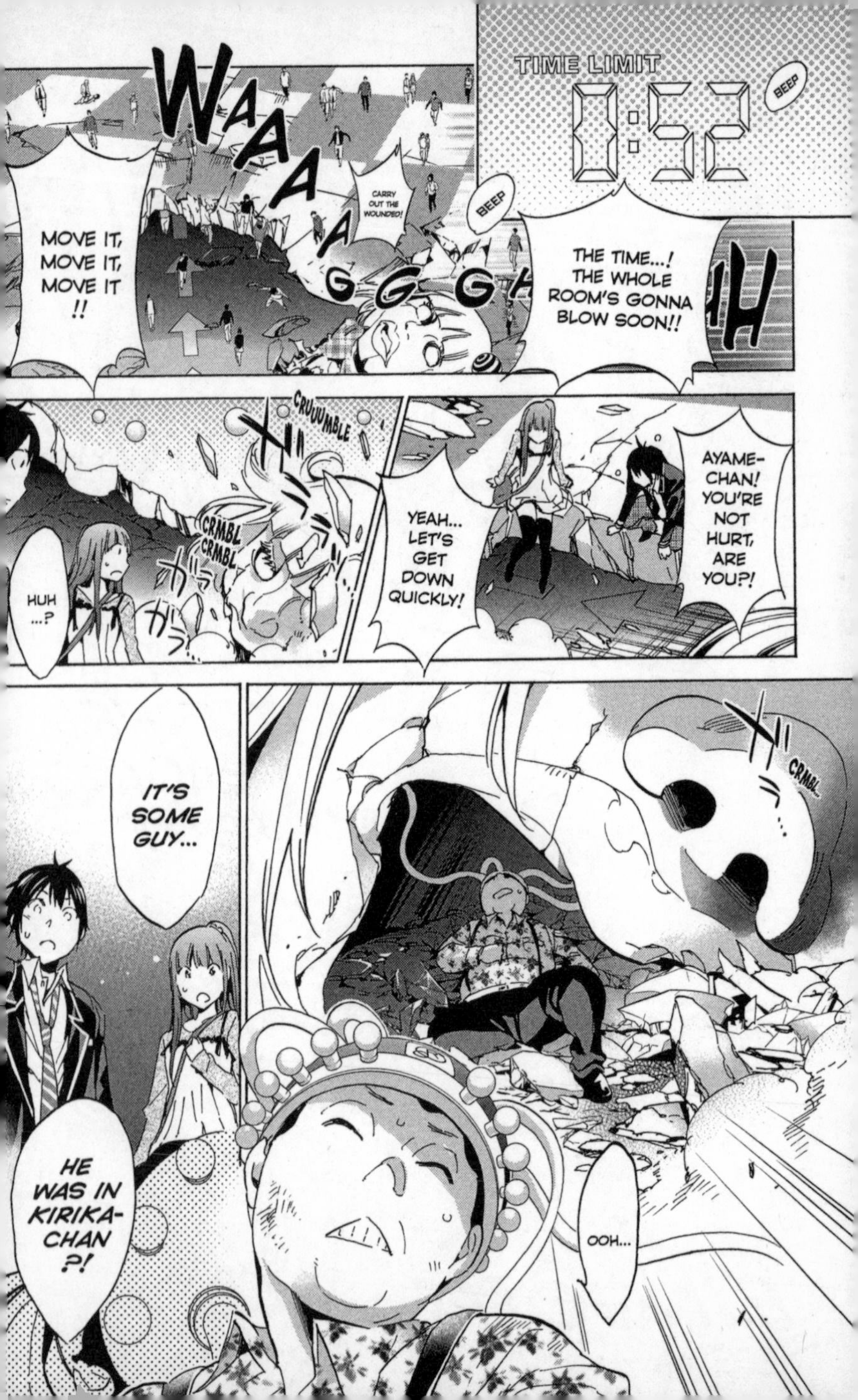
TIME LIMIT
0:52
BEEP
BEEP
THE TIME...! THE WHOLE ROOM'S GONNA BLOW SOON!!
WAAAAAGGGGHH
CARRY OUT THE WOUNDED!
MOVE IT, MOVE IT, MOVE IT !!
AYAME-CHAN! YOU'RE NOT HURT, ARE YOU?!
YEAH... LET'S GET DOWN QUICKLY!
CRUUUMBLE
CRMBL CRMBL
HUH ...?
CRMBL...
OOH...
IT'S SOME GUY...
HE WAS IN KIRIKA-CHAN?!

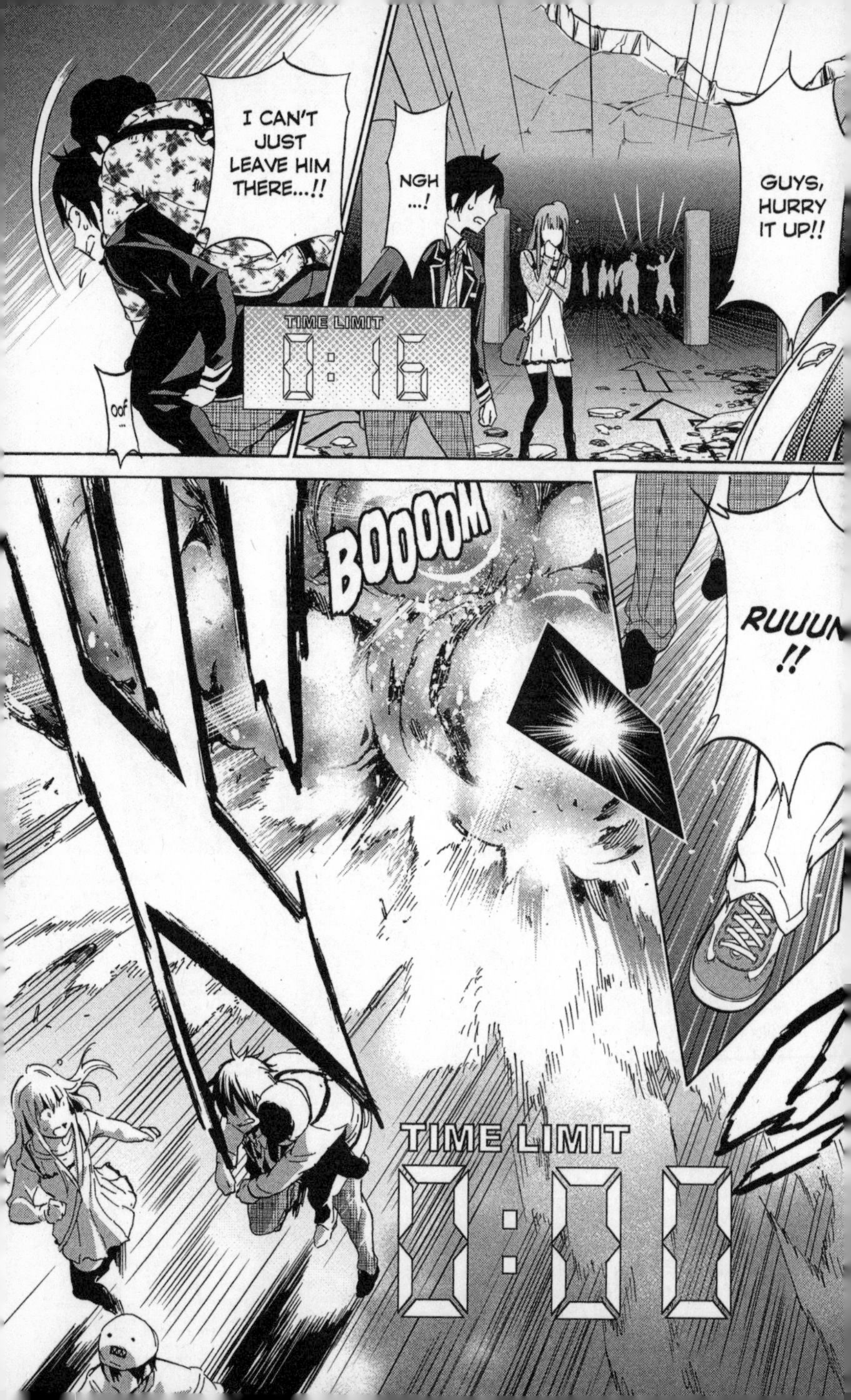
GUYS, HURRY IT UP!!
NGH ...!
I CAN'T JUST LEAVE HIM THERE...!!
Oof ...
TIME LIMIT 0:16
RUUUN !!
BOOOOM
TIME LIMIT 0:00

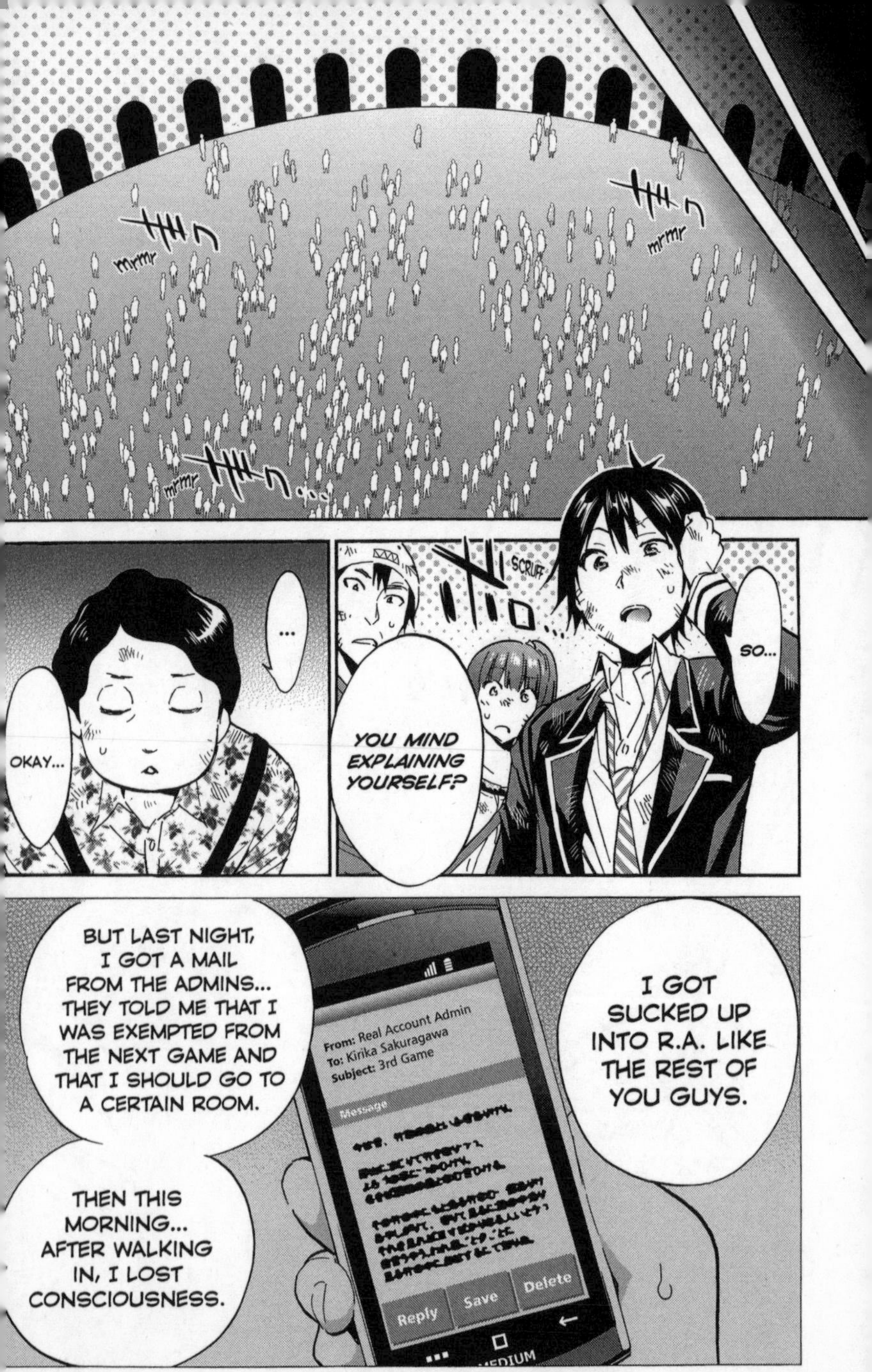
mrmr
mrmr
mrmr
SCRUFF
SO...
YOU MIND EXPLAINING YOURSELF?
...
OKAY...
I GOT SUCKED UP INTO R.A. LIKE THE REST OF YOU GUYS.
BUT LAST NIGHT, I GOT A MAIL FROM THE ADMINS... THEY TOLD ME THAT I WAS EXEMPTED FROM THE NEXT GAME AND THAT I SHOULD GO TO A CERTAIN ROOM.
From: Real Account Admin
To: Kirika Sakuragawa
Subject: 3rd Game
Message
Delete
Save
Reply
THEN THIS MORNING... AFTER WALKING IN, I LOST CONSCIOUSNESS.

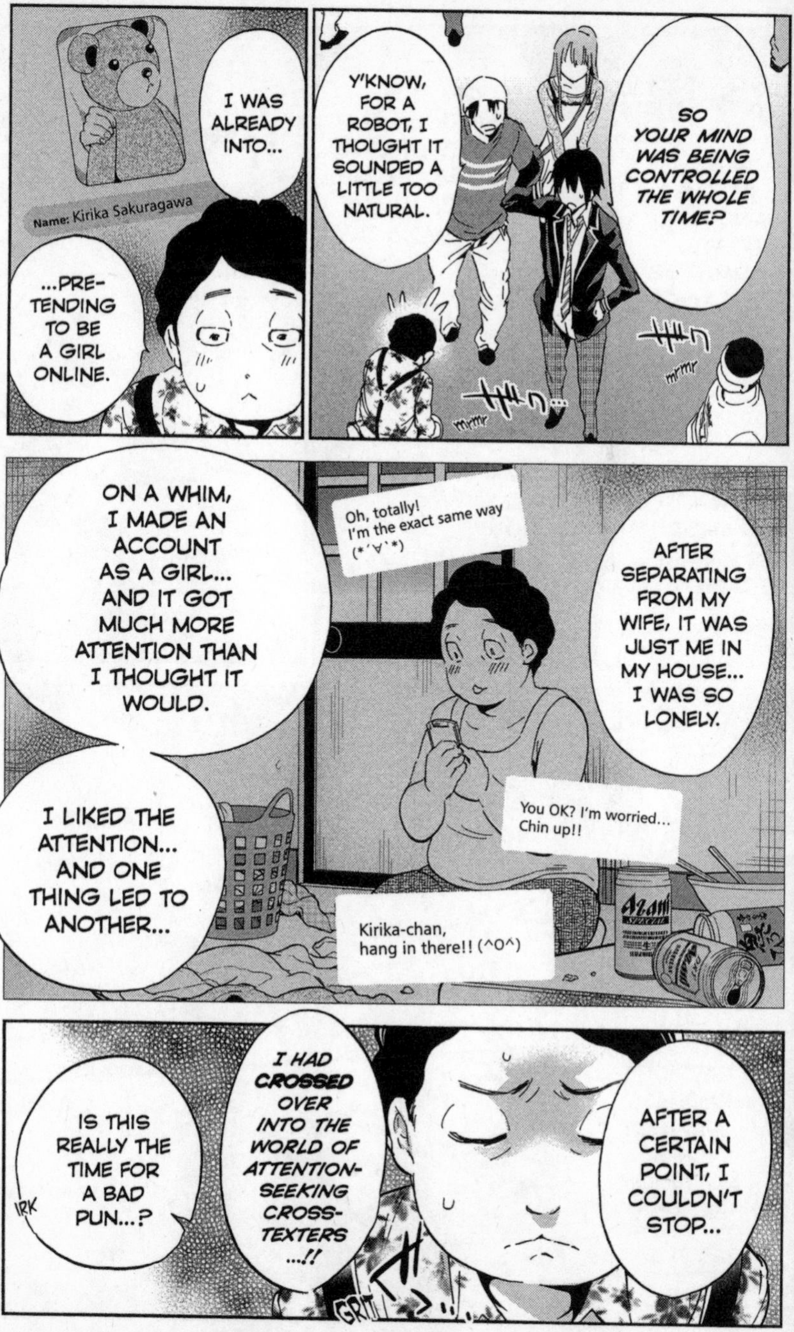
SO YOUR MIND WAS BEING CONTROLLED THE WHOLE TIME?
Y'KNOW, FOR A ROBOT, I THOUGHT IT SOUNDED A LITTLE TOO NATURAL.
mrmr
mrmr
I WAS ALREADY INTO...
Name: Kirika Sakuragawa
...PRE-TENDING TO BE A GIRL ONLINE.
AFTER SEPARATING FROM MY WIFE, IT WAS JUST ME IN MY HOUSE... I WAS SO LONELY.
Oh, totally! I'm the exact same way (*´∀`*)
ON A WHIM, I MADE AN ACCOUNT AS A GIRL... AND IT GOT MUCH MORE ATTENTION THAN I THOUGHT IT WOULD.
You OK? I'm worried... Chin up!!
Kirika-chan, hang in there!! (^O^)
I LIKED THE ATTENTION... AND ONE THING LED TO ANOTHER...
AFTER A CERTAIN POINT, I COULDN'T STOP...
I HAD *CROSSED* OVER INTO THE WORLD OF ATTENTION-SEEKING CROSS-TEXTERS ...!!
GRT
IS THIS REALLY THE TIME FOR A BAD PUN...?
IRK

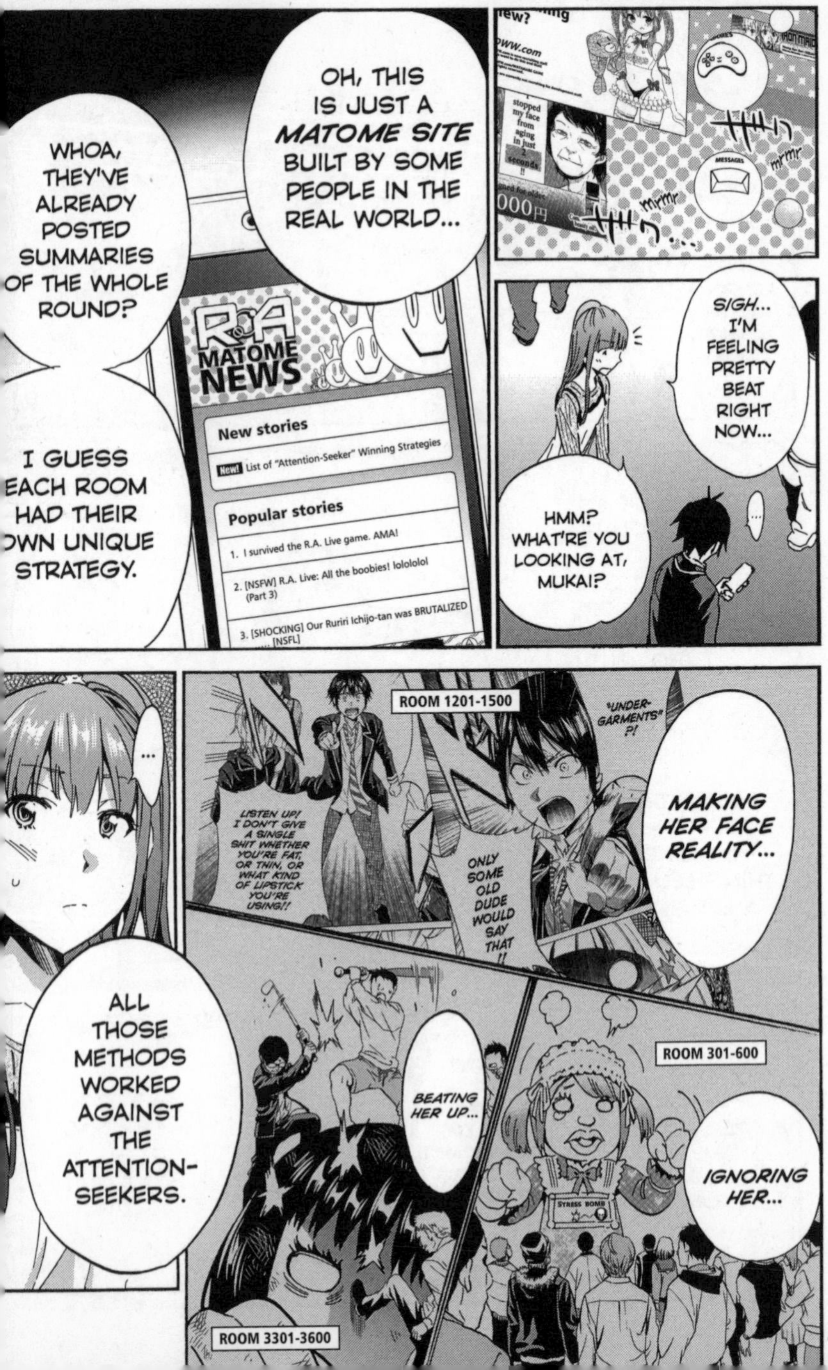
stopped my face from aging in just 2 seconds !!
GAMES
MESSAGES
mrmr
mrmr
SIGH... I'M FEELING PRETTY BEAT RIGHT NOW...
HMM? WHAT'RE YOU LOOKING AT, MUKAI?
...
OH, THIS IS JUST A *MATOME SITE* BUILT BY SOME PEOPLE IN THE REAL WORLD...
WHOA, THEY'VE ALREADY POSTED SUMMARIES OF THE WHOLE ROUND?
R&A MATOME NEWS
New stories
New! List of "Attention-Seeker" Winning Strategies
Popular stories
1. I survived the R.A. Live game. AMA!
2. [NSFW] R.A. Live: All the boobies! lolololol (Part 3)
3. [SHOCKING] Our Ruriri Ichijo-tan was BRUTALIZED
I GUESS EACH ROOM HAD THEIR OWN UNIQUE STRATEGY.
ROOM 1201-1500
MAKING HER FACE REALITY...
"UNDER-GARMENTS" ?!
ONLY SOME OLD DUDE WOULD SAY THAT !!
LISTEN UP! I DON'T GIVE A SINGLE SHIT WHETHER YOU'RE FAT, OR THIN, OR WHAT KIND OF LIPSTICK YOU'RE USING!!
ROOM 301-600
IGNORING HER...
STRESS BOMB
BEATING HER UP...
ROOM 3301-3600
...
ALL THOSE METHODS WORKED AGAINST THE ATTENTION-SEEKERS.

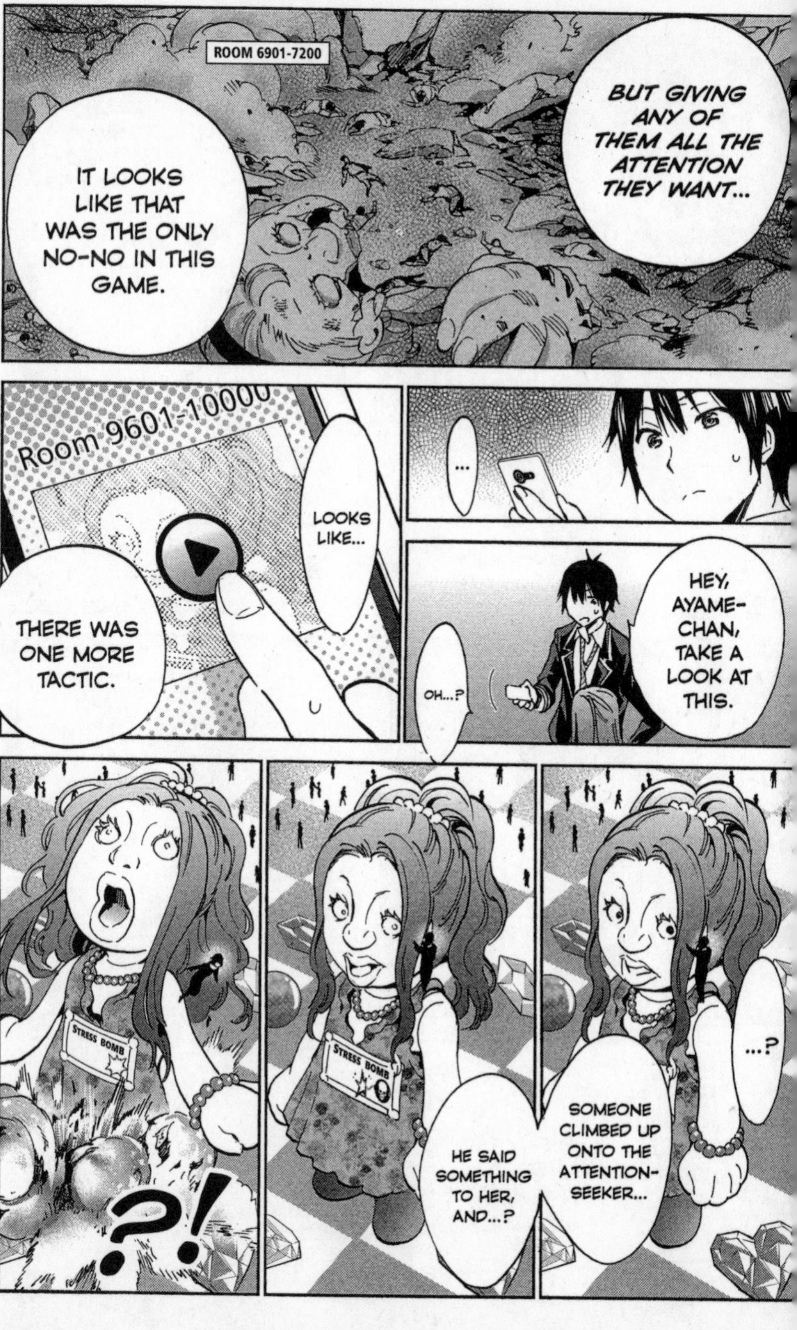
BUT GIVING ANY OF THEM ALL THE ATTENTION THEY WANT...
ROOM 6901-7200
IT LOOKS LIKE THAT WAS THE ONLY NO-NO IN THIS GAME.
...
HEY, AYAME-CHAN, TAKE A LOOK AT THIS.
OH...?
LOOKS LIKE...
Room 9601-10000
THERE WAS ONE MORE TACTIC.
...?
SOMEONE CLIMBED UP ONTO THE ATTENTION-SEEKER...
HE SAID SOMETHING TO HER, AND...?
STRESS BOMB
STRESS BOMB
?!

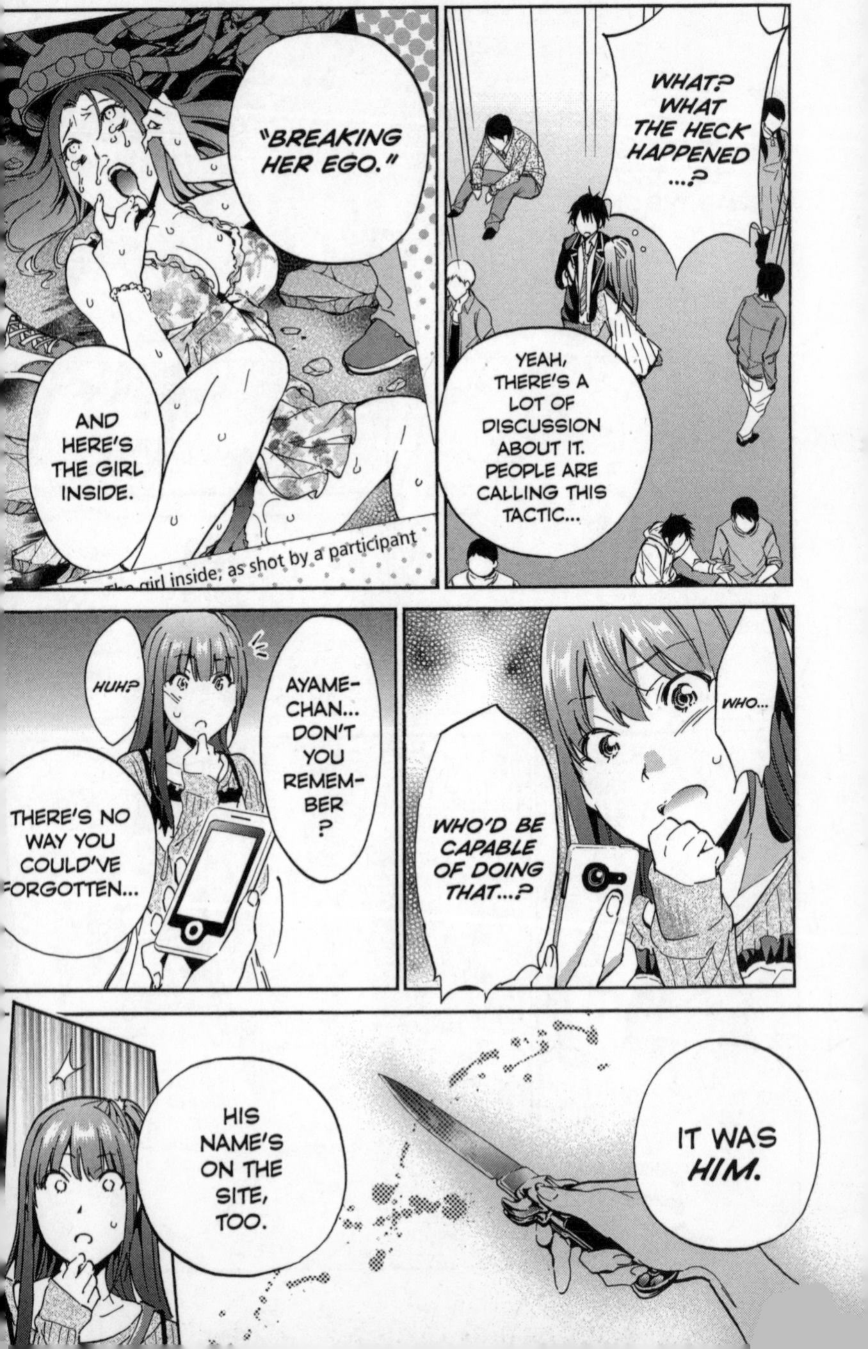
WHAT? WHAT THE HECK HAPPENED ...?
YEAH, THERE'S A LOT OF DISCUSSION ABOUT IT. PEOPLE ARE CALLING THIS TACTIC...
"BREAKING HER EGO."
AND HERE'S THE GIRL INSIDE.
The girl inside, as shot by a participant
WHO...
WHO'D BE CAPABLE OF DOING THAT...?
AYAME-CHAN... DON'T YOU REMEMBER?
HUH?
THERE'S NO WAY YOU COULD'VE FORGOTTEN...
IT WAS HIM.
HIS NAME'S ON THE SITE, TOO.

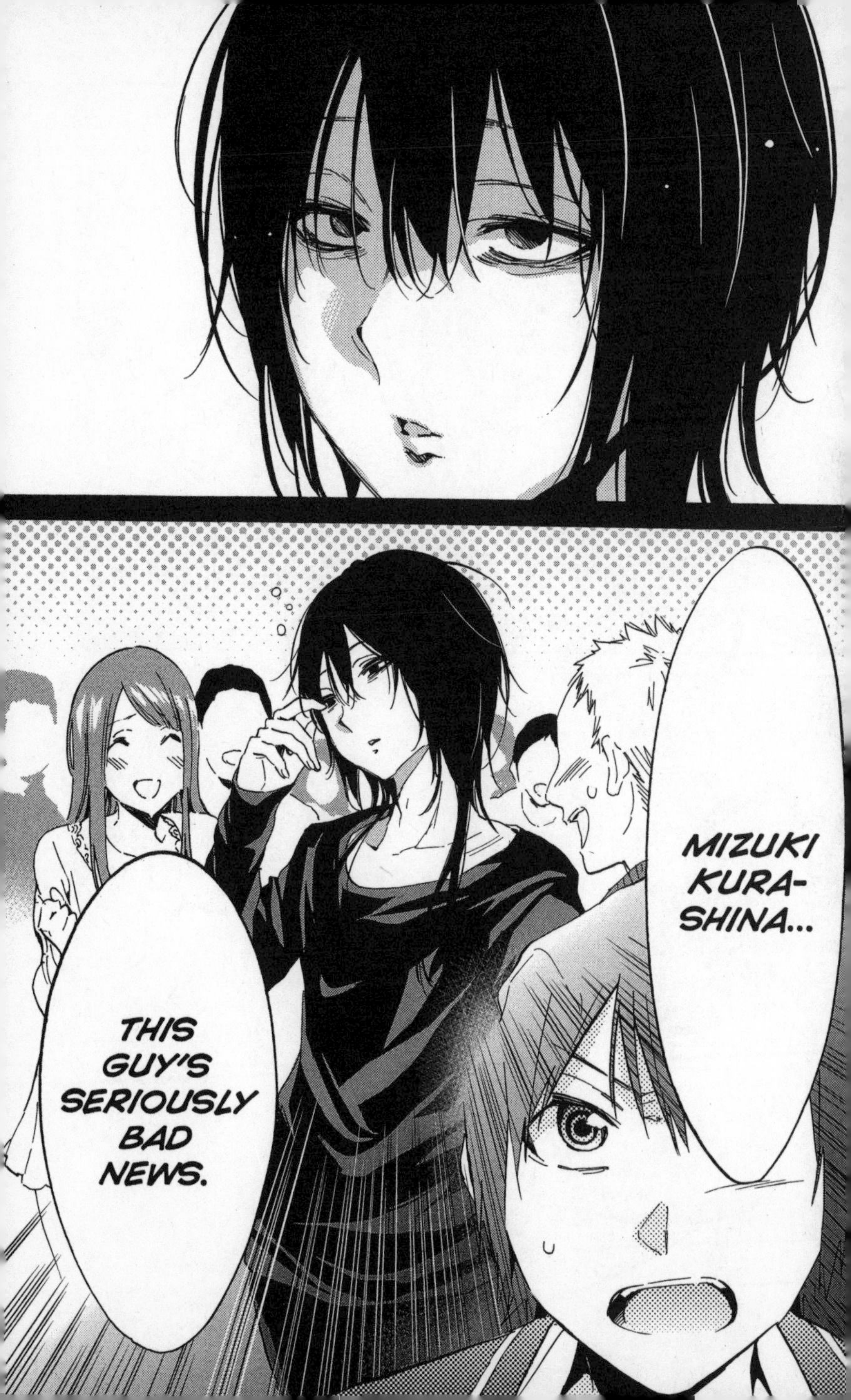
MIZUKI KURA-SHINA...
THIS GUY'S SERIOUSLY BAD NEWS.

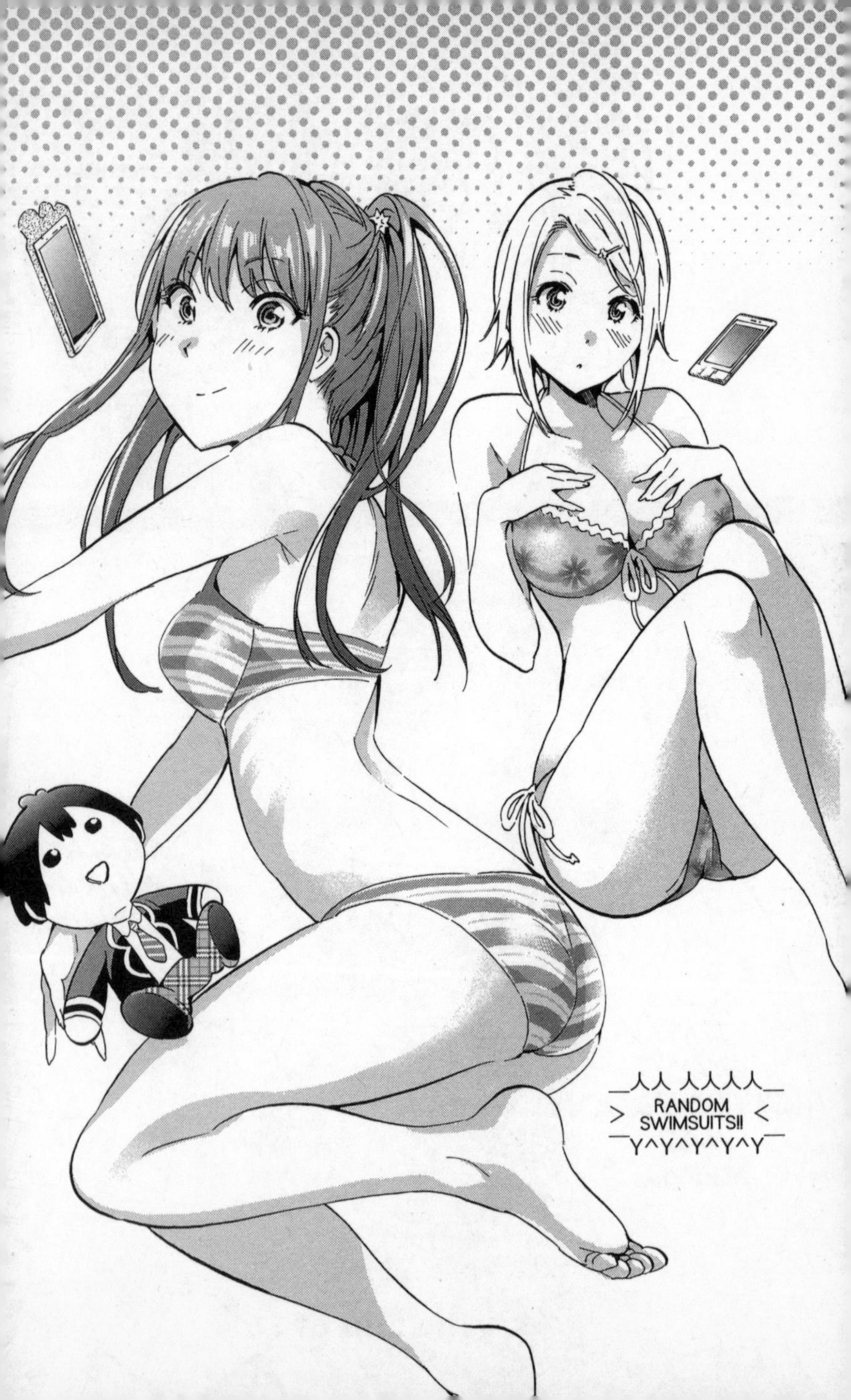
RANDOM SWIMSUITS!!

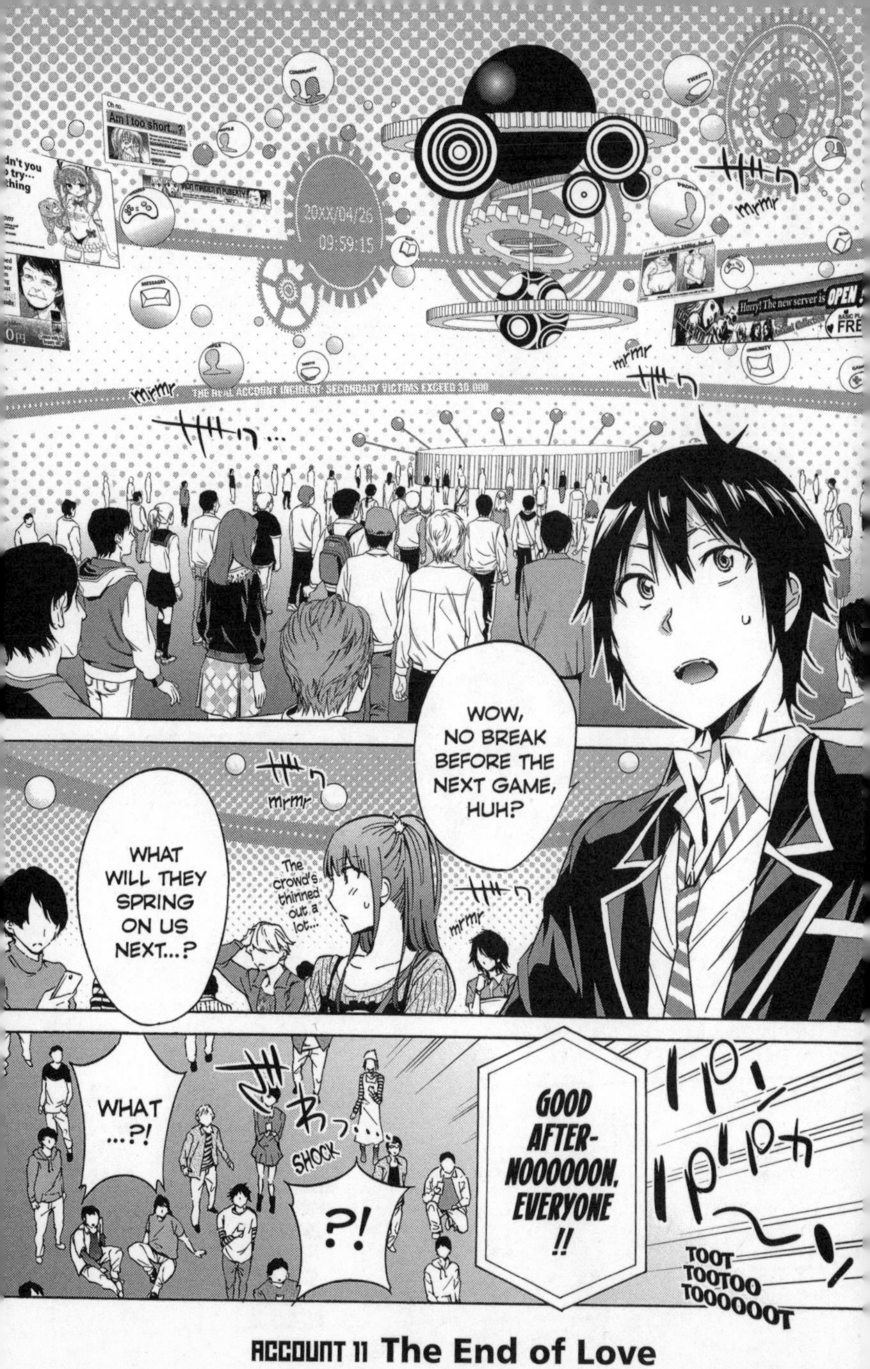
Hurry! The new server is OPEN!
mrmr
20XX/04/26
09:59:15
IRON MAIDEN IN PUBERTY
Oh no...
Am I too short...?
THE REAL ACCOUNT INCIDENT: SECONDARY VICTIMS EXCEED 30,000
mrmr
WOW, NO BREAK BEFORE THE NEXT GAME, HUH?
The crowd's thinned out a lot...
WHAT WILL THEY SPRING ON US NEXT...?
mrmr
GOOD AFTER-NOOOOOON, EVERYONE!!
TOOT TOOTOO TOOOOOOT
?!
SHOCK
WHAT ...?!

ACCOUNT 11 The End of Love

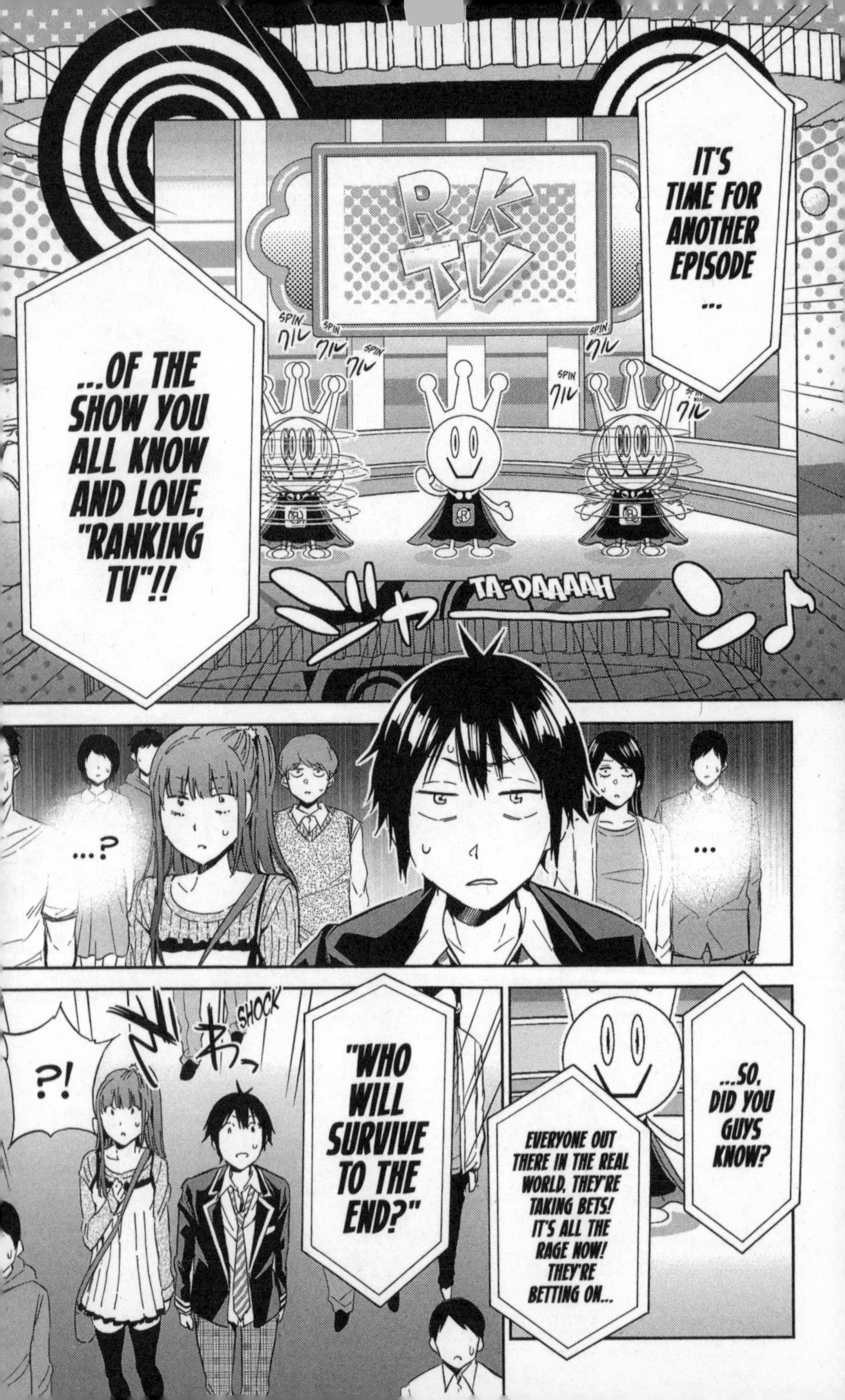
IT'S TIME FOR ANOTHER EPISODE ...
SPIN
SPIN
SPIN
SPIN
SPIN
SPIN
RK TV
...OF THE SHOW YOU ALL KNOW AND LOVE, "RANKING TV"!!
TA-DAAAAH
...
...?
...SO, DID YOU GUYS KNOW?
EVERYONE OUT THERE IN THE REAL WORLD, THEY'RE TAKING BETS! IT'S ALL THE RAGE NOW! THEY'RE BETTING ON...
"WHO WILL SURVIVE TO THE END?"
SHOCK
?!

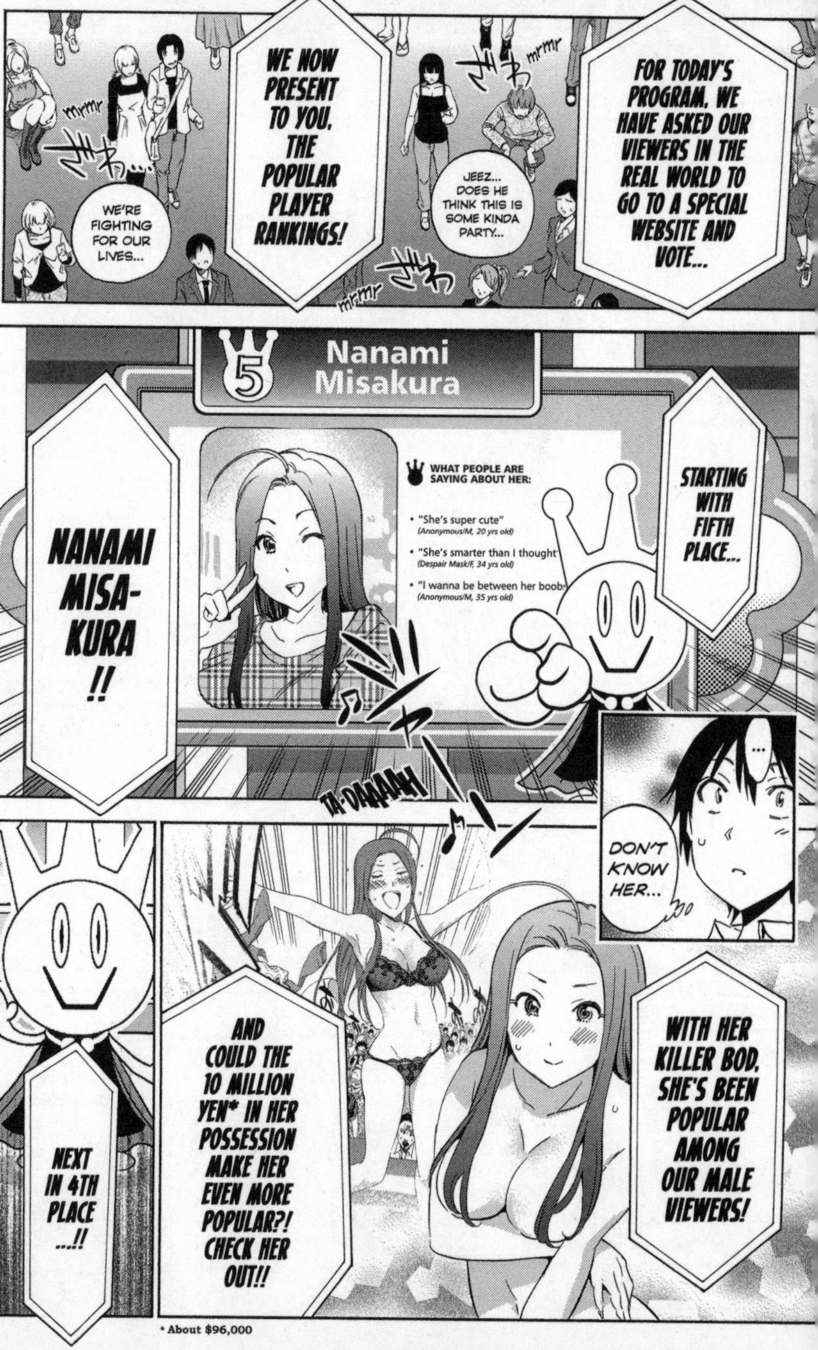
FOR TODAY'S PROGRAM, WE HAVE ASKED OUR VIEWERS IN THE REAL WORLD TO GO TO A SPECIAL WEBSITE AND VOTE...
mrmr
JEEZ... DOES HE THINK THIS IS SOME KINDA PARTY...
WE NOW PRESENT TO YOU, THE POPULAR PLAYER RANKINGS!
mrmr
WE'RE FIGHTING FOR OUR LIVES...
mrmr
5 Nanami Misakura
WHAT PEOPLE ARE SAYING ABOUT HER:
• "She's super cute" (Anonymous/M, 20 yrs old)
• "She's smarter than I thought (Despair Mask/F, 34 yrs old)
• "I wanna be between her boob (Anonymous/M, 35 yrs old)
STARTING WITH FIFTH PLACE...
NANAMI MISA-KURA!!
TA-DAAAAH
...
DON'T KNOW HER...
WITH HER KILLER BOD, SHE'S BEEN POPULAR AMONG OUR MALE VIEWERS!
AND COULD THE 10 MILLION YEN* IN HER POSSESSION MAKE HER EVEN MORE POPULAR?! CHECK HER OUT!!
NEXT IN 4TH PLACE ...!!

* About $96,000

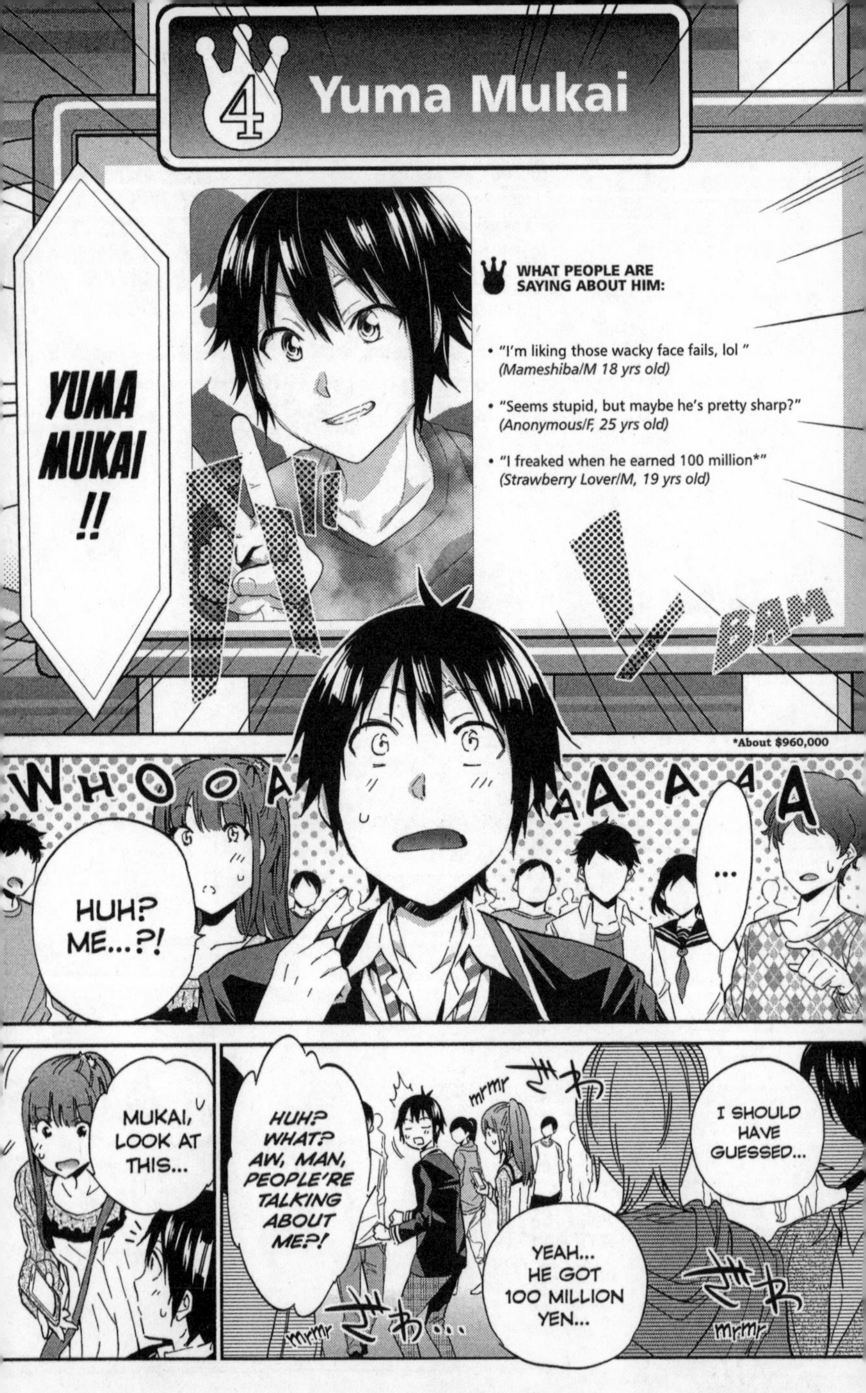
4 Yuma Mukai
WHAT PEOPLE ARE SAYING ABOUT HIM:
• "I'm liking those wacky face fails, lol " (Mameshiba/M 18 yrs old)
• "Seems stupid, but maybe he's pretty sharp?" (Anonymous/F, 25 yrs old)
• "I freaked when he earned 100 million*" (Strawberry Lover/M, 19 yrs old)
BAM
YUMA MUKAI !!
*About $960,000
WHOOAAAAA
...
HUH? ME...?!
I SHOULD HAVE GUESSED...
mrmr
YEAH... HE GOT 100 MILLION YEN...
HUH? WHAT? AW, MAN, PEOPLE'RE TALKING ABOUT ME?!
mrmr
mrmr
MUKAI, LOOK AT THIS...

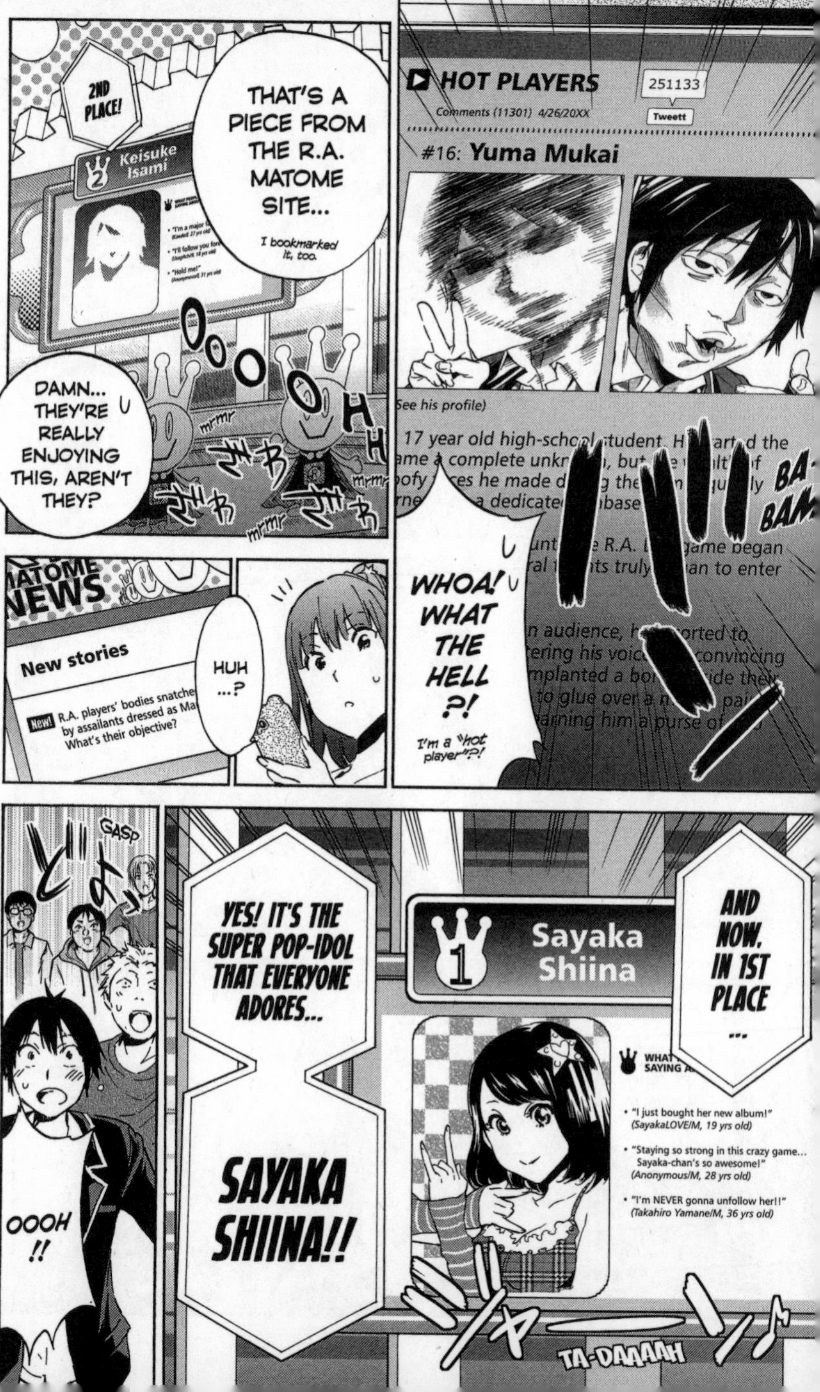
HOT PLAYERS
251133
Tweett
Comments (11301) 4/26/20XX
#16: Yuma Mukai
See his profile)
17 year old high-school student.
BA BAM
WHOA! WHAT THE HELL ?!
I'm a "hot player"?!
2ND PLACE!
Keisuke Isami
THAT'S A PIECE FROM THE R.A. MATOME SITE...
I bookmarked it, too.
OOOOOHH
DAMN... THEY'RE REALLY ENJOYING THIS, AREN'T THEY?
mrmr
mrmr
mrmr
HUH ...?
MATOME NEWS
New stories
New! R.A. players' bodies snatched by assailants dressed as Ma... What's their objective?
AND NOW, IN 1ST PLACE ...
Sayaka Shiina
YES! IT'S THE SUPER POP-IDOL THAT EVERYONE ADORES...
SAYAKA SHIINA!!
• "I just bought her new album!" (SayakaLOVE/M, 19 yrs old)
• "Staying so strong in this crazy game... Sayaka-chan's so awesome!" (Anonymous/M, 28 yrs old)
• "I'm NEVER gonna unfollow her!!" (Takahiro Yamane/M, 36 yrs old)
TA-DAAAAH
GASP
OOOH !!

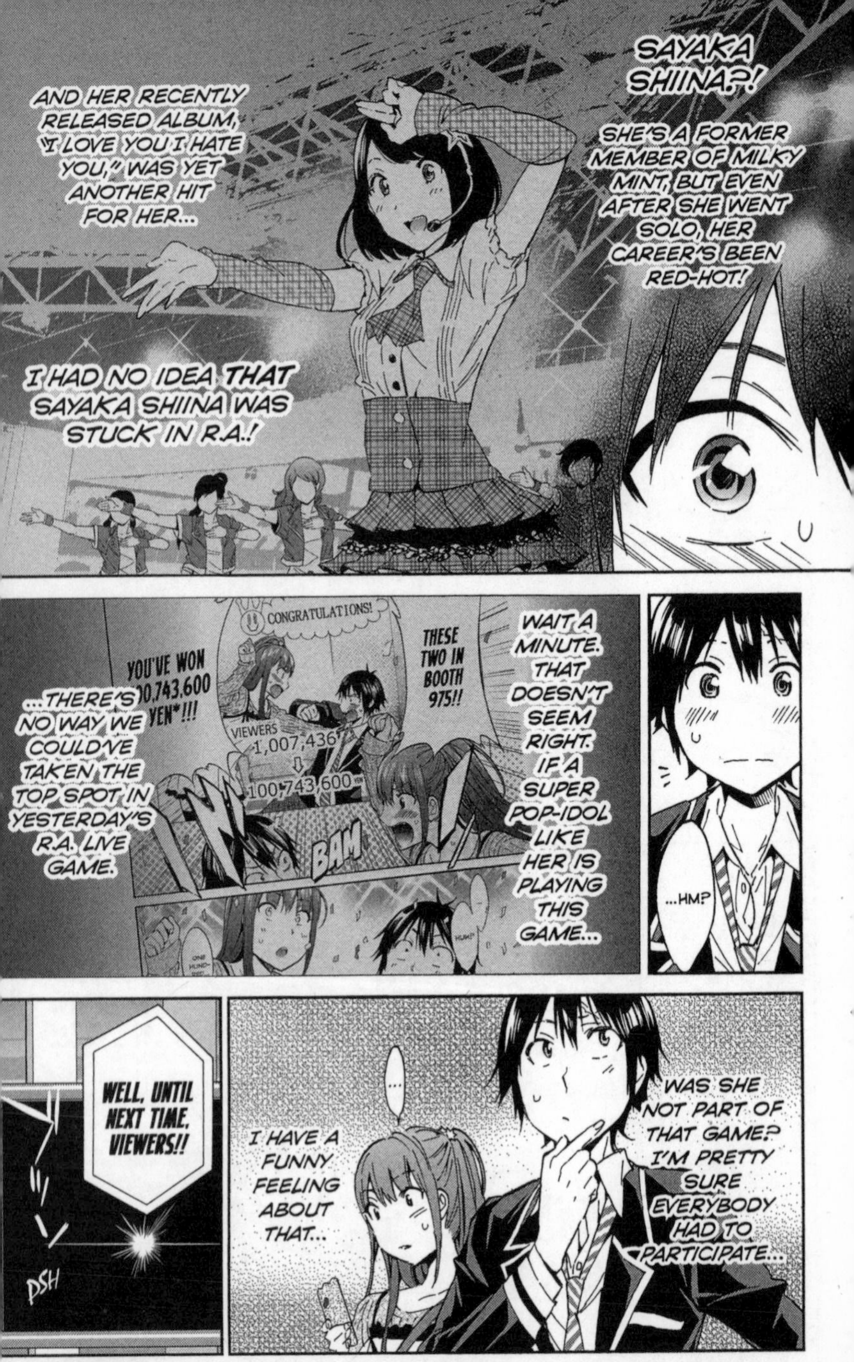
SAYAKA SHIINA?!
SHE'S A FORMER MEMBER OF MILKY MINT, BUT EVEN AFTER SHE WENT SOLO, HER CAREER'S BEEN RED-HOT!
AND HER RECENTLY RELEASED ALBUM, "I LOVE YOU I HATE YOU," WAS YET ANOTHER HIT FOR HER...
I HAD NO IDEA THAT SAYAKA SHIINA WAS STUCK IN R.A.!
...HM?
WAIT A MINUTE. THAT DOESN'T SEEM RIGHT. IF A SUPER POP-IDOL LIKE HER IS PLAYING THIS GAME...
CONGRATULATIONS!
THESE TWO IN BOOTH 975!!
YOU'VE WON
0,743,600
YEN*!!!
...THERE'S NO WAY WE COULD'VE TAKEN THE TOP SPOT IN YESTERDAY'S R.A. LIVE GAME.
VIEWERS
1,007,436
100,743,600
BAM
HUH?
WAS SHE NOT PART OF THAT GAME? I'M PRETTY SURE EVERYBODY HAD TO PARTICIPATE...
...
I HAVE A FUNNY FEELING ABOUT THAT...
WELL, UNTIL NEXT TIME, VIEWERS!!
PSH

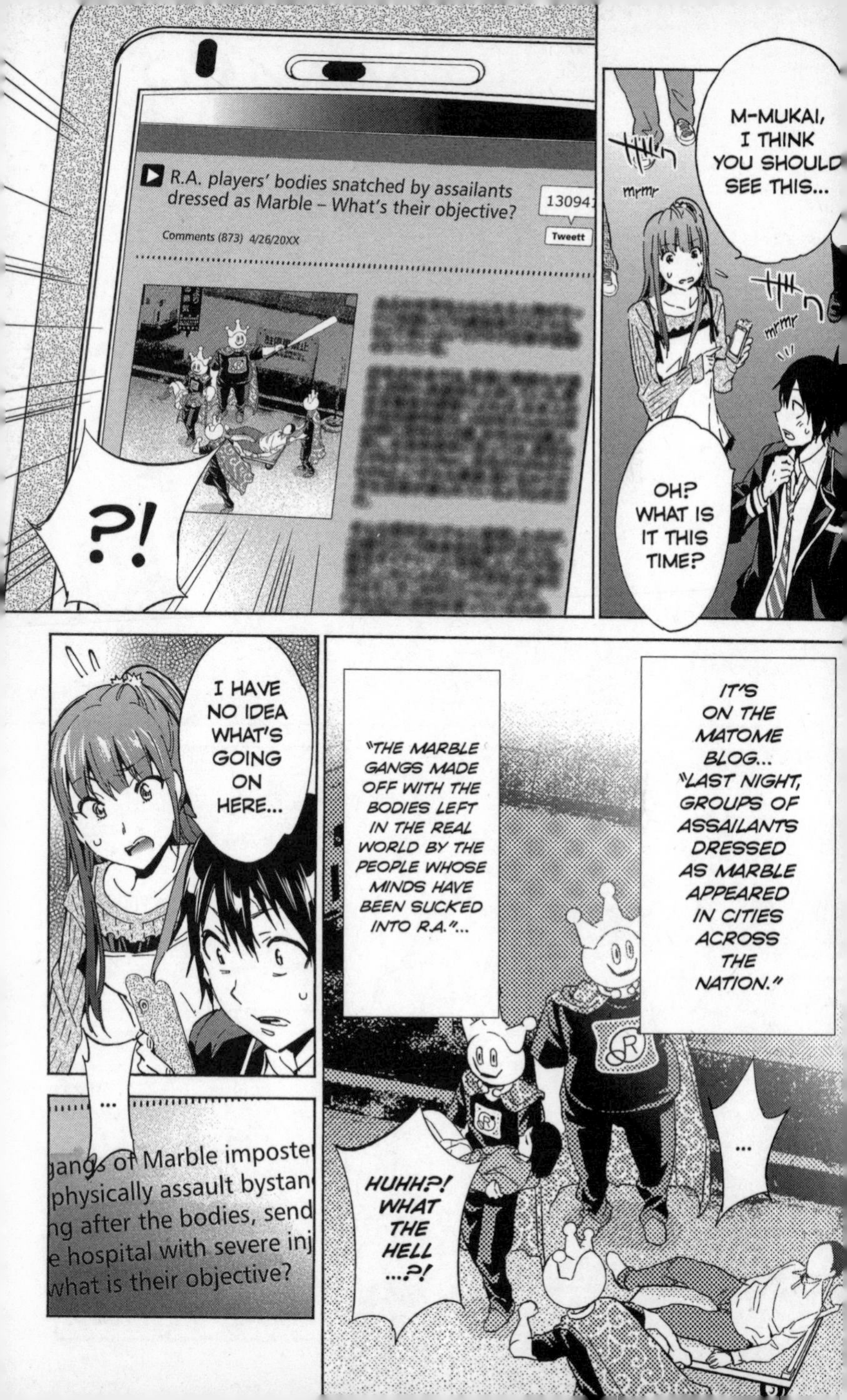
M-MUKAI, I THINK YOU SHOULD SEE THIS...
mrmr
mrmr
OH? WHAT IS IT THIS TIME?
R.A. players' bodies snatched by assailants dressed as Marble – What's their objective?
130941
Tweett
Comments (873) 4/26/20XX
?!
IT'S ON THE MATOME BLOG... "LAST NIGHT, GROUPS OF ASSAILANTS DRESSED AS MARBLE APPEARED IN CITIES ACROSS THE NATION."
"THE MARBLE GANGS MADE OFF WITH THE BODIES LEFT IN THE REAL WORLD BY THE PEOPLE WHOSE MINDS HAVE BEEN SUCKED INTO R.A."...
...
HUHH?! WHAT THE HELL ...?!
I HAVE NO IDEA WHAT'S GOING ON HERE...
...
gangs of Marble imposte
physically assault bystan
ng after the bodies, send
e hospital with severe inj
what is their objective?

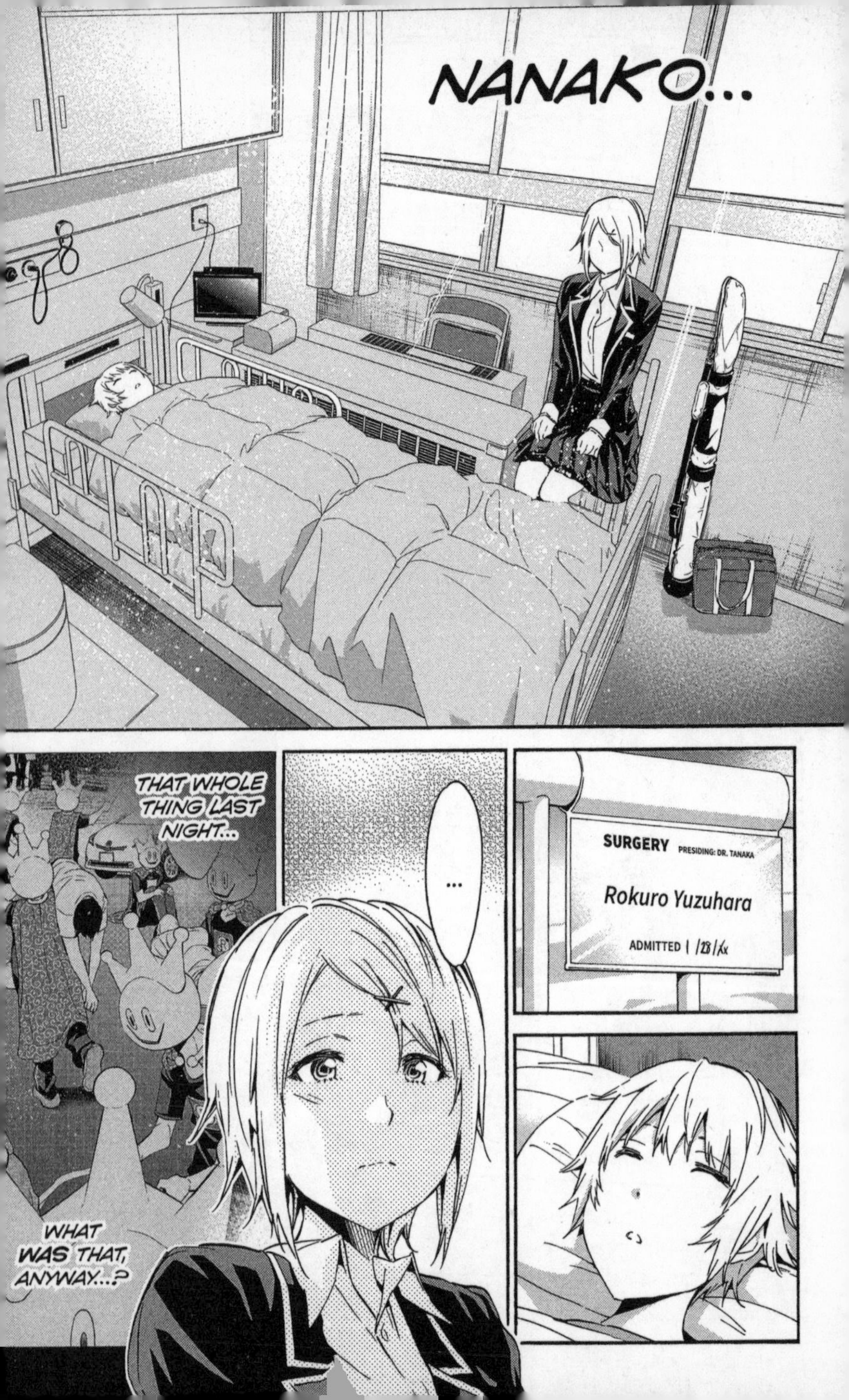
NANAKO...
SURGERY
PRESIDING: DR. TANAKA
Rokuro Yuzuhara
ADMITTED 1 /23/xx
...
THAT WHOLE THING LAST NIGHT...
WHAT WAS THAT, ANYWAY...?

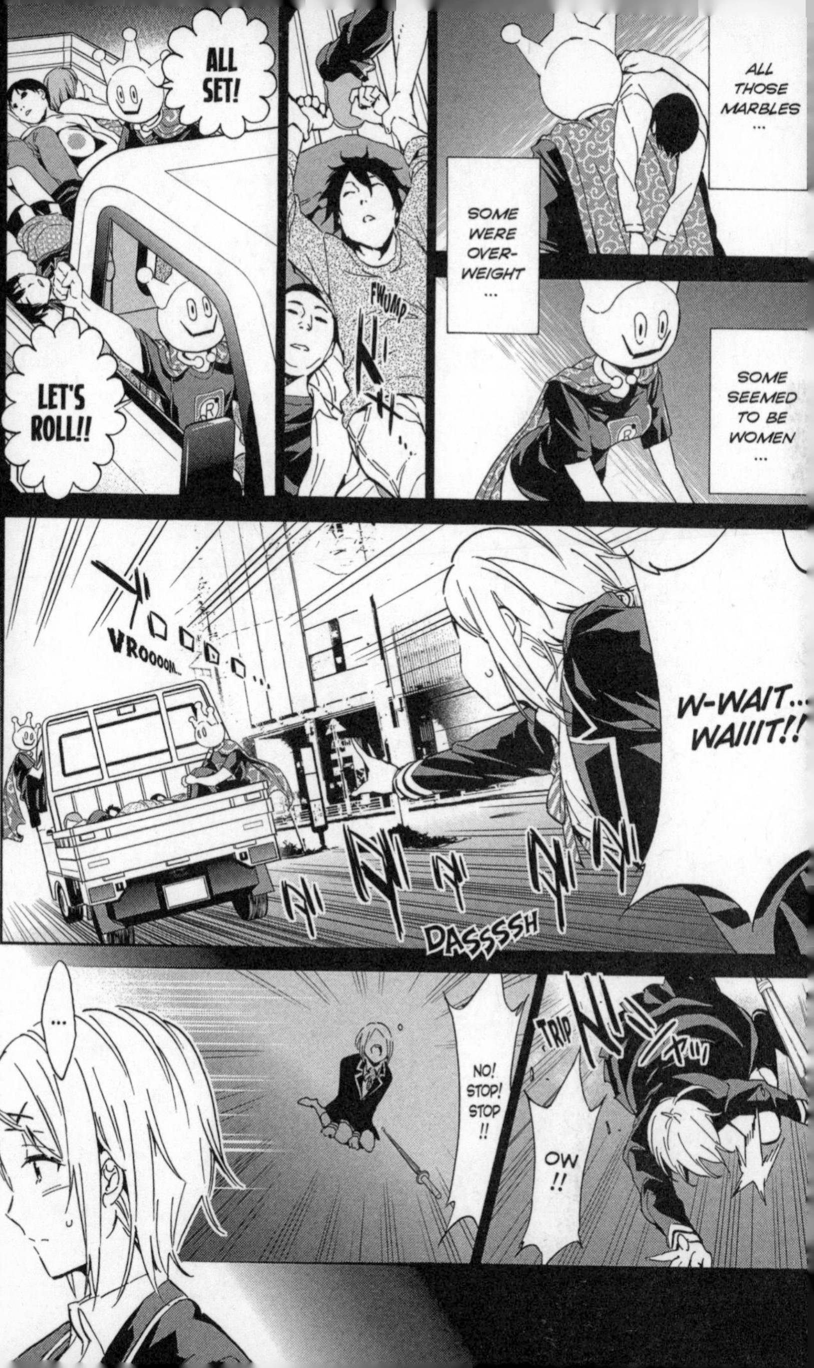
ALL THOSE MARBLES ...
SOME WERE OVER-WEIGHT ...
SOME SEEMED TO BE WOMEN ...
FWUMP
ALL SET!
LET'S ROLL!!
W-WAIT... WAIIIT!!
VROOOOM...
DASSSSH
TRIP
NO! STOP! STOP!!
OW!!
...

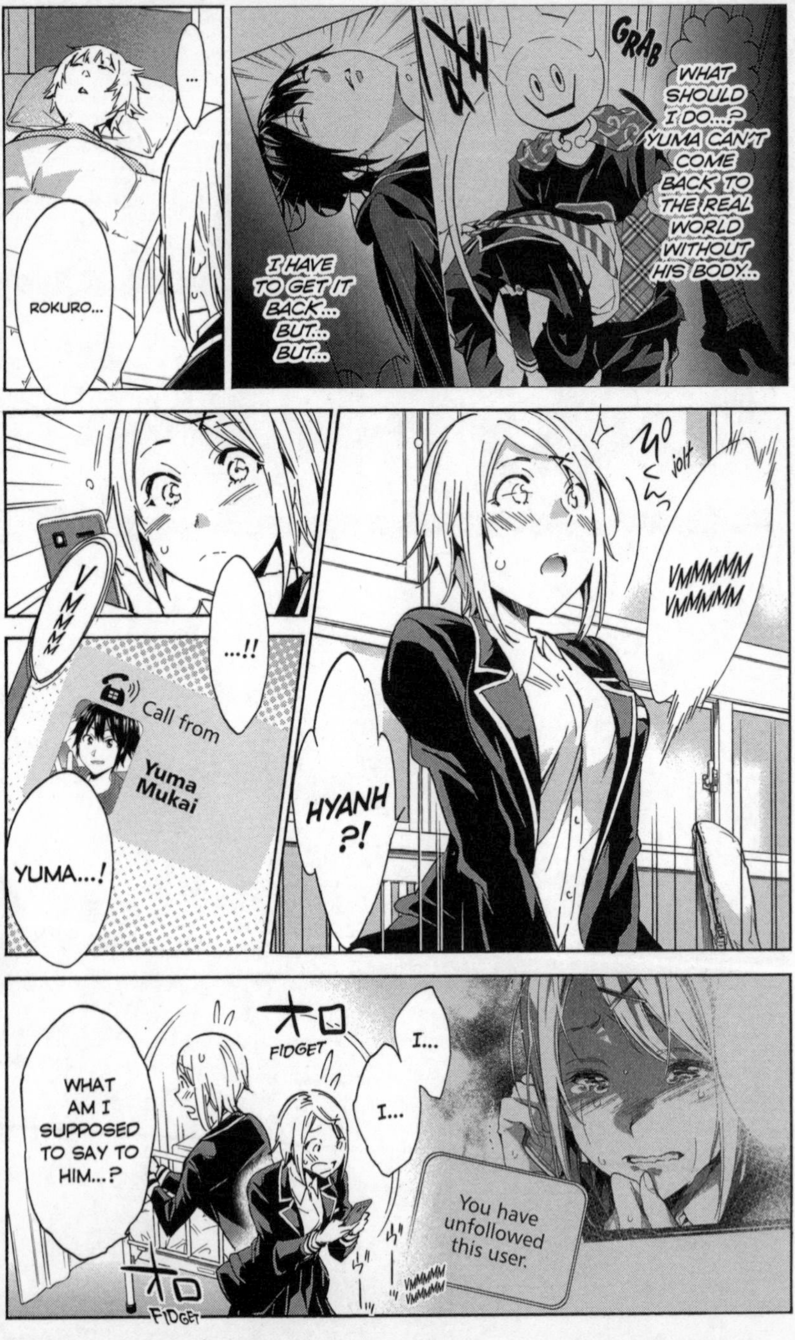
GRAB
WHAT SHOULD I DO...? YUMA CAN'T COME BACK TO THE REAL WORLD WITHOUT HIS BODY...
I HAVE TO GET IT BACK... BUT... BUT...
...
ROKURO...
jolt
VMMMMM VMMMMM
HYANH ?!
...!!
VMMMM
Call from
Yuma Mukai
YUMA...!
You have unfollowed this user.
VMMMMM VMMMMM
I...
I...
FIDGET
WHAT AM I SUPPOSED TO SAY TO HIM...?
FIDGET

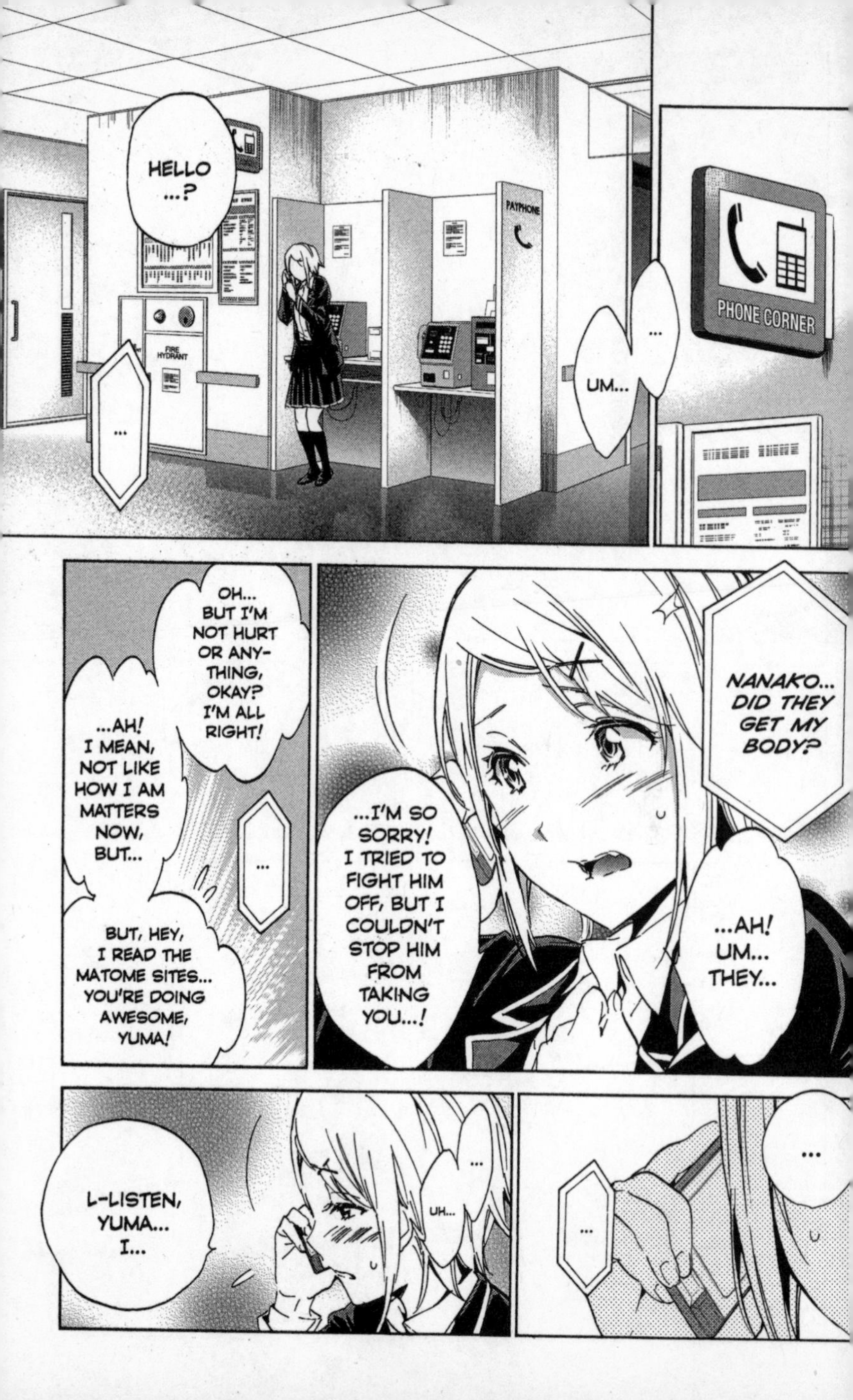
PHONE CORNER
...
UM...
PAYPHONE
FIRE HYDRANT
HELLO ...?
...
NANAKO... DID THEY GET MY BODY?
...AH! UM... THEY...
...I'M SO SORRY! I TRIED TO FIGHT HIM OFF, BUT I COULDN'T STOP HIM FROM TAKING YOU...!
OH... BUT I'M NOT HURT OR ANY-THING, OKAY? I'M ALL RIGHT!
...
...AH! I MEAN, NOT LIKE HOW I AM MATTERS NOW, BUT...
BUT, HEY, I READ THE MATOME SITES... YOU'RE DOING AWESOME, YUMA!
...
...
...
UH...
L-LISTEN, YUMA... I...

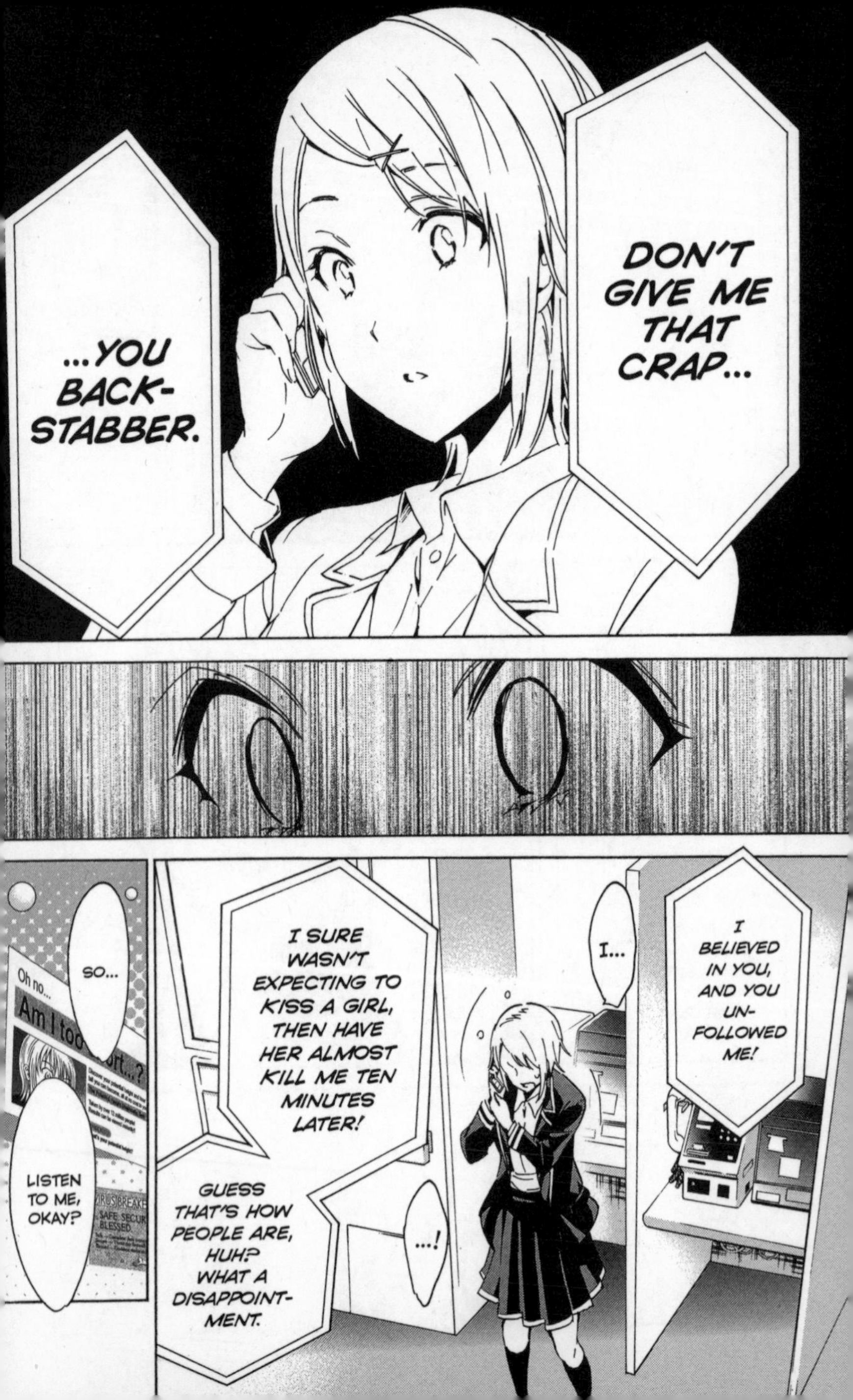
DON'T GIVE ME THAT CRAP...
...YOU BACK-STABBER.
I BELIEVED IN YOU, AND YOU UN-FOLLOWED ME!
I...
I SURE WASN'T EXPECTING TO KISS A GIRL, THEN HAVE HER ALMOST KILL ME TEN MINUTES LATER!
GUESS THAT'S HOW PEOPLE ARE, HUH? WHAT A DISAPPOINT-MENT.
...!
Oh no...
SO...
LISTEN TO ME, OKAY?

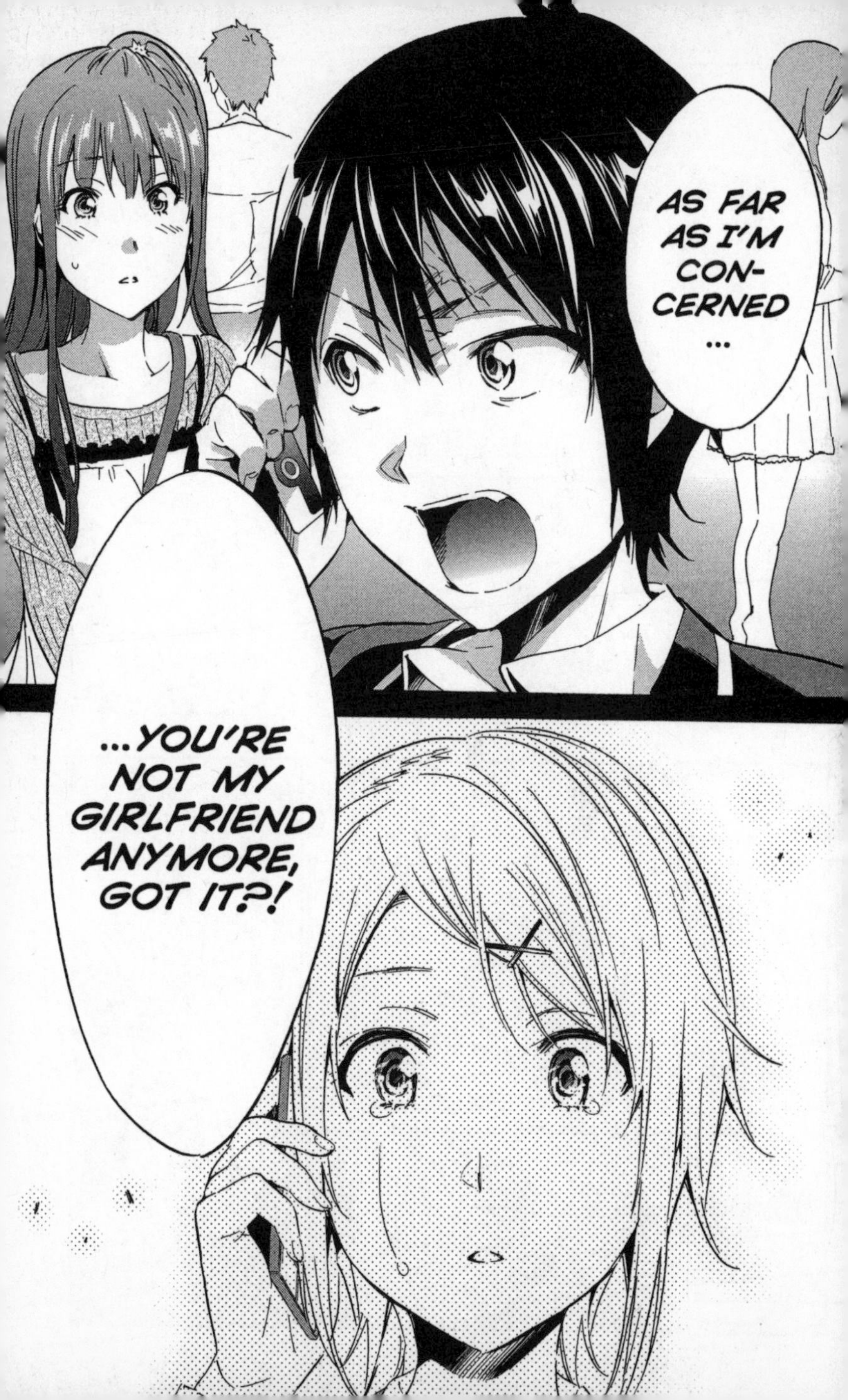
AS FAR AS I'M CON-CERNED ...
...YOU'RE NOT MY GIRLFRIEND ANYMORE, GOT IT?!

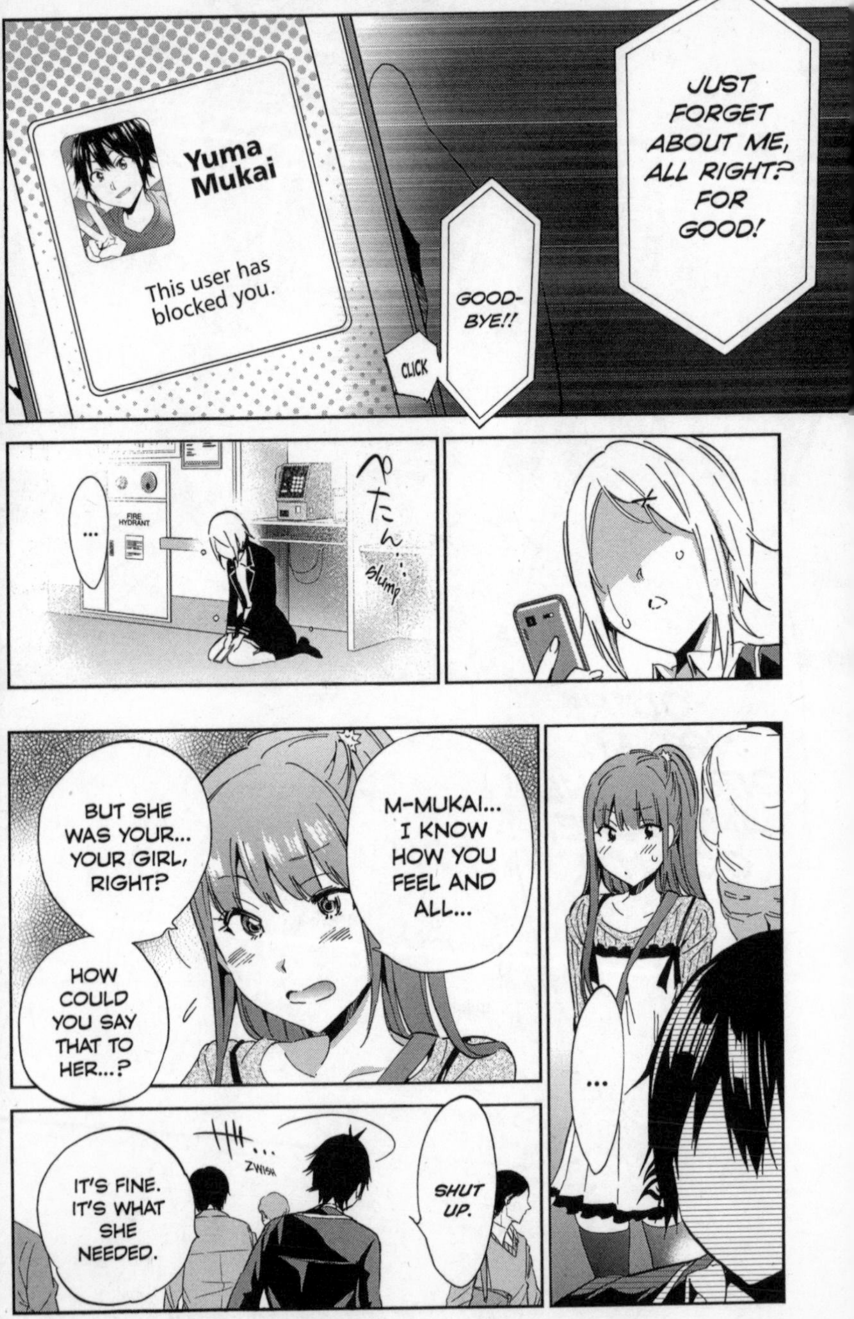
JUST FORGET ABOUT ME, ALL RIGHT? FOR GOOD!
GOOD-BYE!!
CLICK
Yuma Mukai
This user has blocked you.
...
ぺたん…
slump
...
M-MUKAI... I KNOW HOW YOU FEEL AND ALL...
BUT SHE WAS YOUR... YOUR GIRL, RIGHT?
HOW COULD YOU SAY THAT TO HER...?
SHUT UP.
ZWISH
IT'S FINE. IT'S WHAT SHE NEEDED.

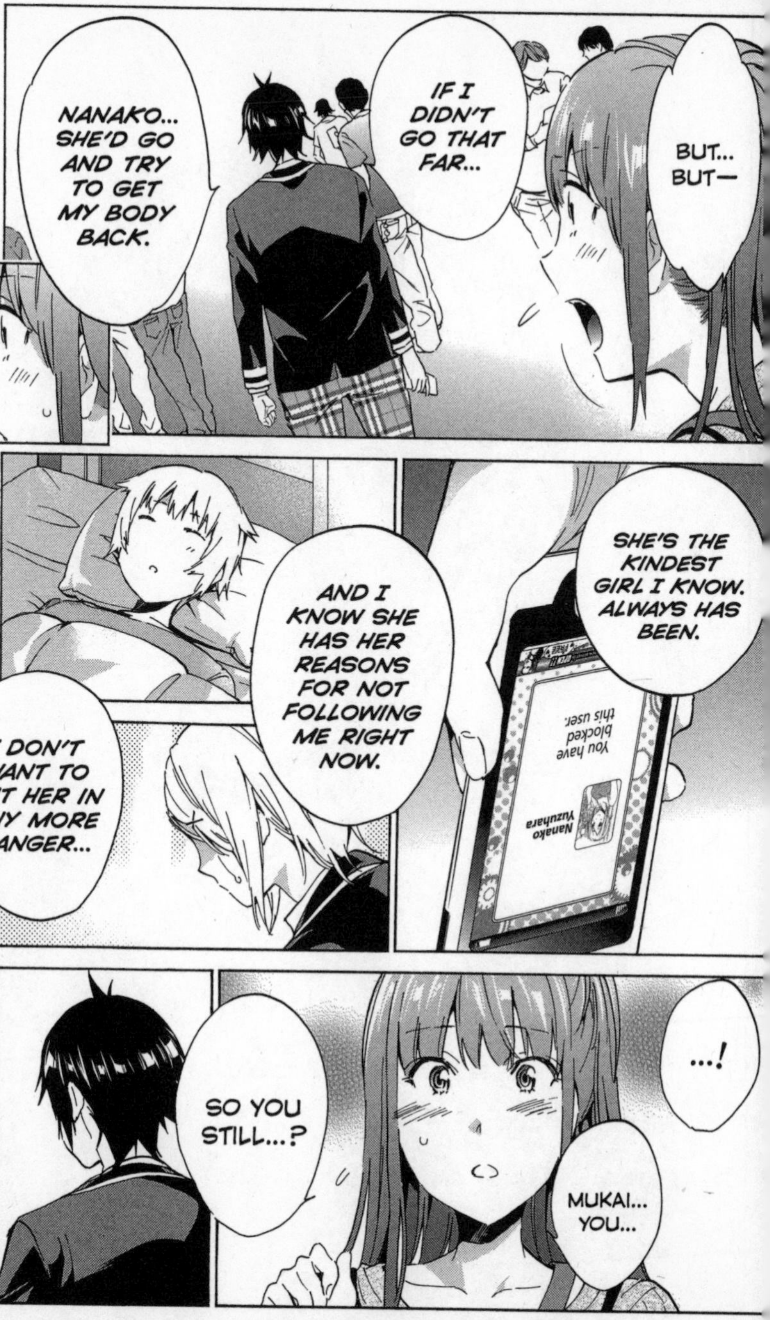
BUT... BUT—
IF I DIDN'T GO THAT FAR...
NANAKO... SHE'D GO AND TRY TO GET MY BODY BACK.
SHE'S THE KINDEST GIRL I KNOW. ALWAYS HAS BEEN.
Nanako Yuzuhara
You have blocked this user.
AND I KNOW SHE HAS HER REASONS FOR NOT FOLLOWING ME RIGHT NOW.
I DON'T WANT TO PUT HER IN ANY MORE DANGER...
...!
MUKAI... YOU...
SO YOU STILL...?

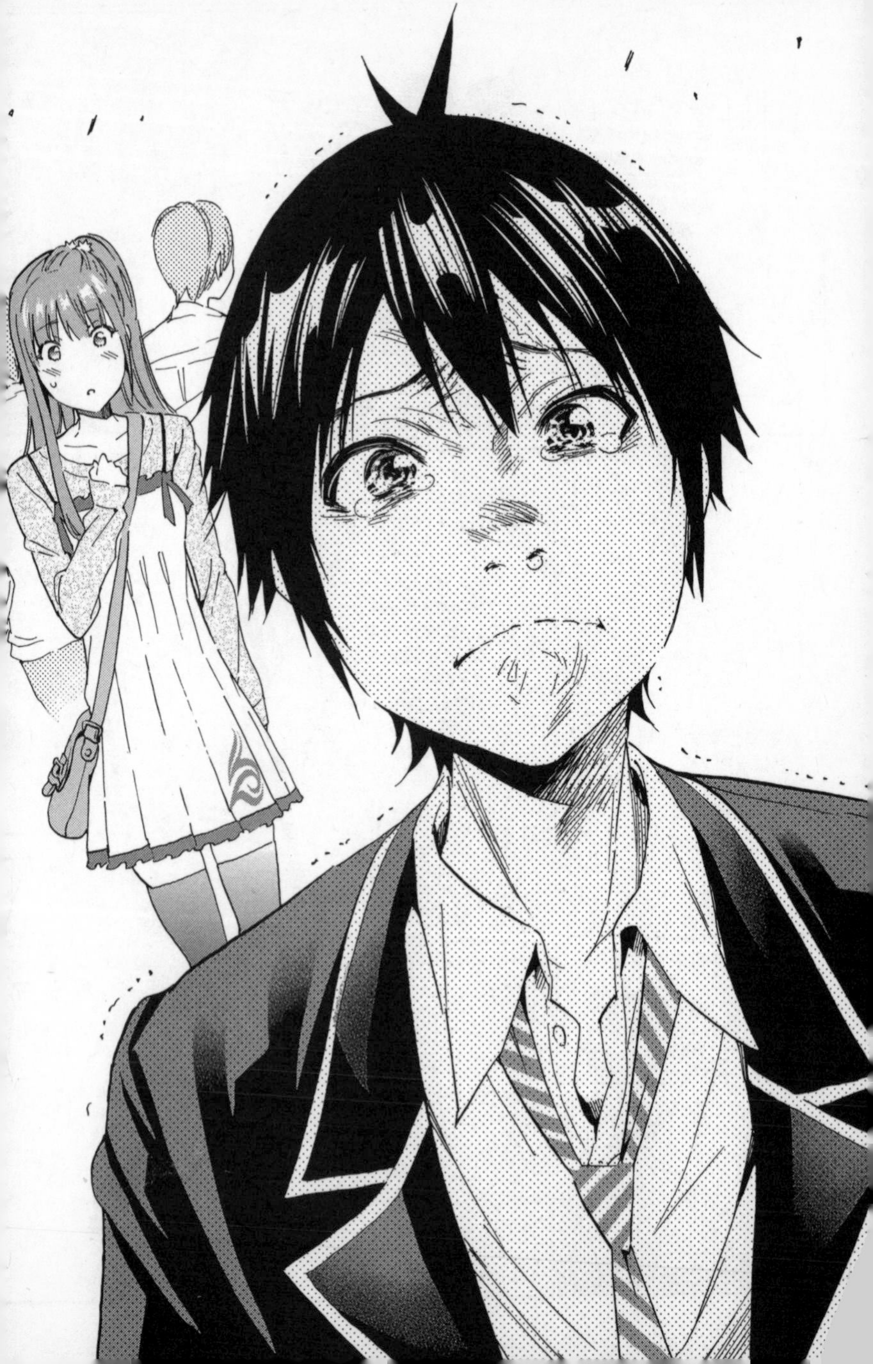

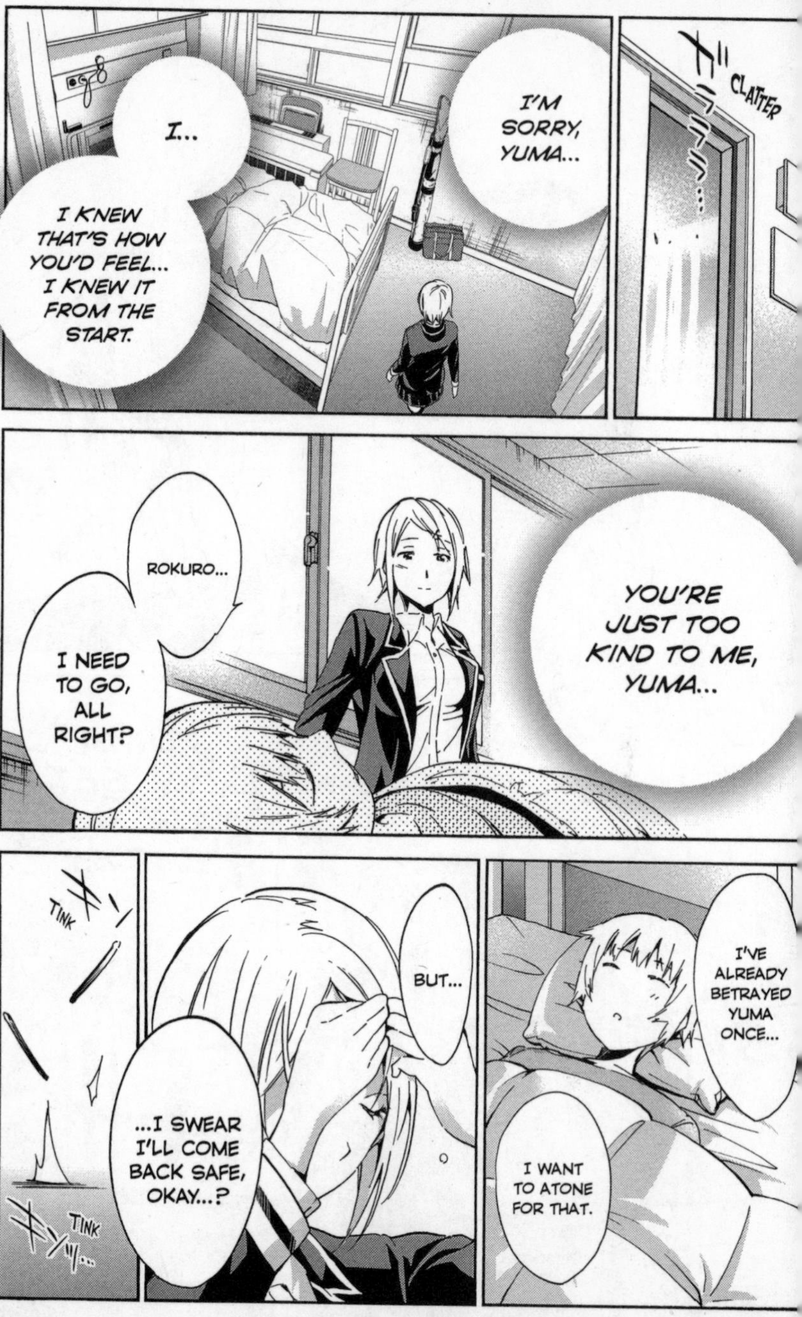
CLATTER
I'M SORRY, YUMA...
I...
I KNEW THAT'S HOW YOU'D FEEL... I KNEW IT FROM THE START.
YOU'RE JUST TOO KIND TO ME, YUMA...
ROKURO...
I NEED TO GO, ALL RIGHT?
I'VE ALREADY BETRAYED YUMA ONCE...
I WANT TO ATONE FOR THAT.
BUT...
...I SWEAR I'LL COME BACK SAFE, OKAY...?
TINK
TINK

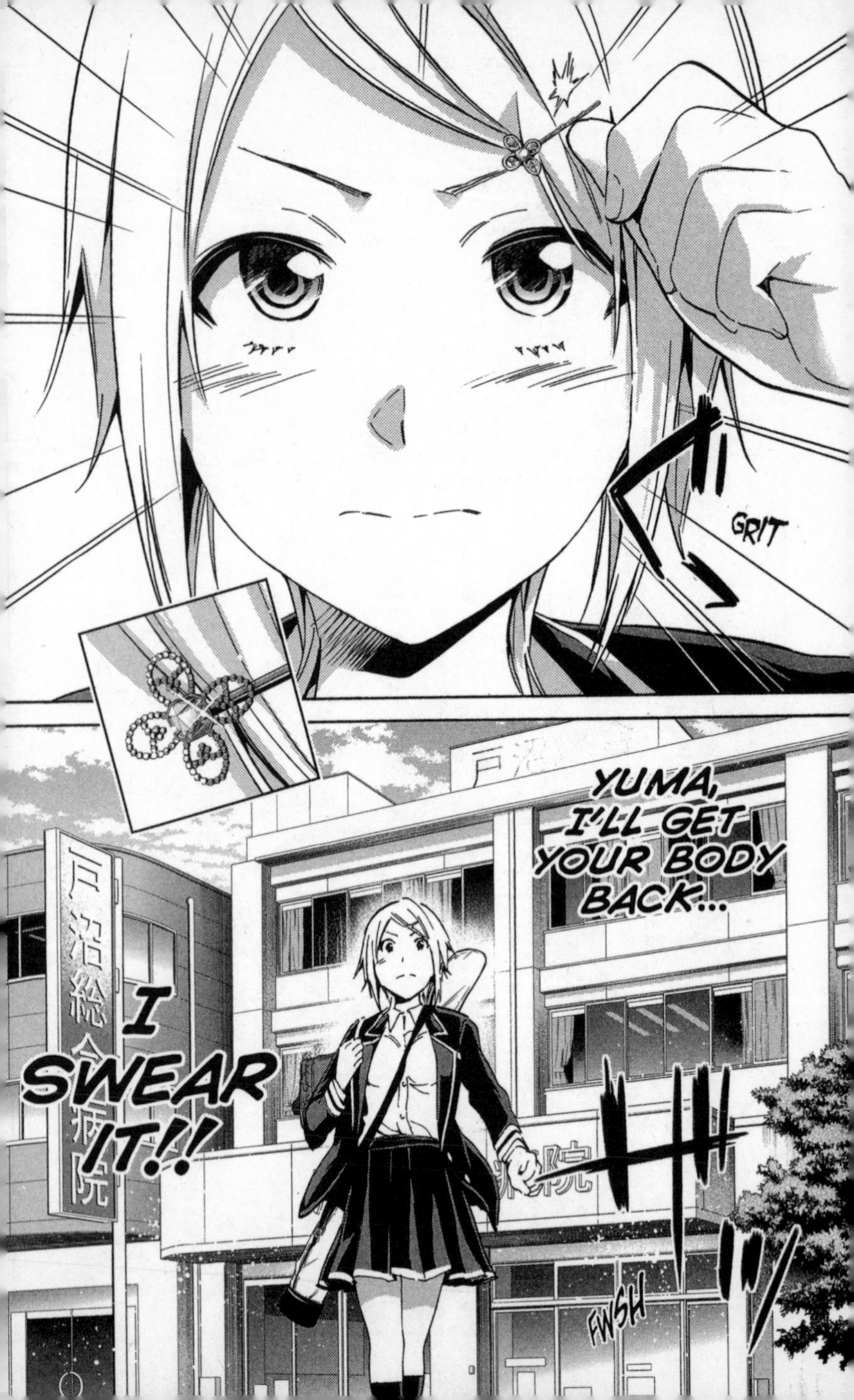
GRIT
YUMA, I'LL GET YOUR BODY BACK...
I SWEAR IT!!
戸沼総合病院
FWSH

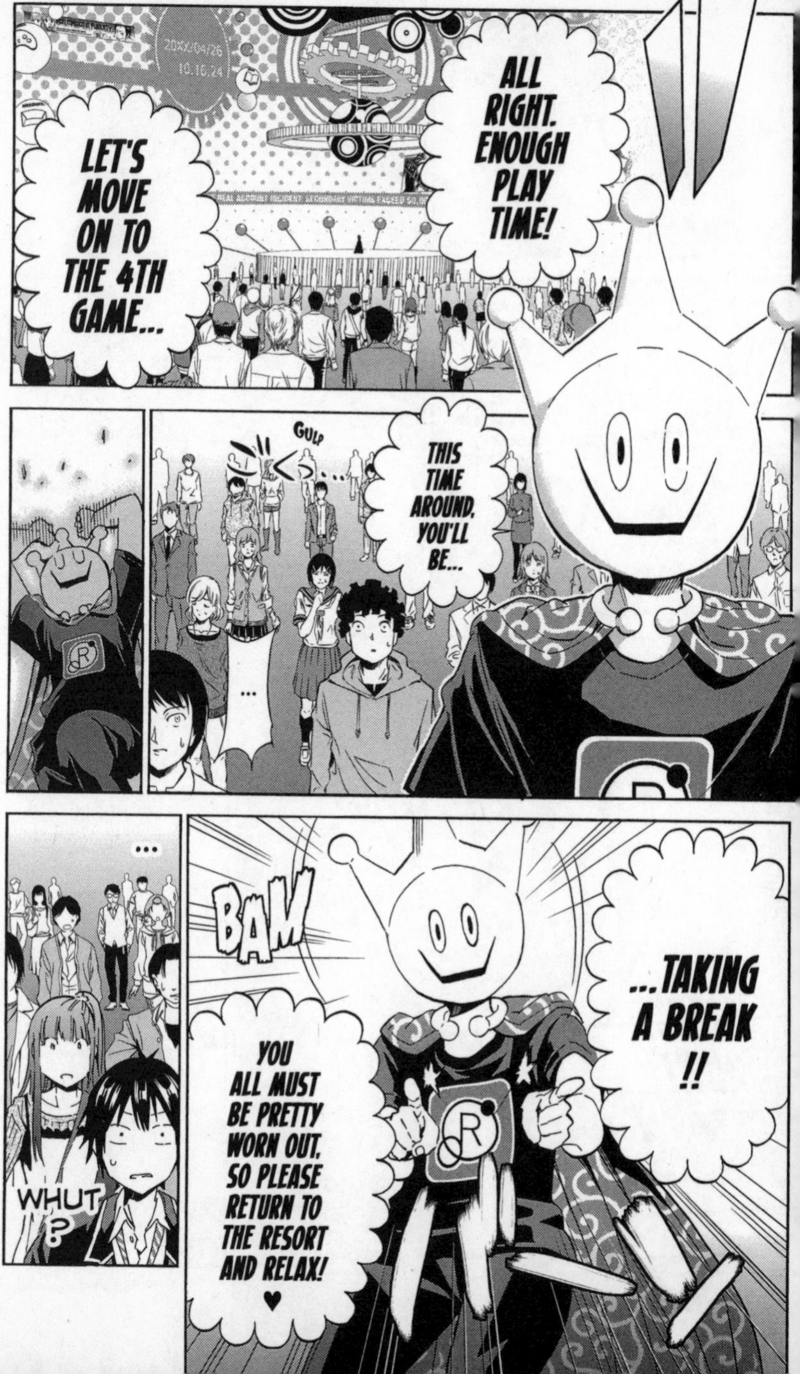
20XX/04/26
10:16:24
ALL RIGHT. ENOUGH PLAY TIME!
LET'S MOVE ON TO THE 4TH GAME...
THIS TIME AROUND, YOU'LL BE...
GULP
...
BAM
...TAKING A BREAK !!
YOU ALL MUST BE PRETTY WORN OUT, SO PLEASE RETURN TO THE RESORT AND RELAX! ♥
...
WHUT?

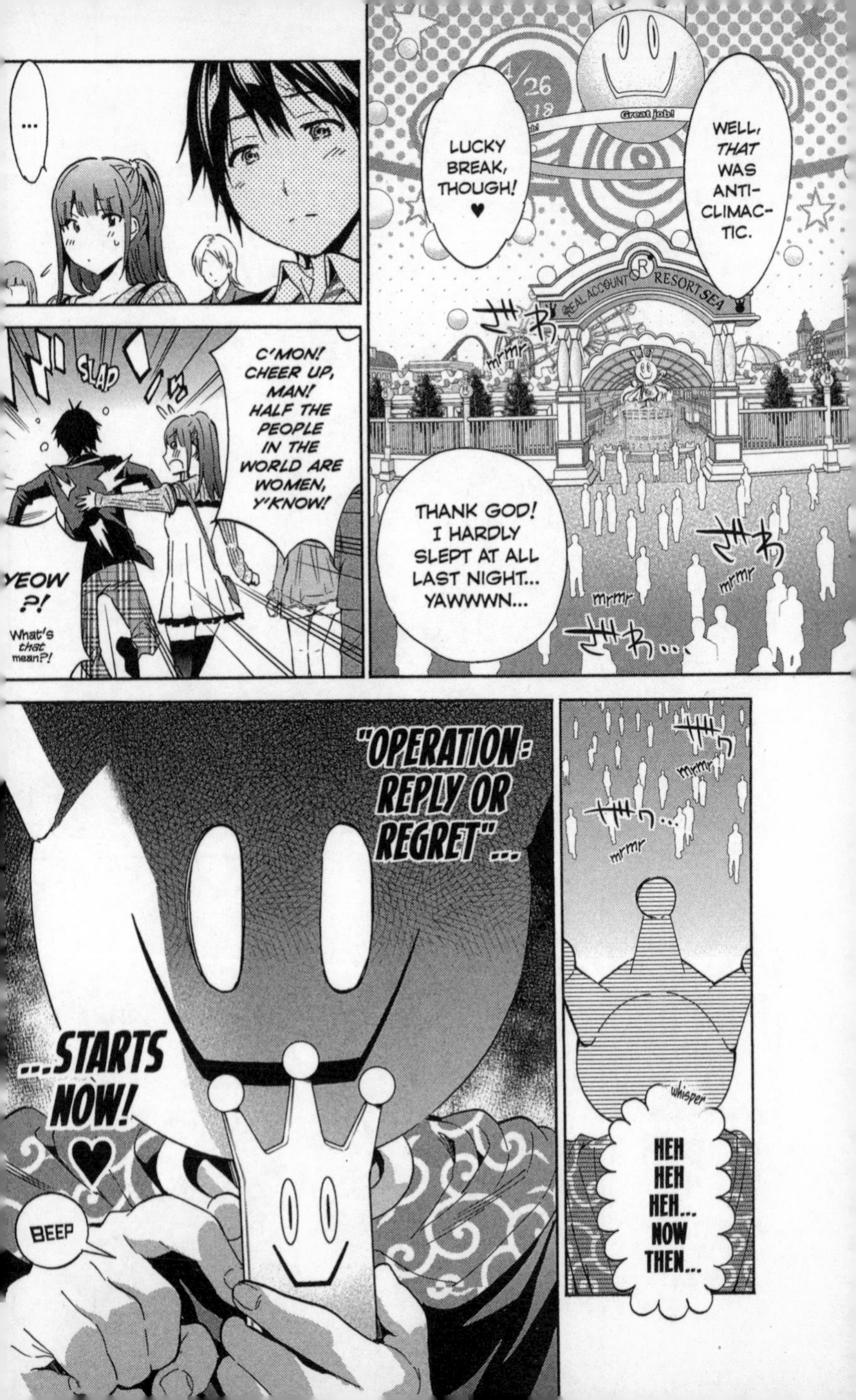
Great job!
RESORT SEA
WELL, THAT WAS ANTI-CLIMACTIC.
LUCKY BREAK, THOUGH! ♥
mrmr
THANK GOD! I HARDLY SLEPT AT ALL LAST NIGHT... YAWWWN...
mrmr
mrmr
...
SLAP
C'MON! CHEER UP, MAN! HALF THE PEOPLE IN THE WORLD ARE WOMEN, Y'KNOW!
YEOW?!
What's that mean?!
mrmr
mrmr
whisper
HEH HEH HEH... NOW THEN...
"OPERATION: REPLY OR REGRET"...
...STARTS NOW! ♥
BEEP

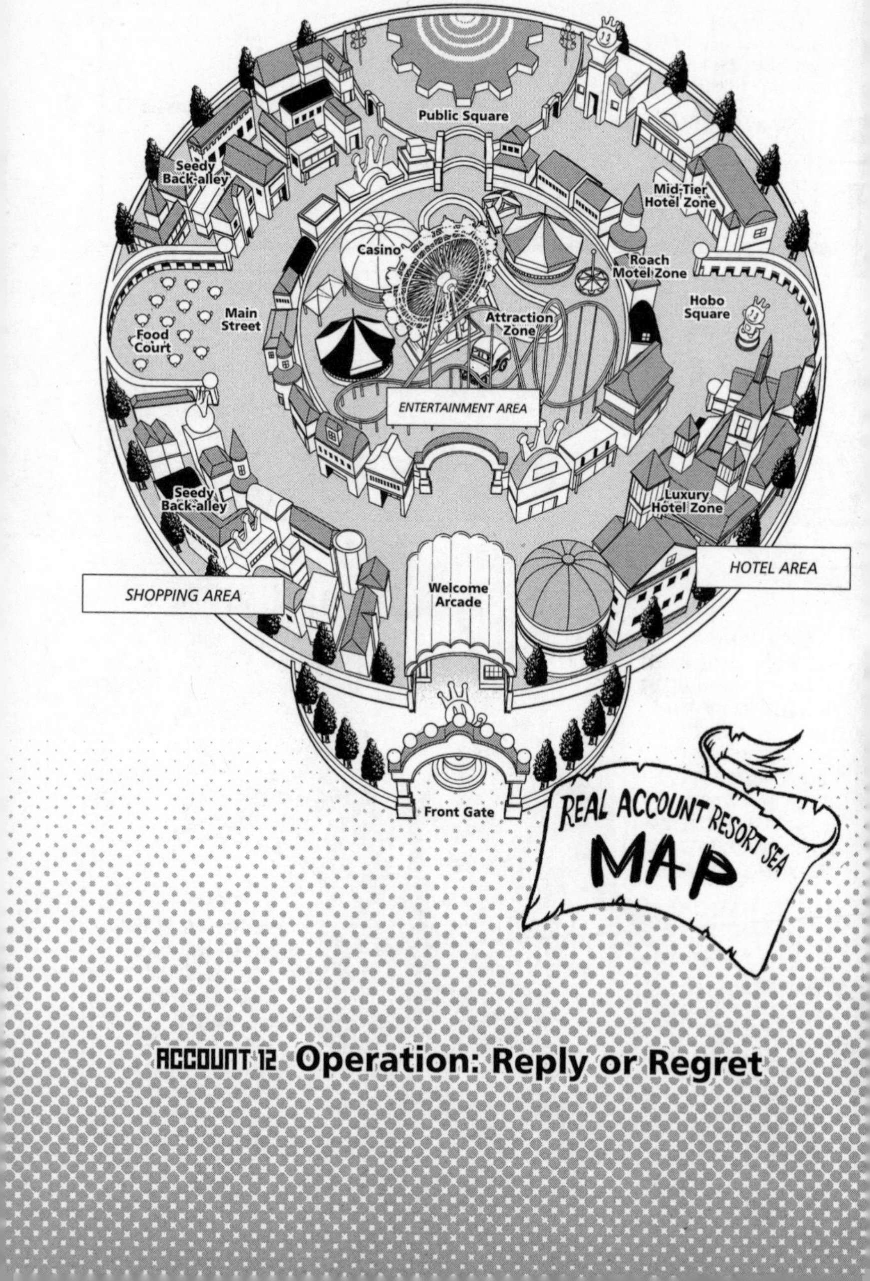
Public Square
Seedy Back-alley
Mid-Tier Hotel Zone
Casino
Roach Motel Zone
Hobo Square
Main Street
Attraction Zone
Food Court
ENTERTAINMENT AREA
Seedy Back-alley
Luxury Hotel Zone
HOTEL AREA
SHOPPING AREA
Welcome Arcade
Front Gate
REAL ACCOUNT RESORT SEA
MAP

ACCOUNT 12 Operation: Reply or Regret

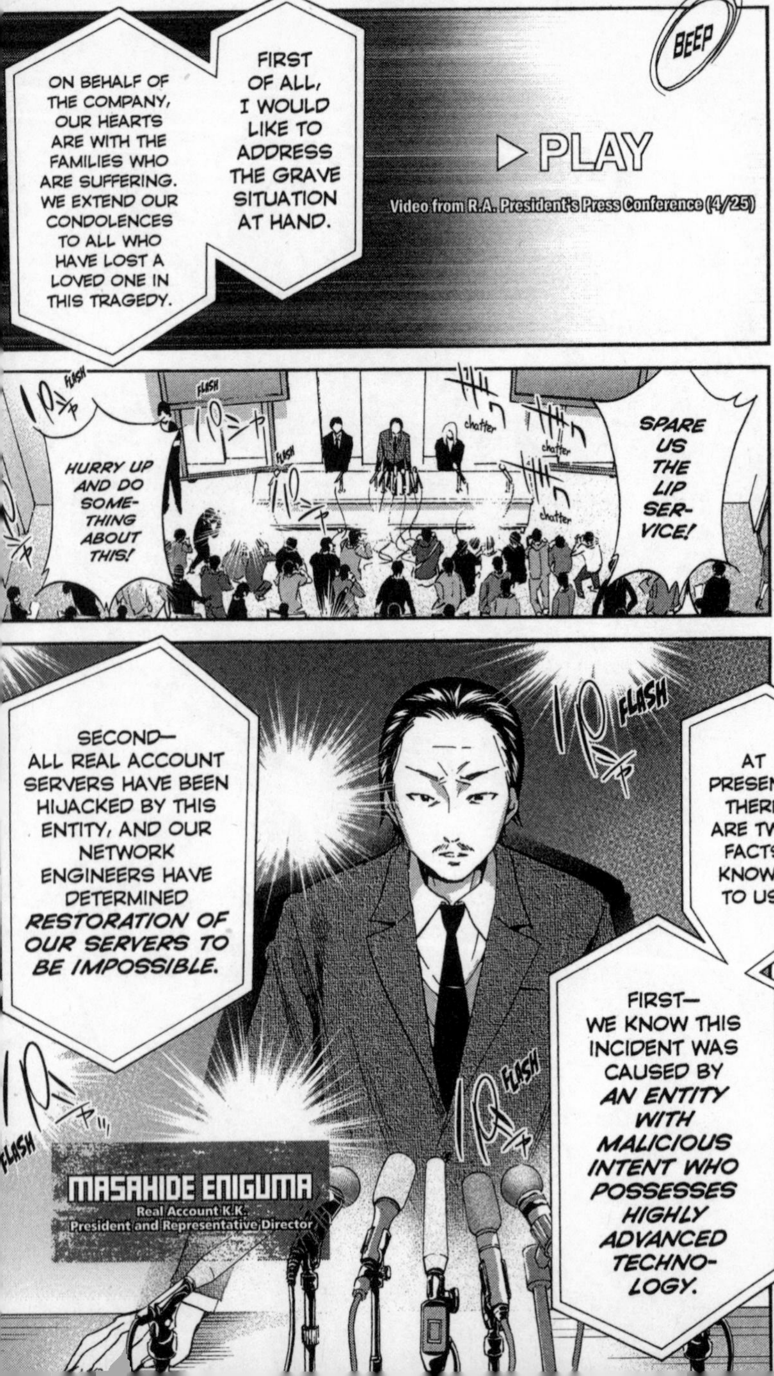
BEEP
▷ PLAY
Video from R.A. President's Press Conference (4/25)
FIRST OF ALL, I WOULD LIKE TO ADDRESS THE GRAVE SITUATION AT HAND.
ON BEHALF OF THE COMPANY, OUR HEARTS ARE WITH THE FAMILIES WHO ARE SUFFERING. WE EXTEND OUR CONDOLENCES TO ALL WHO HAVE LOST A LOVED ONE IN THIS TRAGEDY.
SPARE US THE LIP SERVICE!
chatter
chatter
chatter
FLASH
FLASH
FLASH
HURRY UP AND DO SOMETHING ABOUT THIS!
FLASH
AT PRESENT, THERE ARE TWO FACTS KNOWN TO US.
FIRST— WE KNOW THIS INCIDENT WAS CAUSED BY *AN ENTITY WITH MALICIOUS INTENT WHO POSSESSES HIGHLY ADVANCED TECHNOLOGY.*
SECOND— ALL REAL ACCOUNT SERVERS HAVE BEEN HIJACKED BY THIS ENTITY, AND OUR NETWORK ENGINEERS HAVE DETERMINED *RESTORATION OF OUR SERVERS TO BE IMPOSSIBLE.*
FLASH
FLASH
MASAHIDE ENIGUMA
Real Account K.K.
President and Representative Director

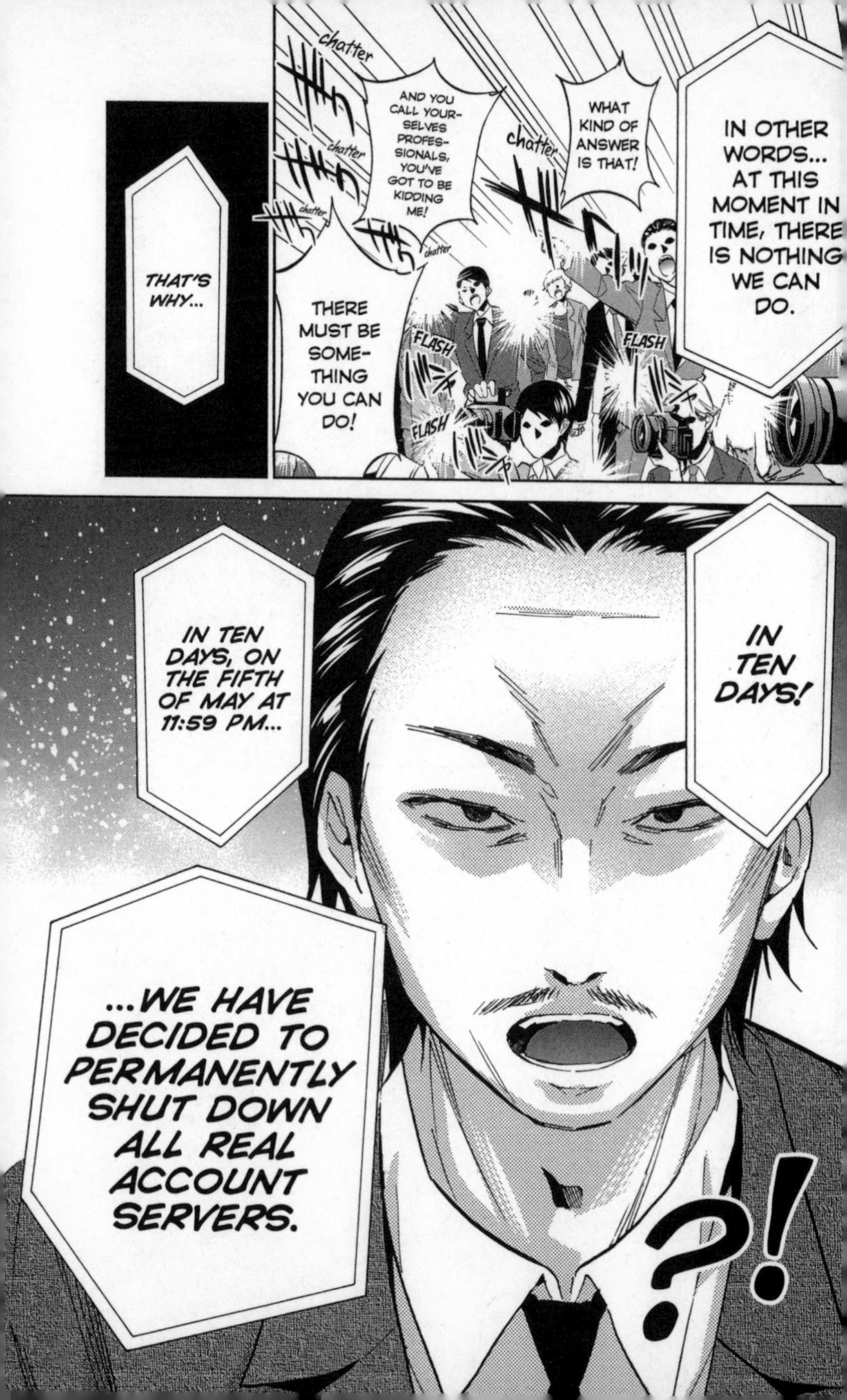
IN OTHER WORDS... AT THIS MOMENT IN TIME, THERE IS NOTHING WE CAN DO.
WHAT KIND OF ANSWER IS THAT!
chatter
chatter
AND YOU CALL YOURSELVES PROFESSIONALS, YOU'VE GOT TO BE KIDDING ME!
chatter
chatter
chatter
FLASH
FLASH
FLASH
THERE MUST BE SOMETHING YOU CAN DO!
THAT'S WHY...
IN TEN DAYS!
IN TEN DAYS, ON THE FIFTH OF MAY AT 11:59 PM...
...WE HAVE DECIDED TO PERMANENTLY SHUT DOWN ALL REAL ACCOUNT SERVERS.
?!

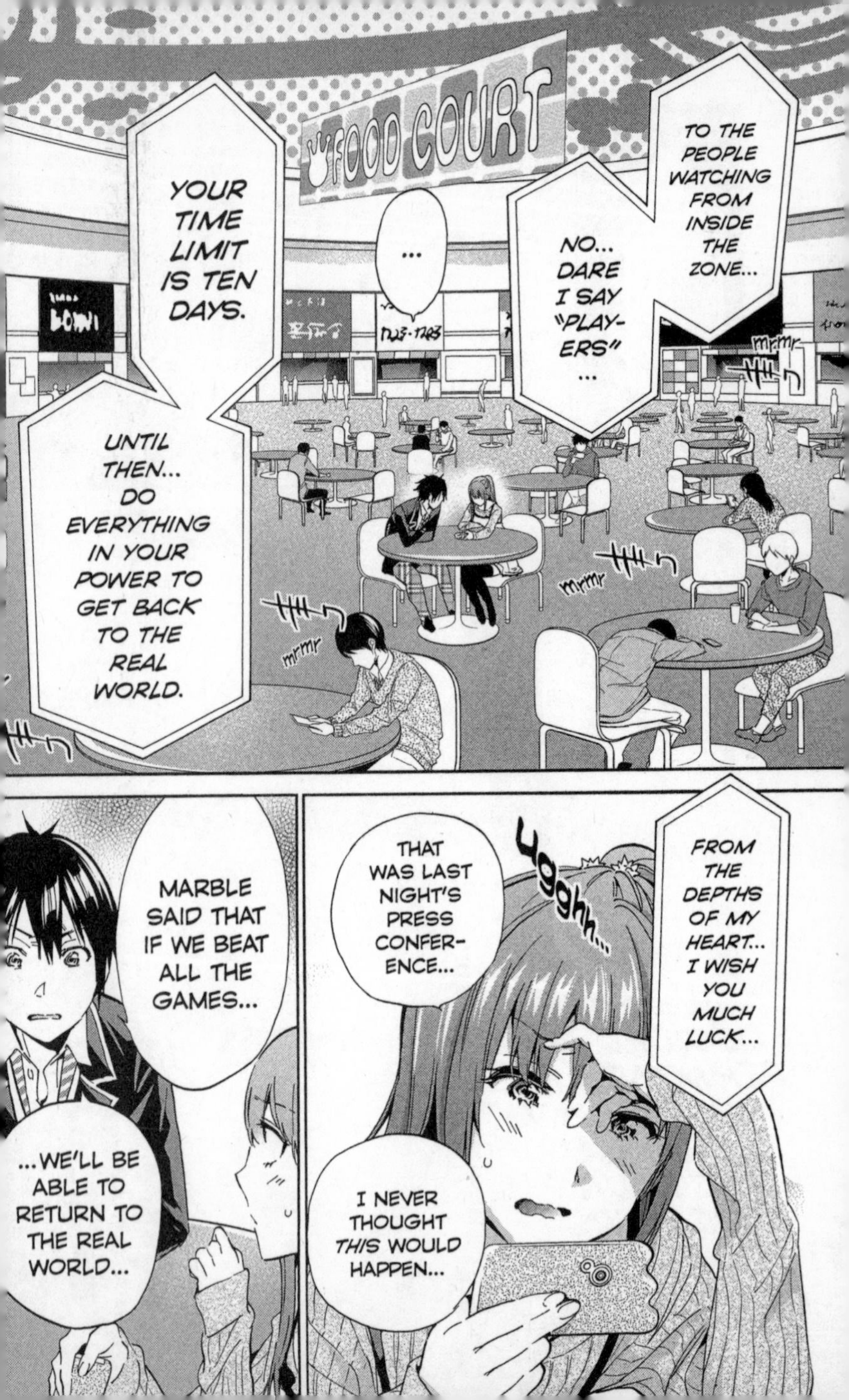
FOOD COURT
TO THE PEOPLE WATCHING FROM INSIDE THE ZONE...
NO... DARE I SAY "PLAYERS"...
...
YOUR TIME LIMIT IS TEN DAYS.
UNTIL THEN... DO EVERYTHING IN YOUR POWER TO GET BACK TO THE REAL WORLD.
mrmr
mrmr
mrmr
FROM THE DEPTHS OF MY HEART... I WISH YOU MUCH LUCK...
Ugghh...
THAT WAS LAST NIGHT'S PRESS CONFERENCE...
I NEVER THOUGHT *THIS* WOULD HAPPEN...
MARBLE SAID THAT IF WE BEAT ALL THE GAMES...
...WE'LL BE ABLE TO RETURN TO THE REAL WORLD...

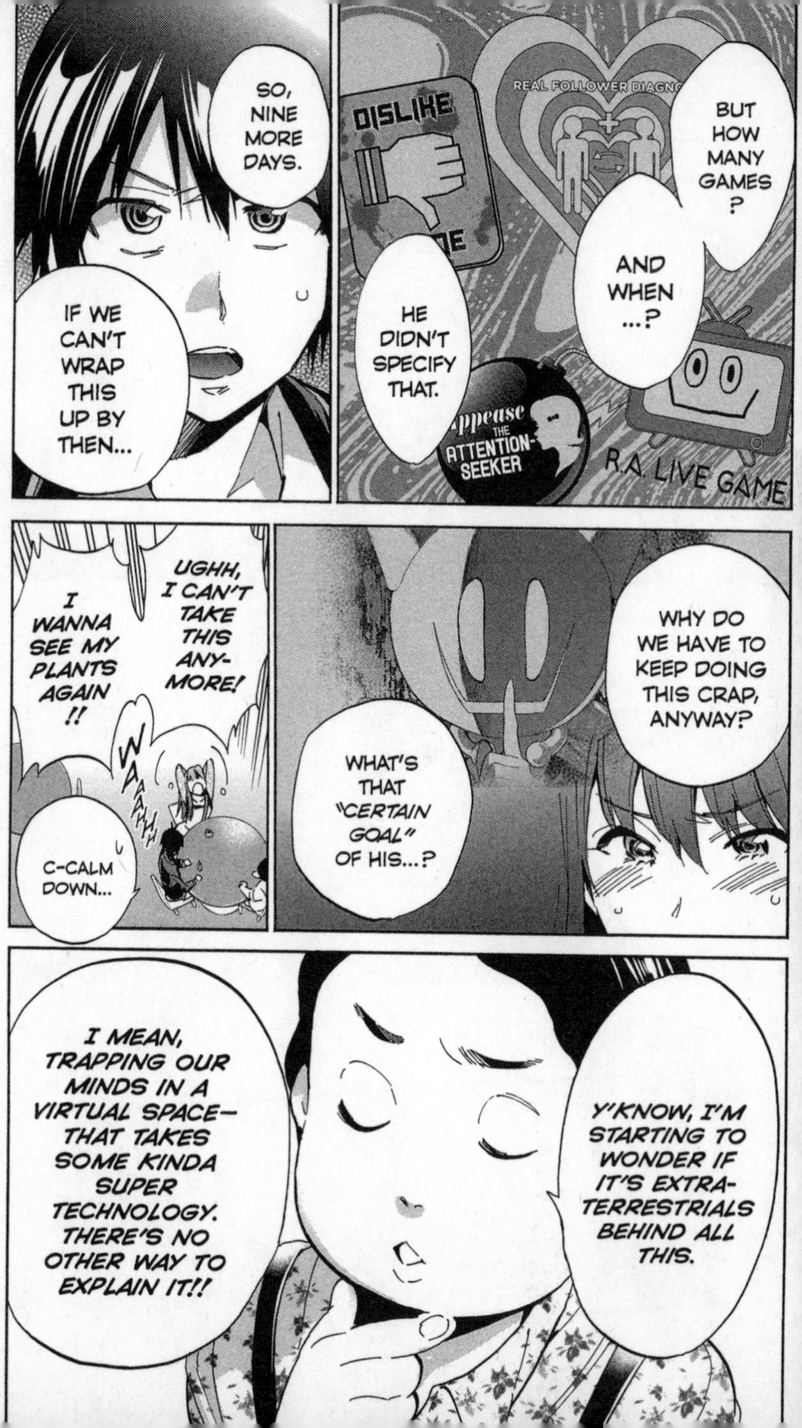

REAL FOLLOWER DIAGNO
DISLIKE
BUT HOW MANY GAMES ?
AND WHEN ...?
HE DIDN'T SPECIFY THAT.
ppease THE ATTENTION-SEEKER
R.A. LIVE GAME
SO, NINE MORE DAYS.
IF WE CAN'T WRAP THIS UP BY THEN...
WHY DO WE HAVE TO KEEP DOING THIS CRAP, ANYWAY?
WHAT'S THAT "CERTAIN GOAL" OF HIS...?
UGHH, I CAN'T TAKE THIS ANY-MORE!
I WANNA SEE MY PLANTS AGAIN !!
WAAAHH
C-CALM DOWN...
Y'KNOW, I'M STARTING TO WONDER IF IT'S EXTRA-TERRESTRIALS BEHIND ALL THIS.
I MEAN, TRAPPING OUR MINDS IN A VIRTUAL SPACE—THAT TAKES SOME KINDA SUPER TECHNOLOGY. THERE'S NO OTHER WAY TO EXPLAIN IT!!

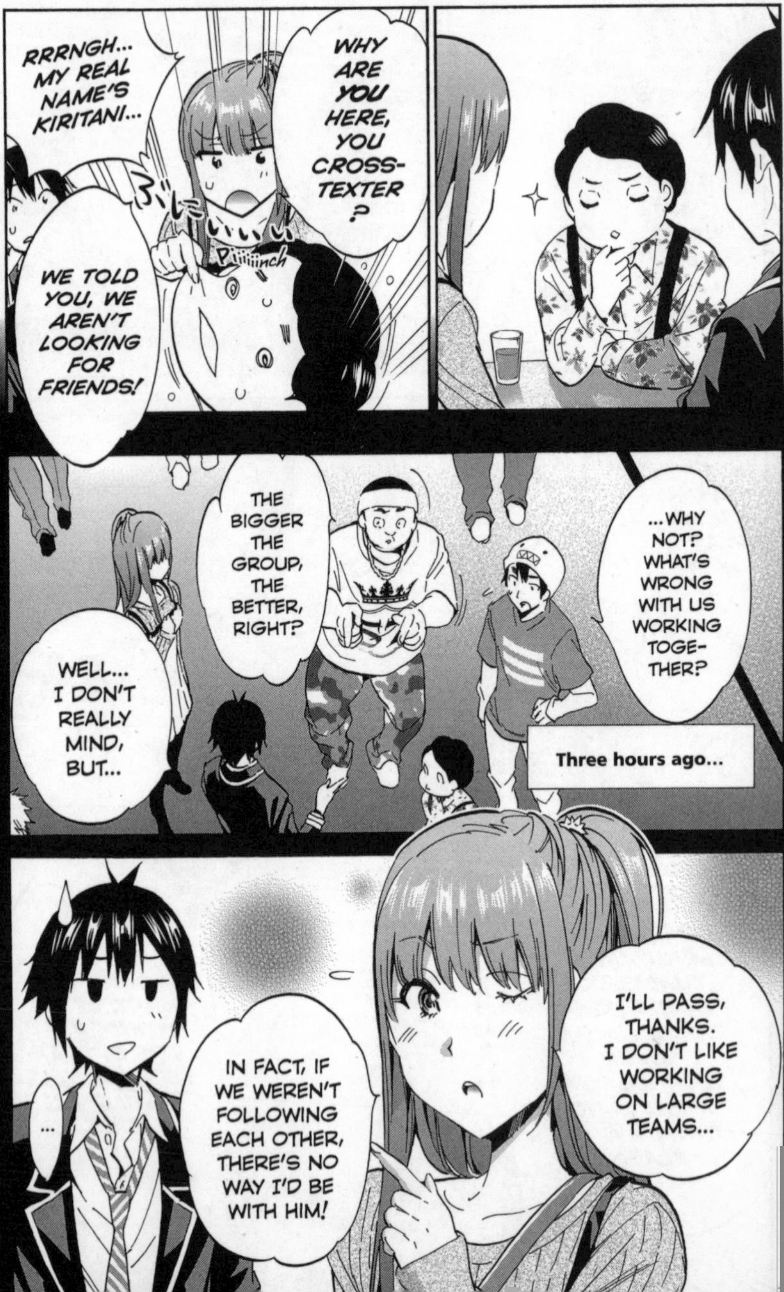
WHY ARE YOU HERE, YOU CROSS-TEXTER?
RRRNGH... MY REAL NAME'S KIRITANI...
Piiiiinch
WE TOLD YOU, WE AREN'T LOOKING FOR FRIENDS!
Three hours ago...
...WHY NOT? WHAT'S WRONG WITH US WORKING TOGE-THER?
THE BIGGER THE GROUP, THE BETTER, RIGHT?
WELL... I DON'T REALLY MIND, BUT...
I'LL PASS, THANKS. I DON'T LIKE WORKING ON LARGE TEAMS...
IN FACT, IF WE WEREN'T FOLLOWING EACH OTHER, THERE'S NO WAY I'D BE WITH HIM!
...

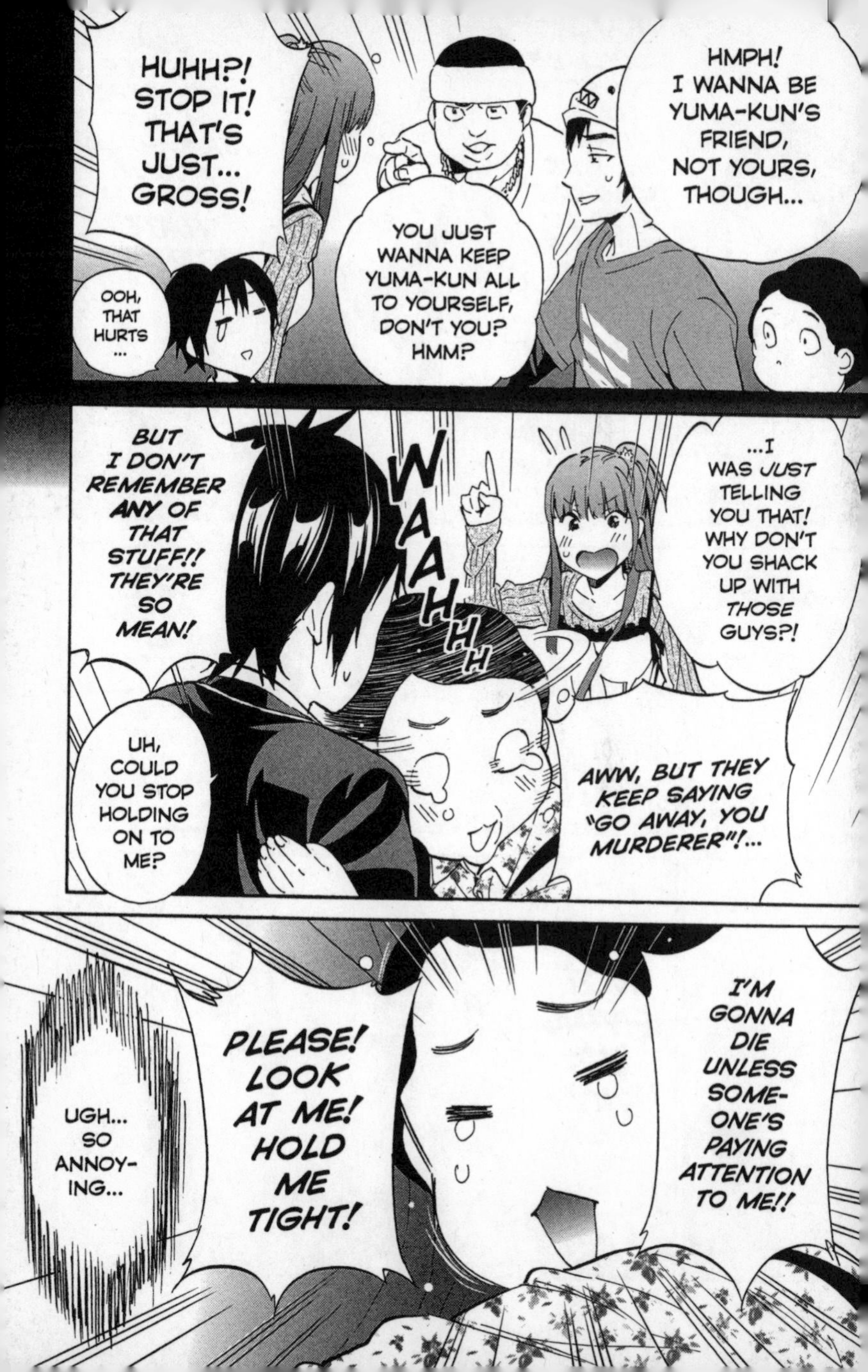
HMPH! I WANNA BE YUMA-KUN'S FRIEND, NOT YOURS, THOUGH...
YOU JUST WANNA KEEP YUMA-KUN ALL TO YOURSELF, DON'T YOU? HMM?
HUHH?! STOP IT! THAT'S JUST... GROSS!
OOH, THAT HURTS ...
...I WAS *JUST* TELLING YOU THAT! WHY DON'T YOU SHACK UP WITH *THOSE* GUYS?!
WAAHHH
*BUT I DON'T REMEMBER **ANY** OF THAT STUFF!! THEY'RE SO MEAN!*
AWW, BUT THEY KEEP SAYING "GO AWAY, YOU MURDERER"!...
UH, COULD YOU STOP HOLDING ON TO ME?
I'M GONNA DIE UNLESS SOME-ONE'S PAYING ATTENTION TO ME!!
PLEASE! LOOK AT ME! HOLD ME TIGHT!
UGH... SO ANNOY-ING...

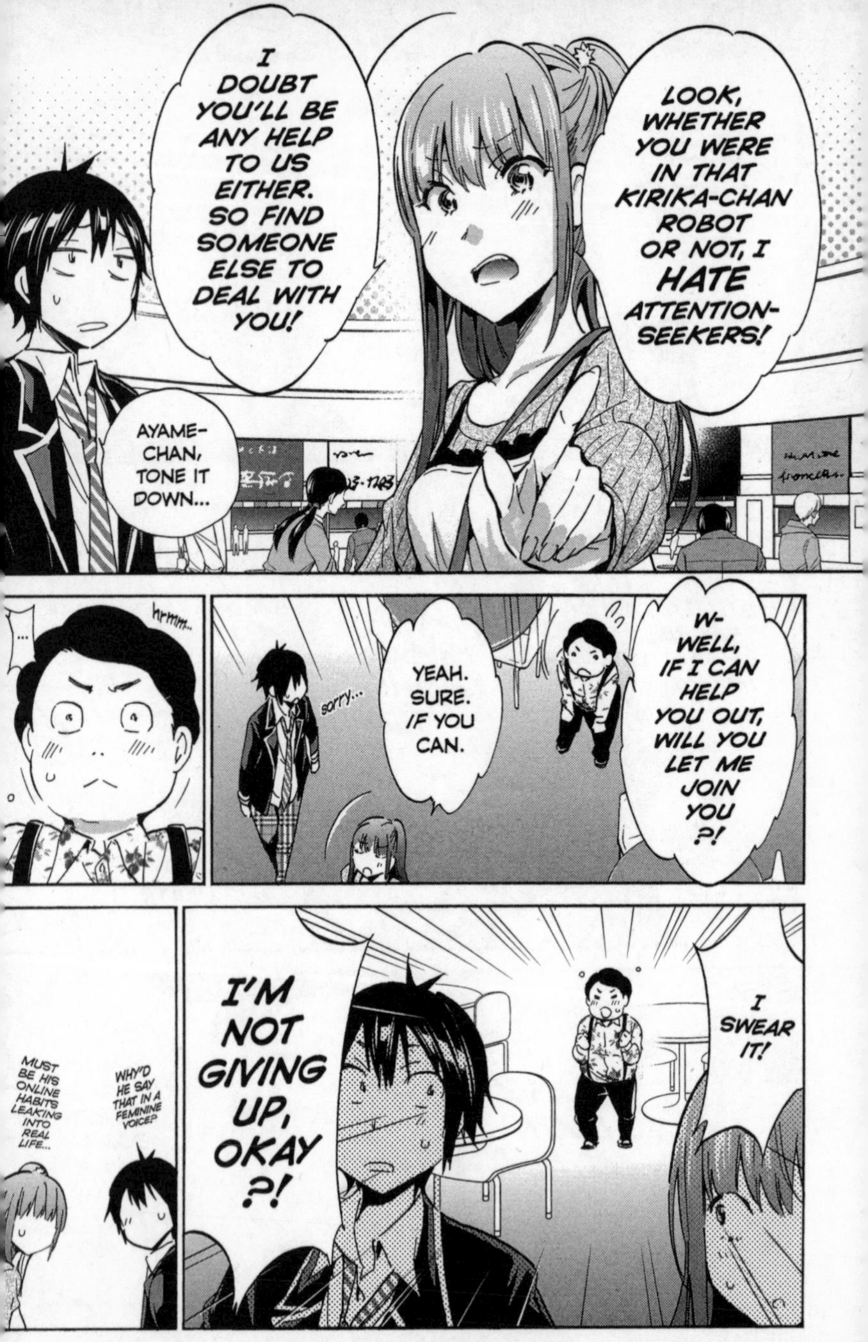
LOOK, WHETHER YOU WERE IN THAT KIRIKA-CHAN ROBOT OR NOT, I HATE ATTENTION-SEEKERS!
I DOUBT YOU'LL BE ANY HELP TO US EITHER. SO FIND SOMEONE ELSE TO DEAL WITH YOU!
AYAME-CHAN, TONE IT DOWN...
W-WELL, IF I CAN HELP YOU OUT, WILL YOU LET ME JOIN YOU?!
YEAH. SURE. IF YOU CAN.
sorry...
hrmm...
...
I SWEAR IT!
I'M NOT GIVING UP, OKAY?!
WHY'D HE SAY THAT IN A FEMININE VOICE?
MUST BE HIS ONLINE HABITS LEAKING INTO REAL LIFE...

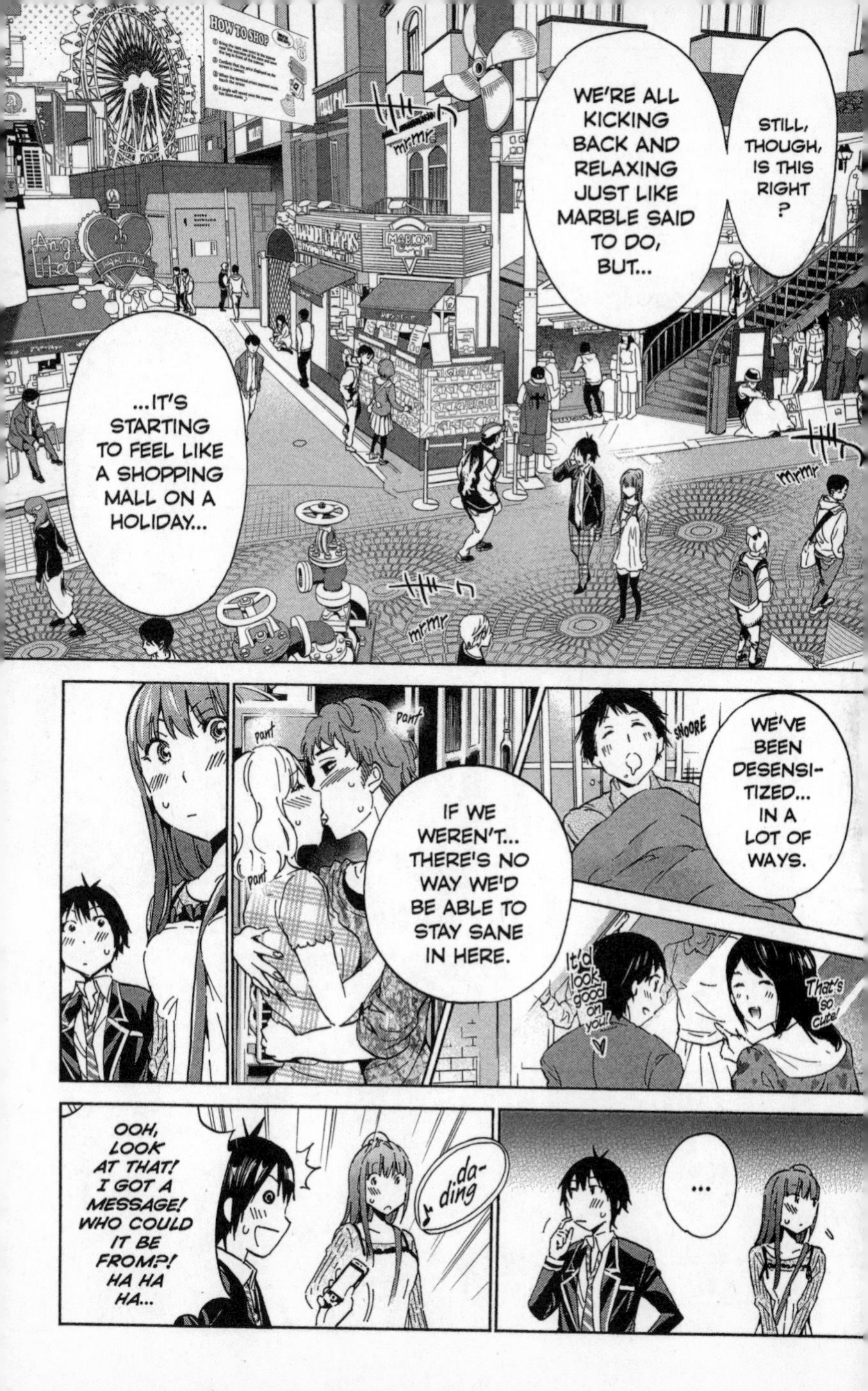
HOW TO SHOP
STILL, THOUGH, IS THIS RIGHT?
WE'RE ALL KICKING BACK AND RELAXING JUST LIKE MARBLE SAID TO DO, BUT...
mrmr
mrmr
...IT'S STARTING TO FEEL LIKE A SHOPPING MALL ON A HOLIDAY...
mrmr
SNOORE
WE'VE BEEN DESENSITIZED... IN A LOT OF WAYS.
That's so cute!
It'd look good on you!
pant
pant
pant
IF WE WEREN'T... THERE'S NO WAY WE'D BE ABLE TO STAY SANE IN HERE.
...
da-ding
OOH, LOOK AT THAT! I GOT A MESSAGE! WHO COULD IT BE FROM?! HA HA HA...

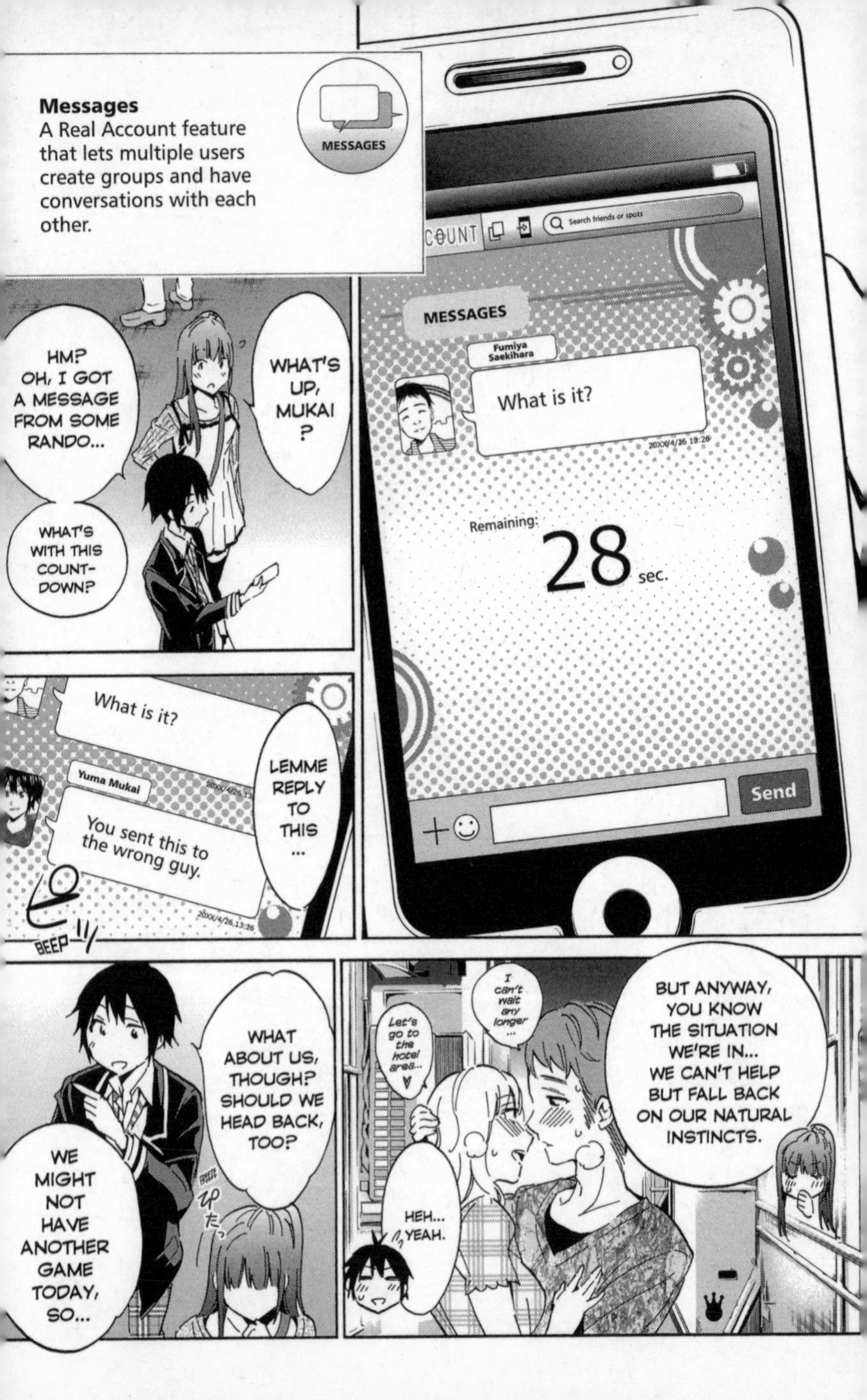

COUNT
Search friends or spots
MESSAGES
Fumiya Saekihara
What is it?
20XX/4/26 13:26
Remaining: 28 sec.
Send
Messages
A Real Account feature that lets multiple users create groups and have conversations with each other.
MESSAGES
WHAT'S UP, MUKAI?
HM? OH, I GOT A MESSAGE FROM SOME RANDO...
WHAT'S WITH THIS COUNTDOWN?
LEMME REPLY TO THIS...
What is it?
Yuma Mukai
You sent this to the wrong guy.
20XX/4/26 13:26
BEEP
BUT ANYWAY, YOU KNOW THE SITUATION WE'RE IN... WE CAN'T HELP BUT FALL BACK ON OUR NATURAL INSTINCTS.
I can't wait any longer...
Let's go to the hotel area...
HEH... YEAH.
WHAT ABOUT US, THOUGH? SHOULD WE HEAD BACK, TOO?
FREEZE
WE MIGHT NOT HAVE ANOTHER GAME TODAY, SO...

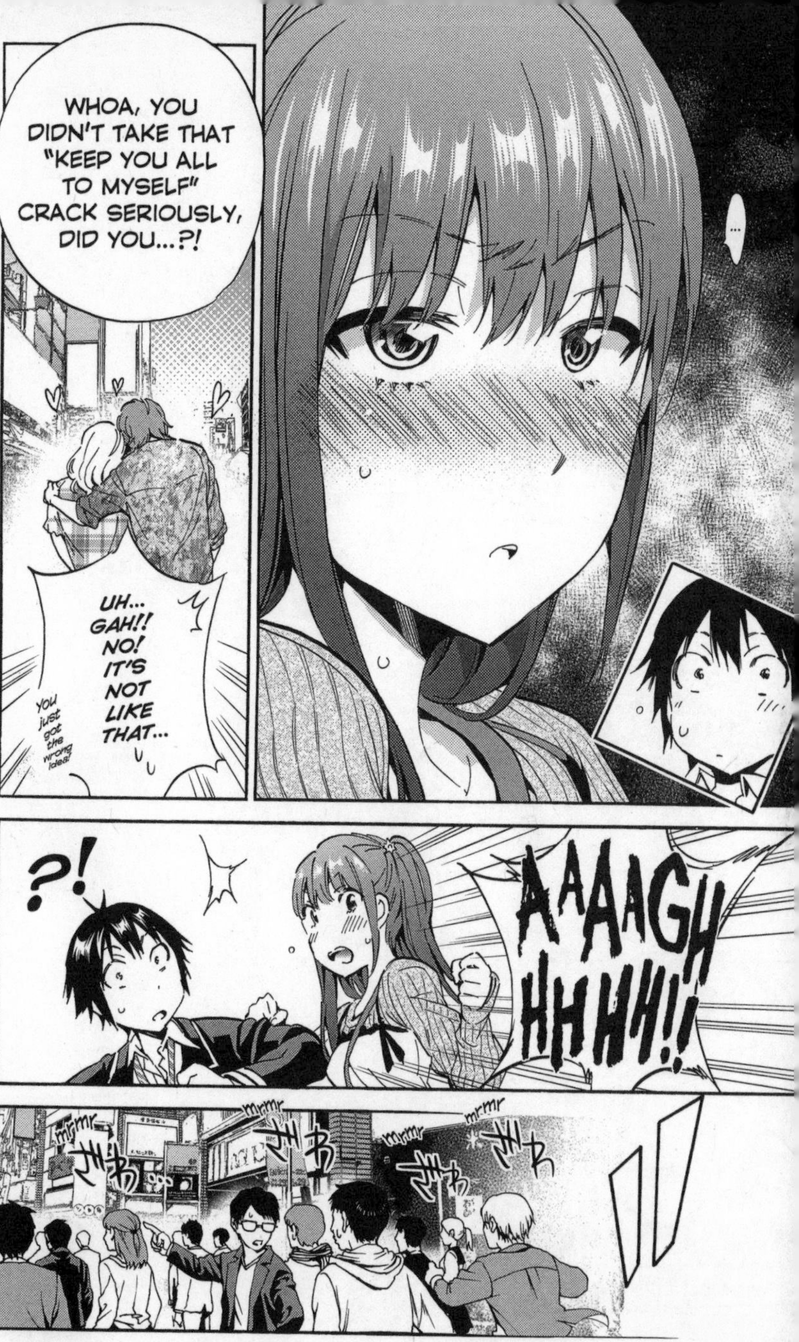
...
WHOA, YOU DIDN'T TAKE THAT "KEEP YOU ALL TO MYSELF" CRACK SERIOUSLY, DID YOU...?!
UH... GAH!! NO! IT'S NOT LIKE THAT...
You just got the wrong idea!
AAAAGH HHHH!!
?!
mrmr
mrmr
mrmr
mrmr

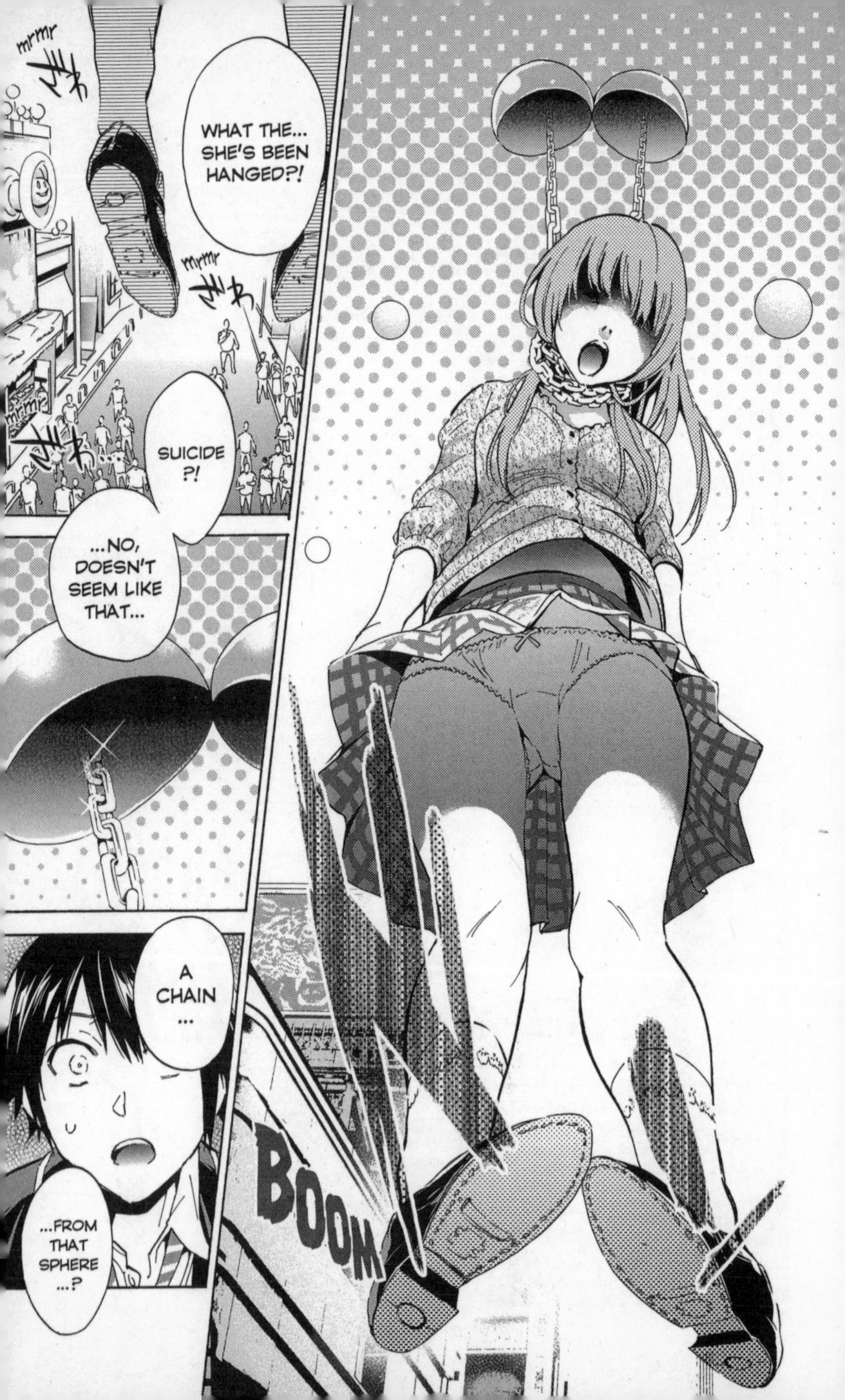

BOOM
mrmr
WHAT THE... SHE'S BEEN HANGED?!
mrmr
mrmr
SUICIDE ?!
...NO, DOESN'T SEEM LIKE THAT...
A CHAIN ...
...FROM THAT SPHERE ...?

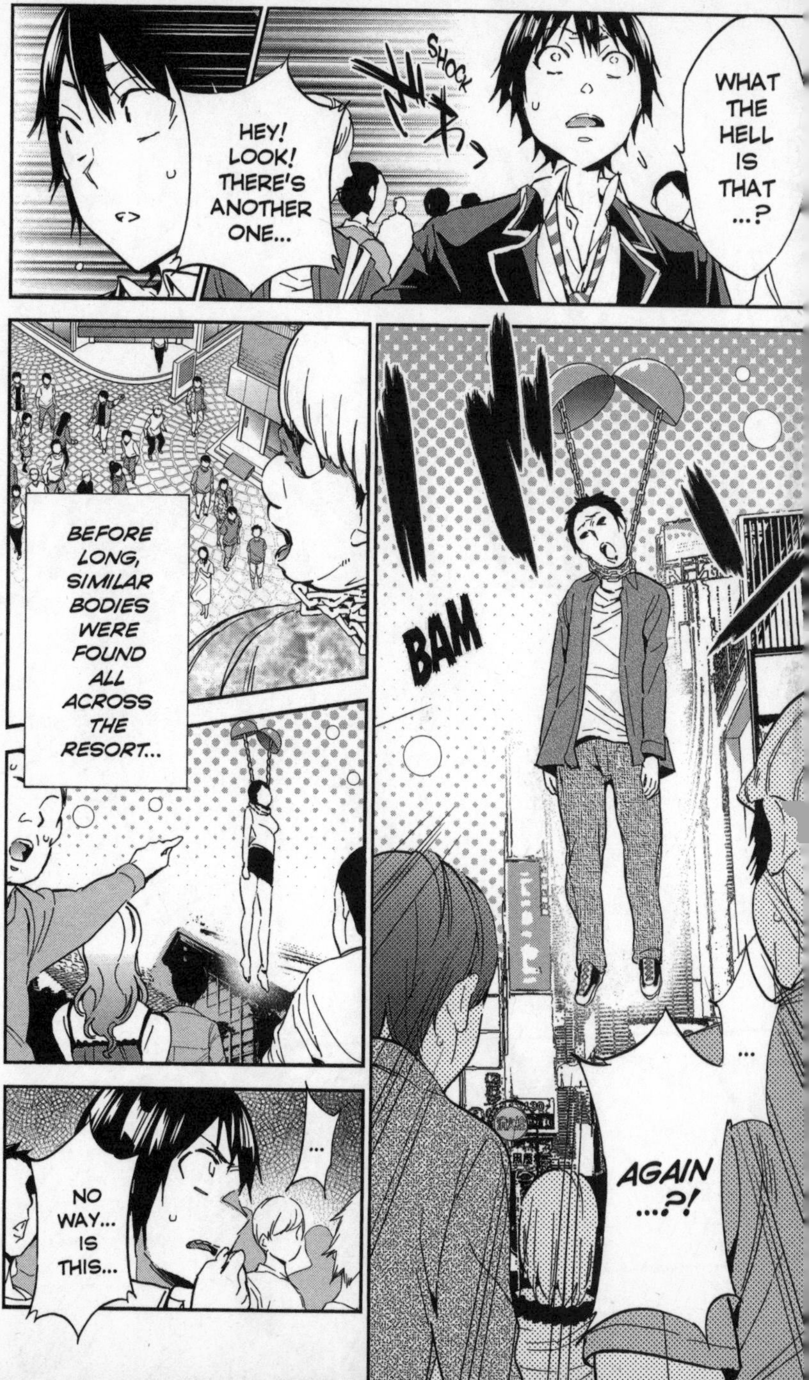
SHOCK
WHAT THE HELL IS THAT ...?
HEY! LOOK! THERE'S ANOTHER ONE...
BAM
...
AGAIN ...?!
BEFORE LONG, SIMILAR BODIES WERE FOUND ALL ACROSS THE RESORT...
...
NO WAY... IS THIS...

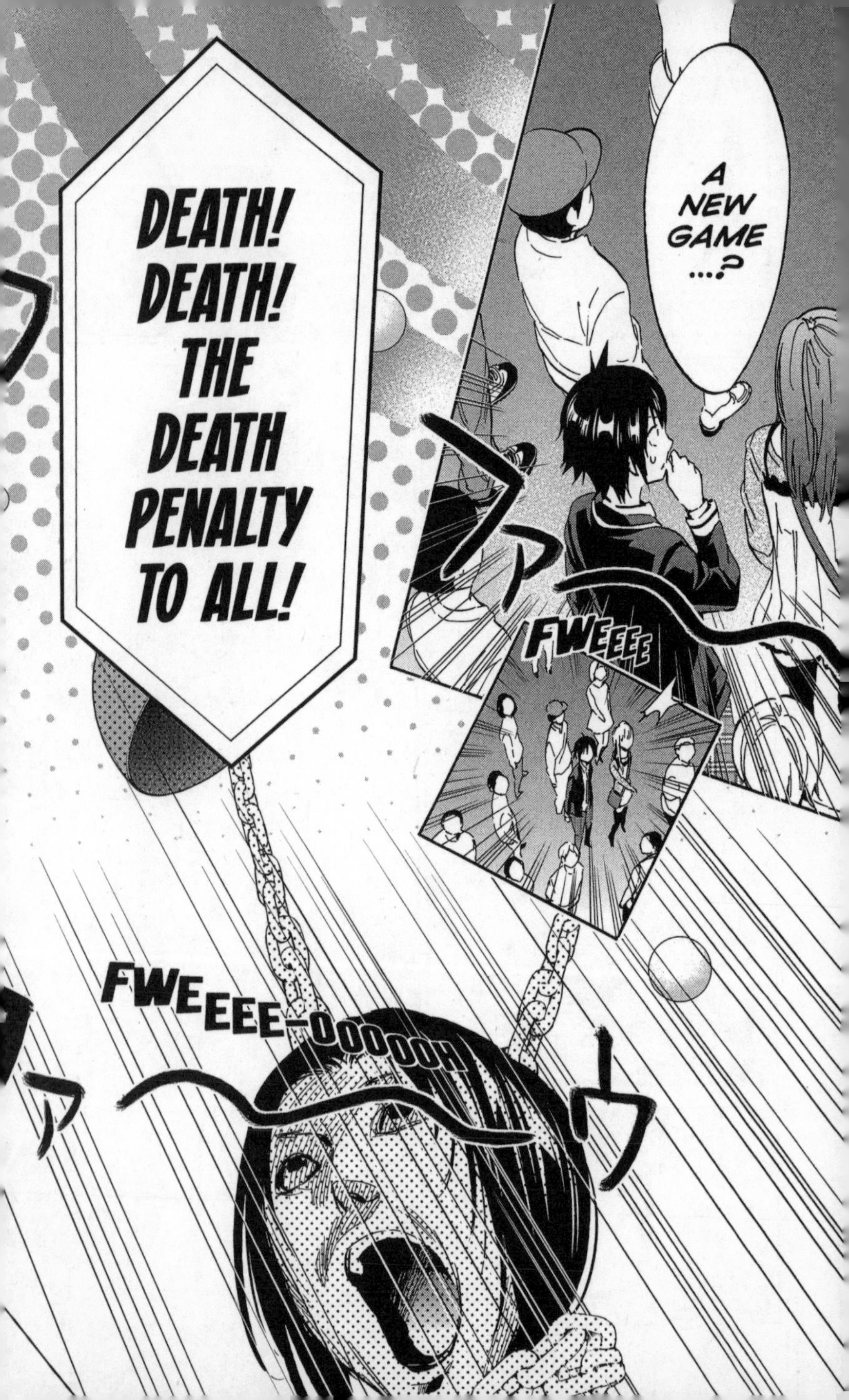
A NEW GAME ...?
DEATH! DEATH! THE DEATH PENALTY TO ALL!
FWEEEE
FWEEEE-OOOOOOH

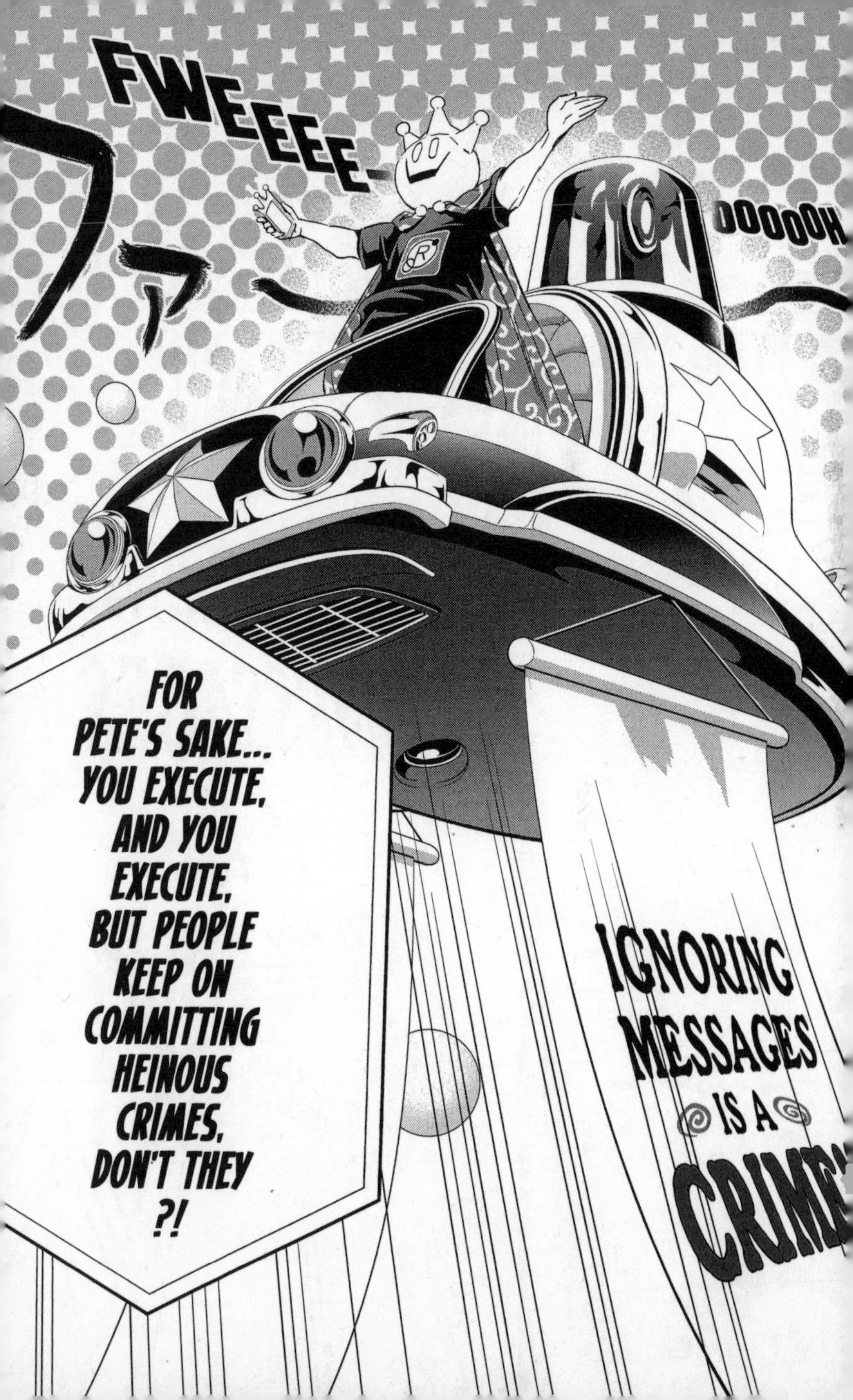
FWEEEEE-
ファ
OOOOOOH
IGNORING MESSAGES IS A CRIME
FOR PETE'S SAKE... YOU EXECUTE, AND YOU EXECUTE, BUT PEOPLE KEEP ON COMMITTING HEINOUS CRIMES, DON'T THEY?!

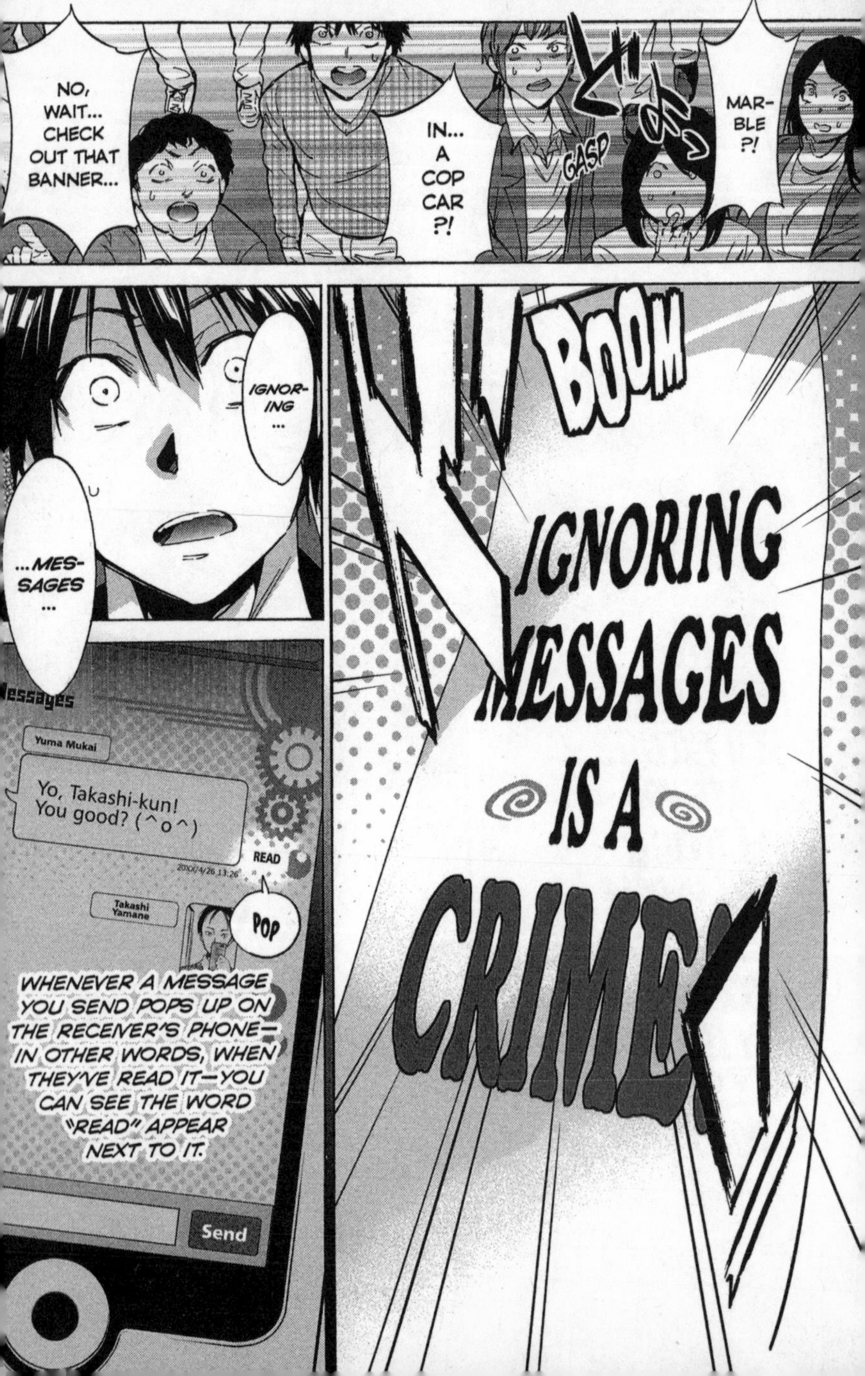
MAR-BLE ?!
GASP
IN... A COP CAR ?!
NO, WAIT... CHECK OUT THAT BANNER...
BOOM
IGNORING MESSAGES IS A CRIME
IGNOR-ING ...
...MES-SAGES ...
essages
Yuma Mukai
Yo, Takashi-kun! You good? (^o^)
READ
20XX/4/26 13:26
Takashi Yamane
POP
WHENEVER A MESSAGE YOU SEND POPS UP ON THE RECEIVER'S PHONE—IN OTHER WORDS, WHEN THEY'VE READ IT—YOU CAN SEE THE WORD "READ" APPEAR NEXT TO IT.
Send

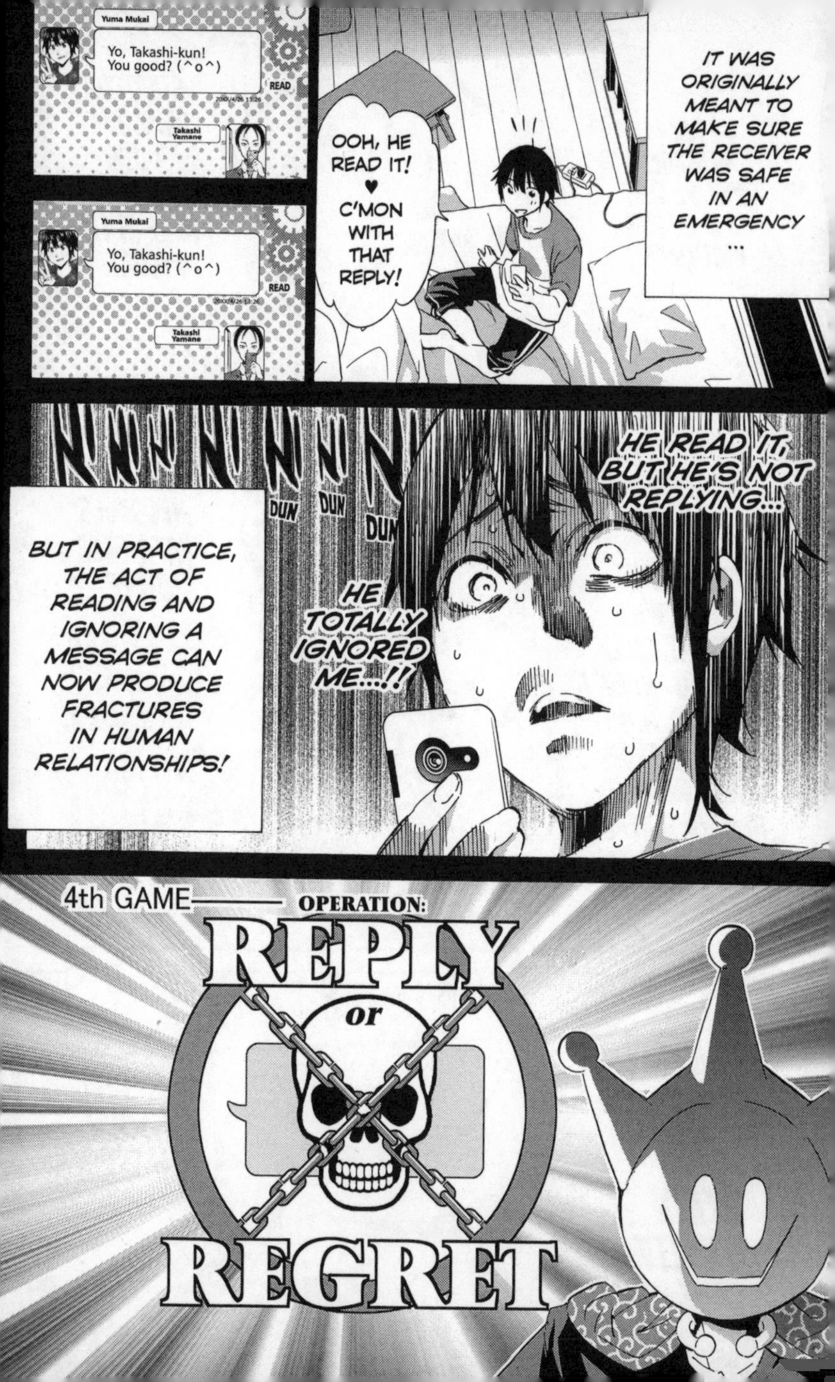

IT WAS ORIGINALLY MEANT TO MAKE SURE THE RECEIVER WAS SAFE IN AN EMERGENCY ...
OOH, HE READ IT! ♥ C'MON WITH THAT REPLY!
Yuma Mukai
Yo, Takashi-kun! You good? (^o^)
READ
Takashi Yamane
Yuma Mukai
Yo, Takashi-kun! You good? (^o^)
READ
Takashi Yamane
HE READ IT, BUT HE'S NOT REPLYING...
DUN DUN DUN
HE TOTALLY IGNORED ME...!!
BUT IN PRACTICE, THE ACT OF READING AND IGNORING A MESSAGE CAN NOW PRODUCE FRACTURES IN HUMAN RELATIONSHIPS!
4th GAME—— OPERATION:
REPLY or REGRET

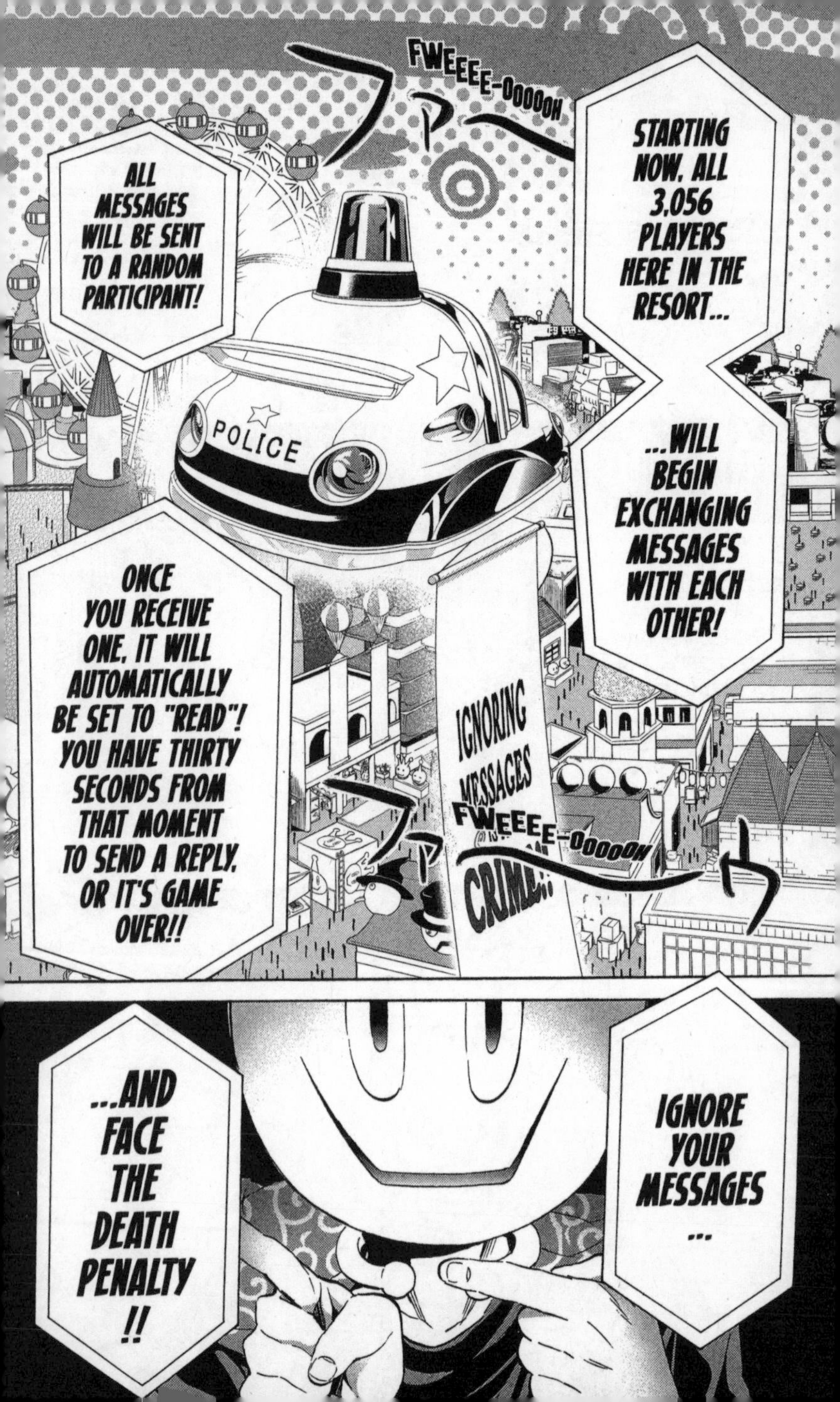
FWEEEE-OOOOOH
STARTING NOW, ALL 3,056 PLAYERS HERE IN THE RESORT...
...WILL BEGIN EXCHANGING MESSAGES WITH EACH OTHER!
ALL MESSAGES WILL BE SENT TO A RANDOM PARTICIPANT!
ONCE YOU RECEIVE ONE, IT WILL AUTOMATICALLY BE SET TO "READ"! YOU HAVE THIRTY SECONDS FROM THAT MOMENT TO SEND A REPLY, OR IT'S GAME OVER!!
POLICE
IGNORING MESSAGES
CRIM
FWEEEE-OOOOOH
IGNORE YOUR MESSAGES ...
...AND FACE THE DEATH PENALTY !!

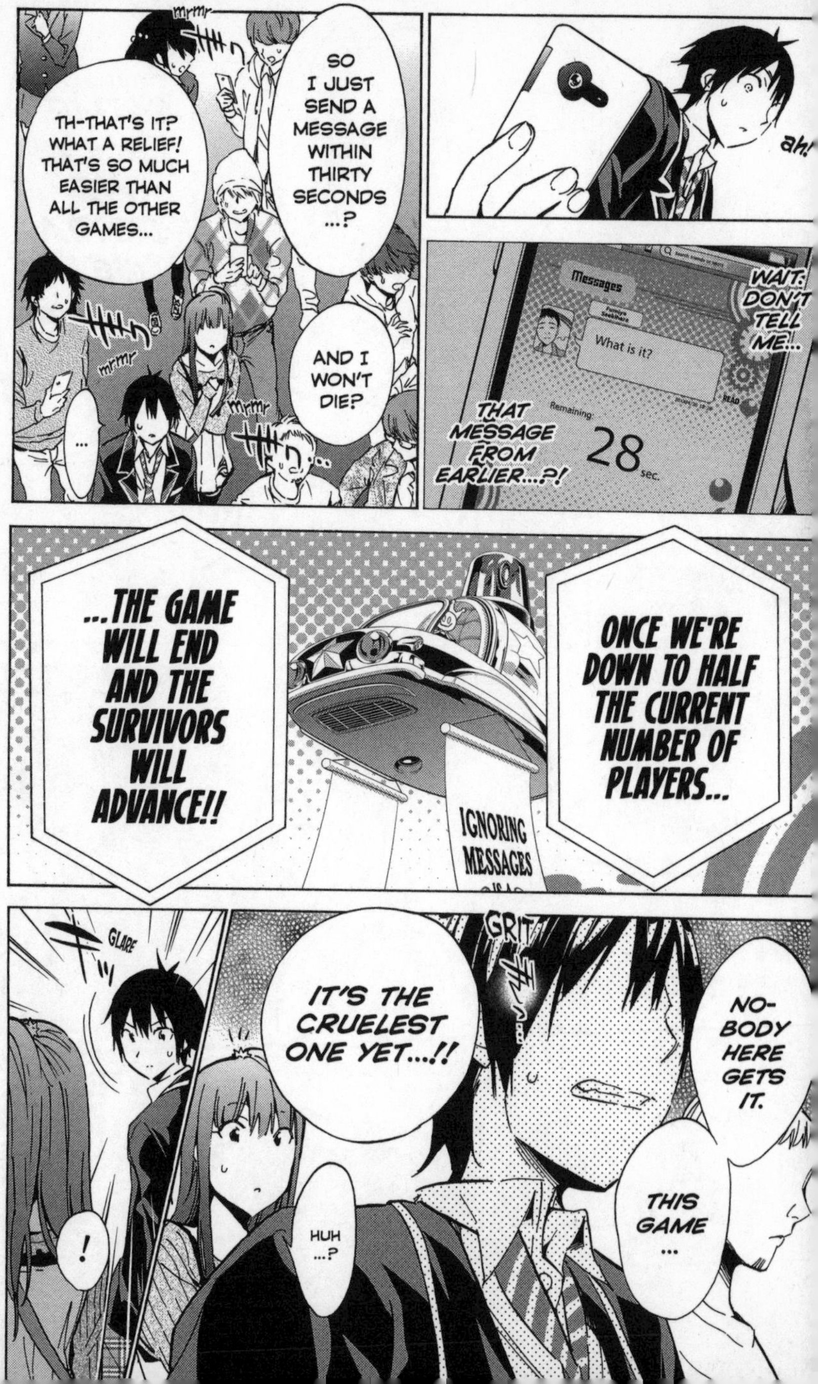
ah!
Messages
What is it?
Remaining:
28 sec.
READ
WAIT. DON'T TELL ME...
THAT MESSAGE FROM EARLIER...?!
mrmr
SO I JUST SEND A MESSAGE WITHIN THIRTY SECONDS ...?
TH-THAT'S IT? WHAT A RELIEF! THAT'S SO MUCH EASIER THAN ALL THE OTHER GAMES...
AND I WON'T DIE?
mrmr
mrmr
...
ONCE WE'RE DOWN TO HALF THE CURRENT NUMBER OF PLAYERS...
IGNORING MESSAGES
...THE GAME WILL END AND THE SURVIVORS WILL ADVANCE!!
NO-BODY HERE GETS IT.
GRIT
THIS GAME ...
IT'S THE CRUELEST ONE YET...!!
HUH ...?
GLARE
!

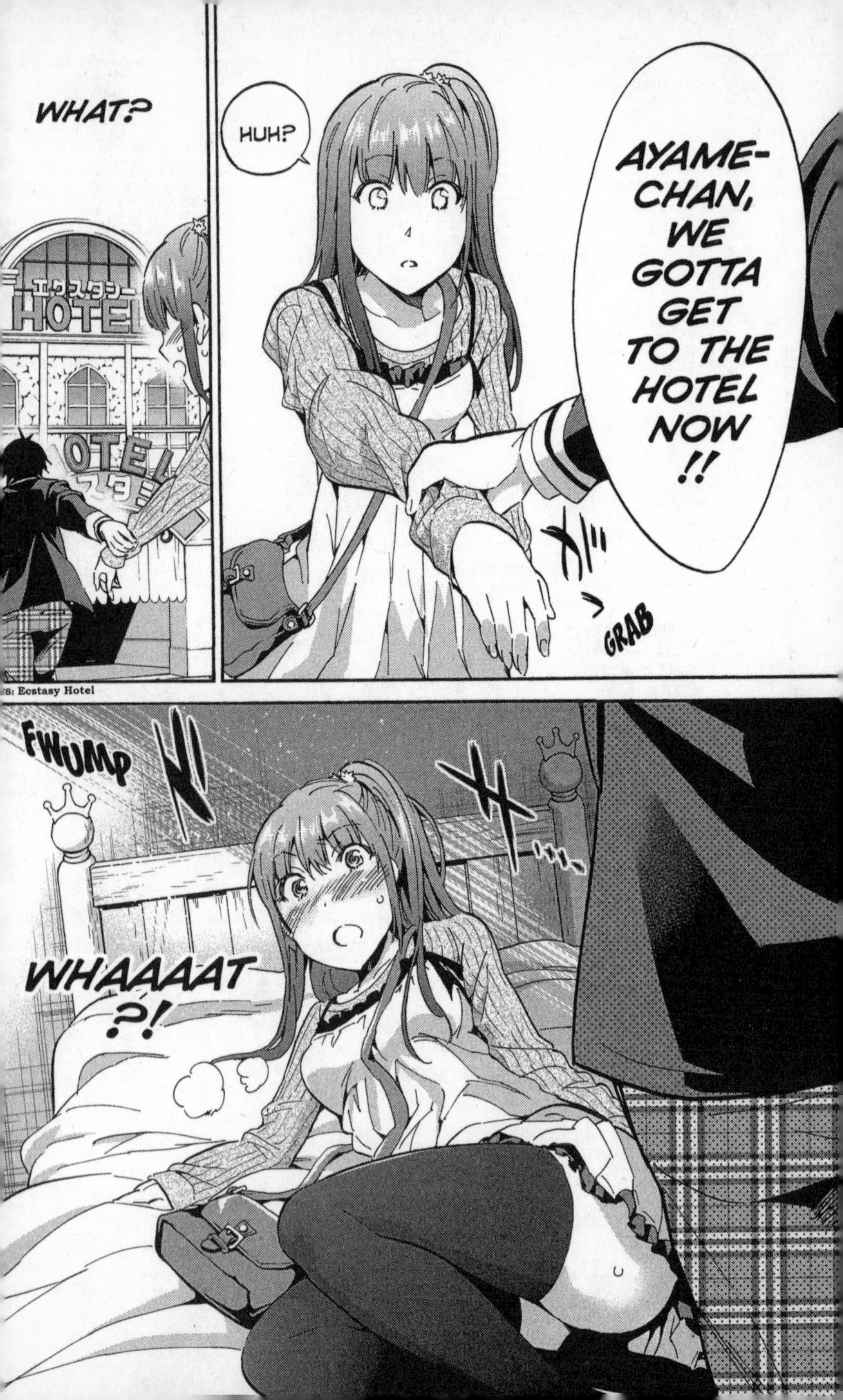
AYAME-CHAN, WE GOTTA GET TO THE HOTEL NOW!!
HUH?
GRAB
WHAT?
HOTEL
FWUMP
WHAAAAT?!

S: Ecstasy Hotel

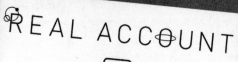

REAL ACCOUNT

4

Shizumu Watanabe   Okushou

STAFF
Shotaro Kunitomo
Iyo Mori
Yushi Takayama
Kazuki Ishihara

HELP STAFF
Yoneko Takamoto

EDITORS
Kazuhiko Otoguro
Sho Igarashi
Hideki Morooka
(Japanese GN)

JAPANESE COVER DESIGN
Tadashi Hisamochi
(HIVE)

Due to the page setup, the staff credits wound up here.
Watanabe

It's All Here! The Complete Guide to Real Account Resort Sea!!

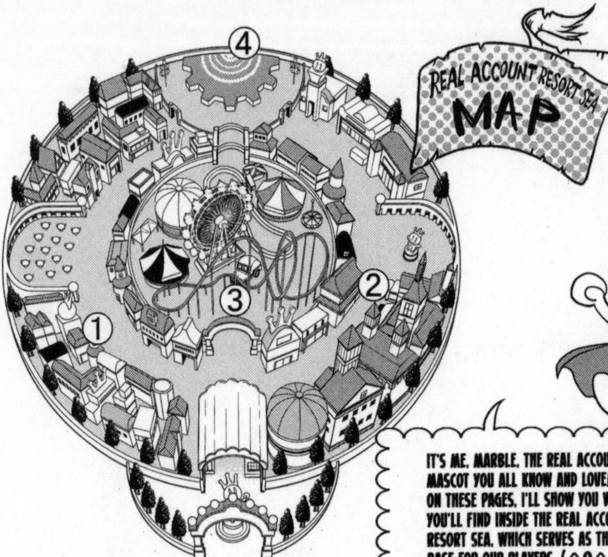
REAL ACCOUNT RESORT SEA
MAP
4
2
3
1

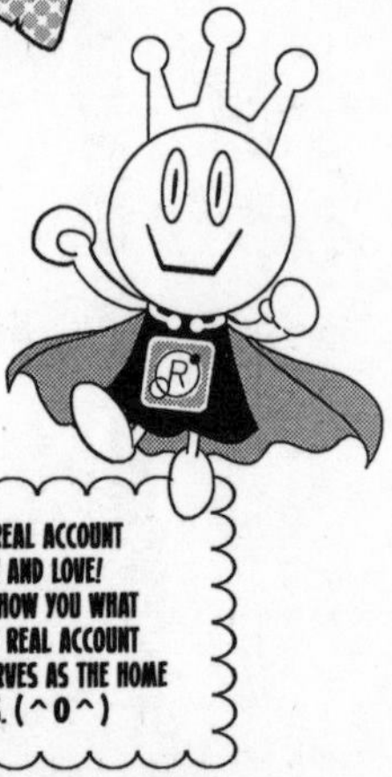
IT'S ME, MARBLE, THE REAL ACCOUNT MASCOT YOU ALL KNOW AND LOVE! ON THESE PAGES, I'LL SHOW YOU WHAT YOU'LL FIND INSIDE THE REAL ACCOUNT RESORT SEA, WHICH SERVES AS THE HOME BASE FOR OUR PLAYERS. (^O^)

① Shopping Area

From broad main streets to narrow, dimly-lit back alleys, this area's packed to the gills with shops big and small! ♪

Whether you're looking for daily necessities or black-market goods, you can get anything you want…as long as you can pay for it! ★

And if you search hard enough, you may just discover an "interesting" shop or two…!

Near the center of the area, you'll find a food court that has all the taste-tempting delights you could possibly hope for! (^O^)

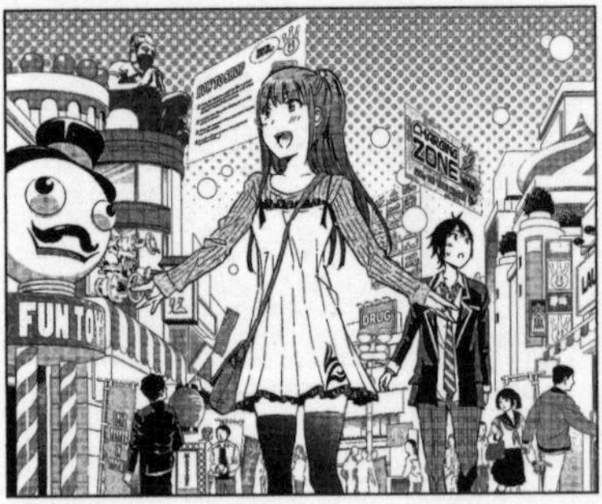
CHARGING ZONE
FUN TO
DRUG

▲ Main Street

HOW TO SHOP

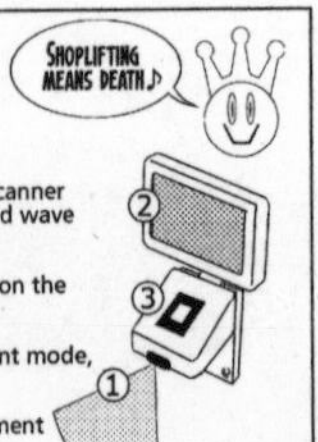
SHOPLIFTING MEANS DEATH ♪
2
3
1

① Bring the item you want to the scanner near the entrance of the store and wave the tag in front of the scanner.

② Confirm that the price displayed on the screen is correct.

③ When the terminal enters payment mode, touch the sensor.

④ A jingle will sound once the payment has been made.

▲ Purchasing methods are explained on signs floating in each area.

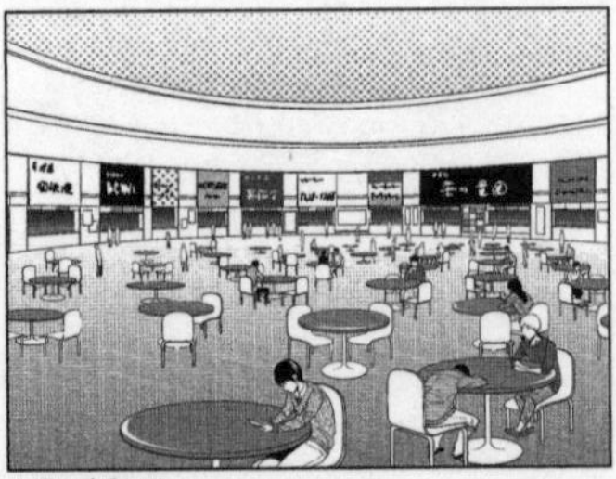

▲ Food Court

GOOD MORNING, EVERYONE! RISE AND SHINE!

[Y]ONE LATE [FO]R THE START [OF] THE GAME [AT] NINE A.M.'S [GON]NA GO OUT [W]ITH A REAL "BANG"!

▲ Look at all the mid-tier hotels available!

② Hotel Area

This area is where all our players stay between games! ♪

It's divided into three areas—luxury, mid-tier, and roach motel—depending on the cost. Viewers from the real world checking in on our players through our live broadcasts can't peek inside the hotels and other designated private spaces, so take a load off and have fun! ♥

If you're a little short on cash, no worries there—you'll also find Hobo Square near the middle, where you can huddle together for warmth to your heart's delight!

▲ Hobo Square

③ Entertainment Area

From Ferris wheels to roller coasters, visitors can enjoy all kinds of thrilling attractions in this area!

Too bad many of our contestants aren't making much use of the facilities! If you ask me, I think it's important that you take the time to play a little when your life's on the line! \(^0^)/

There's even a casino in the area, too! If you're out of money, there's no better place to try and make a big financial comeback!

THIS IS SOOO FUUUUNN!! ♡

▲ That coaster looks like a blast! ♥

④ Public Square

▲ A place for gatherings and other events! ♪ It can hold around 500 people.

💡 TOPIC

☞

Have you found any "Hidden Marbles" around the resort yet? Players who spot them earn 100 yen for each one they discover!

Why don't you give it a shot too?

SO WHAT DO YOU THINK? PROVIDING SUCH A LAVISH PARADISE FOR PLAYERS TO HANG OUT IN, YOU'D EXPECT THEM TO BE AT LEAST A LITTLE BIT GRATEFUL, WOULDN'T YOU? ANYWAY, THIS RESORT IS THE STAGE FOR OUR LATEST GAME, OPERATION: REPLY OR REGRET! HOW WILL IT TURN OUT? STAY TUNED TO FIND OUT!!

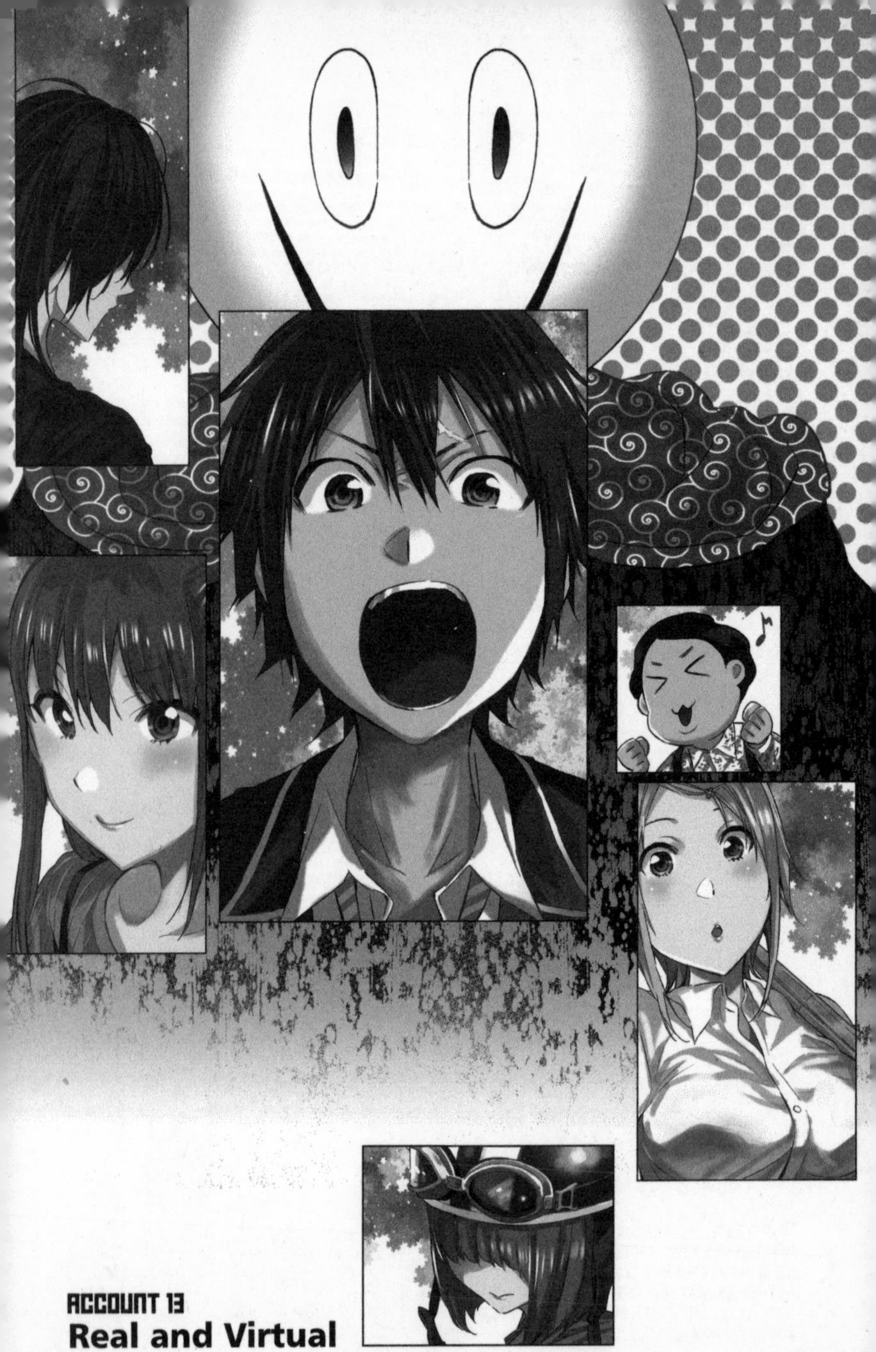

ACCOUNT 13
Real and Virtual

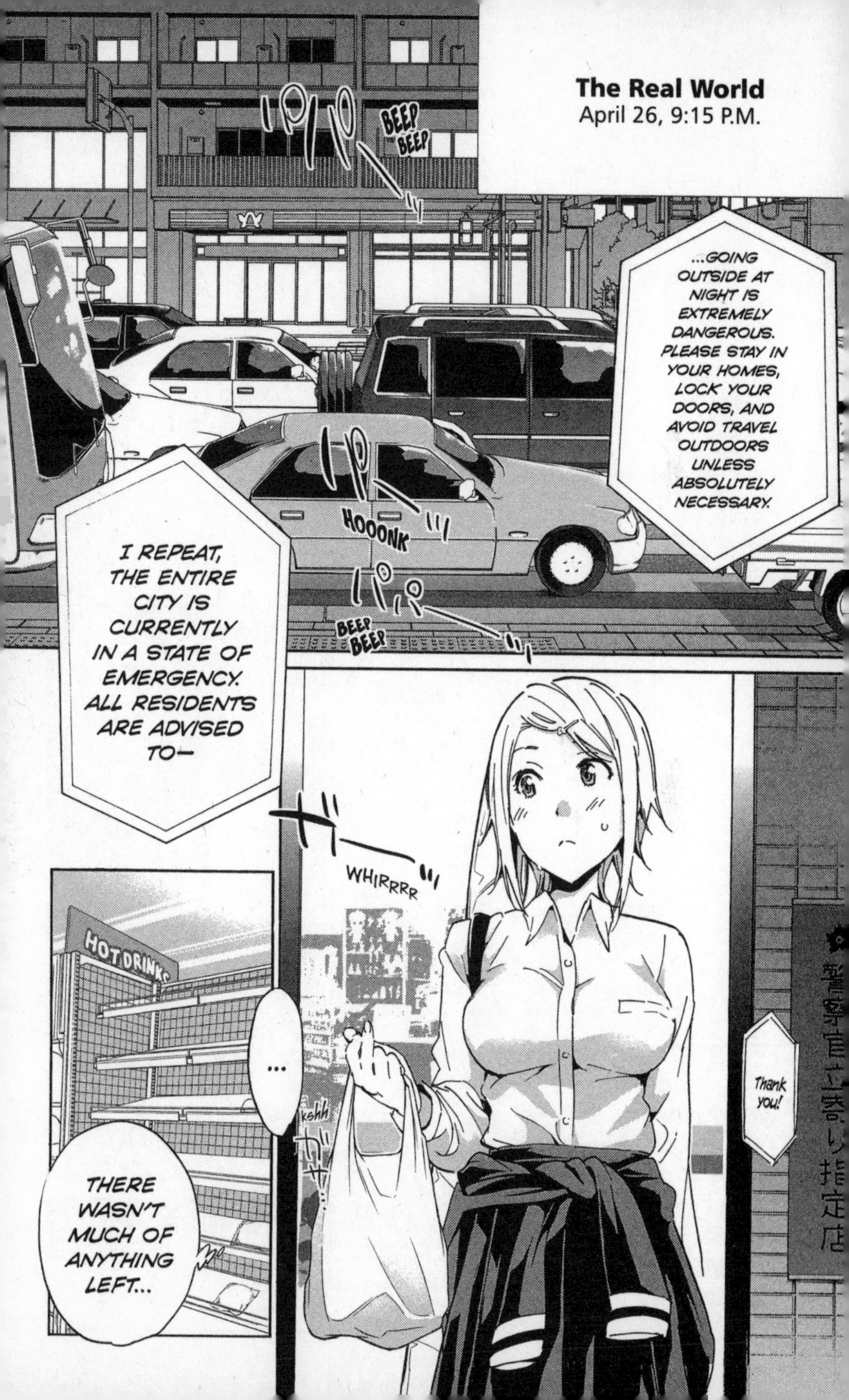
The Real World
April 26, 9:15 P.M.
BEEP BEEP
...GOING OUTSIDE AT NIGHT IS EXTREMELY DANGEROUS. PLEASE STAY IN YOUR HOMES, LOCK YOUR DOORS, AND AVOID TRAVEL OUTDOORS UNLESS ABSOLUTELY NECESSARY.
HOOONK
BEEP BEEP
I REPEAT, THE ENTIRE CITY IS CURRENTLY IN A STATE OF EMERGENCY. ALL RESIDENTS ARE ADVISED TO—
警察官立寄り指定店
Thank you!
WHIRRRR
kshh
...
HOT DRINKS
THERE WASN'T MUCH OF ANYTHING LEFT...

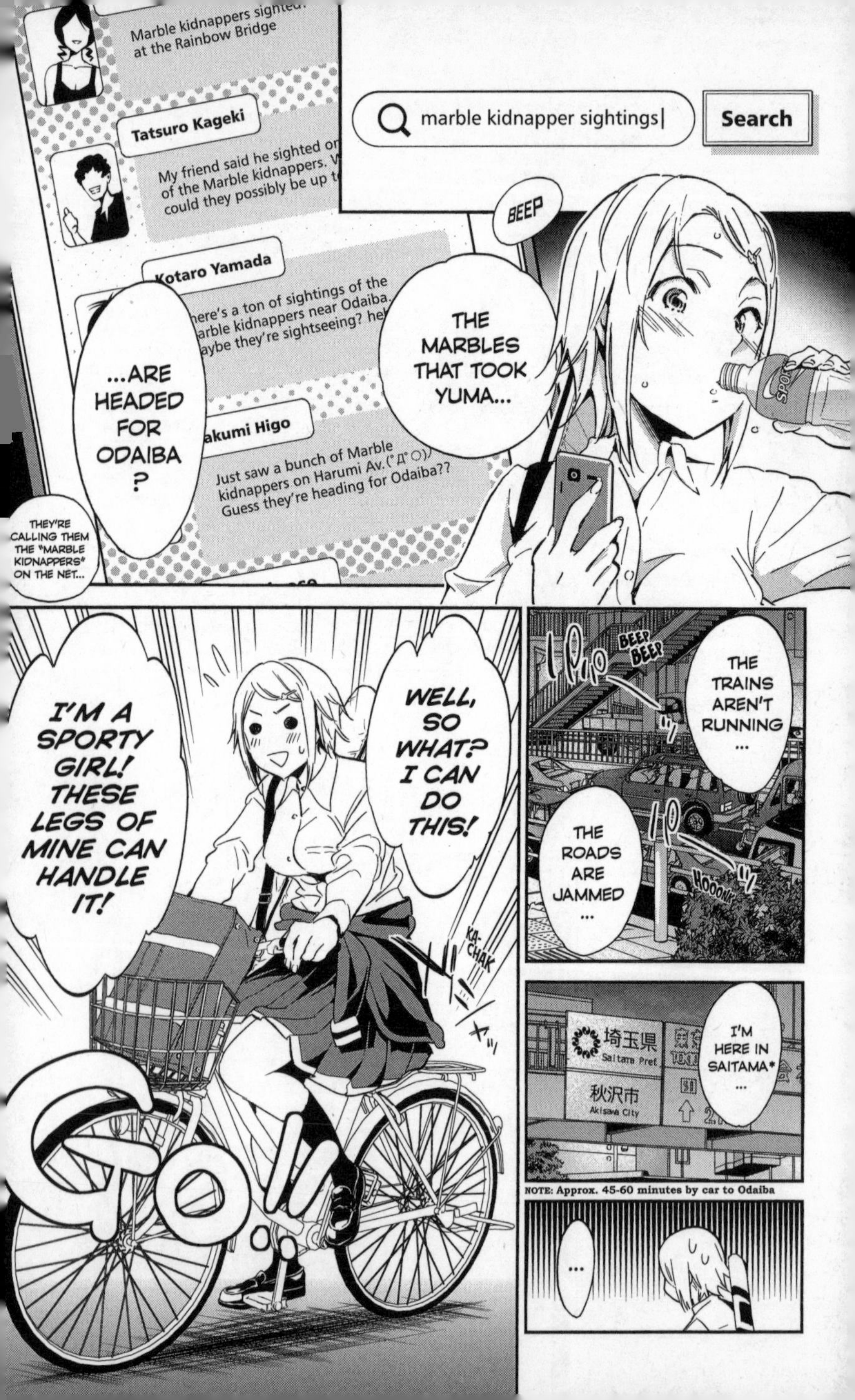
marble kidnapper sightings|
Search
BEEP
THE MARBLES THAT TOOK YUMA...
Marble kidnappers sighted at the Rainbow Bridge
Tatsuro Kageki
My friend said he sighted o of the Marble kidnappers. could they possibly be up t
Kotaro Yamada
here's a ton of sightings of the arble kidnappers near Odaiba. aybe they're sightseeing? he
akumi Higo
Just saw a bunch of Marble kidnappers on Harumi Av.(°Д°○) Guess they're heading for Odaiba??
...ARE HEADED FOR ODAIBA ?
THEY'RE CALLING THEM THE "MARBLE KIDNAPPERS" ON THE NET...
BEEP BEEP
THE TRAINS AREN'T RUNNING ...
THE ROADS ARE JAMMED ...
HOOONK
埼玉県
Saitama Pref
秋沢市
Akisawa City
I'M HERE IN SAITAMA* ...
NOTE: Approx. 45-60 minutes by car to Odaiba
...
WELL, SO WHAT? I CAN DO THIS!
I'M A SPORTY GIRL! THESE LEGS OF MINE CAN HANDLE IT!
KA-CHAK
GO!

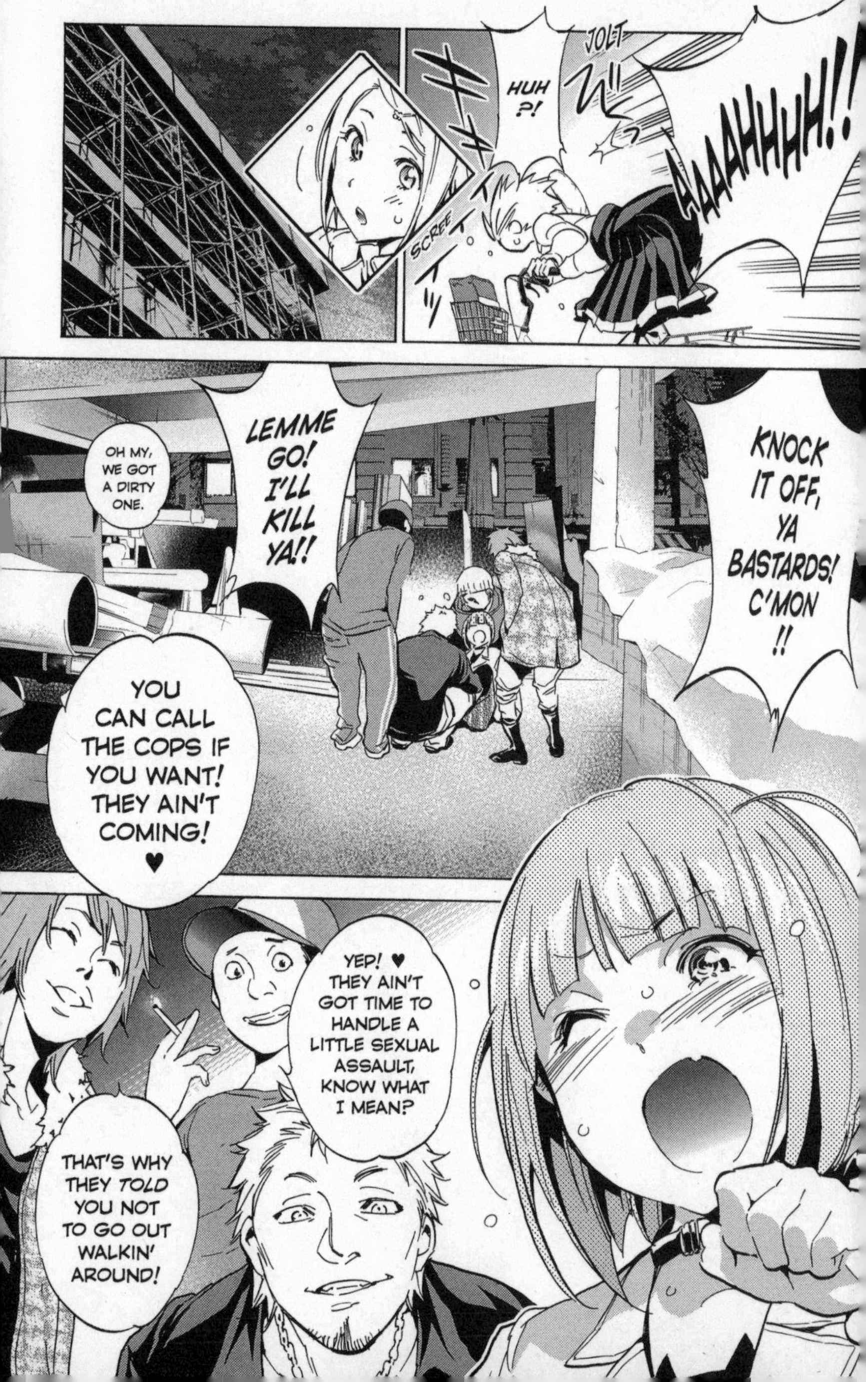
JOLT
HUH ?!
AAAAHHHH!!
SCREE
KNOCK IT OFF, YA BASTARDS! C'MON !!
LEMME GO! I'LL KILL YA!!
OH MY, WE GOT A DIRTY ONE.
YOU CAN CALL THE COPS IF YOU WANT! THEY AIN'T COMING! ♥
YEP! ♥ THEY AIN'T GOT TIME TO HANDLE A LITTLE SEXUAL ASSAULT, KNOW WHAT I MEAN?
THAT'S WHY THEY *TOLD* YOU NOT TO GO OUT WALKIN' AROUND!

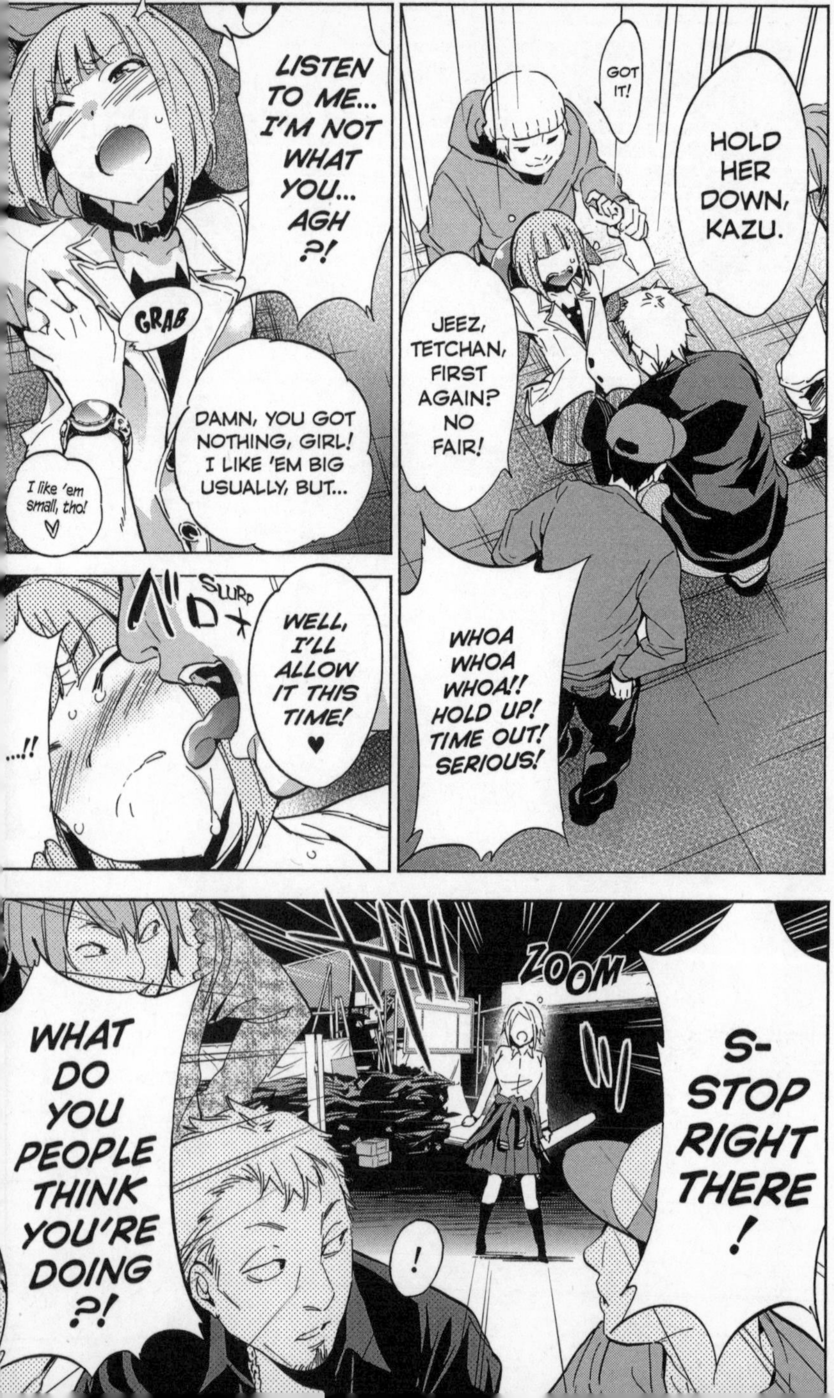
HOLD HER DOWN, KAZU.
GOT IT!
JEEZ, TETCHAN, FIRST AGAIN? NO FAIR!
WHOA WHOA WHOA!! HOLD UP! TIME OUT! SERIOUS!
LISTEN TO ME... I'M NOT WHAT YOU... AGH ?!
GRAB
DAMN, YOU GOT NOTHING, GIRL! I LIKE 'EM BIG USUALLY, BUT...
I like 'em small, tho! ♥
WELL, I'LL ALLOW IT THIS TIME! ♥
SLURP
...!!
S-STOP RIGHT THERE!
ZOOM
!
WHAT DO YOU PEOPLE THINK YOU'RE DOING?!

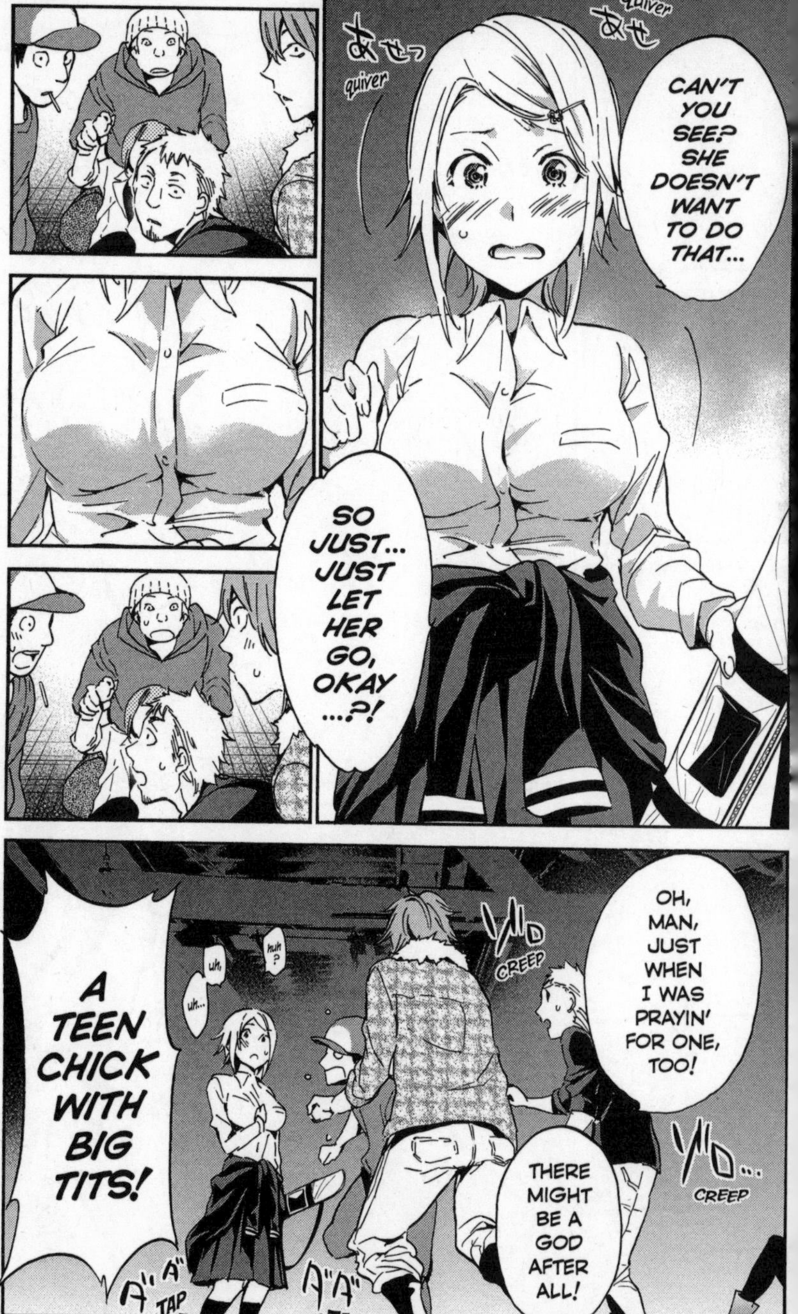
あせ quiver
あせっ quiver
CAN'T YOU SEE? SHE DOESN'T WANT TO DO THAT...
SO JUST... JUST LET HER GO, OKAY ...?!
OH, MAN, JUST WHEN I WAS PRAYIN' FOR ONE, TOO!
CREEP
THERE MIGHT BE A GOD AFTER ALL!
CREEP
huh?
uh,
uh...
A TEEN CHICK WITH BIG TITS!
TAP-TAP
TAP-TAP

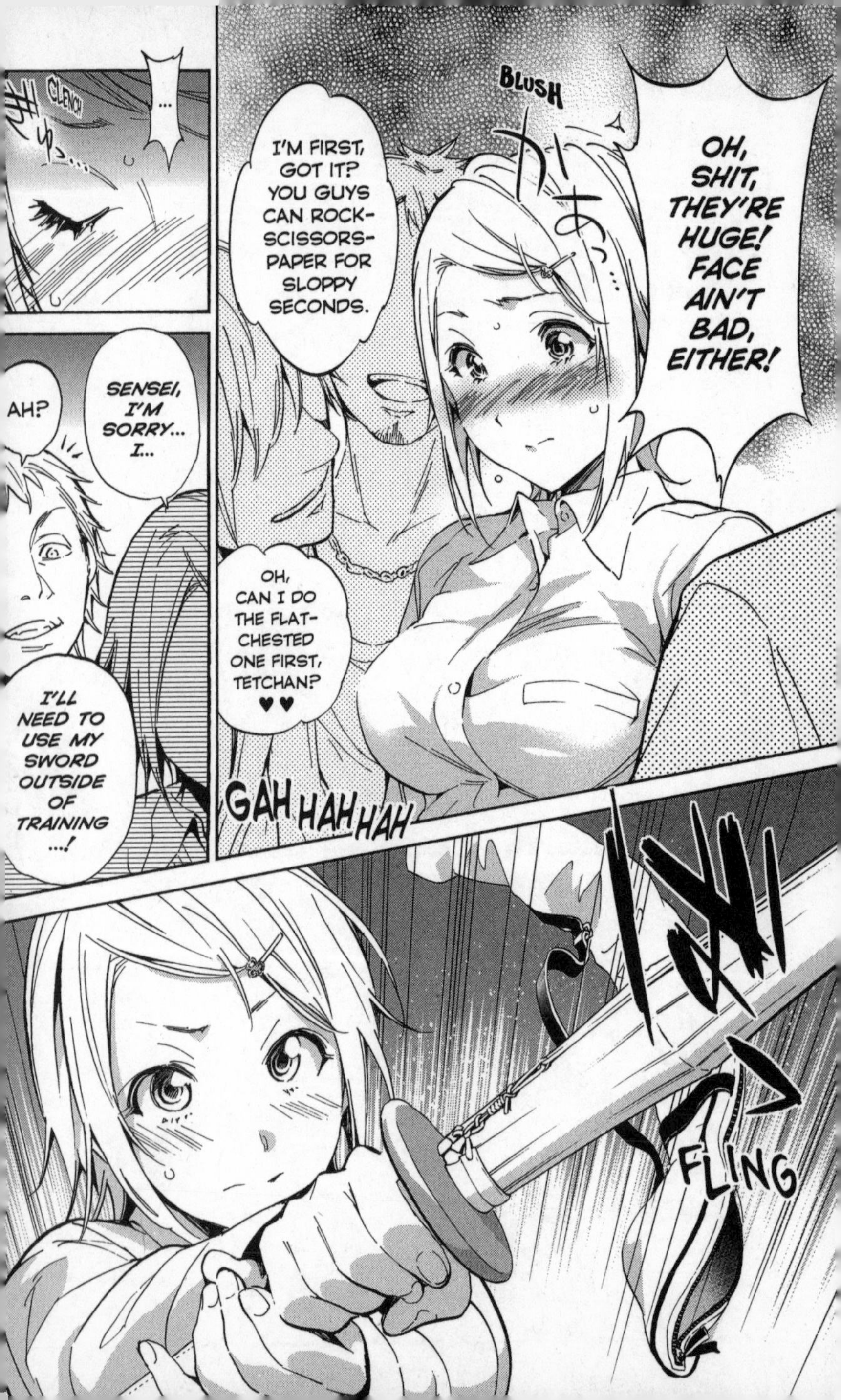
OH, SHIT, THEY'RE HUGE! FACE AIN'T BAD, EITHER!
BLUSH
I'M FIRST, GOT IT? YOU GUYS CAN ROCK-SCISSORS-PAPER FOR SLOPPY SECONDS.
OH, CAN I DO THE FLAT-CHESTED ONE FIRST, TETCHAN? ♥♥
GAH HAH HAH
CLENCH
...
SENSEI, I'M SORRY... I...
AH?
I'LL NEED TO USE MY SWORD OUTSIDE OF TRAINING ...!
FLING

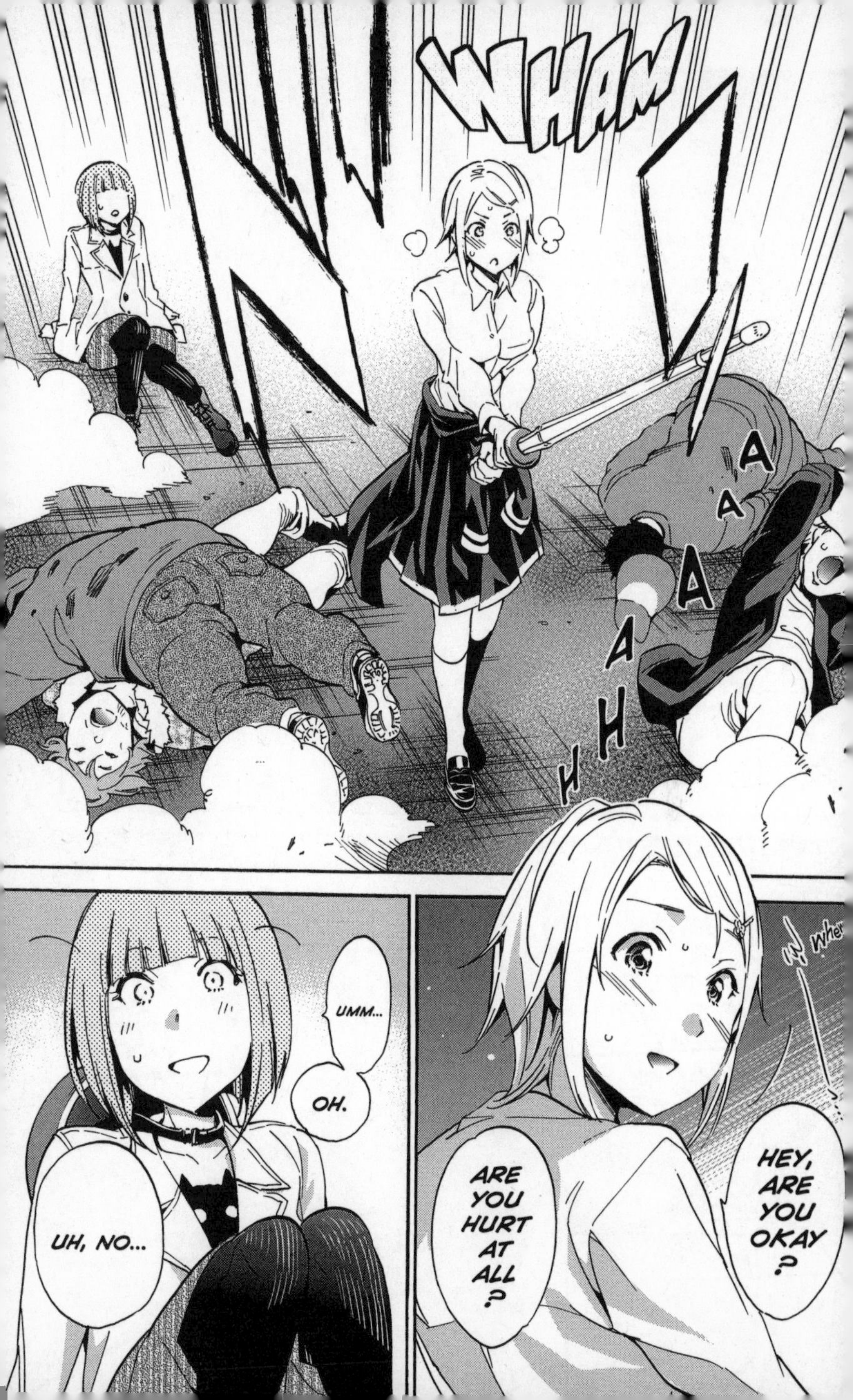
WHAM
AAAAHHH
HEY, ARE YOU OKAY?
ARE YOU HURT AT ALL?
UMM...
OH.
UH, NO...

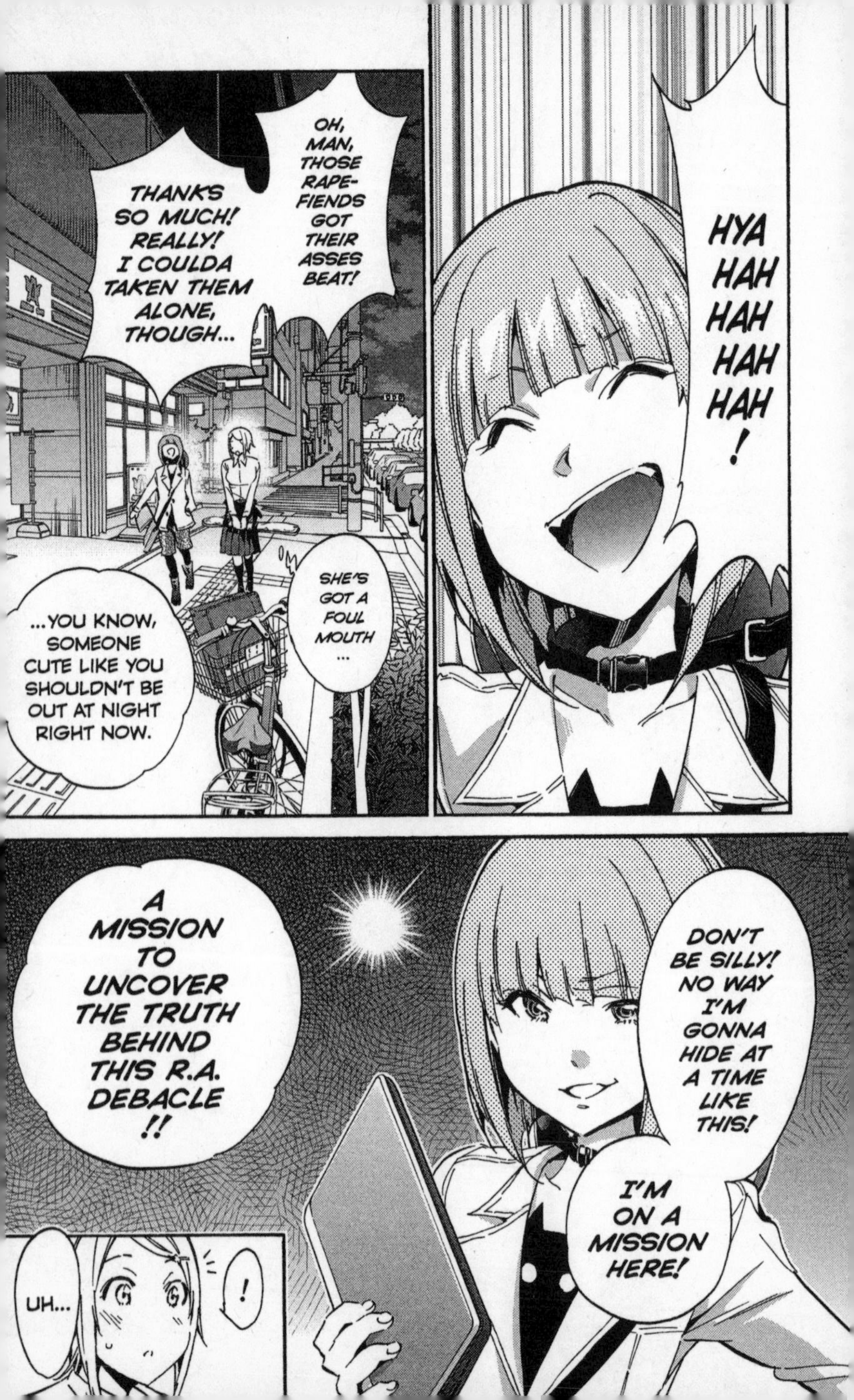
HYA HAH HAH HAH HAH!
OH, MAN, THOSE RAPE-FIENDS GOT THEIR ASSES BEAT!
THANKS SO MUCH! REALLY! I COULDA TAKEN THEM ALONE, THOUGH...
SHE'S GOT A FOUL MOUTH...
...YOU KNOW, SOMEONE CUTE LIKE YOU SHOULDN'T BE OUT AT NIGHT RIGHT NOW.
DON'T BE SILLY! NO WAY I'M GONNA HIDE AT A TIME LIKE THIS!
I'M ON A MISSION HERE!
A MISSION TO UNCOVER THE TRUTH BEHIND THIS R.A. DEBACLE!!
!
UH...

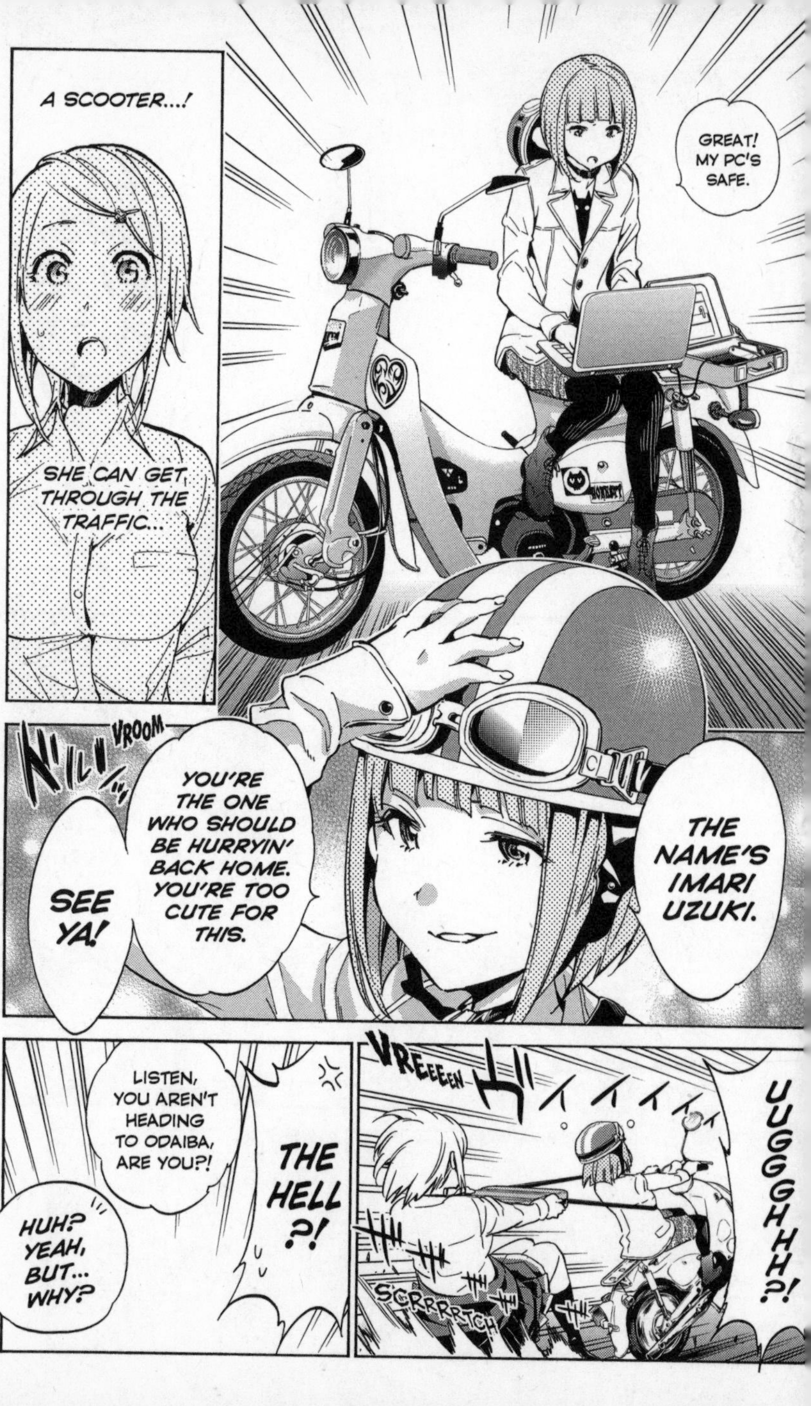
GREAT! MY PC'S SAFE.
A SCOOTER...!
SHE CAN GET THROUGH THE TRAFFIC...
VROOM
THE NAME'S IMARI UZUKI.
YOU'RE THE ONE WHO SHOULD BE HURRYIN' BACK HOME. YOU'RE TOO CUTE FOR THIS.
SEE YA!
VREEEEEN
UUGGGHHH?!
SCRRRRTCH
LISTEN, YOU AREN'T HEADING TO ODAIBA, ARE YOU?!
THE HELL?!
HUH? YEAH, BUT... WHY?

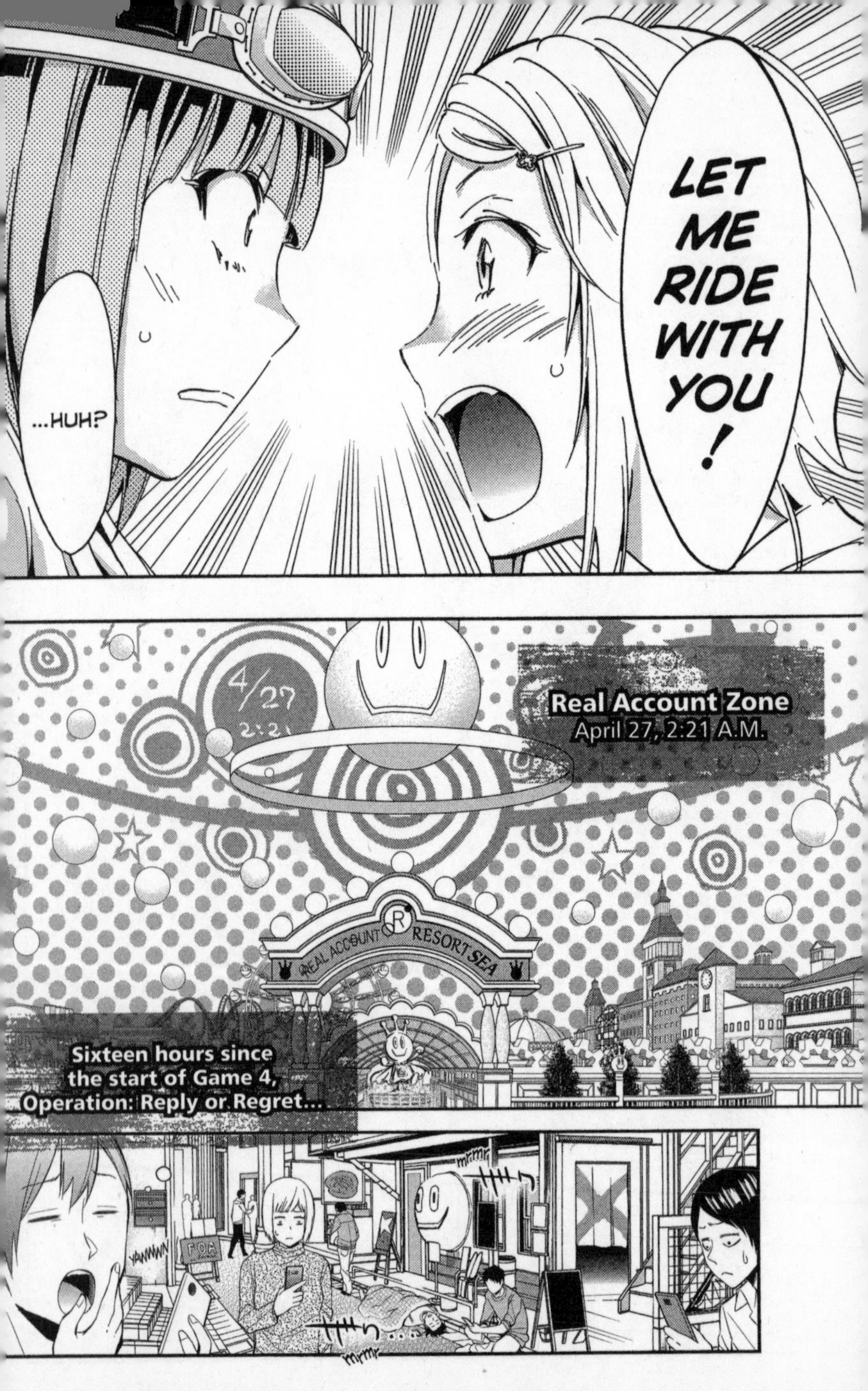
LET ME RIDE WITH YOU!
...HUH?
Real Account Zone
April 27, 2:21 A.M.
4/27 2:21
REAL ACCOUNT RESORT SEA
Sixteen hours since the start of Game 4, Operation: Reply or Regret...
mrmr
YAWWWN
mrmr

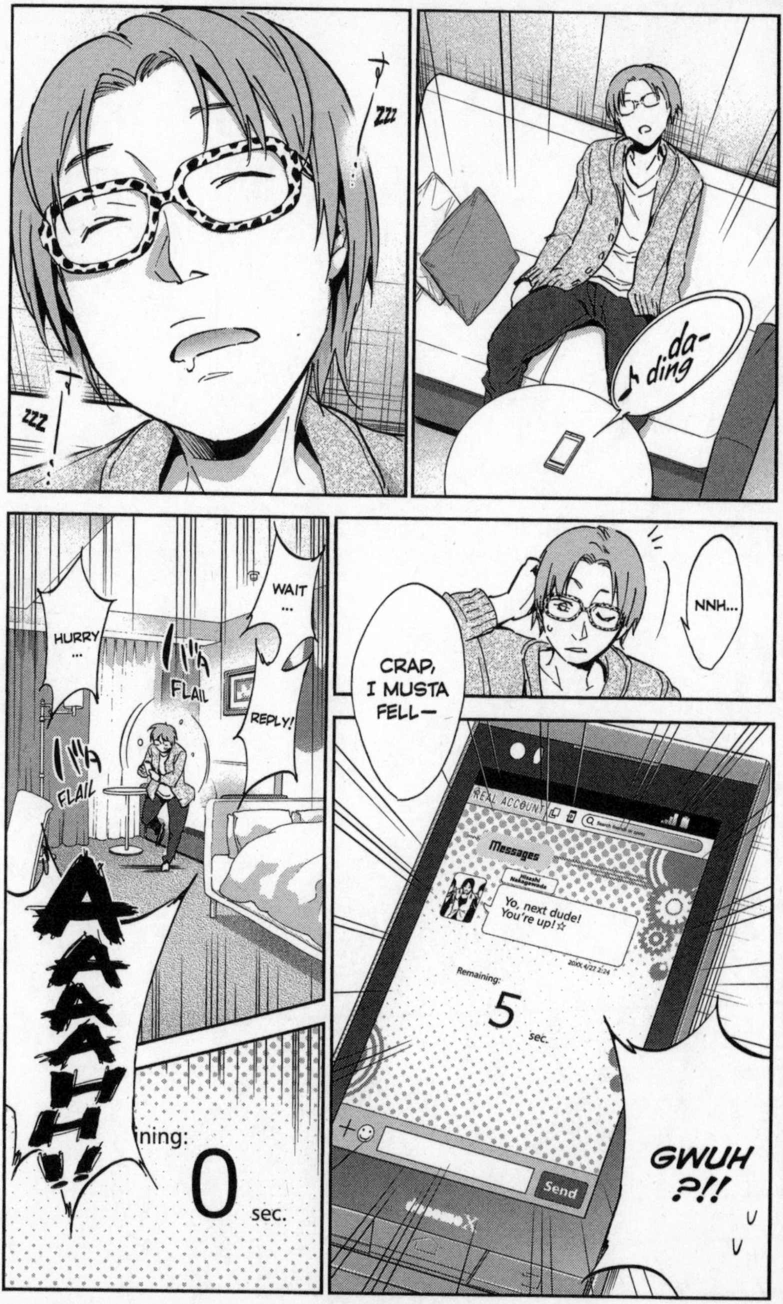
♪ da-ding
zzz
zzz
NNH...
CRAP, I MUSTA FELL—
REAL ACCOUNT
Messages
Hisashi Nakagawada
Yo, next dude! You're up!☆
20XX 4/27 2:24
Remaining:
5
sec.
Send
GWUH ?!!
WAIT ... REPLY!
HURRY ...
FLAIL
FLAIL
AAAAHH!!
ning:
0
sec.

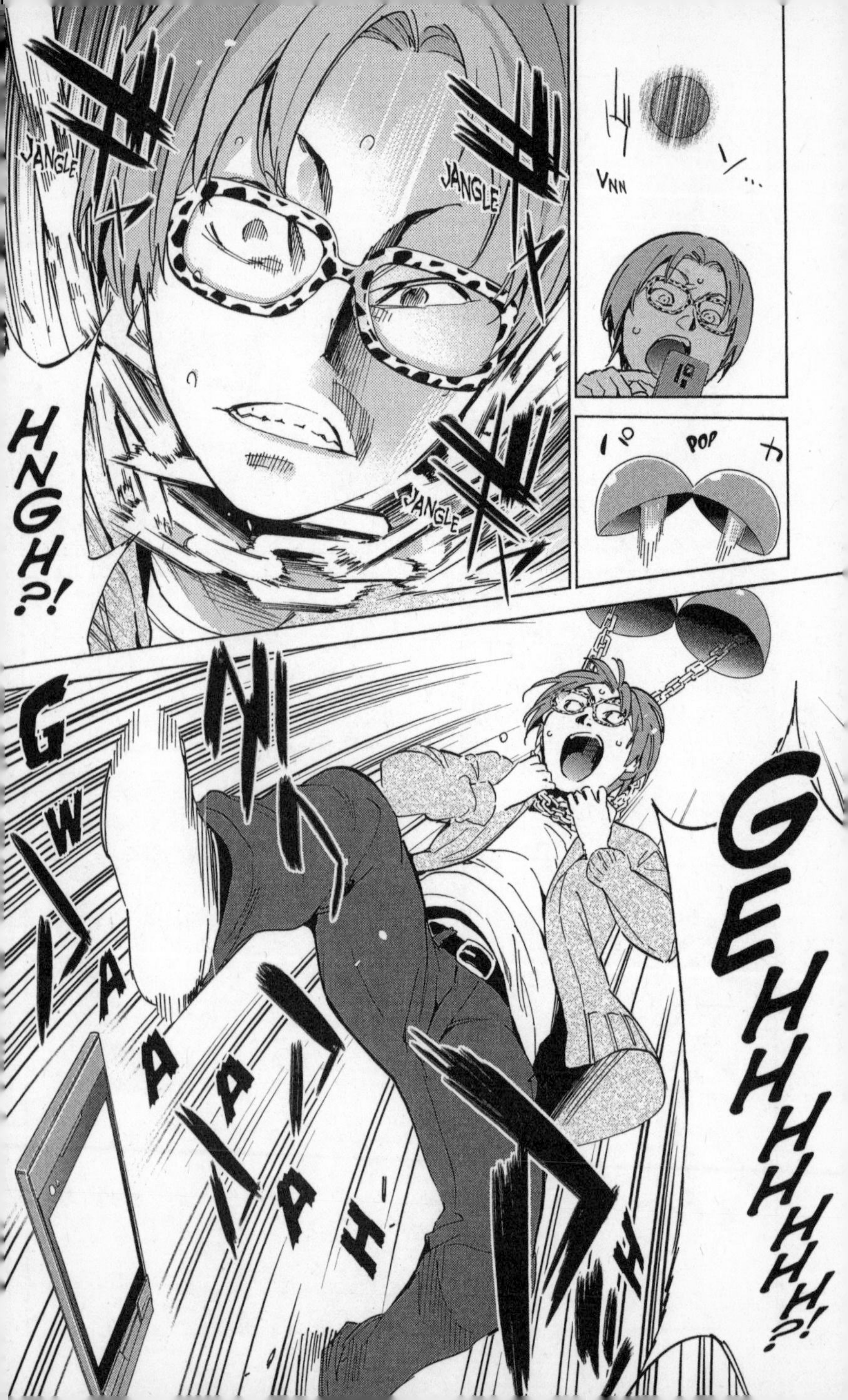
VNN
POP
JANGLE
JANGLE
JANGLE
HNGH?!
GEHHHHHHH?!
GWAAAAH

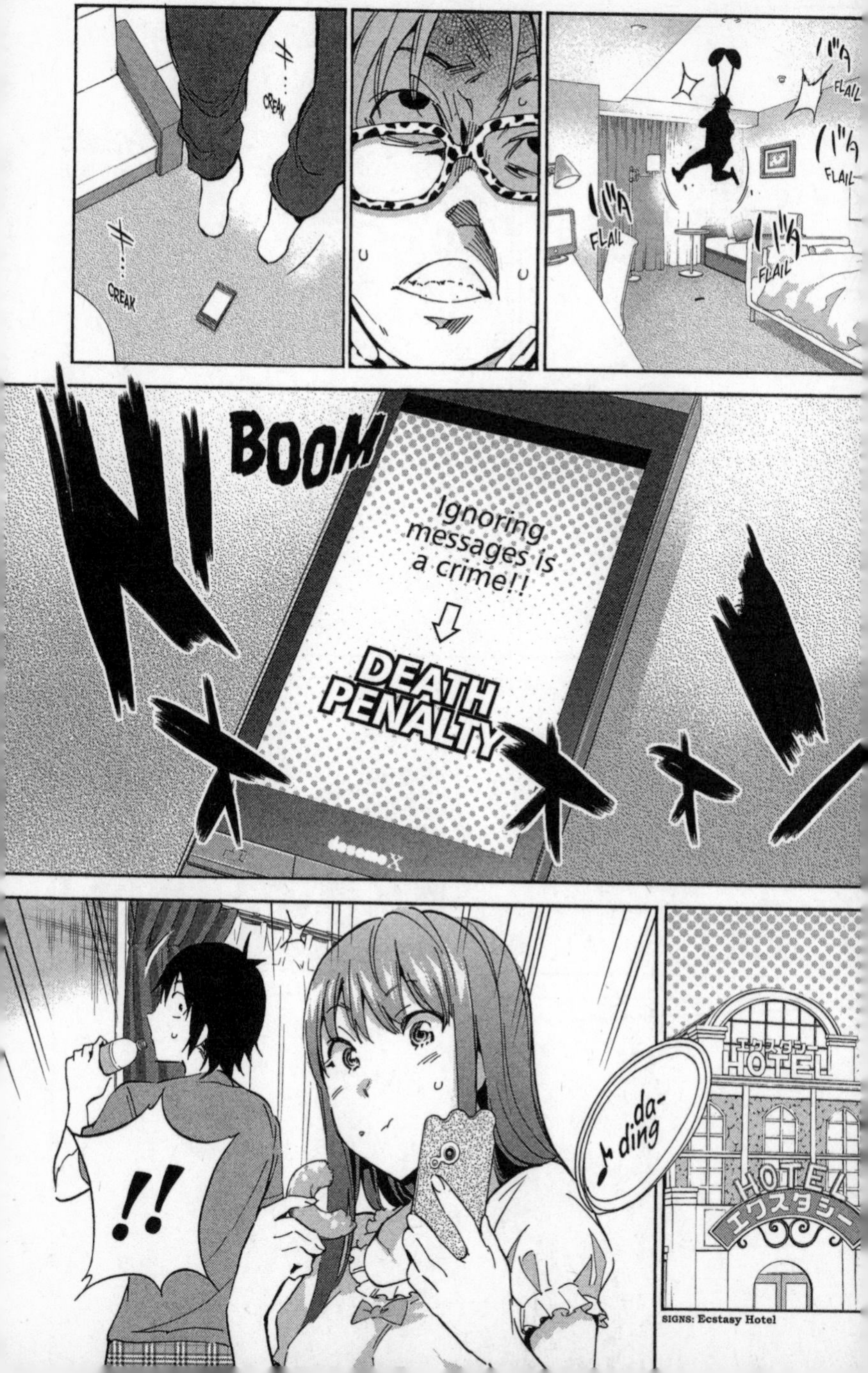

バタ FLAIL
バタ FLAIL
バタ FLAIL
バタ FLAIL
CREAK
CREAK
BOOM
Ignoring messages is a crime!!
DEATH PENALTY
エクスタシー HOTEL
HOTEL エクスタシー
SIGNS: Ecstasy Hotel
♪ da-ding
!!

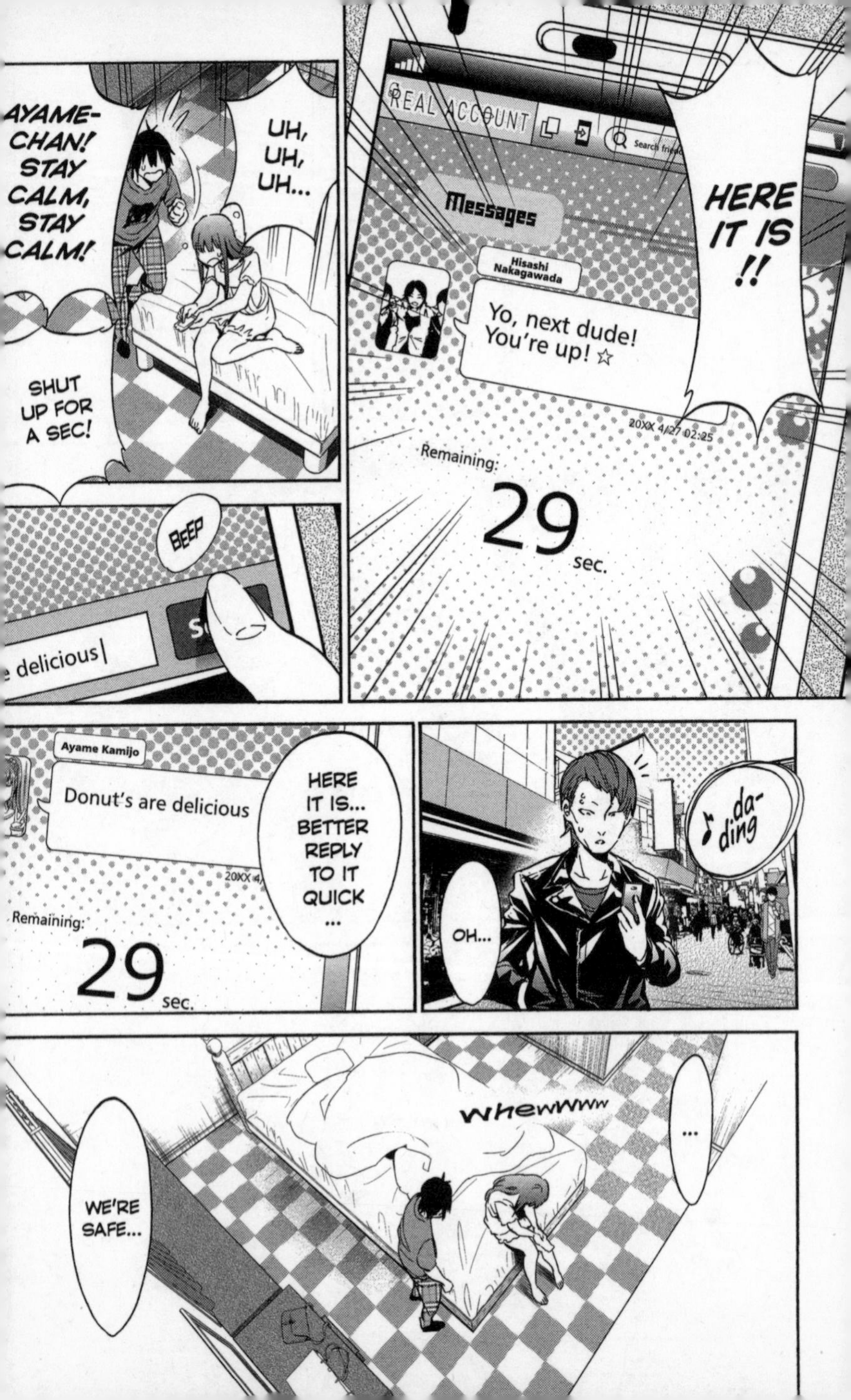
REAL ACCOUNT
Search friends
HERE IT IS!!
Messages
Hisashi Nakagawada
Yo, next dude! You're up! ☆
20XX 4/27 02:25
Remaining:
29 sec.
UH, UH, UH...
AYAME-CHAN! STAY CALM, STAY CALM!
SHUT UP FOR A SEC!
BEEP
e delicious
♪ da-ding
OH...
HERE IT IS... BETTER REPLY TO IT QUICK...
Ayame Kamijo
Donut's are delicious
20XX 4/
Remaining:
29 sec.
...
WHEWWWW
WE'RE SAFE...

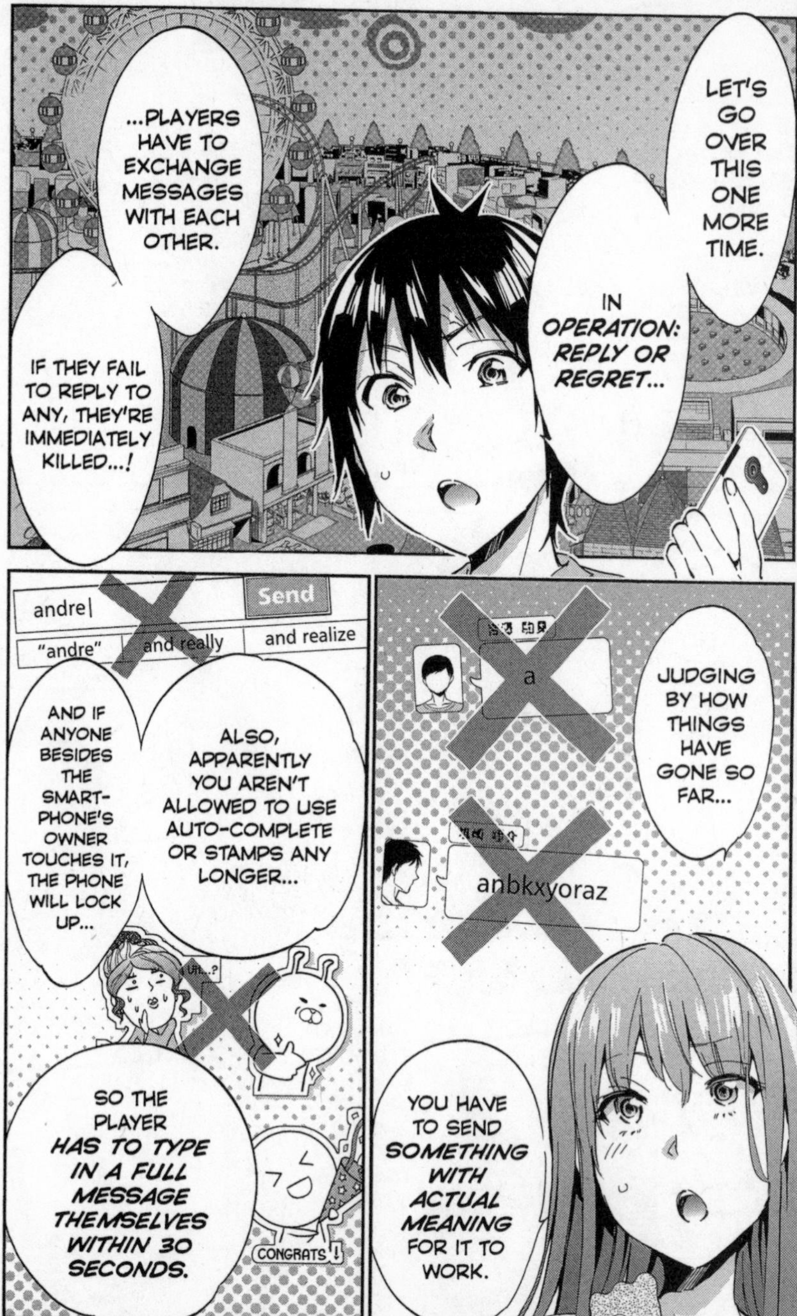
LET'S GO OVER THIS ONE MORE TIME.
IN OPERATION: REPLY OR REGRET...
...PLAYERS HAVE TO EXCHANGE MESSAGES WITH EACH OTHER.
IF THEY FAIL TO REPLY TO ANY, THEY'RE IMMEDIATELY KILLED...!
a
anbkxyoraz
JUDGING BY HOW THINGS HAVE GONE SO FAR...
YOU HAVE TO SEND SOMETHING WITH ACTUAL MEANING FOR IT TO WORK.
andre|
Send
"andre"
and really
and realize
ALSO, APPARENTLY YOU AREN'T ALLOWED TO USE AUTO-COMPLETE OR STAMPS ANY LONGER...
AND IF ANYONE BESIDES THE SMART-PHONE'S OWNER TOUCHES IT, THE PHONE WILL LOCK UP...
SO THE PLAYER HAS TO TYPE IN A FULL MESSAGE THEMSELVES WITHIN 30 SECONDS.
CONGRATS!

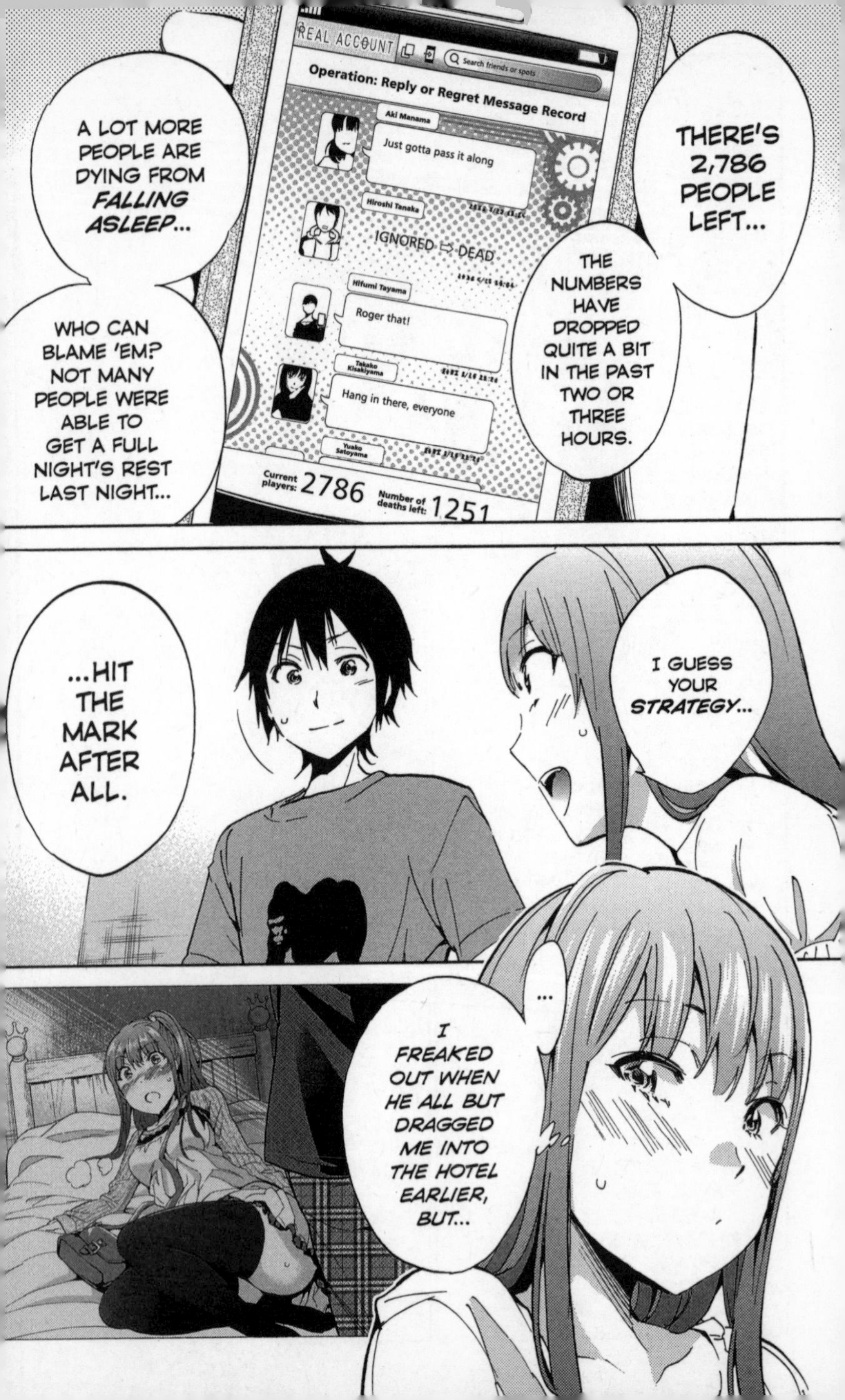
THERE'S 2,786 PEOPLE LEFT...
THE NUMBERS HAVE DROPPED QUITE A BIT IN THE PAST TWO OR THREE HOURS.
REAL ACCOUNT
Search friends or spots
Operation: Reply or Regret Message Record
Aki Manama
Just gotta pass it along
Hiroshi Tanaka
IGNORED ⇨ DEAD
Hifumi Tayama
Roger that!
Takako Kisakiyama
Hang in there, everyone
Yuako Satoyama
Current players: 2786
Number of deaths left: 1251
A LOT MORE PEOPLE ARE DYING FROM *FALLING ASLEEP*...
WHO CAN BLAME 'EM? NOT MANY PEOPLE WERE ABLE TO GET A FULL NIGHT'S REST LAST NIGHT...
I GUESS YOUR *STRATEGY*...
...HIT THE MARK AFTER ALL.
...
I FREAKED OUT WHEN HE ALL BUT DRAGGED ME INTO THE HOTEL EARLIER, BUT...

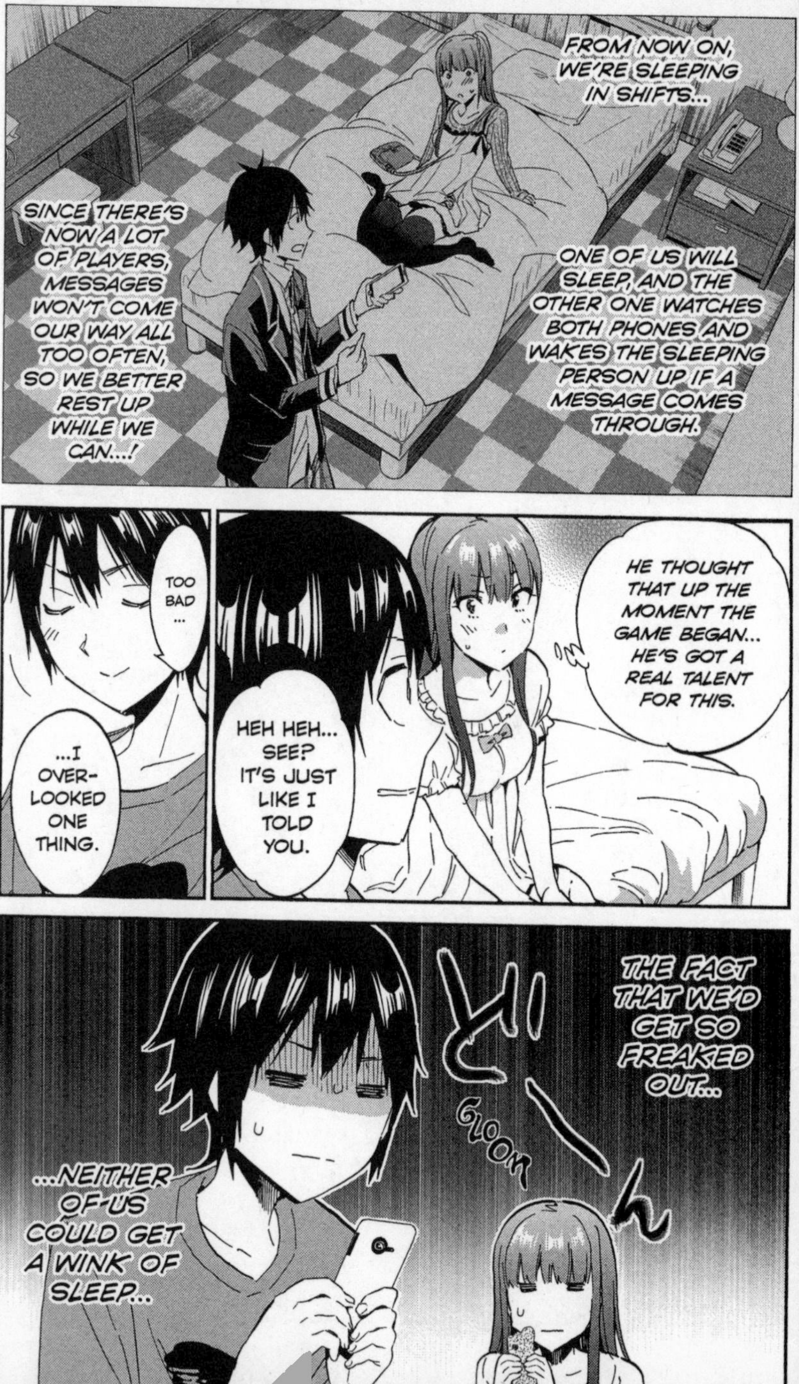
FROM NOW ON, WE'RE SLEEPING IN SHIFTS...
ONE OF US WILL SLEEP, AND THE OTHER ONE WATCHES BOTH PHONES AND WAKES THE SLEEPING PERSON UP IF A MESSAGE COMES THROUGH.
SINCE THERE'S NOW A LOT OF PLAYERS, MESSAGES WON'T COME OUR WAY ALL TOO OFTEN, SO WE BETTER REST UP WHILE WE CAN...!
HE THOUGHT THAT UP THE MOMENT THE GAME BEGAN... HE'S GOT A REAL TALENT FOR THIS.
HEH HEH... SEE? IT'S JUST LIKE I TOLD YOU.
TOO BAD...
...I OVERLOOKED ONE THING.
THE FACT THAT WE'D GET SO FREAKED OUT...
GLOOM
...NEITHER OF US COULD GET A WINK OF SLEEP...

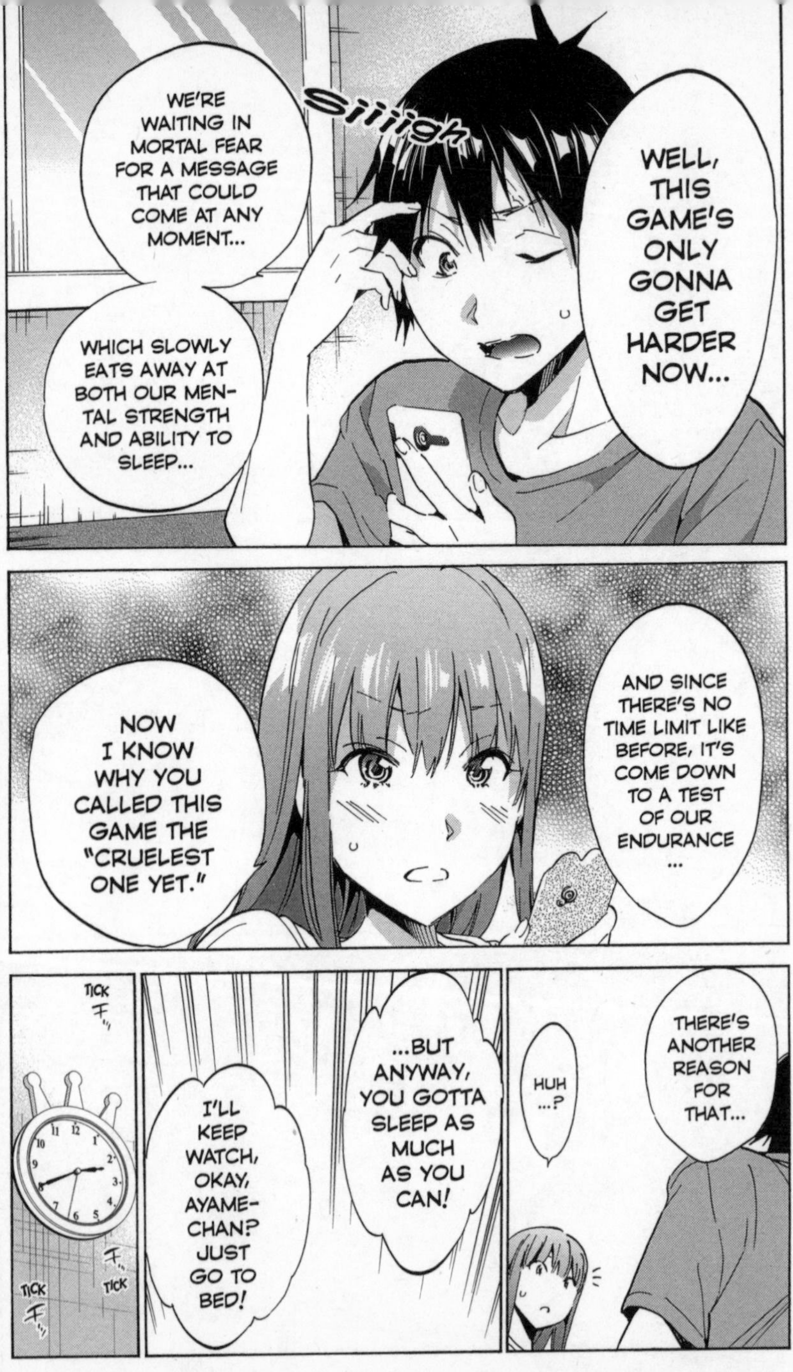
WELL, THIS GAME'S ONLY GONNA GET HARDER NOW...
Siiiigh
WE'RE WAITING IN MORTAL FEAR FOR A MESSAGE THAT COULD COME AT ANY MOMENT...
WHICH SLOWLY EATS AWAY AT BOTH OUR MEN-TAL STRENGTH AND ABILITY TO SLEEP...
AND SINCE THERE'S NO TIME LIMIT LIKE BEFORE, IT'S COME DOWN TO A TEST OF OUR ENDURANCE ...
NOW I KNOW WHY YOU CALLED THIS GAME THE "CRUELEST ONE YET."
THERE'S ANOTHER REASON FOR THAT...
HUH ...?
...BUT ANYWAY, YOU GOTTA SLEEP AS MUCH AS YOU CAN!
I'LL KEEP WATCH, OKAY, AYAME-CHAN? JUST GO TO BED!
TICK
TICK
TICK

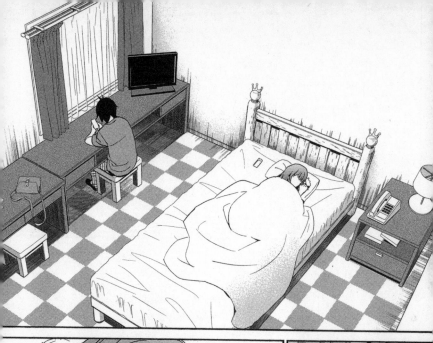

WOW... ME, ALONE WITH A GUY IN A HOTEL...

IF MY BIG BROTHER SAW ME, WHAT WOULD HE SAY...?

...

THE REASON I COULDN'T SLEEP BEFORE...

...ISN'T JUST BECAUSE I'M AFRAID OF THIS GAME.

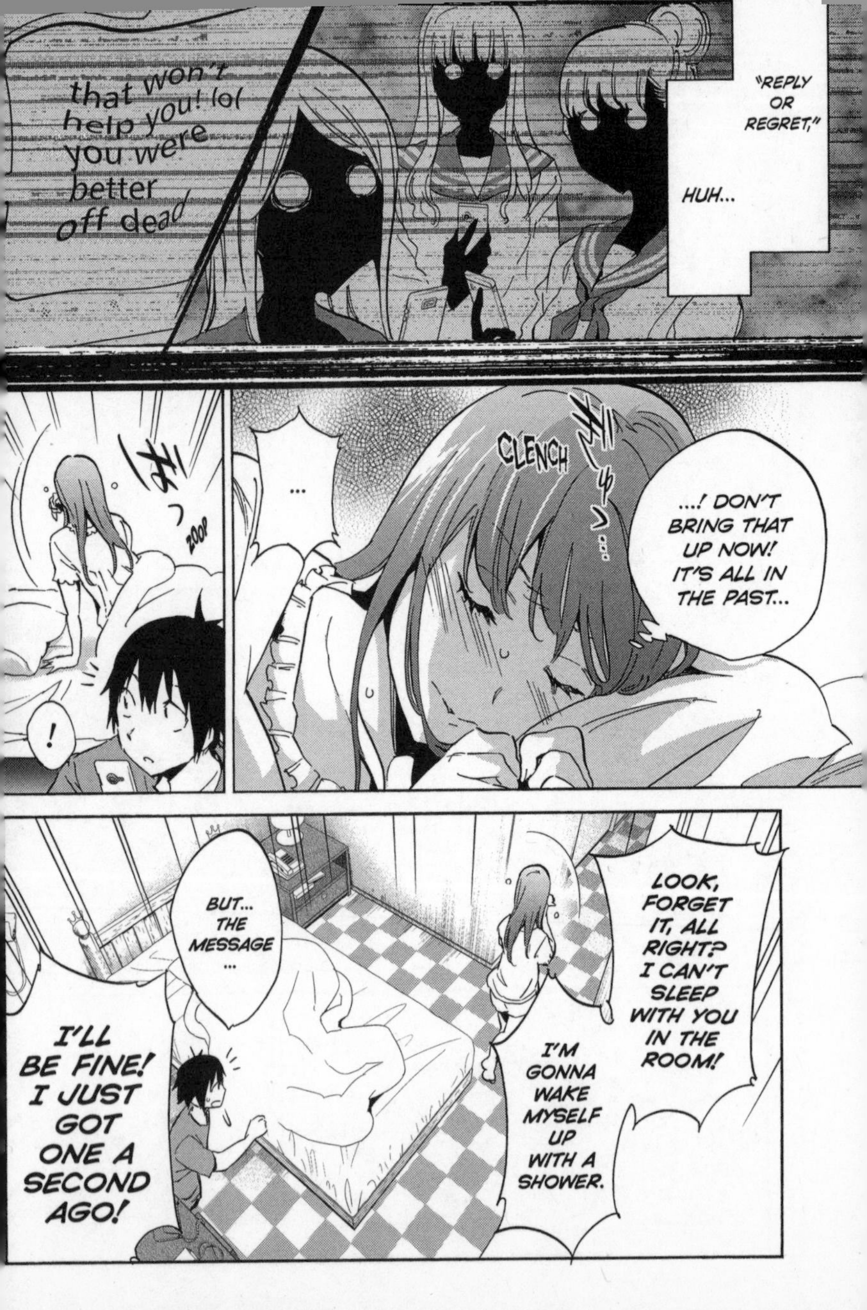
"REPLY OR REGRET,"
HUH...
that won't help you! lol you were better off dead
CLENCH
...! DON'T BRING THAT UP NOW! IT'S ALL IN THE PAST...
...
ZOOP
!
LOOK, FORGET IT, ALL RIGHT? I CAN'T SLEEP WITH YOU IN THE ROOM!
I'M GONNA WAKE MYSELF UP WITH A SHOWER.
BUT... THE MESSAGE...
I'LL BE FINE! I JUST GOT ONE A SECOND AGO!

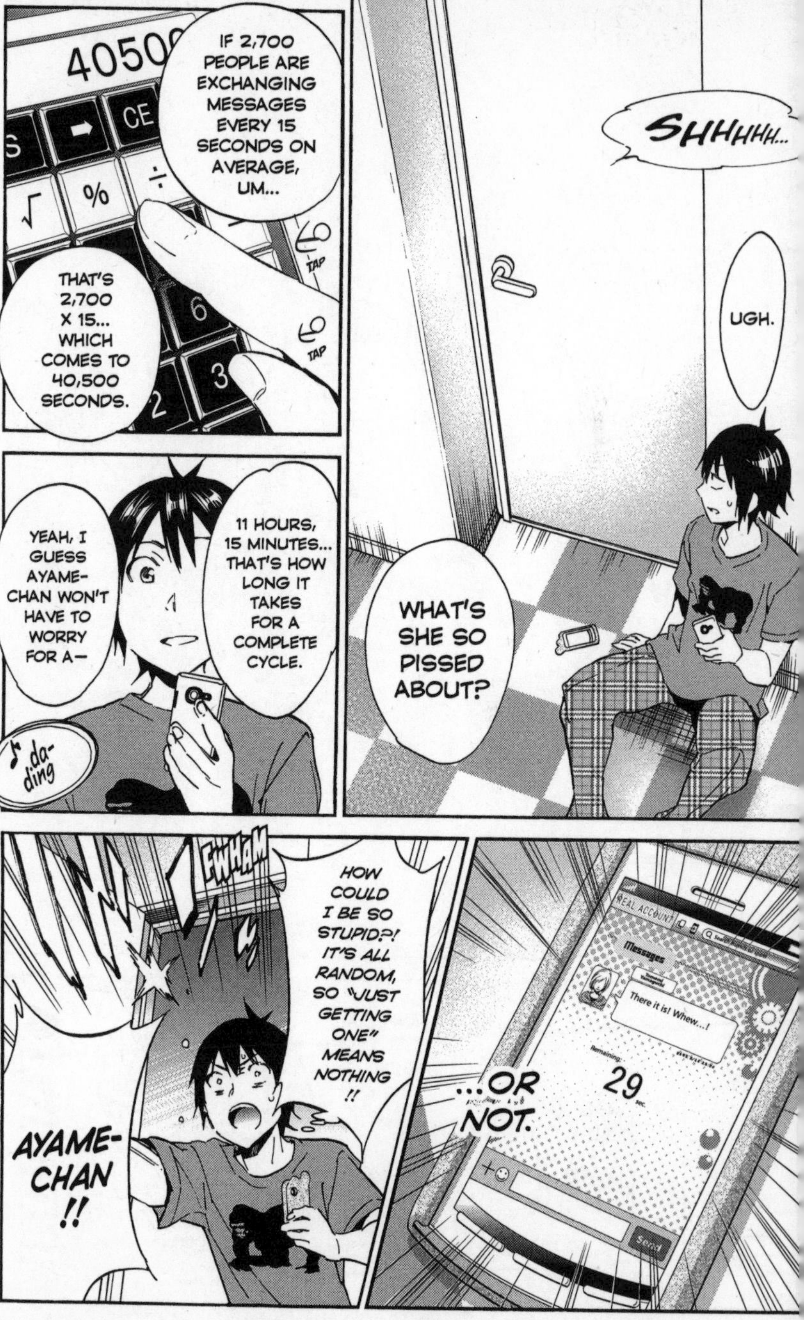
SHHHHH...
UGH.
WHAT'S SHE SO PISSED ABOUT?
40500
IF 2,700 PEOPLE ARE EXCHANGING MESSAGES EVERY 15 SECONDS ON AVERAGE, UM...
TAP
TAP
THAT'S 2,700 X 15... WHICH COMES TO 40,500 SECONDS.
11 HOURS, 15 MINUTES... THAT'S HOW LONG IT TAKES FOR A COMPLETE CYCLE.
YEAH, I GUESS AYAME-CHAN WON'T HAVE TO WORRY FOR A—
♪ da-ding
REAL ACCOUNT
Messages
There it is! Whew...!
Remaining:
29 sec
Send
...OR NOT.
EWHAM
HOW COULD I BE SO STUPID?! IT'S ALL RANDOM, SO "JUST GETTING ONE" MEANS NOTHING!!
AYAME-CHAN!!

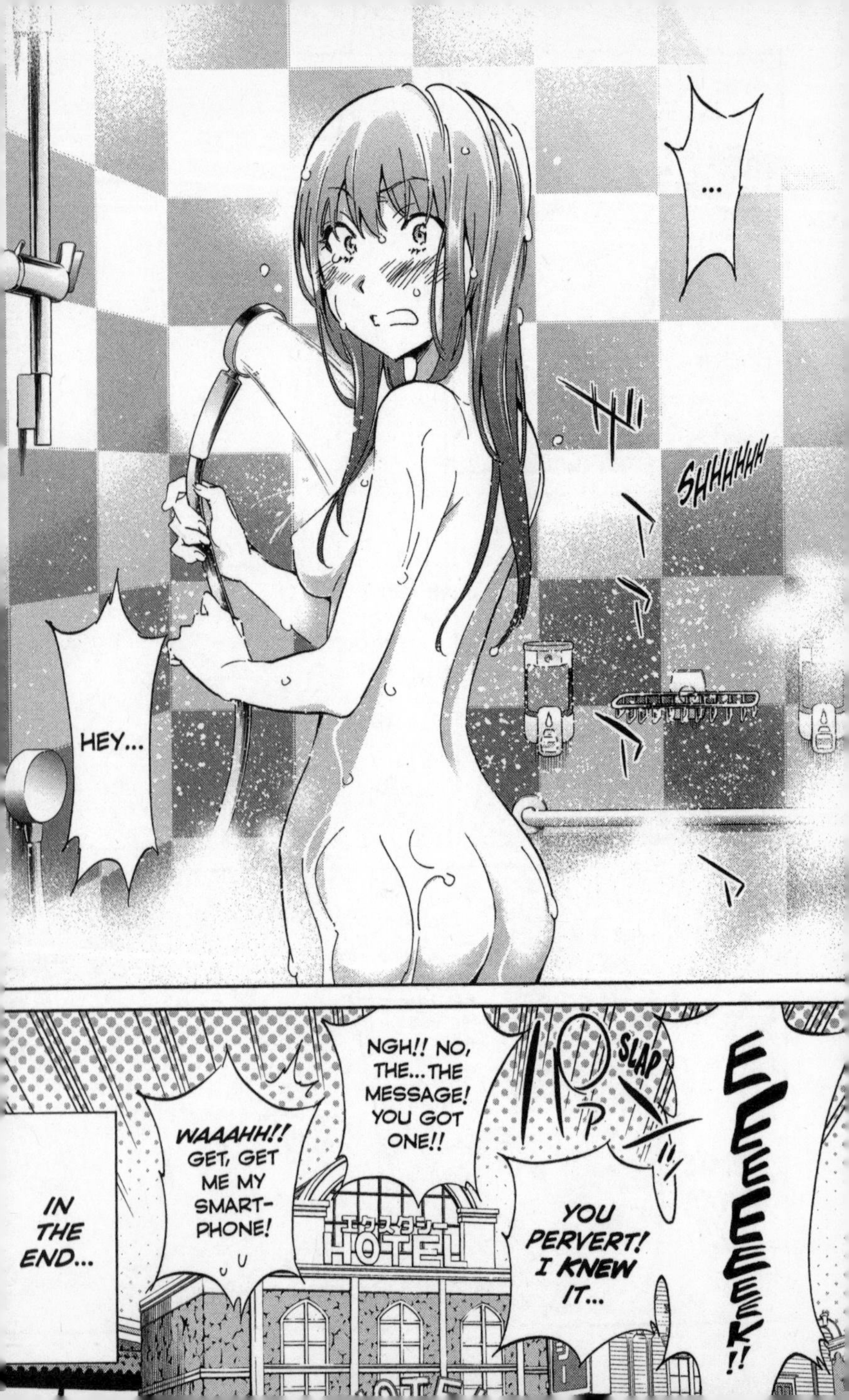
...
SHHHHHH
HEY...
EEEEEEEK!!
SLAP
YOU PERVERT! I KNEW IT...
NGH!! NO, THE...THE MESSAGE! YOU GOT ONE!!
WAAAHH!! GET, GET ME MY SMART-PHONE!
HOTEL
IN THE END...

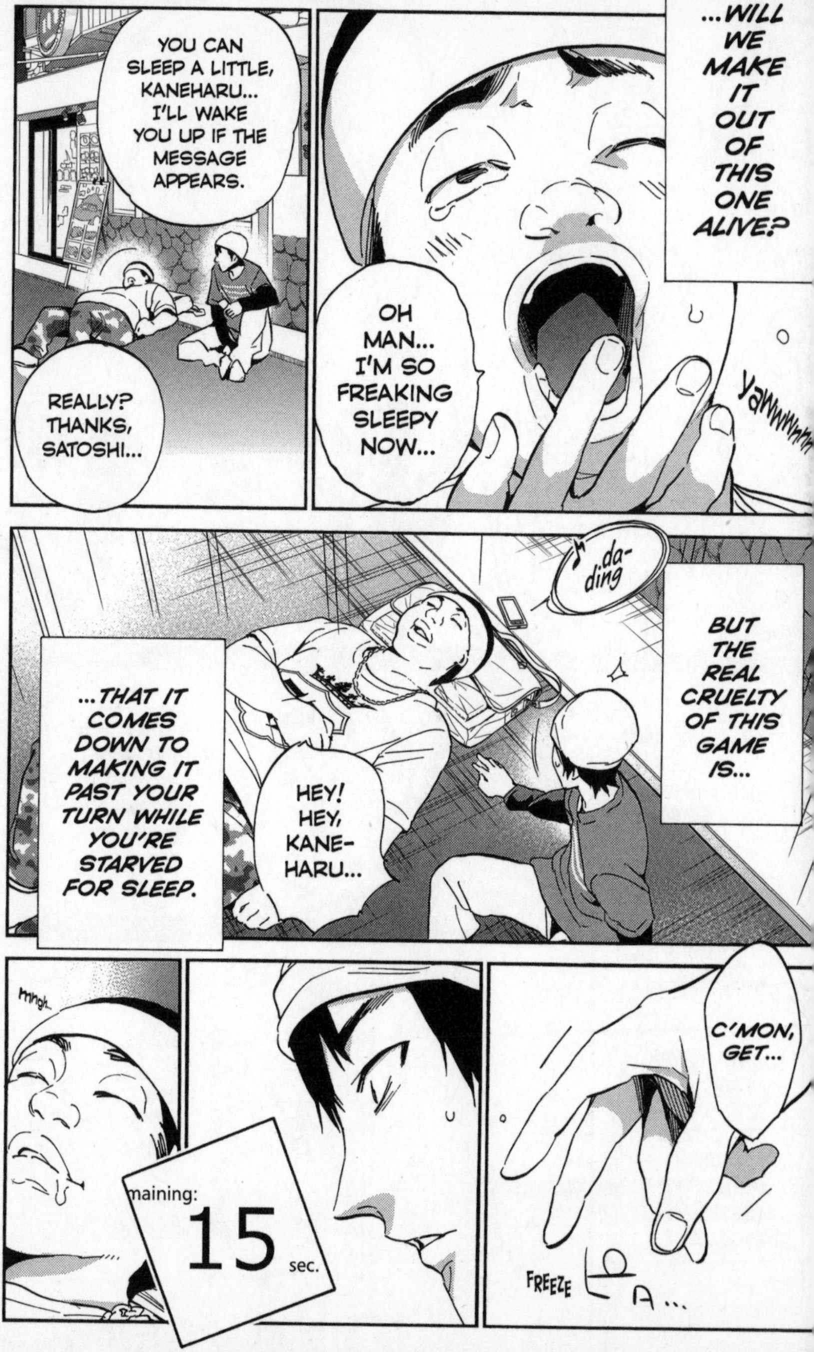
...WILL WE MAKE IT OUT OF THIS ONE ALIVE?
OH MAN... I'M SO FREAKING SLEEPY NOW...
YAWWWNNN
YOU CAN SLEEP A LITTLE, KANEHARU... I'LL WAKE YOU UP IF THE MESSAGE APPEARS.
REALLY? THANKS, SATOSHI...
♪ ..da-ding
BUT THE REAL CRUELTY OF THIS GAME IS...
HEY! HEY, KANE-HARU...
...THAT IT COMES DOWN TO MAKING IT PAST YOUR TURN WHILE YOU'RE STARVED FOR SLEEP.
C'MON, GET...
FREEZE
ピタ...
mngh..
maining:
15
sec.

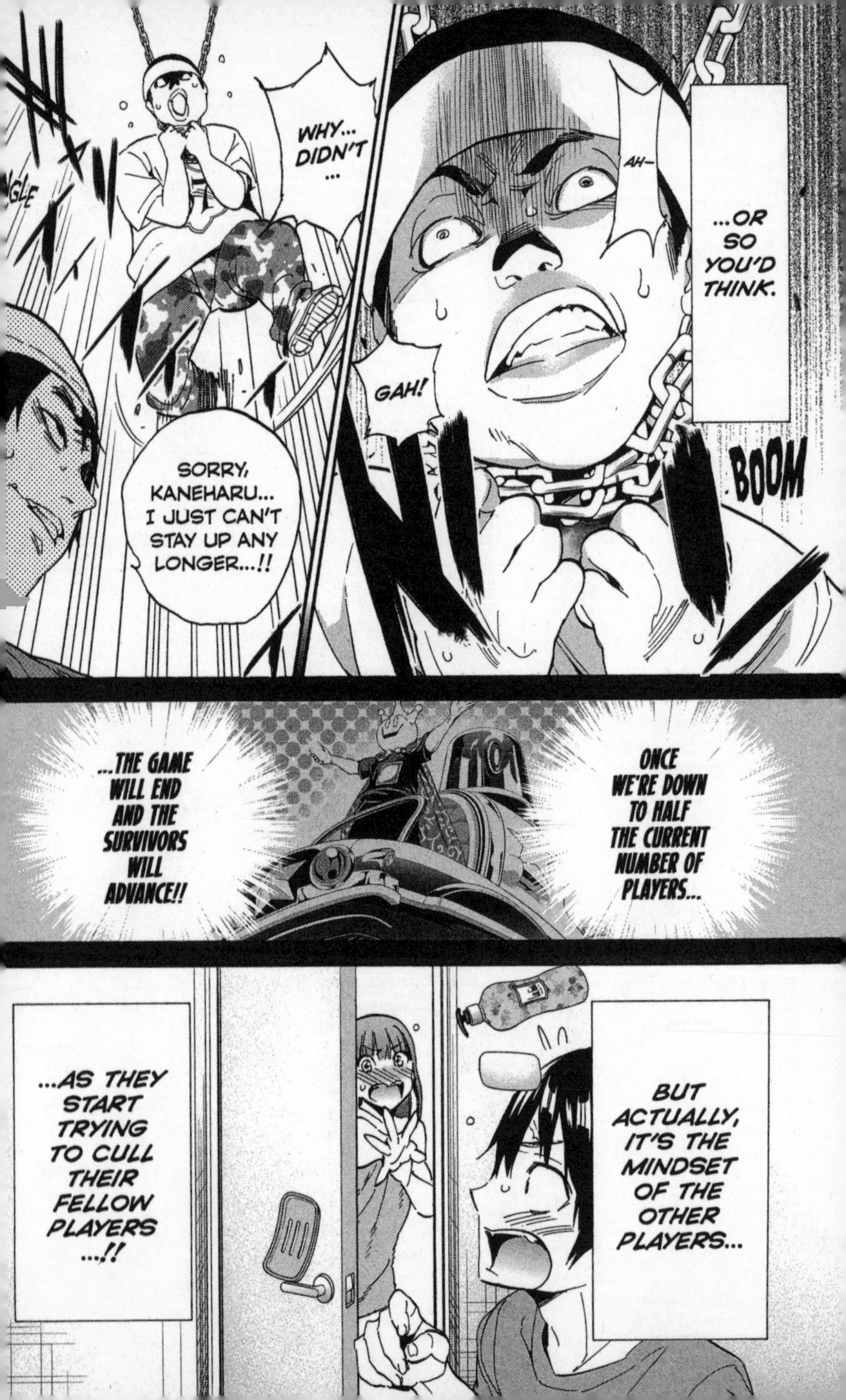
...OR SO YOU'D THINK.
AH—
BOOM
GAH!
WHY... DIDN'T ...
SORRY, KANEHARU... I JUST CAN'T STAY UP ANY LONGER...!!
ONCE WE'RE DOWN TO HALF THE CURRENT NUMBER OF PLAYERS...
...THE GAME WILL END AND THE SURVIVORS WILL ADVANCE!!
BUT ACTUALLY, IT'S THE MINDSET OF THE OTHER PLAYERS...
...AS THEY START TRYING TO CULL THEIR FELLOW PLAYERS ...!!

ACCOUNT 14 The Reply Police

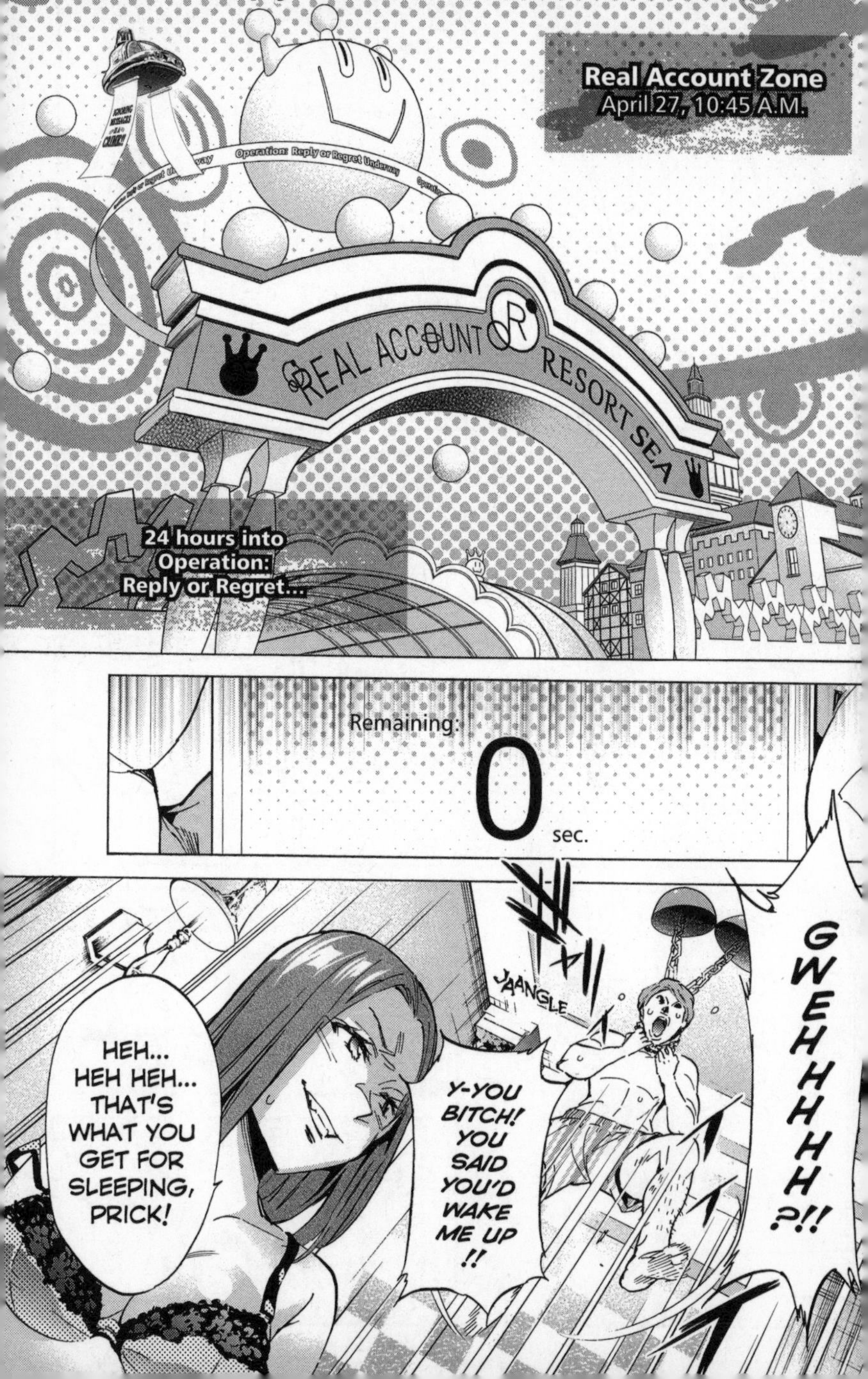
Real Account Zone
April 27, 10:45 A.M.
Operation: Reply or Regret Underway
REAL ACCOUNT RESORT SEA
24 hours into Operation: Reply or Regret...
Remaining: 0 sec.
GWEHHHHHH?!!
Y-YOU BITCH! YOU SAID YOU'D WAKE ME UP!!
JAANGLE
HEH... HEH HEH... THAT'S WHAT YOU GET FOR SLEEPING, PRICK!

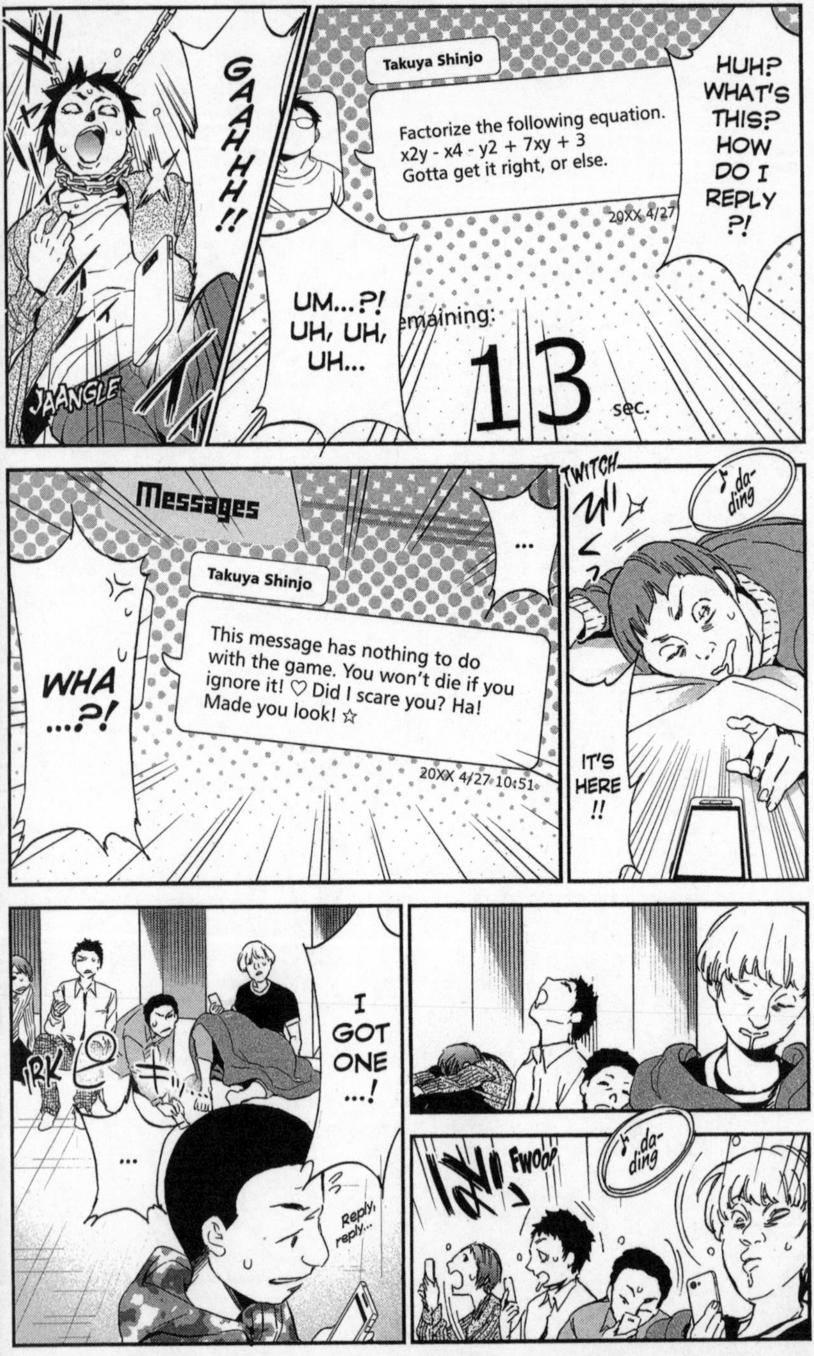
HUH? WHAT'S THIS? HOW DO I REPLY?!
Takuya Shinjo
Factorize the following equation.
x2y - x4 - y2 + 7xy + 3
Gotta get it right, or else.
20XX 4/27
UM...?! UH, UH, UH...
emaining:
13
sec.
GAAHHH!!
JAANGLE
TWITCH
da-ding
IT'S HERE!!
...
Messages
Takuya Shinjo
This message has nothing to do with the game. You won't die if you ignore it! ♡ Did I scare you? Ha! Made you look! ☆
20XX 4/27 10:51
WHA...?!
da-ding
FWOOP
I GOT ONE...!
IRK
...
Reply, reply...

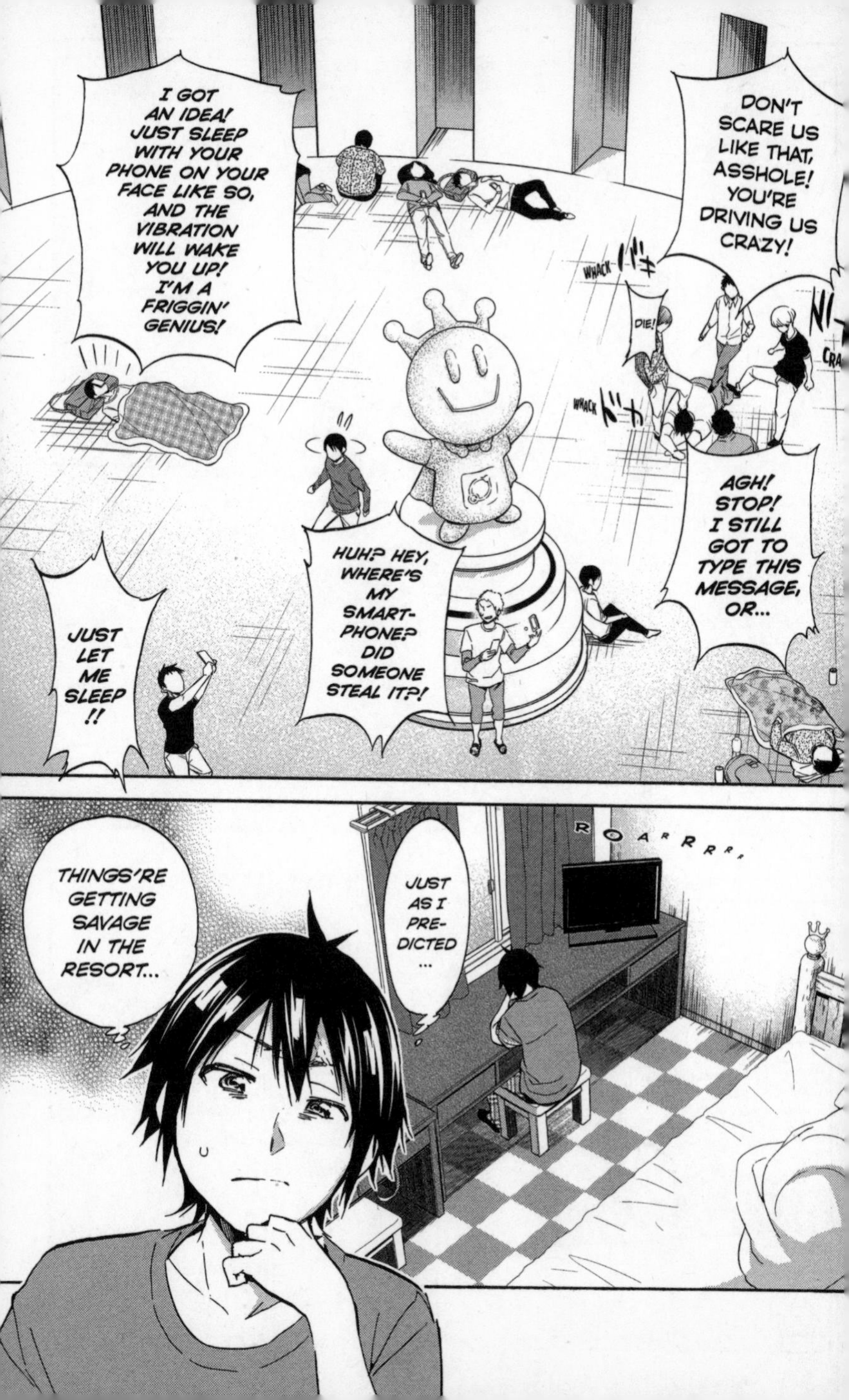
DON'T SCARE US LIKE THAT, ASSHOLE! YOU'RE DRIVING US CRAZY!
WHACK
DIE!
CRA
WHACK
AGH! STOP! I STILL GOT TO TYPE THIS MESSAGE, OR...
I GOT AN IDEA! JUST SLEEP WITH YOUR PHONE ON YOUR FACE LIKE SO, AND THE VIBRATION WILL WAKE YOU UP! I'M A FRIGGIN' GENIUS!
HUH? HEY, WHERE'S MY SMART-PHONE? DID SOMEONE STEAL IT?!
JUST LET ME SLEEP!!
ROARRRRR
JUST AS I PRE-DICTED...
THINGS'RE GETTING SAVAGE IN THE RESORT...

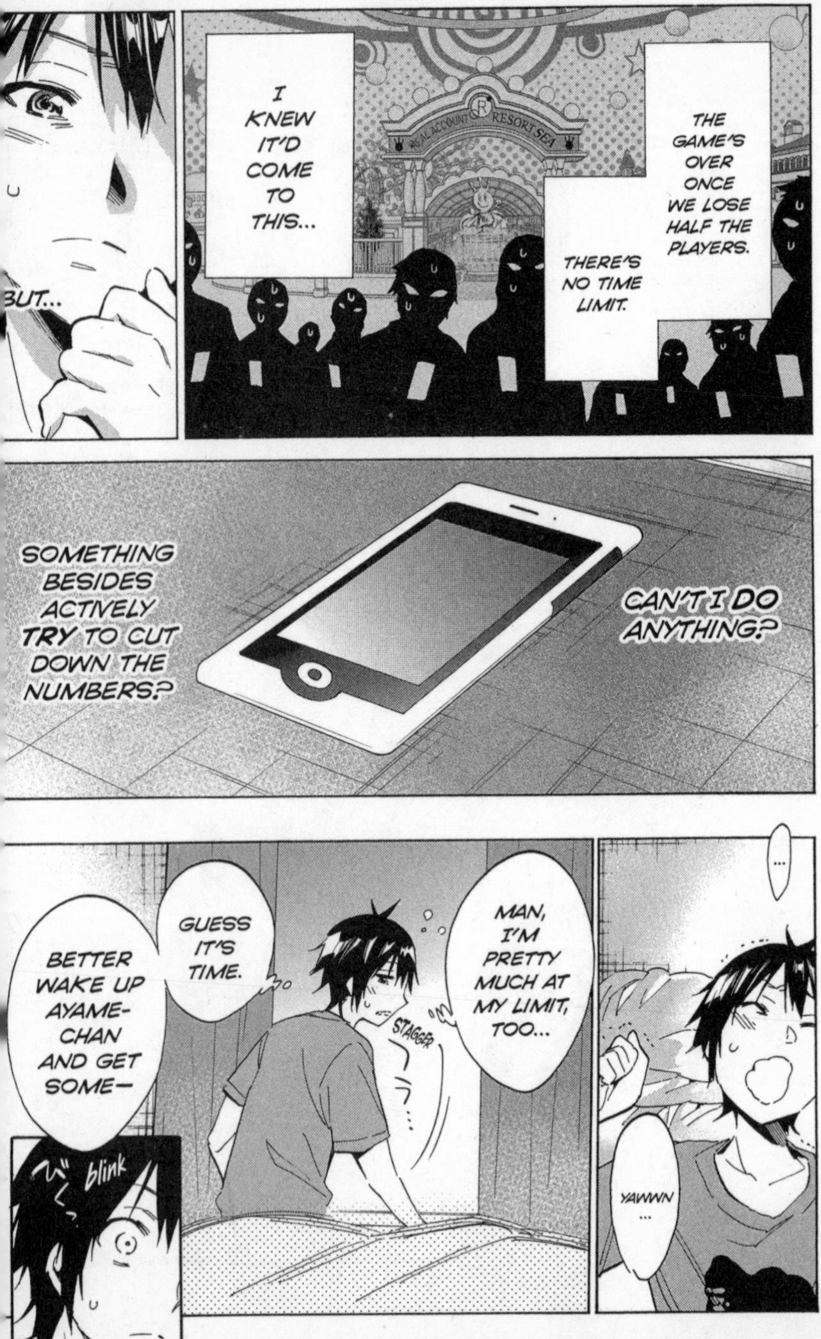
THE GAME'S OVER ONCE WE LOSE HALF THE PLAYERS.
THERE'S NO TIME LIMIT.
I KNEW IT'D COME TO THIS...
BUT...
CAN'T I DO ANYTHING?
SOMETHING BESIDES ACTIVELY TRY TO CUT DOWN THE NUMBERS?
...
YAWWN ...
MAN, I'M PRETTY MUCH AT MY LIMIT, TOO...
STAGGER
GUESS IT'S TIME.
BETTER WAKE UP AYAME-CHAN AND GET SOME—
blink

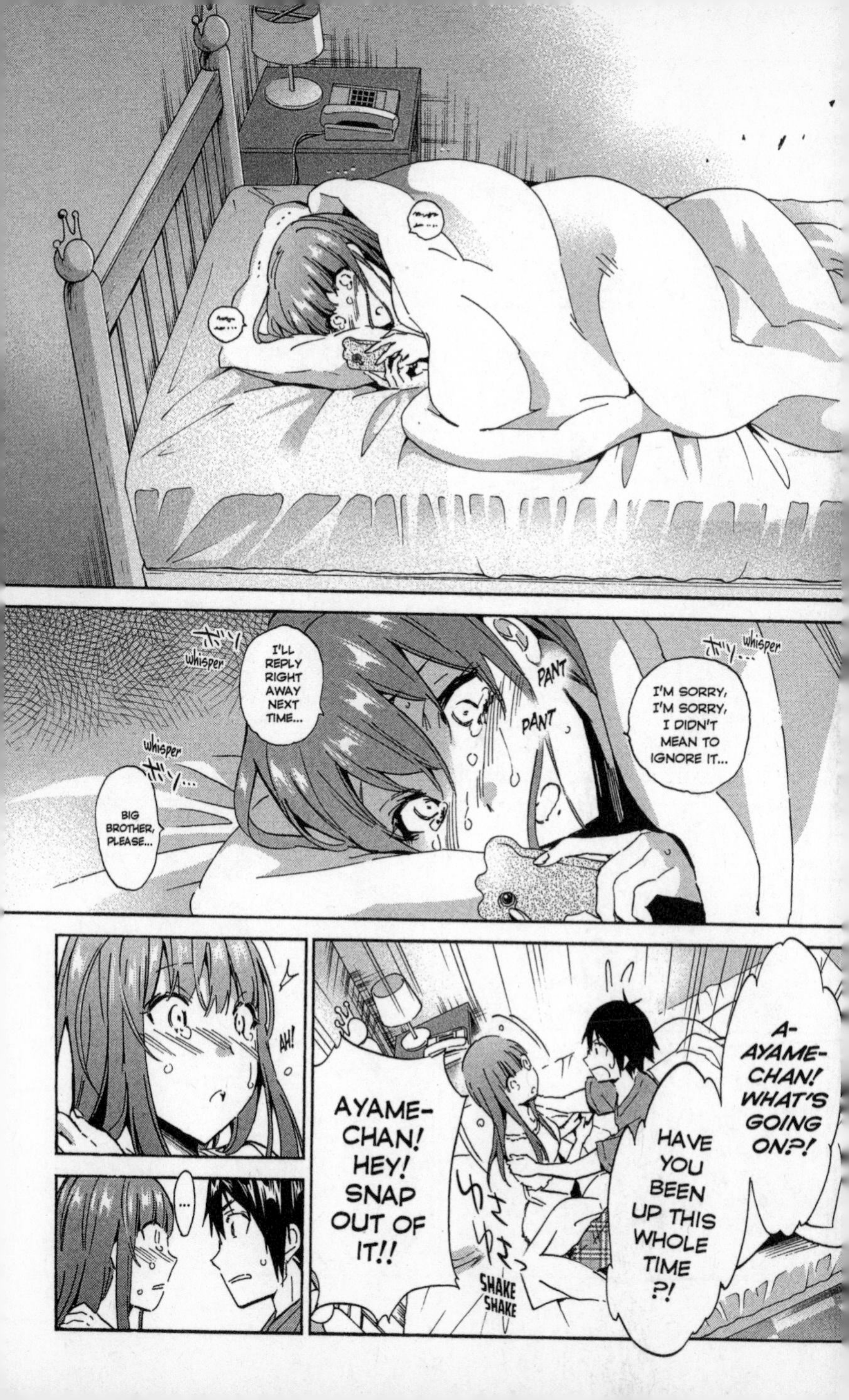
ボソ… whisper
I'M SORRY, I'M SORRY, I DIDN'T MEAN TO IGNORE IT...
PANT
PANT
I'LL REPLY RIGHT AWAY NEXT TIME...
ボソ whisper
whisper ボソ…
BIG BROTHER, PLEASE...
A-AYAME-CHAN! WHAT'S GOING ON?!
HAVE YOU BEEN UP THIS WHOLE TIME?!
AYAME-CHAN! HEY! SNAP OUT OF IT!!
SHAKE SHAKE
AH!
...

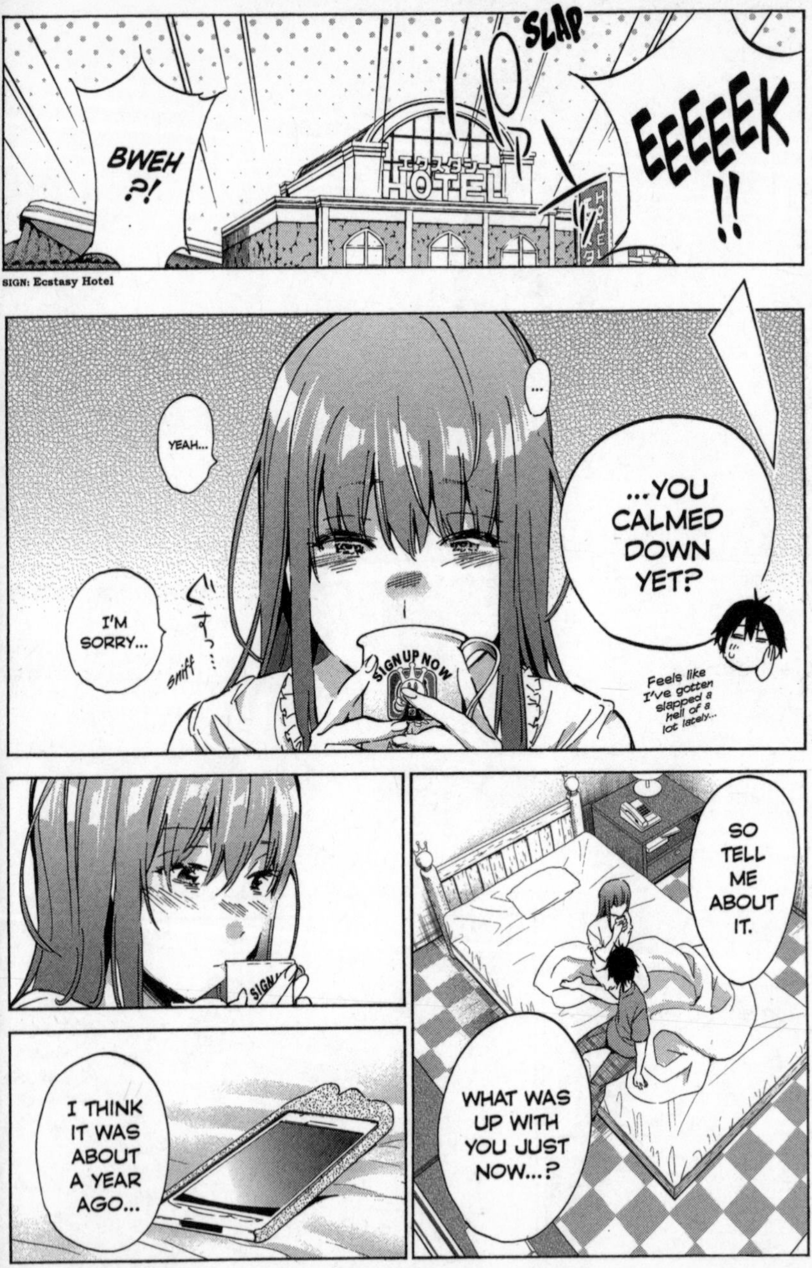
EEEEEK!!
SLAP
BWEH?!
...YOU CALMED DOWN YET?
Feels like I've gotten slapped a hell of a lot lately...
...
YEAH...
I'M SORRY...
sniff
SIGN UP NOW
SO TELL ME ABOUT IT.
WHAT WAS UP WITH YOU JUST NOW...?
I THINK IT WAS ABOUT A YEAR AGO...

SIGN: Ecstasy Hotel

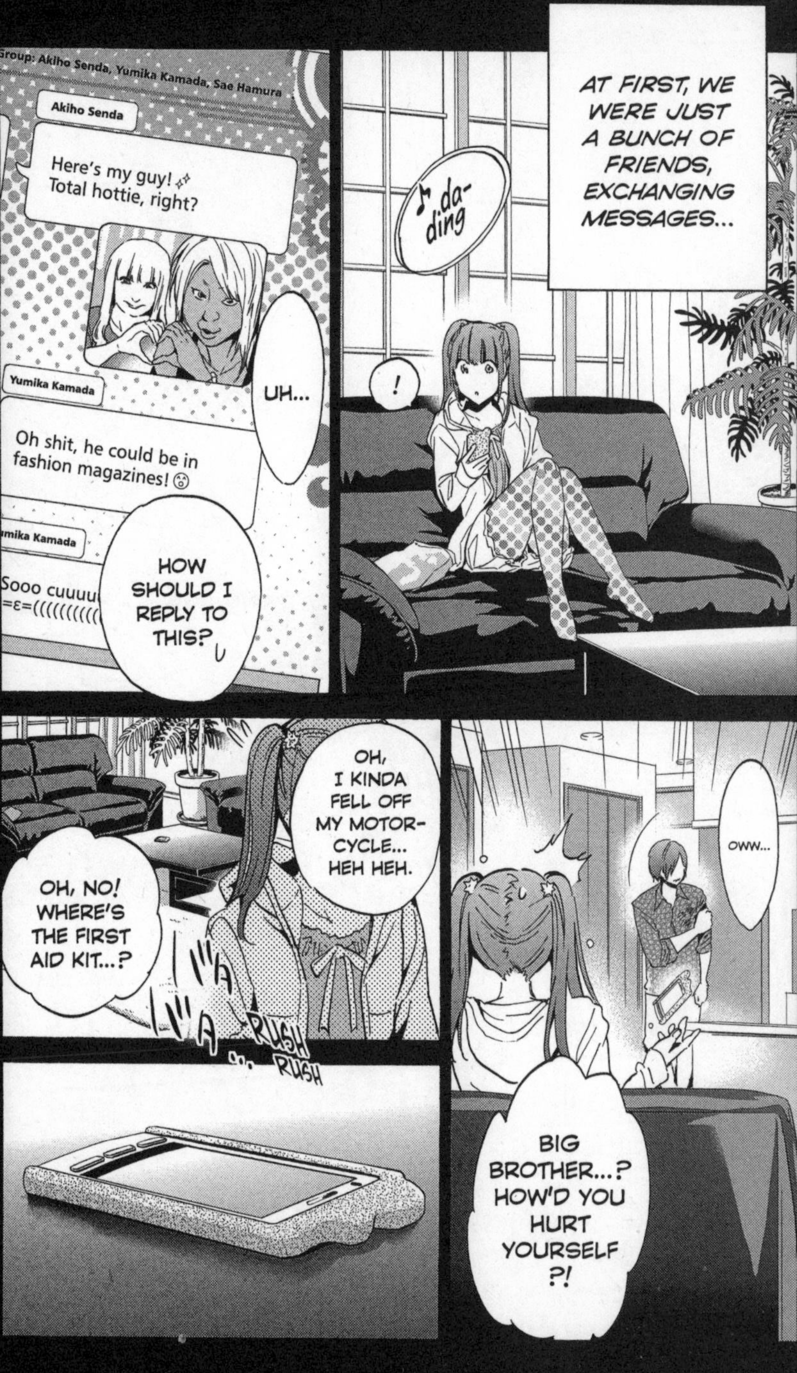
AT FIRST, WE WERE JUST A BUNCH OF FRIENDS, EXCHANGING MESSAGES...
♪ da-ding
!
Group: Akiho Senda, Yumika Kamada, Sae Hamura
Akiho Senda
Here's my guy! Total hottie, right?
Yumika Kamada
Oh shit, he could be in fashion magazines!
UH...
umika Kamada
Sooo cuuuu
HOW SHOULD I REPLY TO THIS?
OWW...
BIG BROTHER...? HOW'D YOU HURT YOURSELF ?!
OH, I KINDA FELL OFF MY MOTOR-CYCLE... HEH HEH.
OH, NO! WHERE'S THE FIRST AID KIT...?
RUSH RUSH

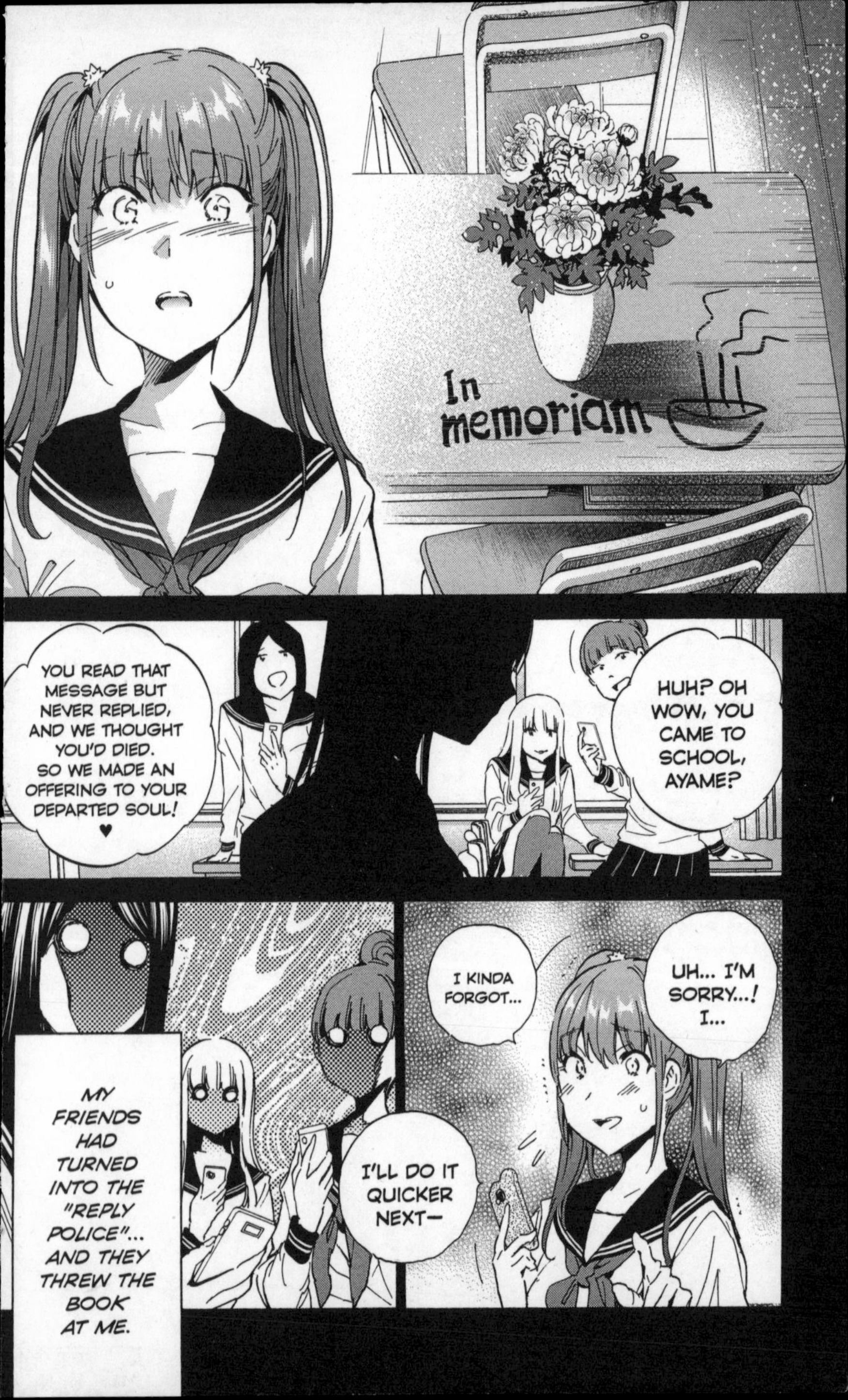
In memoriam
HUH? OH WOW, YOU CAME TO SCHOOL, AYAME?
YOU READ THAT MESSAGE BUT NEVER REPLIED, AND WE THOUGHT YOU'D DIED. SO WE MADE AN OFFERING TO YOUR DEPARTED SOUL! ♥
UH... I'M SORRY...! I...
I KINDA FORGOT...
I'LL DO IT QUICKER NEXT—
MY FRIENDS HAD TURNED INTO THE "REPLY POLICE"... AND THEY THREW THE BOOK AT ME.

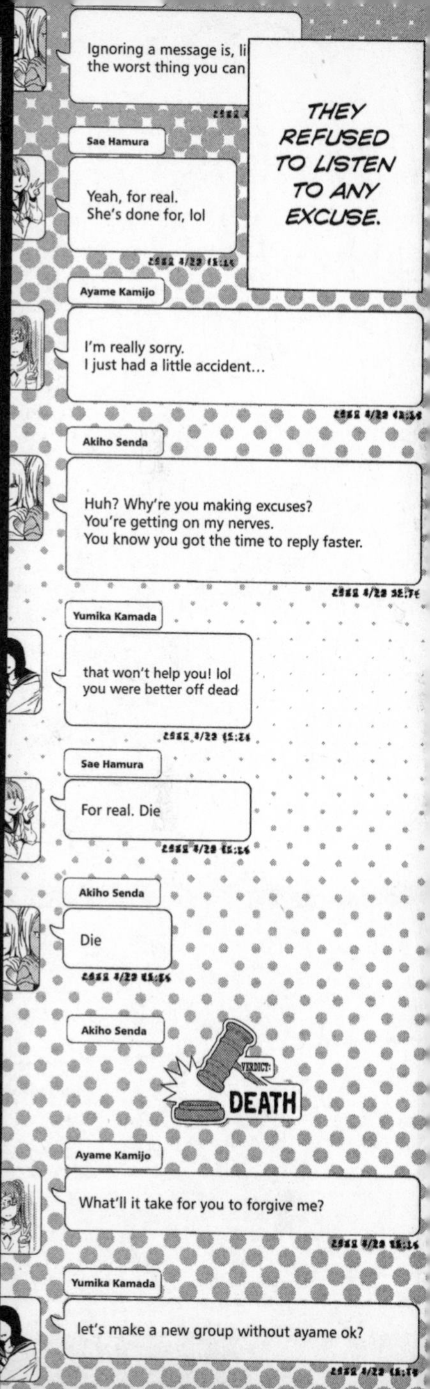
Ignoring a message is, li
the worst thing you can
THEY REFUSED TO LISTEN TO ANY EXCUSE.
Sae Hamura
Yeah, for real.
She's done for, lol
Ayame Kamijo
I'm really sorry.
I just had a little accident...
Akiho Senda
Huh? Why're you making excuses?
You're getting on my nerves.
You know you got the time to reply faster.
Yumika Kamada
that won't help you! lol
you were better off dead
Sae Hamura
For real. Die
Akiho Senda
Die
Akiho Senda
VERDICT:
DEATH
Ayame Kamijo
What'll it take for you to forgive me?
Yumika Kamada
let's make a new group without ayame ok?
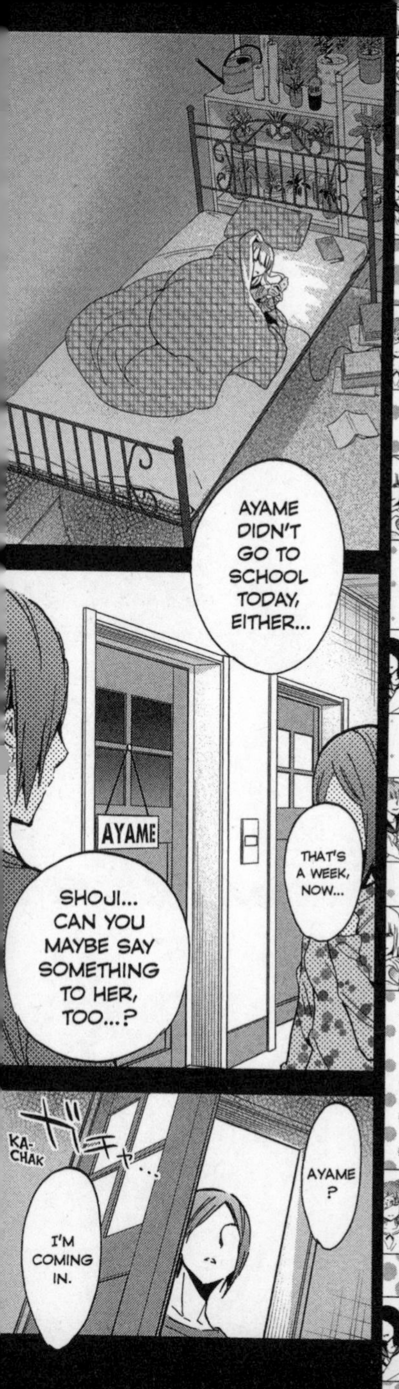
AYAME DIDN'T GO TO SCHOOL TODAY, EITHER...
AYAME
THAT'S A WEEK, NOW...
SHOJI... CAN YOU MAYBE SAY SOMETHING TO HER, TOO...?
AYAME ?
KA-CHAK
I'M COMING IN.

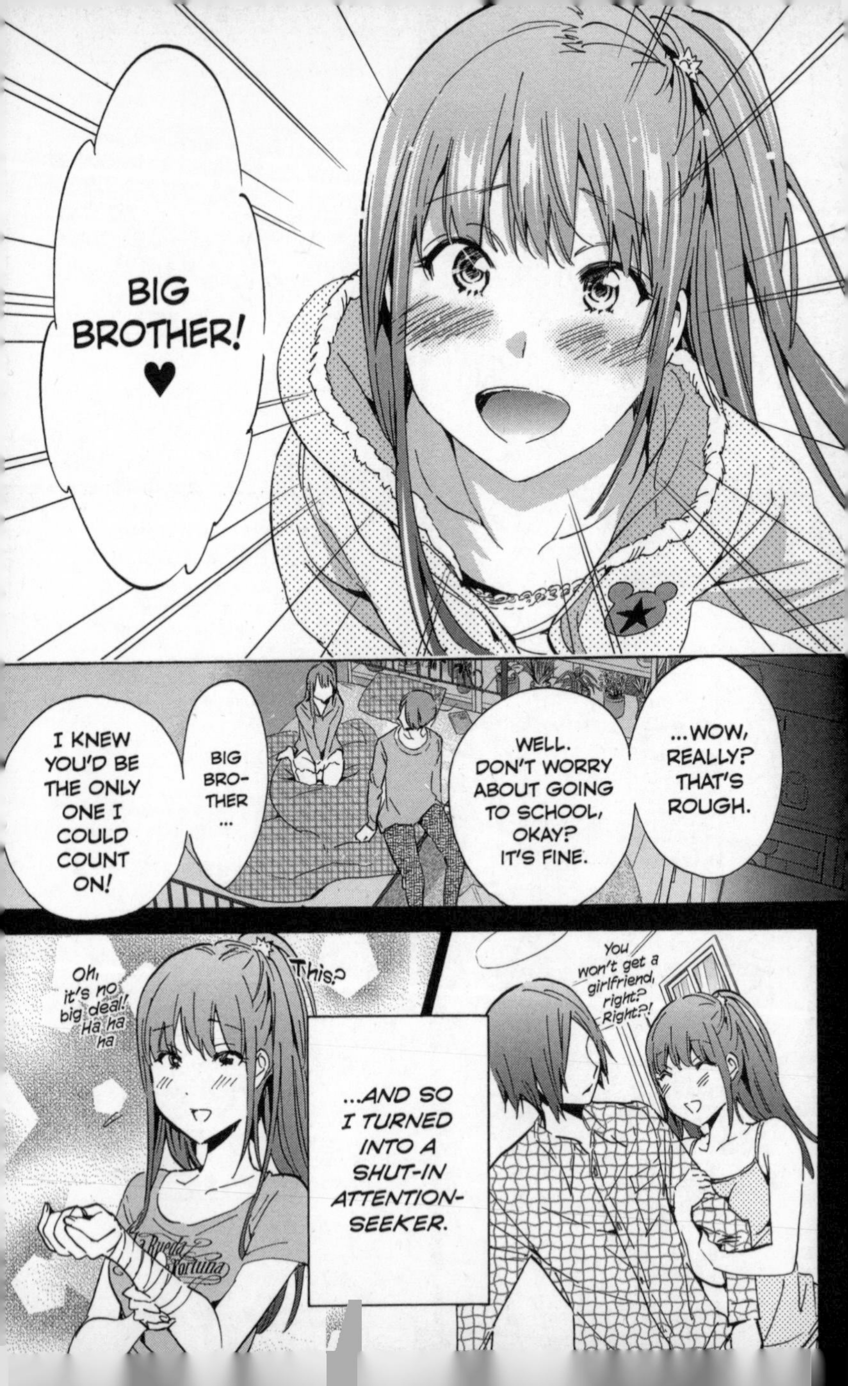
BIG BROTHER! ♥
...WOW, REALLY? THAT'S ROUGH.
WELL. DON'T WORRY ABOUT GOING TO SCHOOL, OKAY? IT'S FINE.
BIG BROTHER...
I KNEW YOU'D BE THE ONLY ONE I COULD COUNT ON!
You won't get a girlfriend, right? Right?!
...AND SO I TURNED INTO A SHUT-IN ATTENTION-SEEKER.
This?
Oh, it's no big deal! Ha ha ha

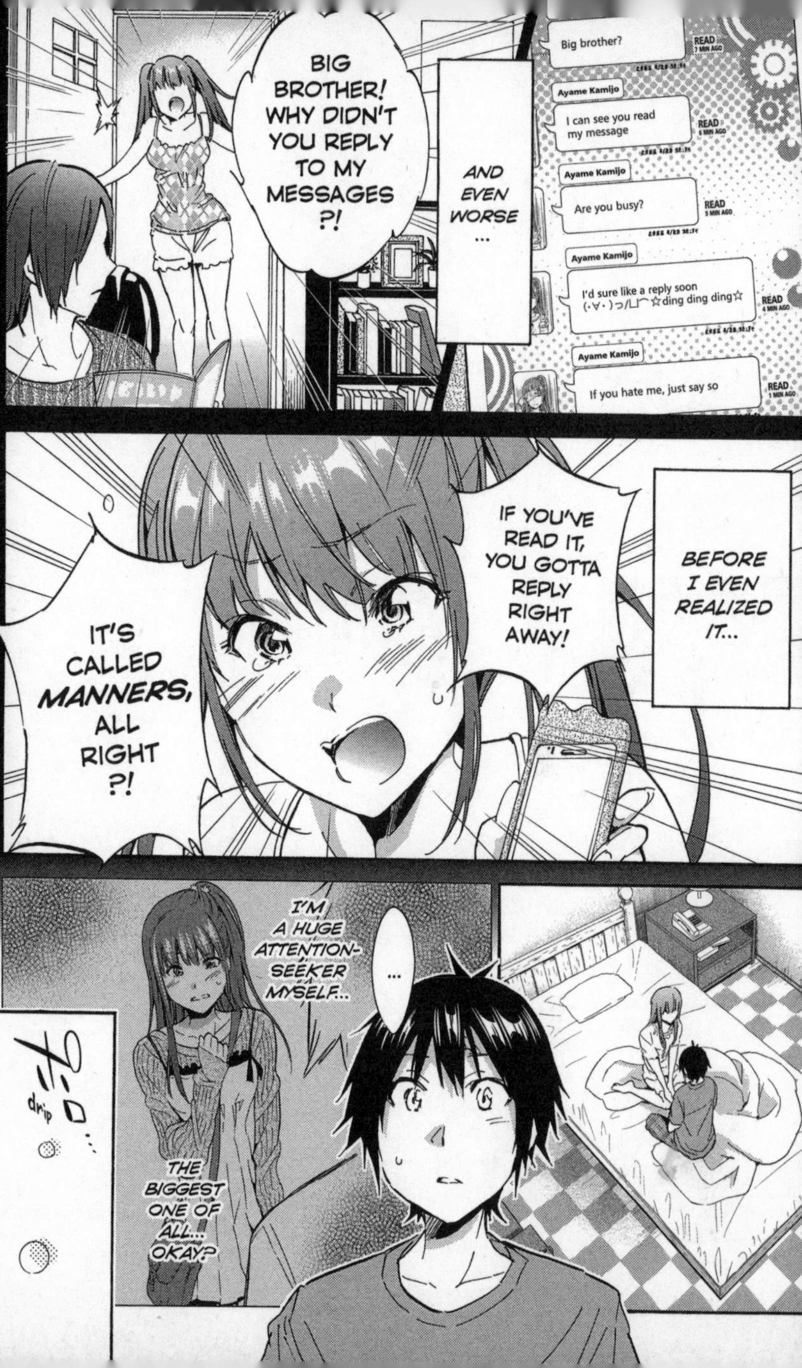
Big brother?
READ 7 MIN AGO
Ayame Kamijo
I can see you read my message
READ 6 MIN AGO
Ayame Kamijo
Are you busy?
READ 5 MIN AGO
Ayame Kamijo
I'd sure like a reply soon (･∀･)っ/凵⌒☆ding ding ding☆
READ 4 MIN AGO
Ayame Kamijo
If you hate me, just say so
READ 1 MIN AGO
AND EVEN WORSE...
BIG BROTHER! WHY DIDN'T YOU REPLY TO MY MESSAGES?!
BEFORE I EVEN REALIZED IT...
IF YOU'VE READ IT, YOU GOTTA REPLY RIGHT AWAY!
IT'S CALLED MANNERS, ALL RIGHT?!
...
I'M A HUGE ATTENTION-SEEKER MYSELF...
THE BIGGEST ONE OF ALL... OKAY?
drip

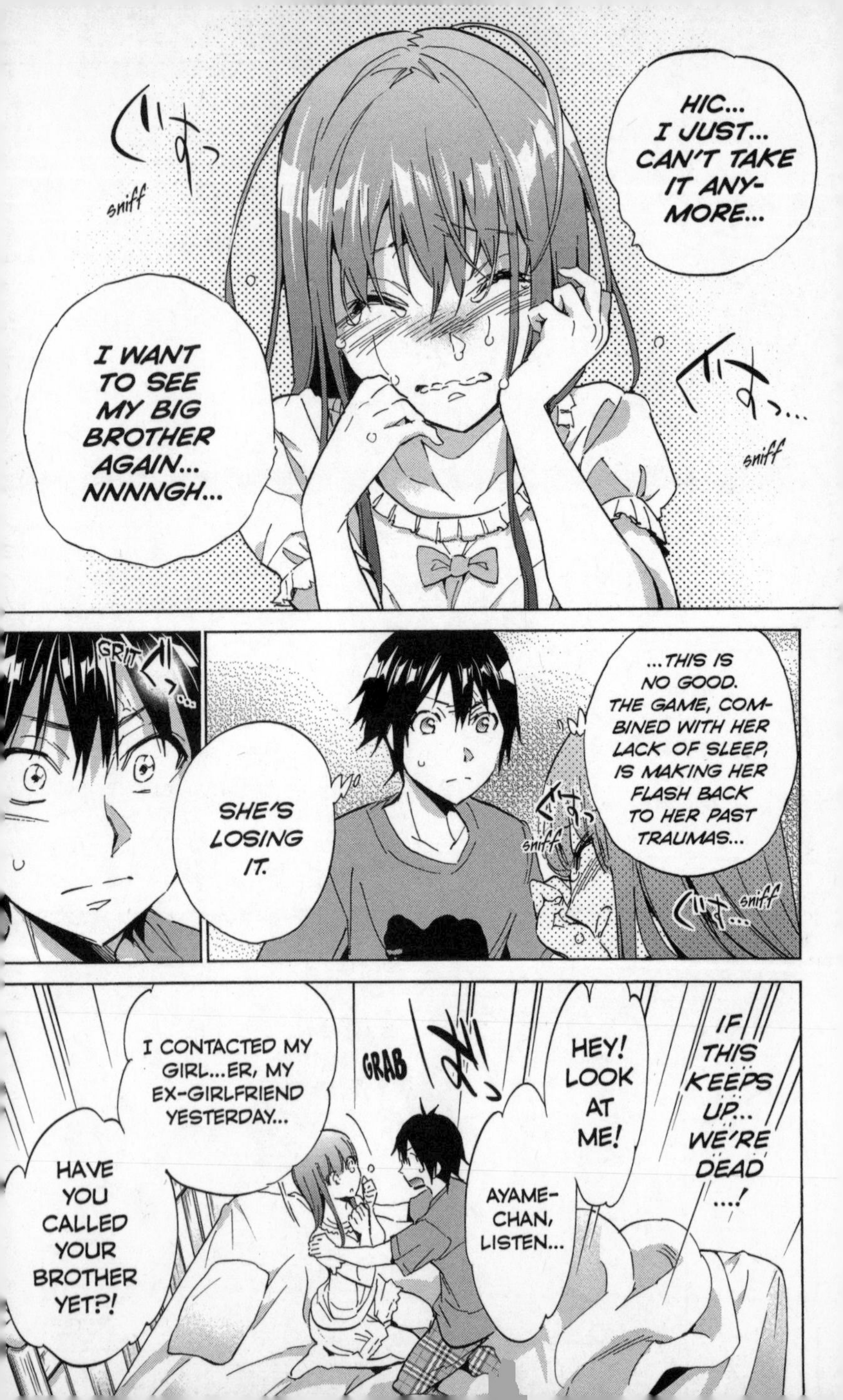
HIC... I JUST... CAN'T TAKE IT ANY-MORE...
sniff
I WANT TO SEE MY BIG BROTHER AGAIN... NNNNGH...
sniff
...THIS IS NO GOOD. THE GAME, COM-BINED WITH HER LACK OF SLEEP, IS MAKING HER FLASH BACK TO HER PAST TRAUMAS...
sniff
sniff
SHE'S LOSING IT.
GRIT
IF THIS KEEPS UP... WE'RE DEAD ...!
HEY! LOOK AT ME!
GRAB
AYAME-CHAN, LISTEN...
I CONTACTED MY GIRL...ER, MY EX-GIRLFRIEND YESTERDAY...
HAVE YOU CALLED YOUR BROTHER YET?!

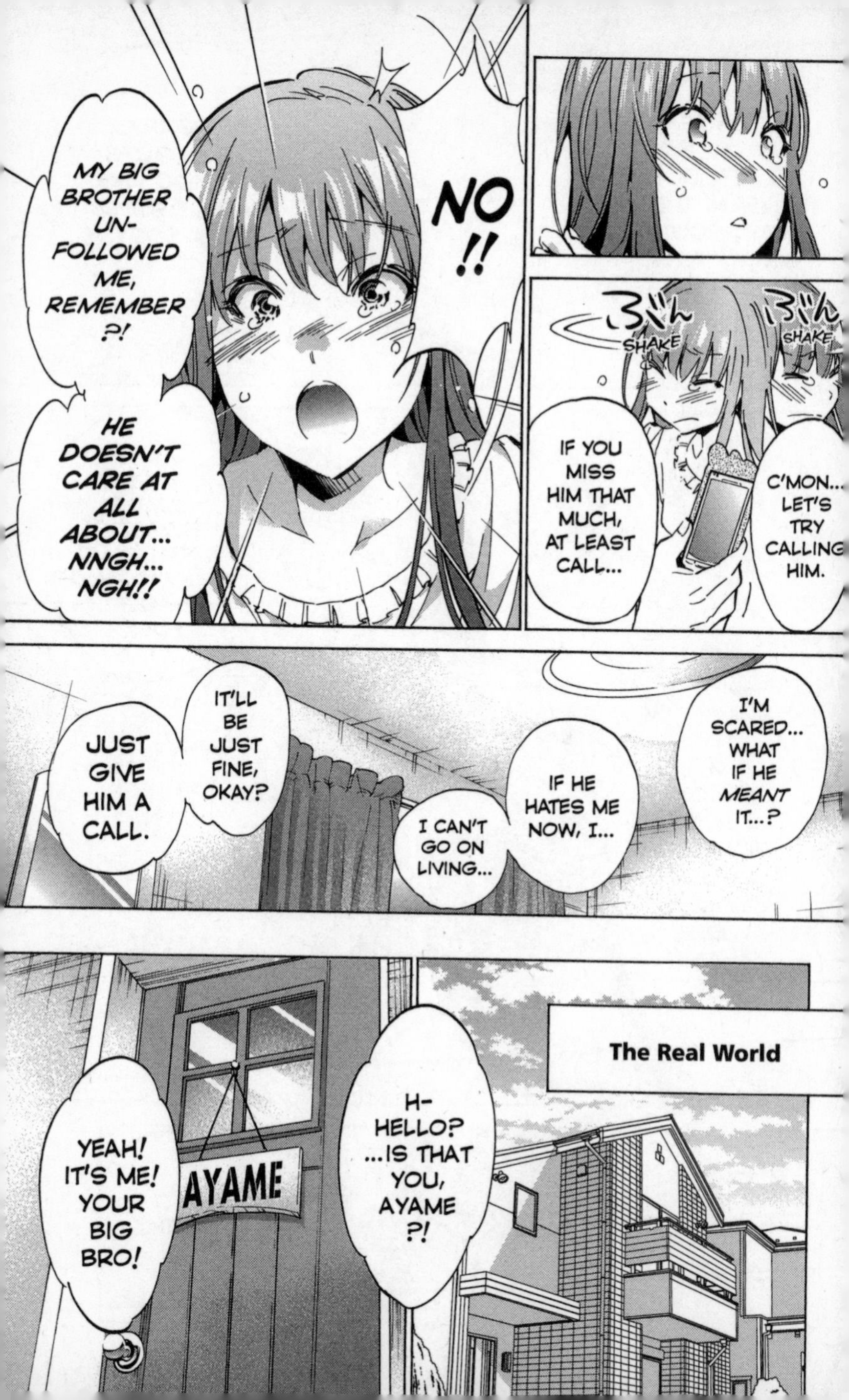

ぶん
SHAKE
ぶん
SHAKE
C'MON... LET'S TRY CALLING HIM.
IF YOU MISS HIM THAT MUCH, AT LEAST CALL...
NO!!
MY BIG BROTHER UN-FOLLOWED ME, REMEMBER?!
HE DOESN'T CARE AT ALL ABOUT... NNGH... NGH!!
I'M SCARED... WHAT IF HE *MEANT* IT...?
IF HE HATES ME NOW, I...
I CAN'T GO ON LIVING...
IT'LL BE JUST FINE, OKAY?
JUST GIVE HIM A CALL.
The Real World
H-HELLO? ...IS THAT YOU, AYAME?!
AYAME
YEAH! IT'S ME! YOUR BIG BRO!

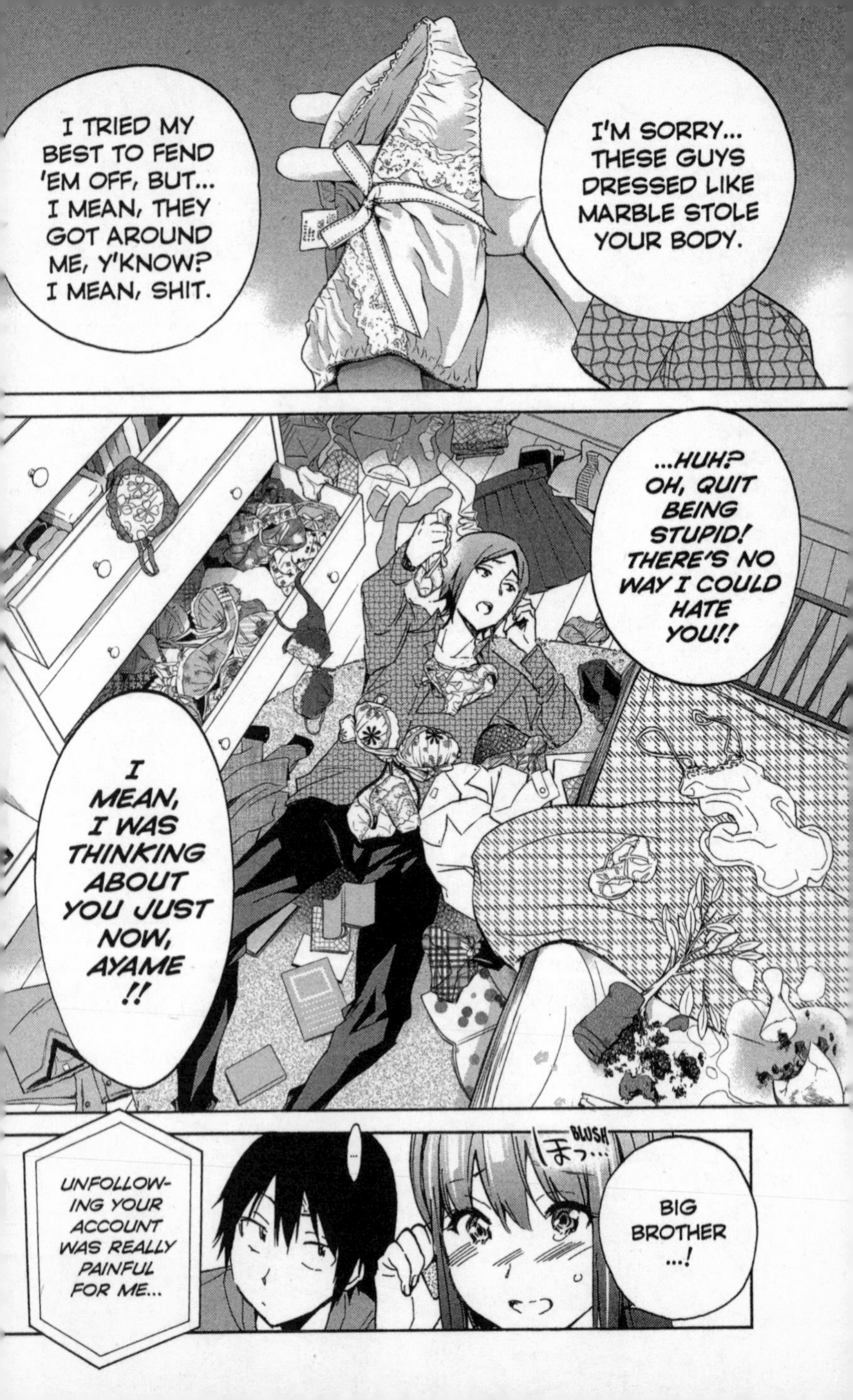
I'M SORRY... THESE GUYS DRESSED LIKE MARBLE STOLE YOUR BODY.
I TRIED MY BEST TO FEND 'EM OFF, BUT... I MEAN, THEY GOT AROUND ME, Y'KNOW? I MEAN, SHIT.
...HUH? OH, QUIT BEING STUPID! THERE'S NO WAY I COULD HATE YOU!!
I MEAN, I WAS THINKING ABOUT YOU JUST NOW, AYAME!!
BLUSH
BIG BROTHER ...!
...
UNFOLLOWING YOUR ACCOUNT WAS REALLY PAINFUL FOR ME...

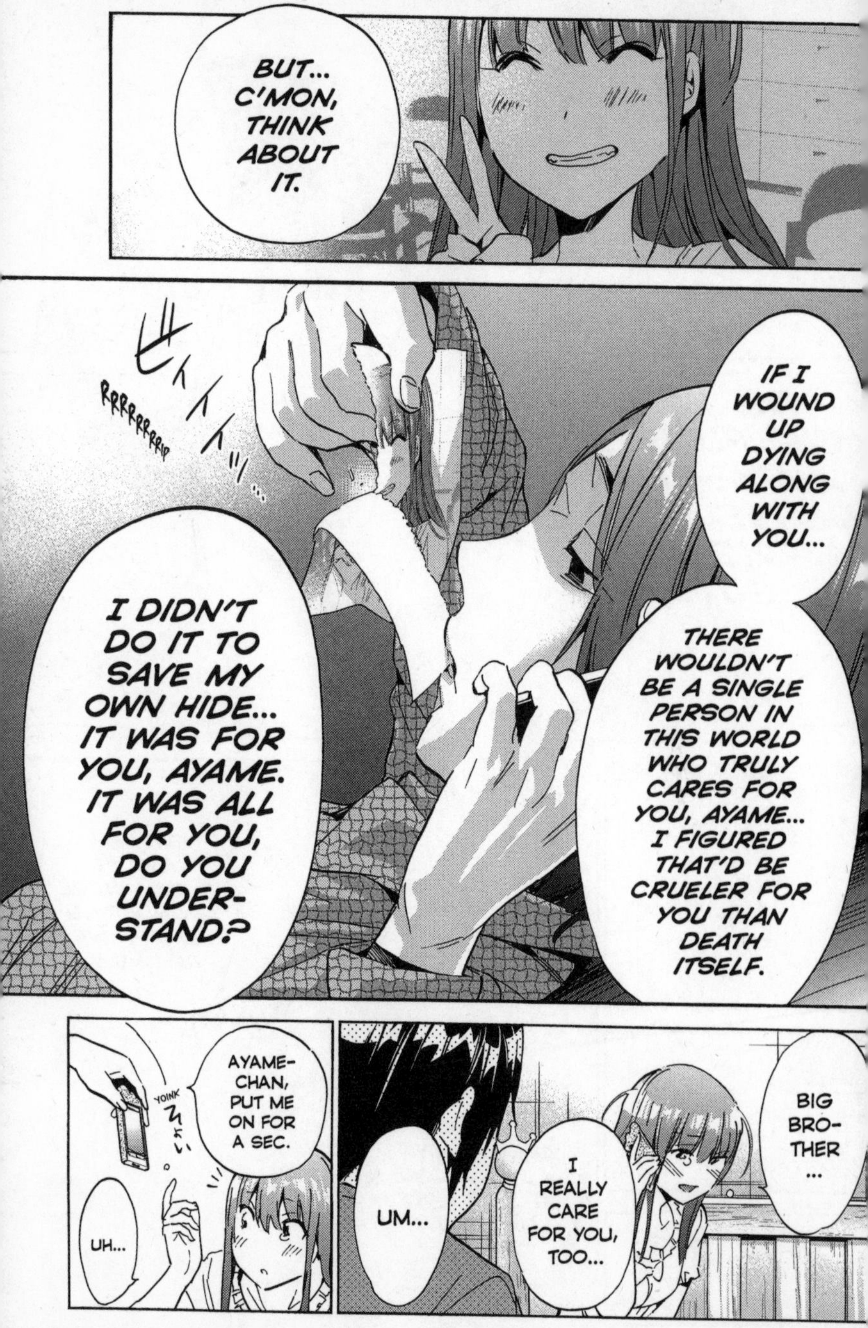
BUT... C'MON, THINK ABOUT IT.
IF I WOUND UP DYING ALONG WITH YOU...
THERE WOULDN'T BE A SINGLE PERSON IN THIS WORLD WHO TRULY CARES FOR YOU, AYAME... I FIGURED THAT'D BE CRUELER FOR YOU THAN DEATH ITSELF.
RRRRRRRRRIP
I DIDN'T DO IT TO SAVE MY OWN HIDE... IT WAS FOR YOU, AYAME. IT WAS ALL FOR YOU, DO YOU UNDER-STAND?
BIG BRO-THER...
I REALLY CARE FOR YOU, TOO...
UM...
AYAME-CHAN, PUT ME ON FOR A SEC.
YOINK
UH...

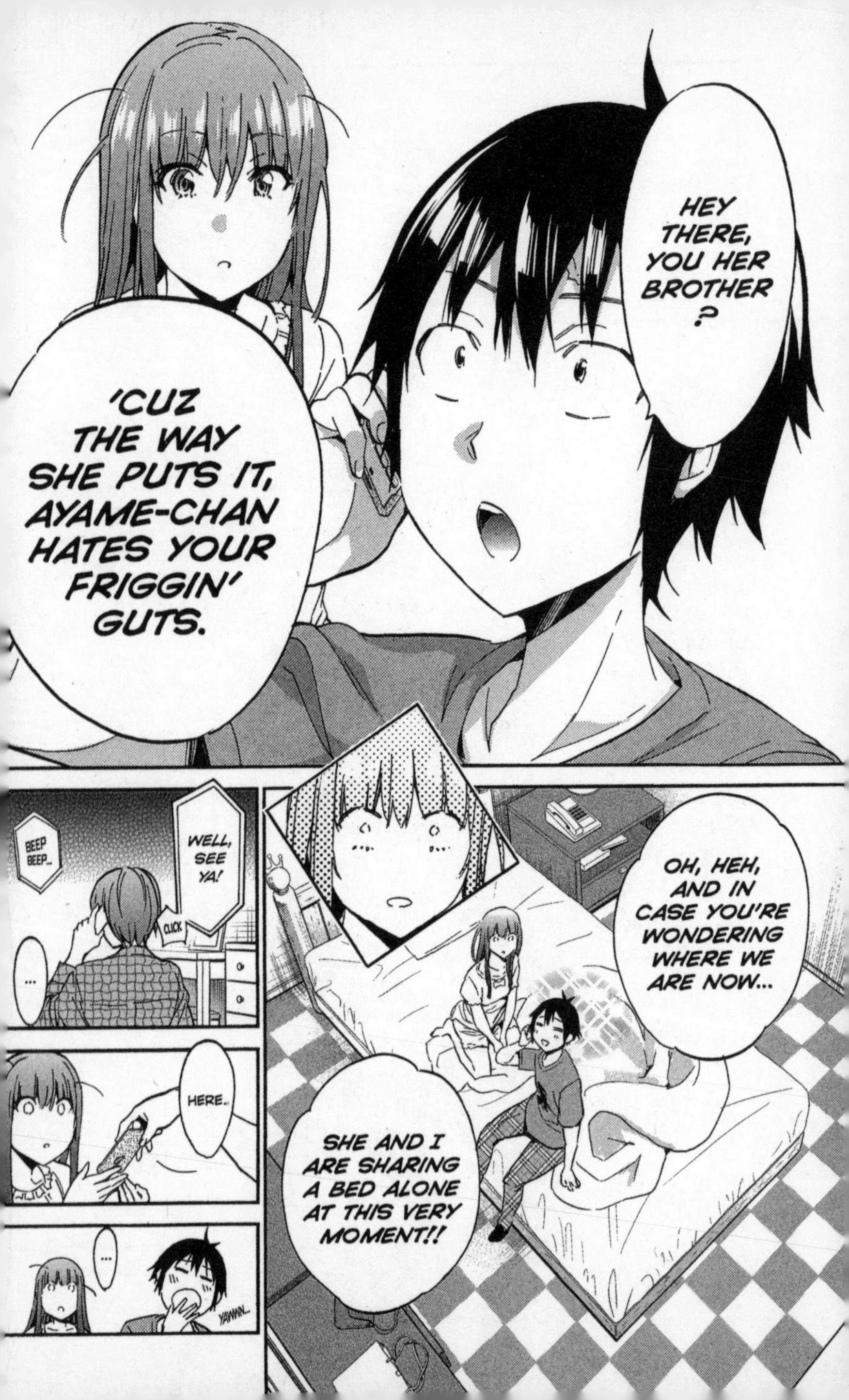
HEY THERE, YOU HER BROTHER?
'CUZ THE WAY SHE PUTS IT, AYAME-CHAN HATES YOUR FRIGGIN' GUTS.
OH, HEH, AND IN CASE YOU'RE WONDERING WHERE WE ARE NOW...
SHE AND I ARE SHARING A BED ALONE AT THIS VERY MOMENT!!
WELL, SEE YA!
BEEP BEEP...
CLICK
...
HERE..
...
YAWWN...

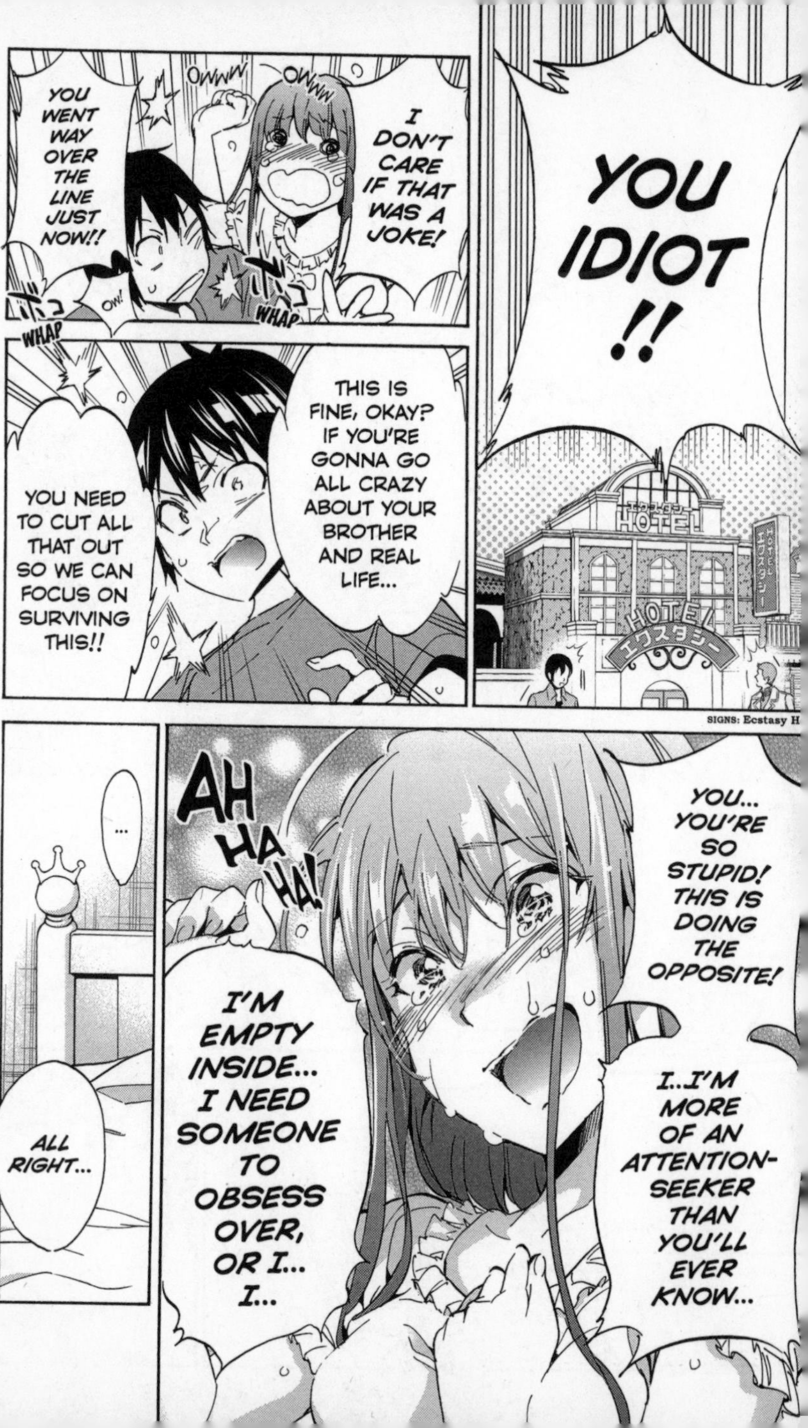
YOU IDIOT!!
HOTEL
HOTEL エクスタシー
OWWW
OWWW
I DON'T CARE IF THAT WAS A JOKE!
YOU WENT WAY OVER THE LINE JUST NOW!!
WHAP
OW!
WHAP
THIS IS FINE, OKAY? IF YOU'RE GONNA GO ALL CRAZY ABOUT YOUR BROTHER AND REAL LIFE...
YOU NEED TO CUT ALL THAT OUT SO WE CAN FOCUS ON SURVIVING THIS!!
YOU... YOU'RE SO STUPID! THIS IS DOING THE OPPOSITE!
AH HA HA!
I..I'M MORE OF AN ATTENTION-SEEKER THAN YOU'LL EVER KNOW...
I'M EMPTY INSIDE... I NEED SOMEONE TO OBSESS OVER, OR I... I...
...
ALL RIGHT...
SIGNS: Ecstasy H

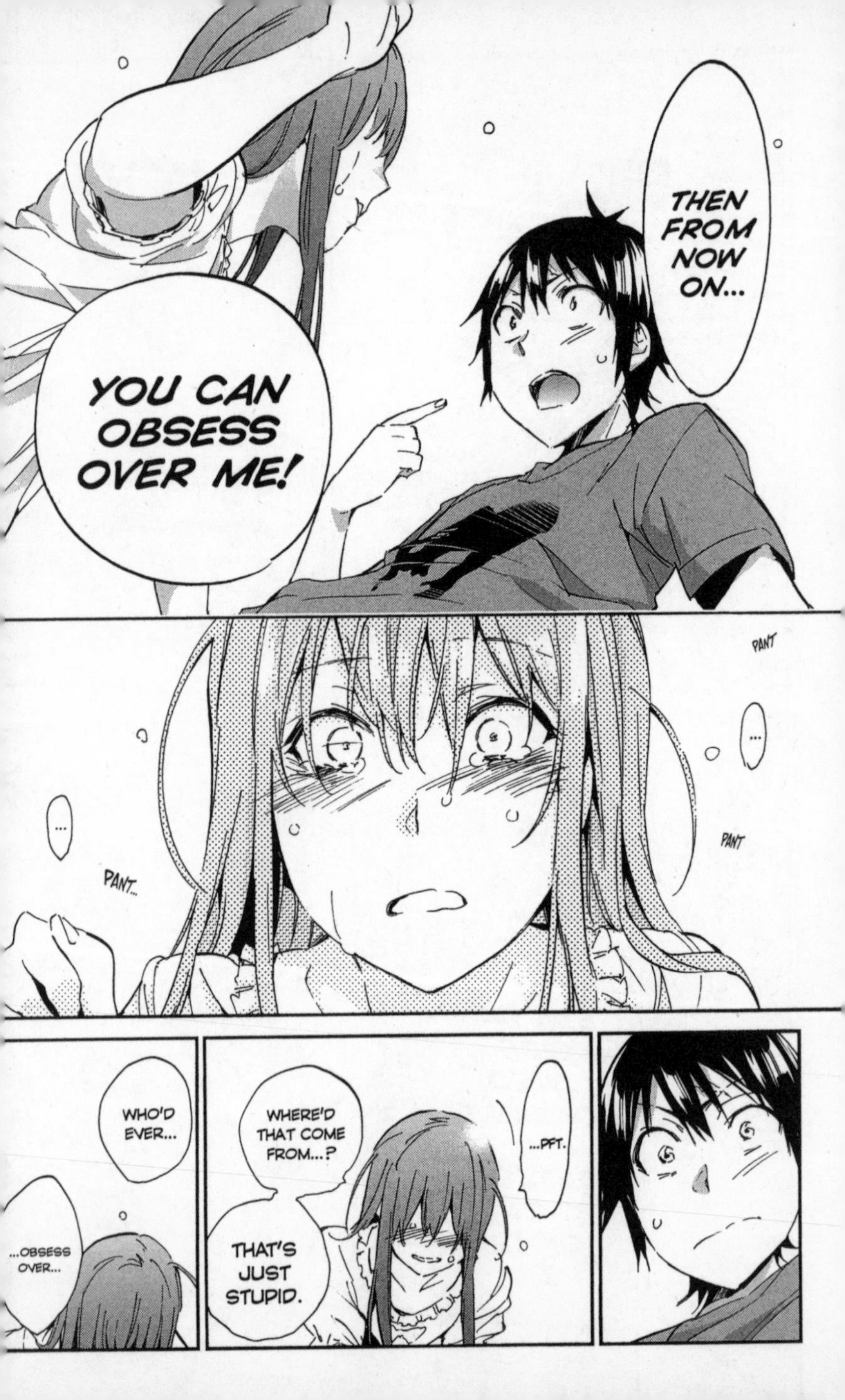
THEN FROM NOW ON...
YOU CAN OBSESS OVER ME!
PANT
...
PANT
...
PANT...
...PFT.
WHERE'D THAT COME FROM...?
THAT'S JUST STUPID.
WHO'D EVER...
...OBSESS OVER...

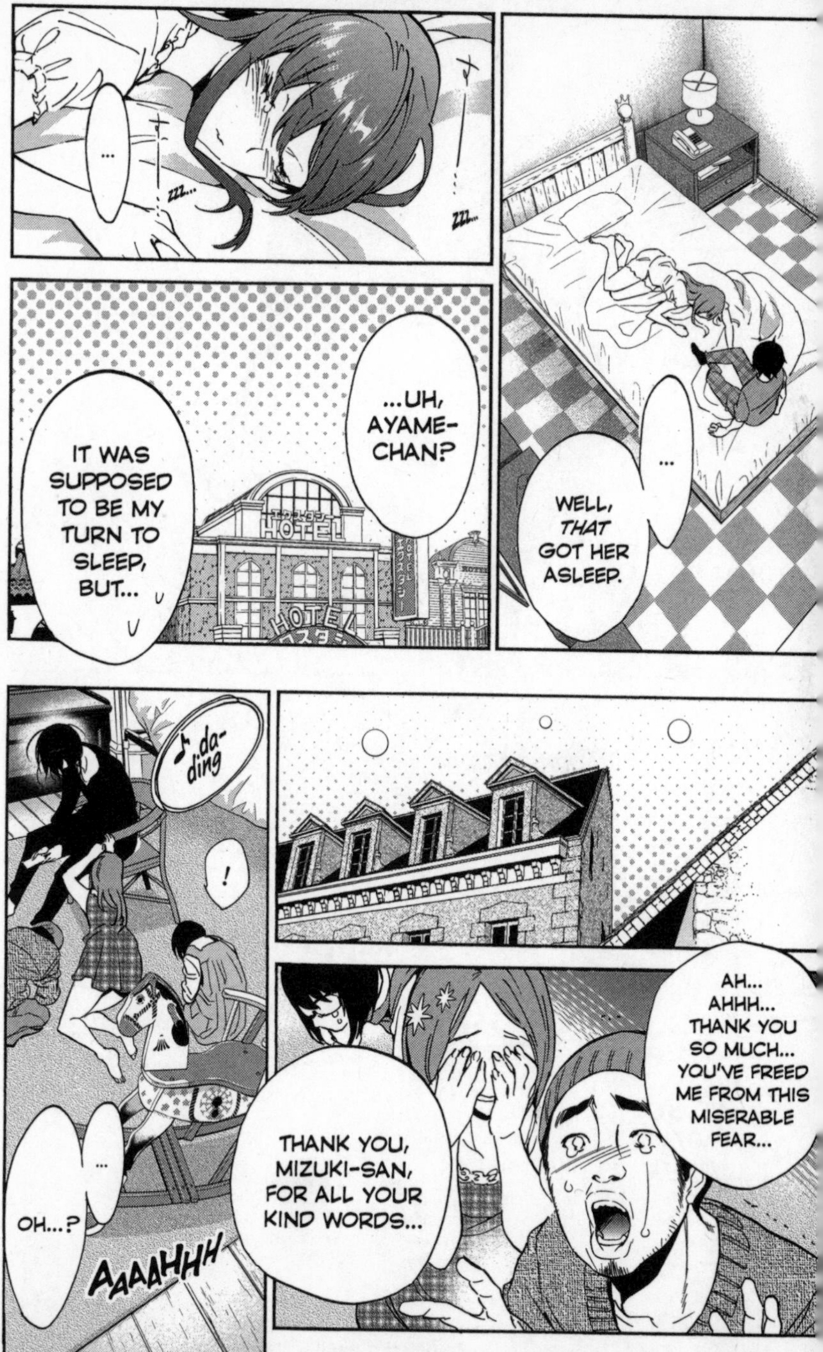
...
WELL, *THAT* GOT HER ASLEEP.
...
zzz...
zzz...
...UH, AYAME-CHAN?
IT WAS SUPPOSED TO BE MY TURN TO SLEEP, BUT...
AH... AHHH... THANK YOU SO MUCH... YOU'VE FREED ME FROM THIS MISERABLE FEAR...
THANK YOU, MIZUKI-SAN, FOR ALL YOUR KIND WORDS...
♪ da-ding
!
...
OH...?
AAAAHHH

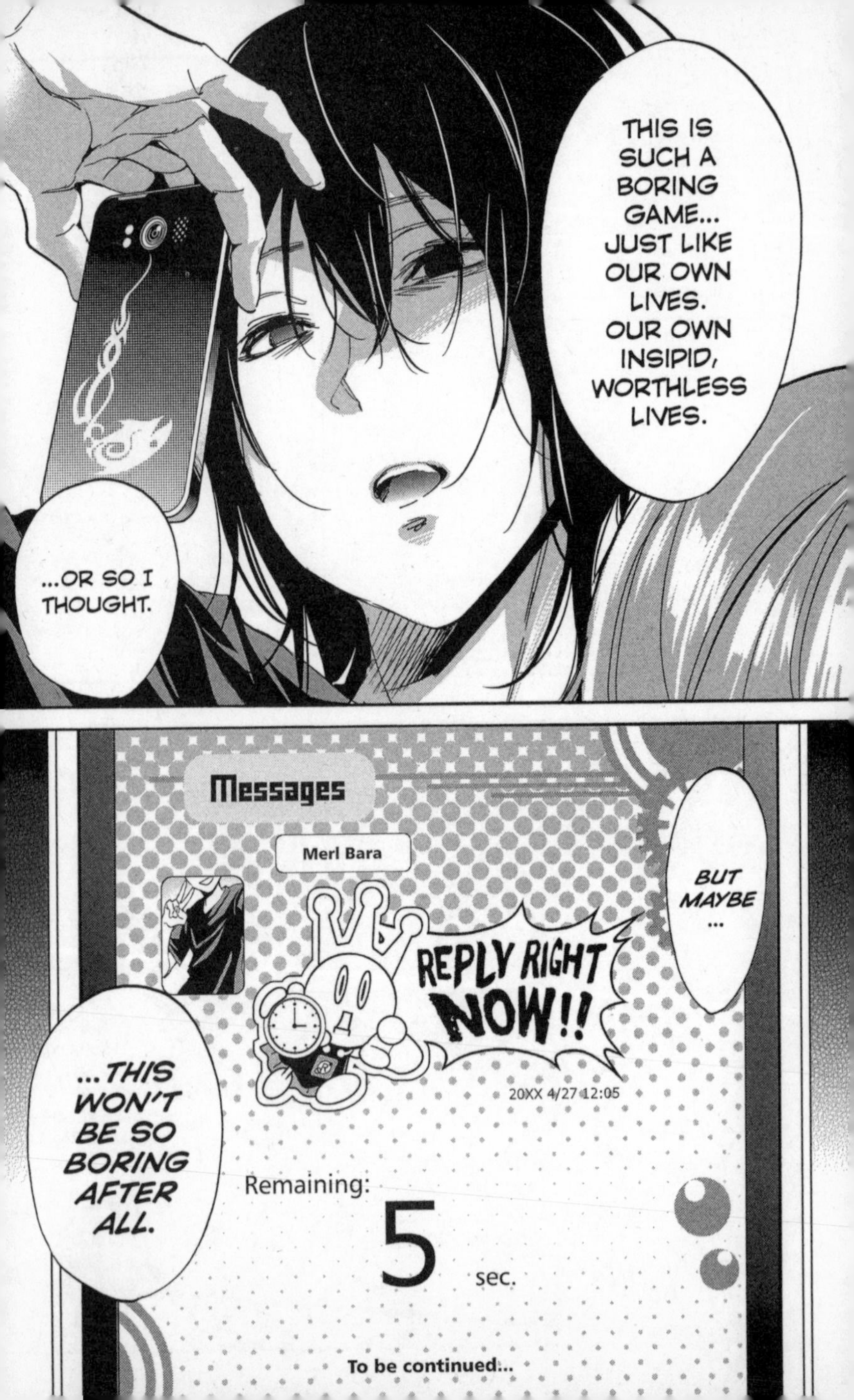
THIS IS SUCH A BORING GAME... JUST LIKE OUR OWN LIVES. OUR OWN INSIPID, WORTHLESS LIVES.
...OR SO I THOUGHT.
BUT MAYBE ...
Messages
Merl Bara
REPLY RIGHT NOW!!
20XX 4/27 12:05
...THIS WON'T BE SO BORING AFTER ALL.
Remaining:
5 sec.
To be continued...

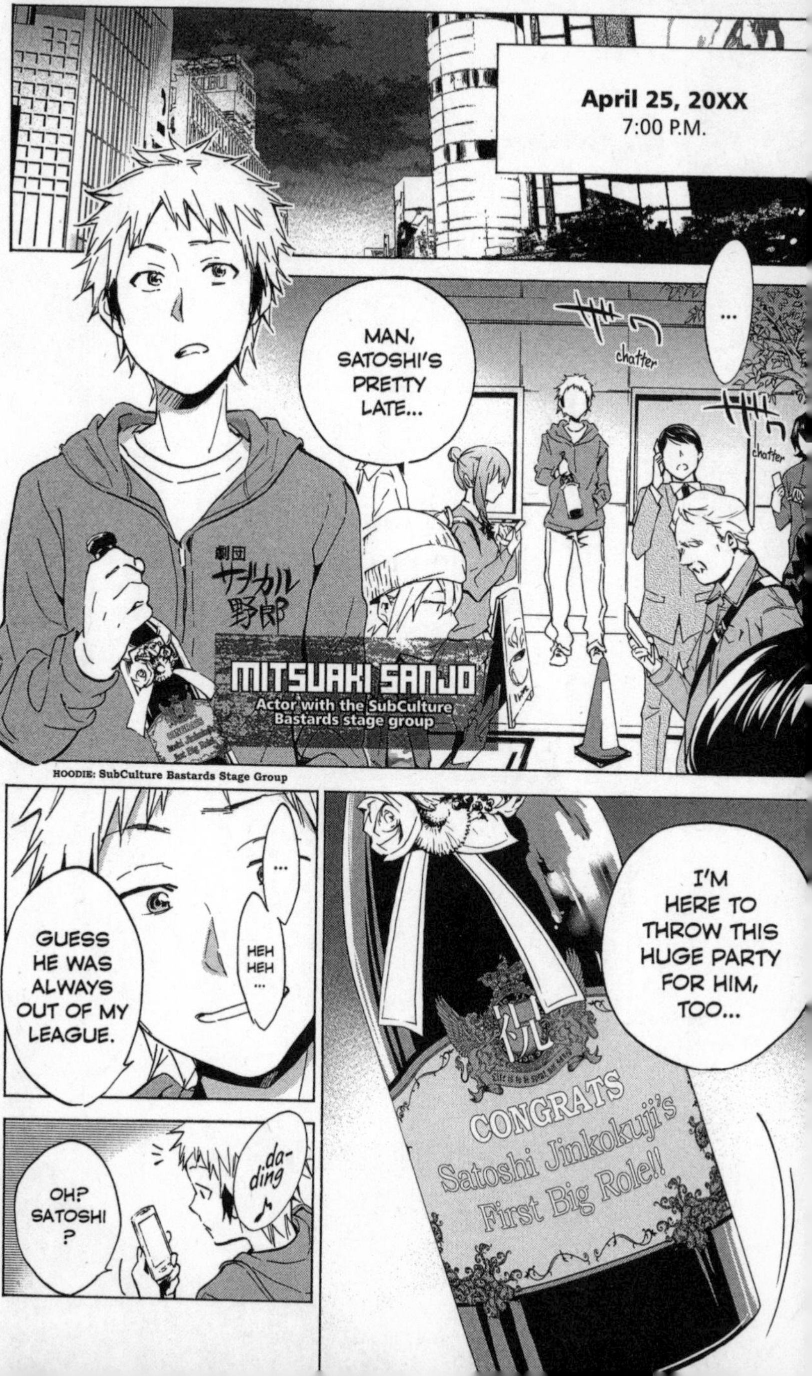
April 25, 20XX
7:00 P.M.
...
chatter
MAN, SATOSHI'S PRETTY LATE...
chatter
劇団
サブカル野郎
MITSUAKI SANJO
Actor with the SubCulture Bastards stage group
HOODIE: SubCulture Bastards Stage Group
I'M HERE TO THROW THIS HUGE PARTY FOR HIM, TOO...
祝
CONGRATS
Satoshi Jinkokuji's
First Big Role!!
...
HEH HEH ...
GUESS HE WAS ALWAYS OUT OF MY LEAGUE.
da-ding
OH? SATOSHI ?

EXTRA Live from Reality

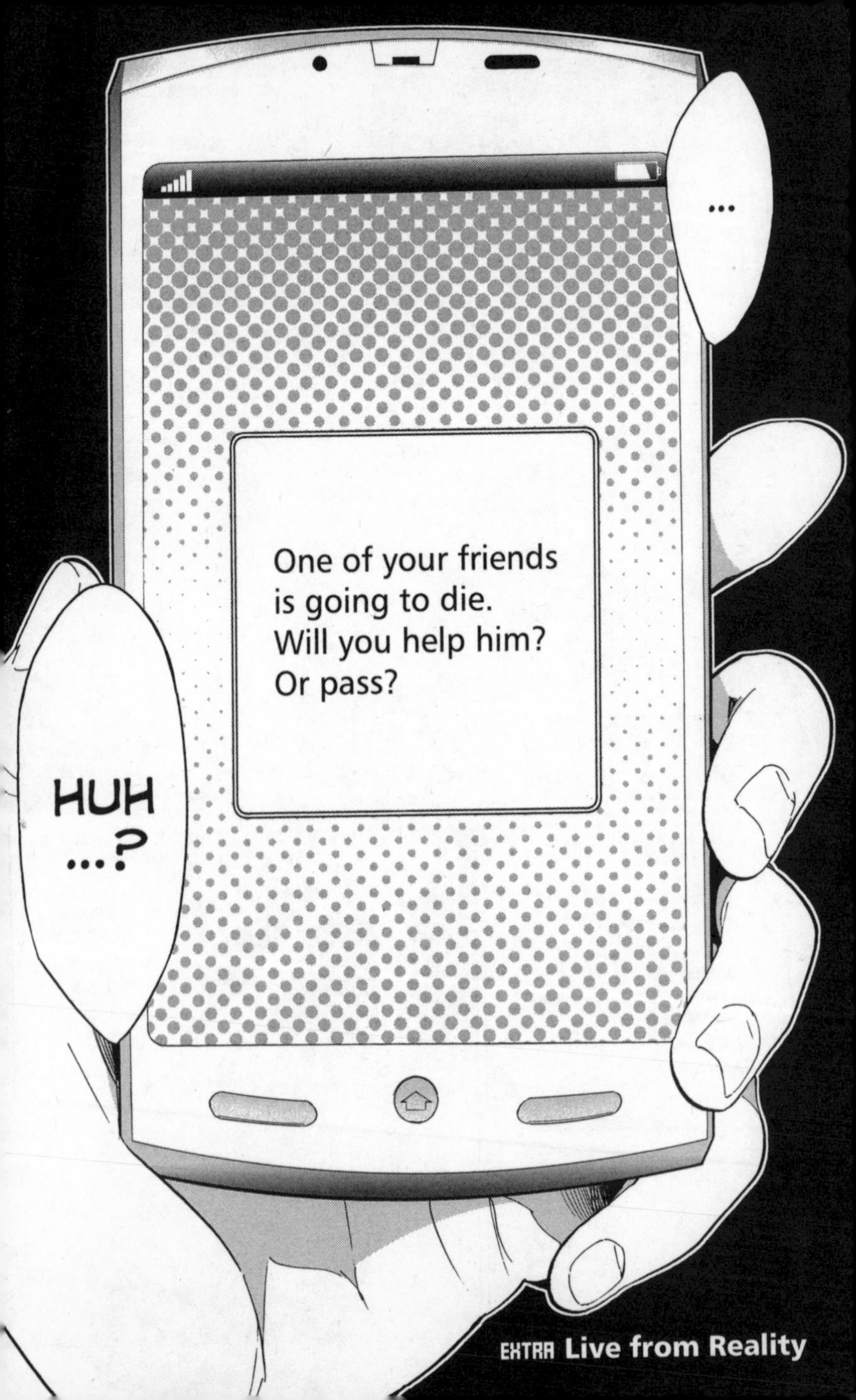
...
One of your friends is going to die. Will you help him? Or pass?
HUH ...?

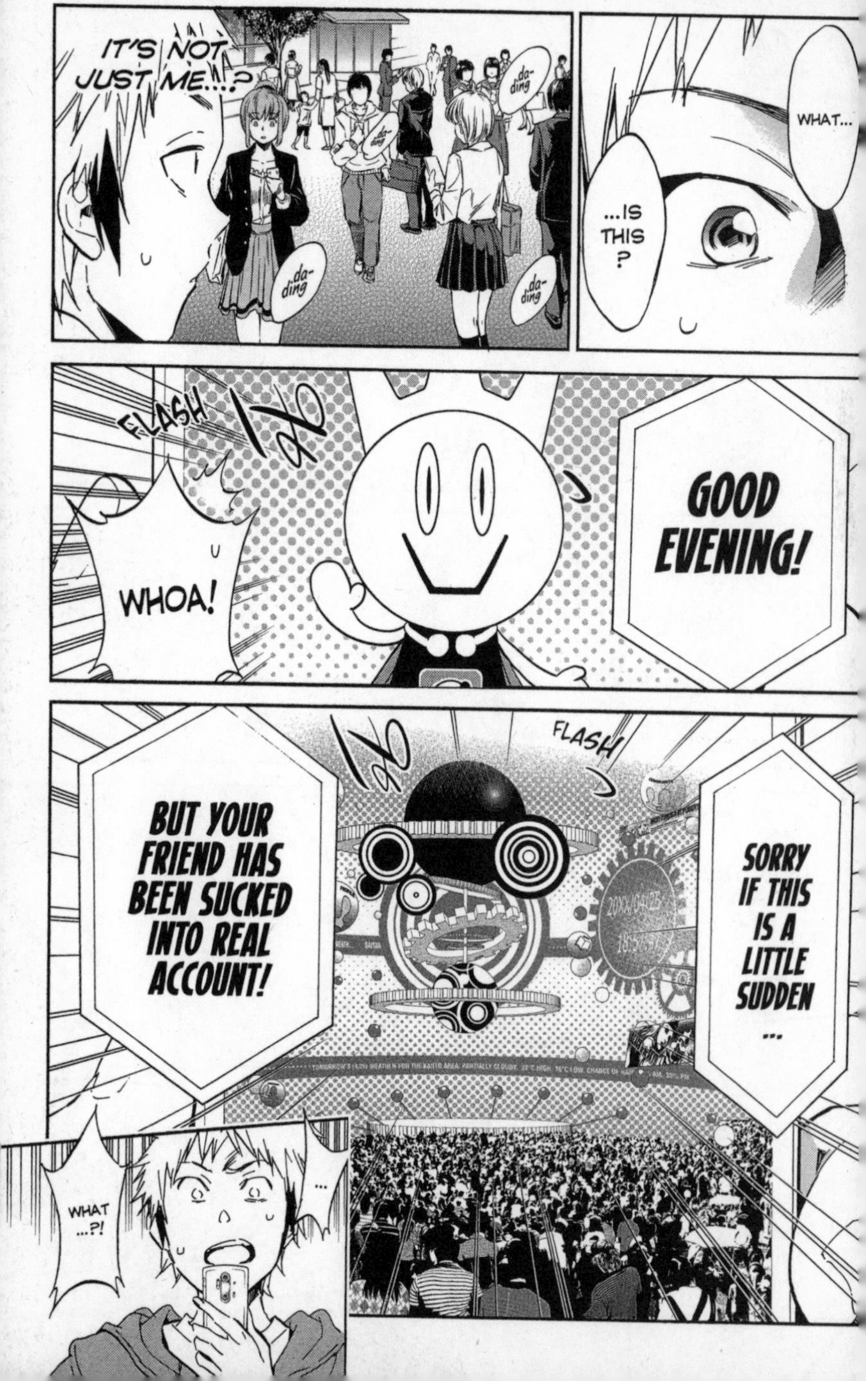
WHAT...
...IS THIS?
IT'S NOT JUST ME...!?
da-ding
da-ding
da-ding
da-ding
GOOD EVENING!
FLASH
WHOA!
SORRY IF THIS IS A LITTLE SUDDEN...
FLASH
BUT YOUR FRIEND HAS BEEN SUCKED INTO REAL ACCOUNT!
...
WHAT...?!

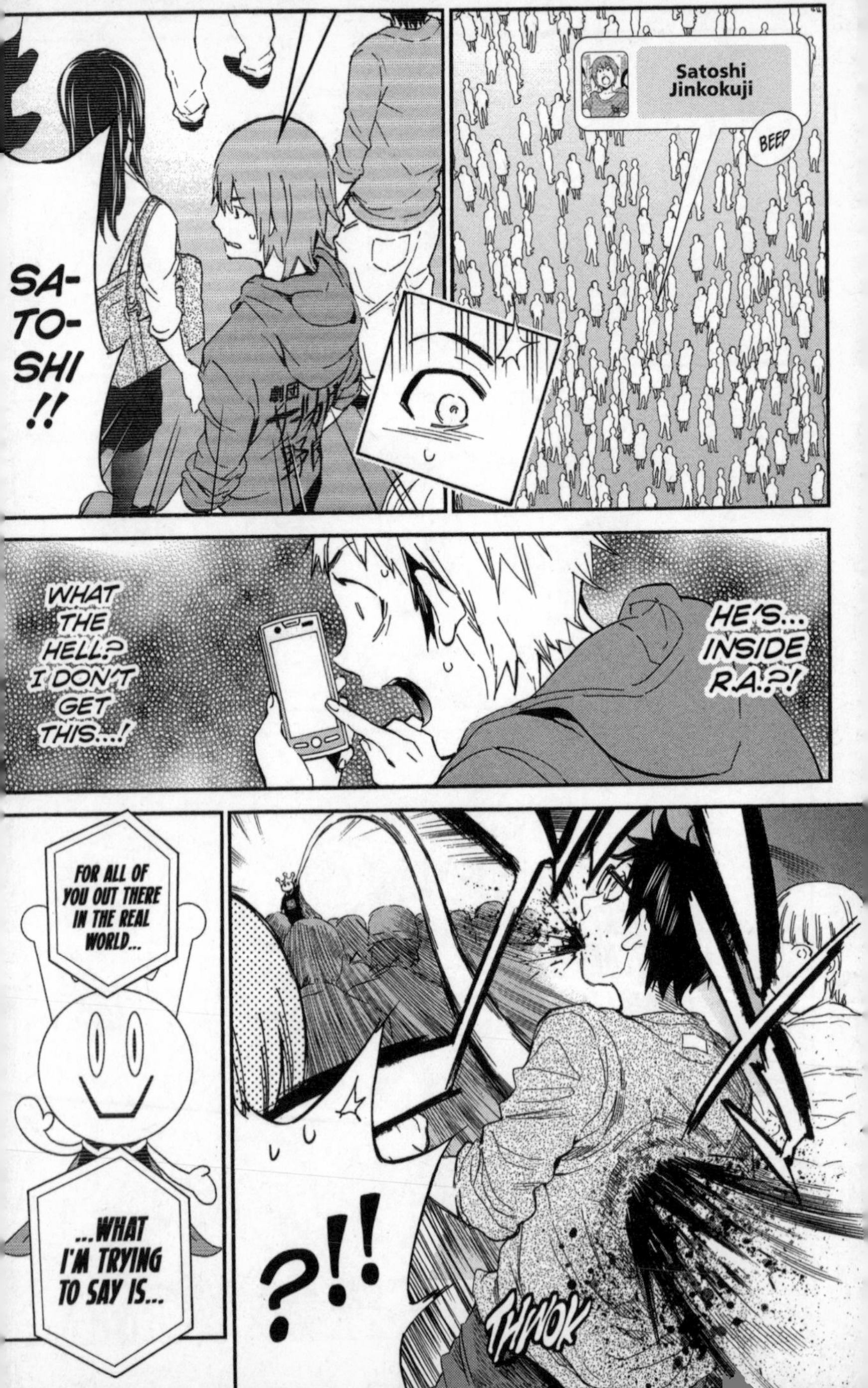
Satoshi Jinkokuji
BEEP
SA-TO-SHI !!
HE'S... INSIDE R.A.?!
WHAT THE HELL? I DON'T GET THIS...!
?!!
THWOK
FOR ALL OF YOU OUT THERE IN THE REAL WORLD...
...WHAT I'M TRYING TO SAY IS...

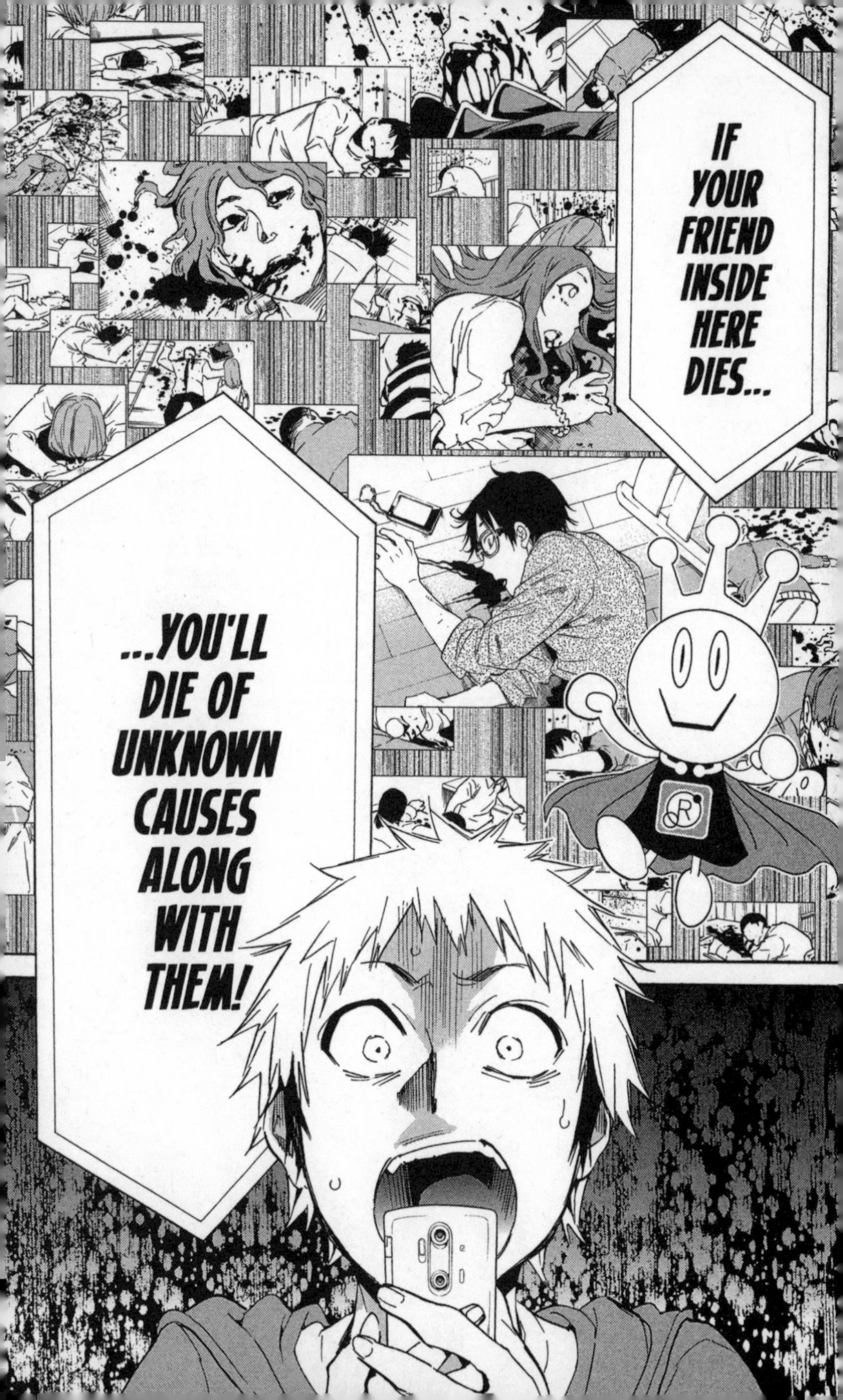
IF YOUR FRIEND INSIDE HERE DIES...
...YOU'LL DIE OF UNKNOWN CAUSES ALONG WITH THEM!

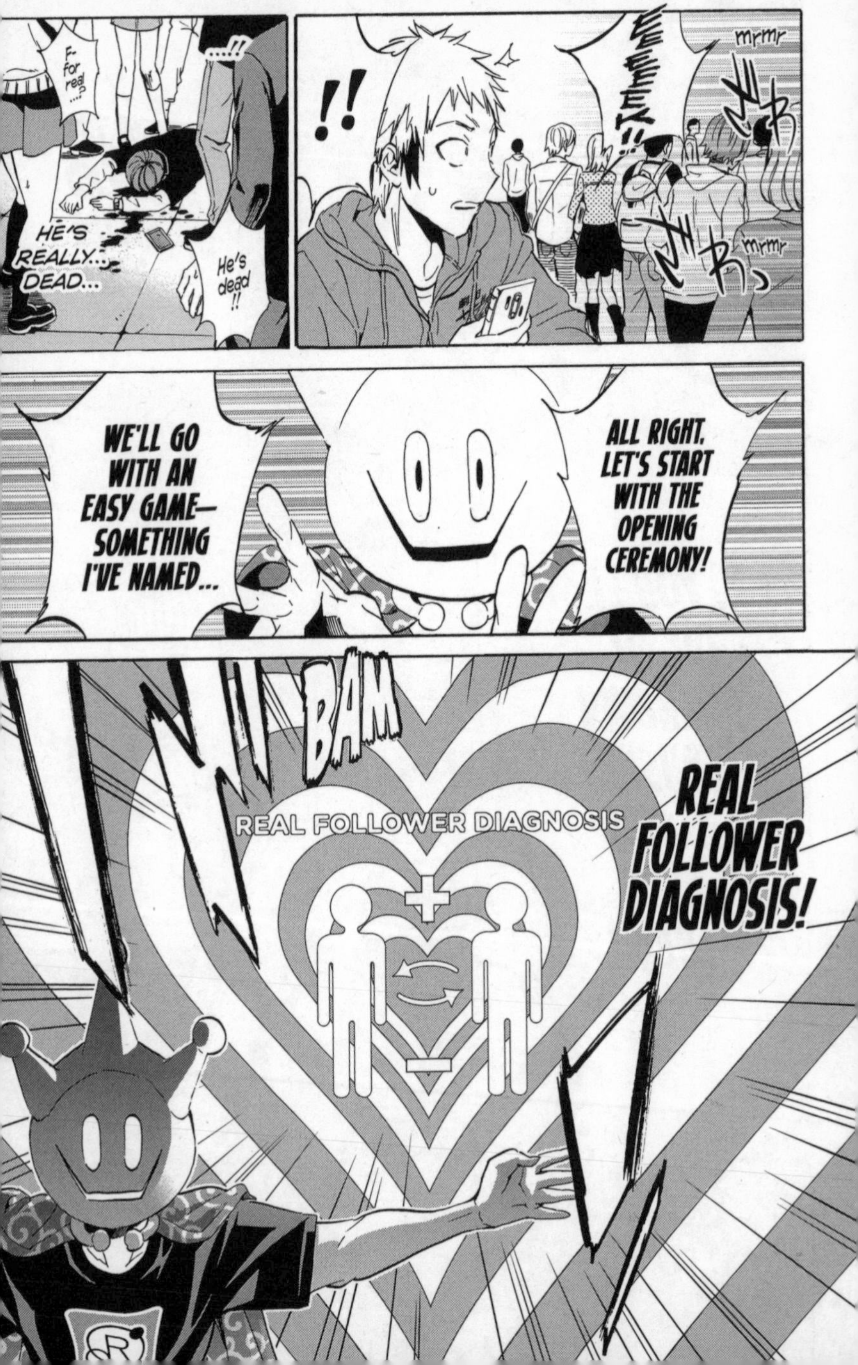
EEEEEY!!
mrmr
mrmr
!!
...!!
F-for real...?
HE'S REALLY... DEAD...
He's dead!!
ALL RIGHT. LET'S START WITH THE OPENING CEREMONY!
WE'LL GO WITH AN EASY GAME—SOMETHING I'VE NAMED...
REAL FOLLOWER DIAGNOSIS!
BAM
REAL FOLLOWER DIAGNOSIS

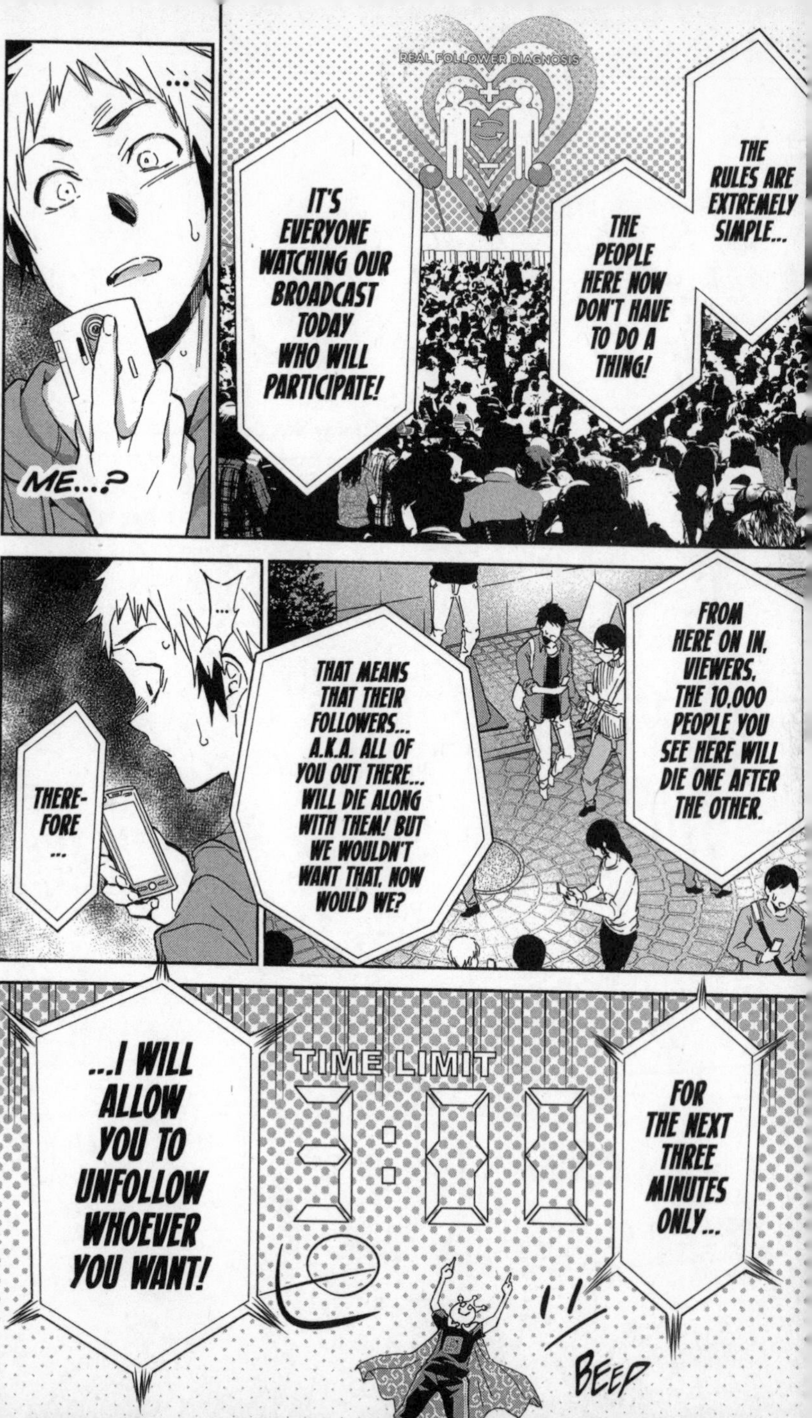
REAL FOLLOWER DIAGNOSIS
THE RULES ARE EXTREMELY SIMPLE...
THE PEOPLE HERE NOW DON'T HAVE TO DO A THING!
IT'S EVERYONE WATCHING OUR BROADCAST TODAY WHO WILL PARTICIPATE!
...
ME...?
FROM HERE ON IN, VIEWERS, THE 10,000 PEOPLE YOU SEE HERE WILL DIE ONE AFTER THE OTHER.
THAT MEANS THAT THEIR FOLLOWERS... A.K.A. ALL OF YOU OUT THERE... WILL DIE ALONG WITH THEM! BUT WE WOULDN'T WANT THAT, NOW WOULD WE?
...
THERE-FORE ...
FOR THE NEXT THREE MINUTES ONLY...
TIME LIMIT
3:00
...I WILL ALLOW YOU TO UNFOLLOW WHOEVER YOU WANT!
BEEP

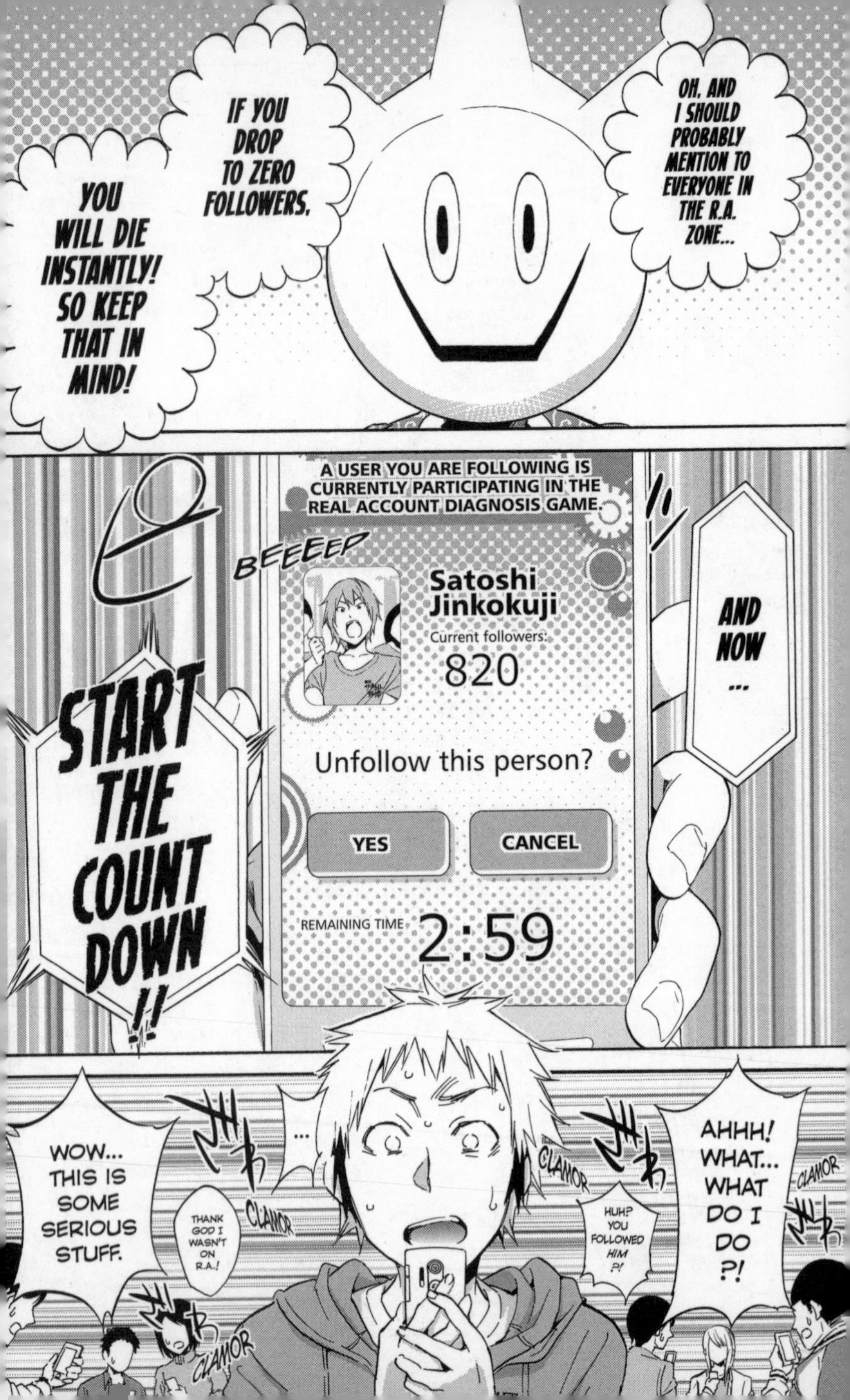
OH, AND I SHOULD PROBABLY MENTION TO EVERYONE IN THE R.A. ZONE...
IF YOU DROP TO ZERO FOLLOWERS,
YOU WILL DIE INSTANTLY! SO KEEP THAT IN MIND!
AND NOW ...
A USER YOU ARE FOLLOWING IS CURRENTLY PARTICIPATING IN THE REAL ACCOUNT DIAGNOSIS GAME.
Satoshi Jinkokuji
Current followers:
820
Unfollow this person?
YES
CANCEL
REMAINING TIME
2:59
BEEEEEP
START THE COUNT DOWN!!
AHHH! WHAT... WHAT DO I DO?!
CLAMOR
HUH? YOU FOLLOWED HIM?!
CLAMOR
...
THANK GOD I WASN'T ON R.A.!
CLAMOR
WOW... THIS IS SOME SERIOUS STUFF.
CLAMOR

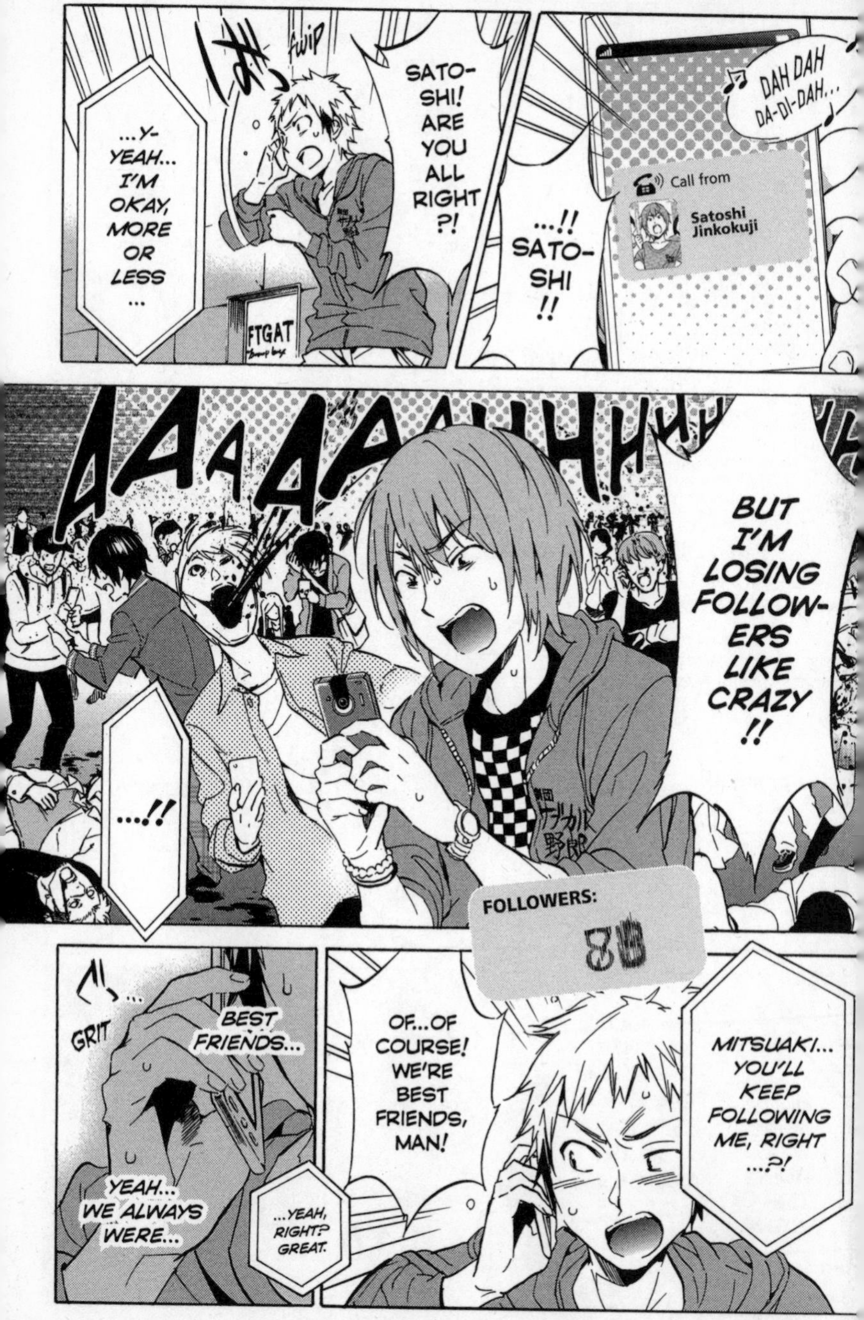
DAH DAH DA-DI-DAH...
Call from
Satoshi Jinkokuji
...!! SATO-SHI !!
fwip
SATO-SHI! ARE YOU ALL RIGHT?!
...Y-YEAH... I'M OKAY, MORE OR LESS...
FTGAT
AAAAAHHHH
BUT I'M LOSING FOLLOW-ERS LIKE CRAZY!!
...!!
FOLLOWERS:
MITSUAKI... YOU'LL KEEP FOLLOWING ME, RIGHT...?!
OF...OF COURSE! WE'RE BEST FRIENDS, MAN!
...YEAH, RIGHT? GREAT.
BEST FRIENDS...
GRIT
YEAH... WE ALWAYS WERE...

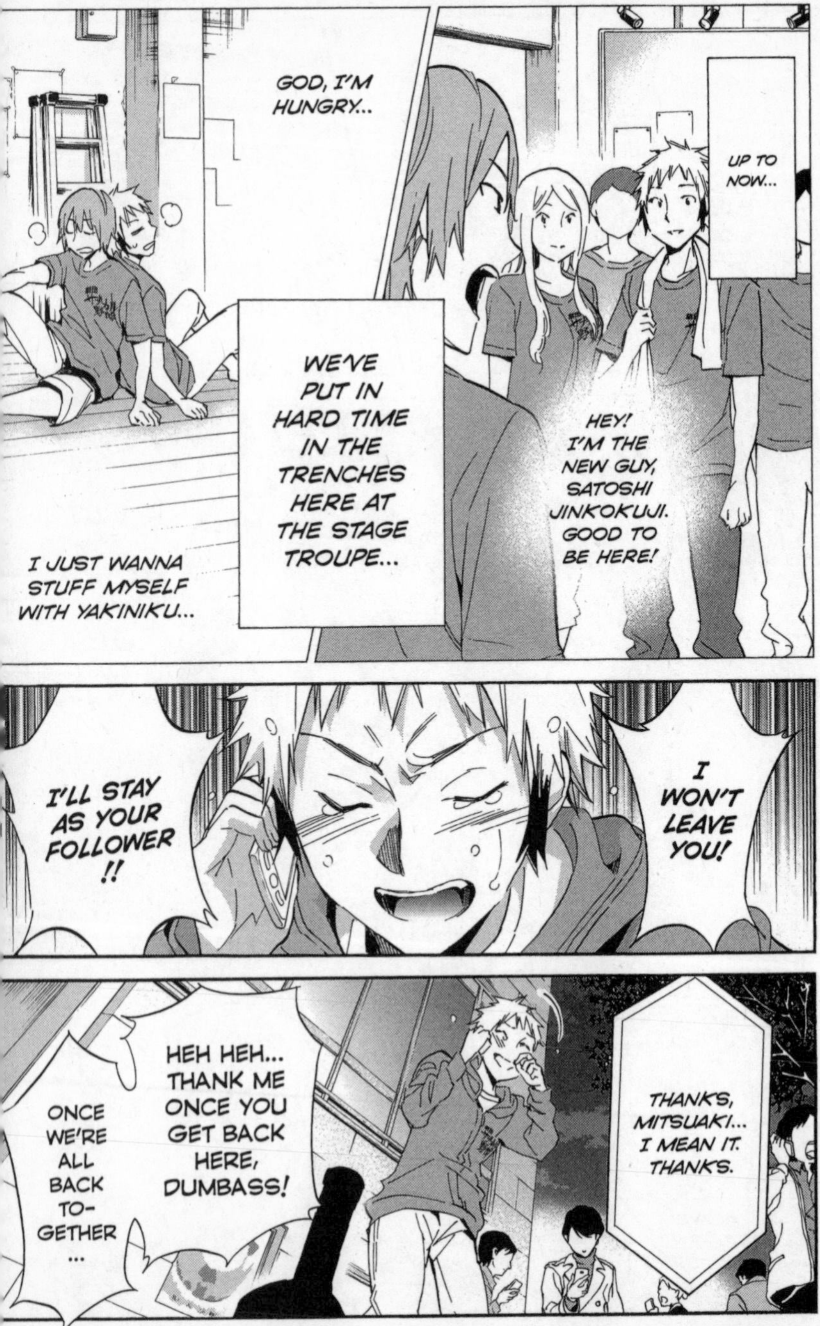
UP TO NOW...
HEY! I'M THE NEW GUY, SATOSHI JINKOKUJI. GOOD TO BE HERE!
WE'VE PUT IN HARD TIME IN THE TRENCHES HERE AT THE STAGE TROUPE...
GOD, I'M HUNGRY...
I JUST WANNA STUFF MYSELF WITH YAKINIKU...
I WON'T LEAVE YOU!
I'LL STAY AS YOUR FOLLOWER!!
THANKS, MITSUAKI... I MEAN IT. THANKS.
HEH HEH... THANK ME ONCE YOU GET BACK HERE, DUMBASS!
ONCE WE'RE ALL BACK TO-GETHER...

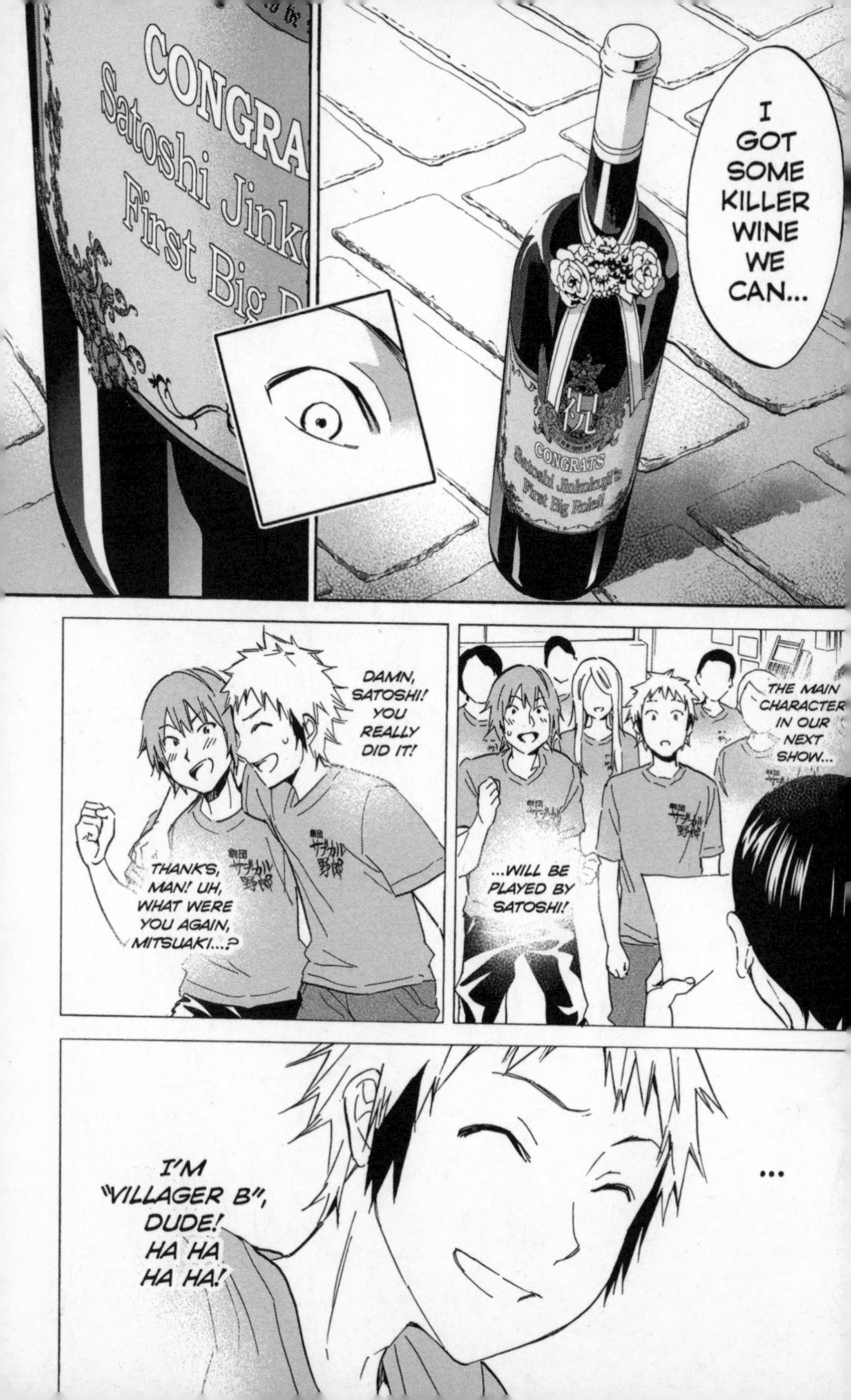
CONGRA
Satoshi Jink
First Big R
祝
CONGRATS
Satoshi Jinkokuji's
First Big Role!!
I GOT SOME KILLER WINE WE CAN...
THE MAIN CHARACTER IN OUR NEXT SHOW...
...WILL BE PLAYED BY SATOSHI!
DAMN, SATOSHI! YOU REALLY DID IT!
THANKS, MAN! UH, WHAT WERE YOU AGAIN, MITSUAKI...?
...
I'M "VILLAGER B", DUDE! HA HA HA HA!

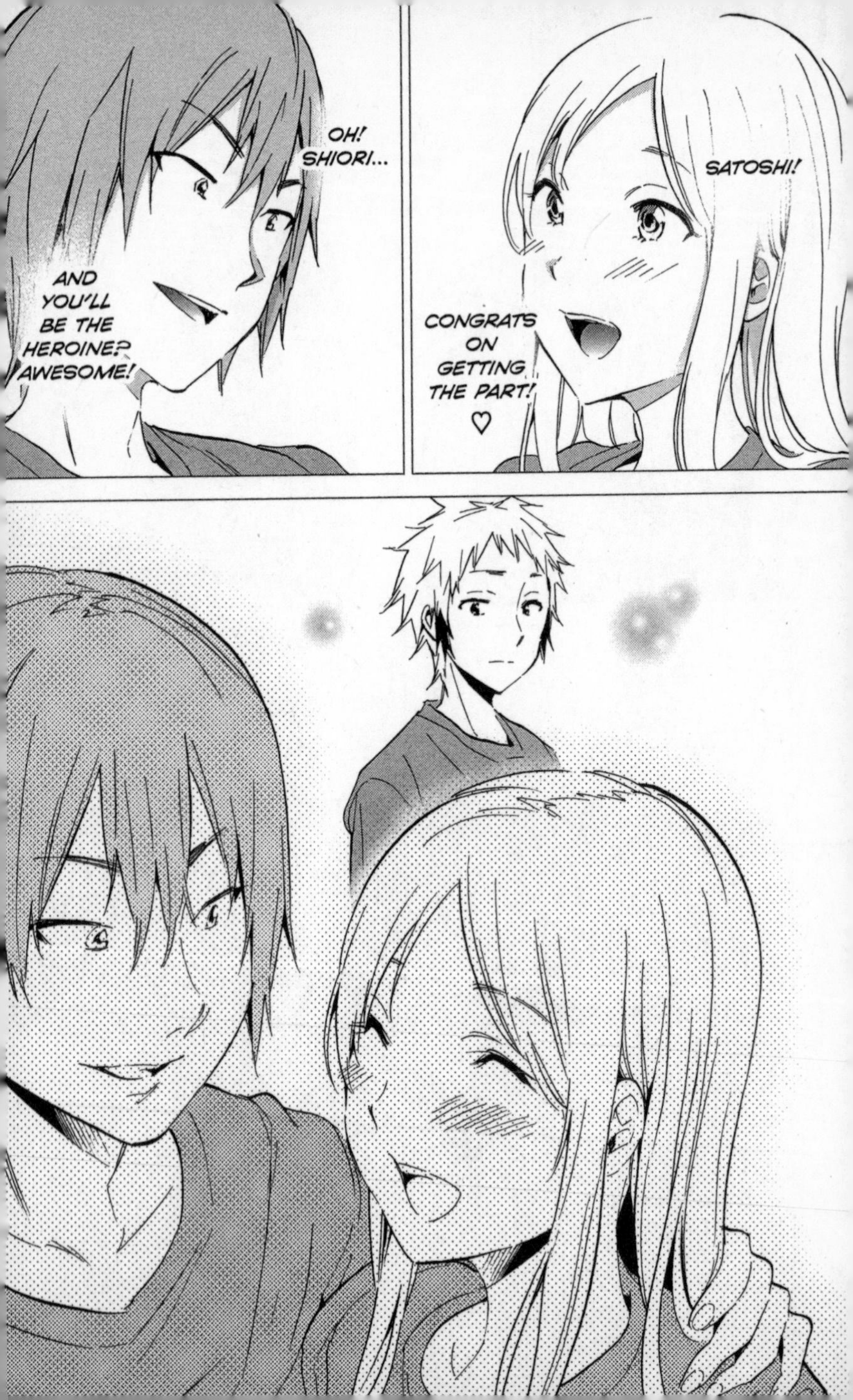
SATOSHI!
CONGRATS ON GETTING THE PART! ♡
OH! SHIORI...
AND YOU'LL BE THE HEROINE? AWESOME!

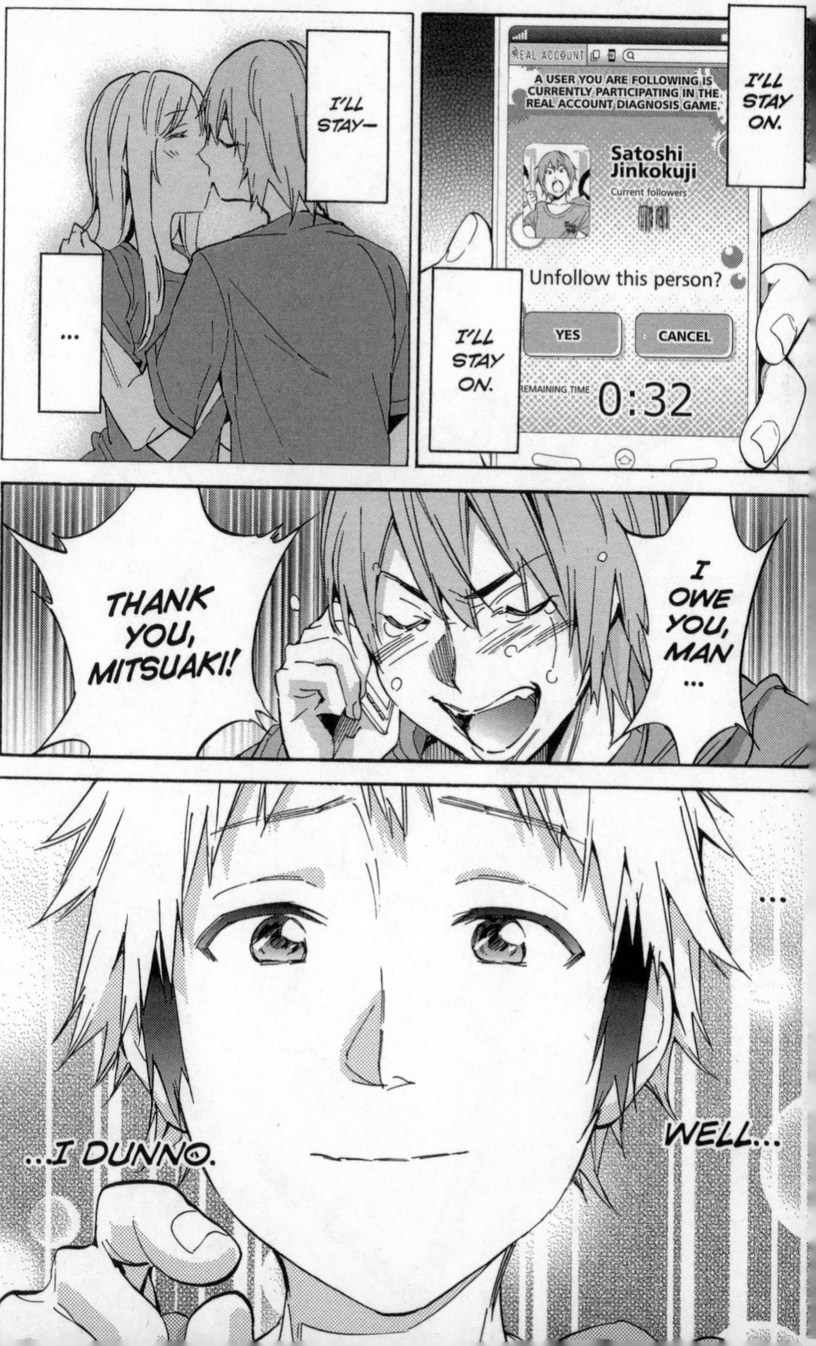
I'LL STAY ON.
REAL ACCOUNT
A USER YOU ARE FOLLOWING IS CURRENTLY PARTICIPATING IN THE REAL ACCOUNT DIAGNOSIS GAME.
Satoshi Jinkokuji
Current followers
Unfollow this person?
YES
CANCEL
REMAINING TIME
0:32
I'LL STAY ON.
I'LL STAY—
...
I OWE YOU, MAN ...
THANK YOU, MITSUAKI!
...
WELL...
...I DUNNO.

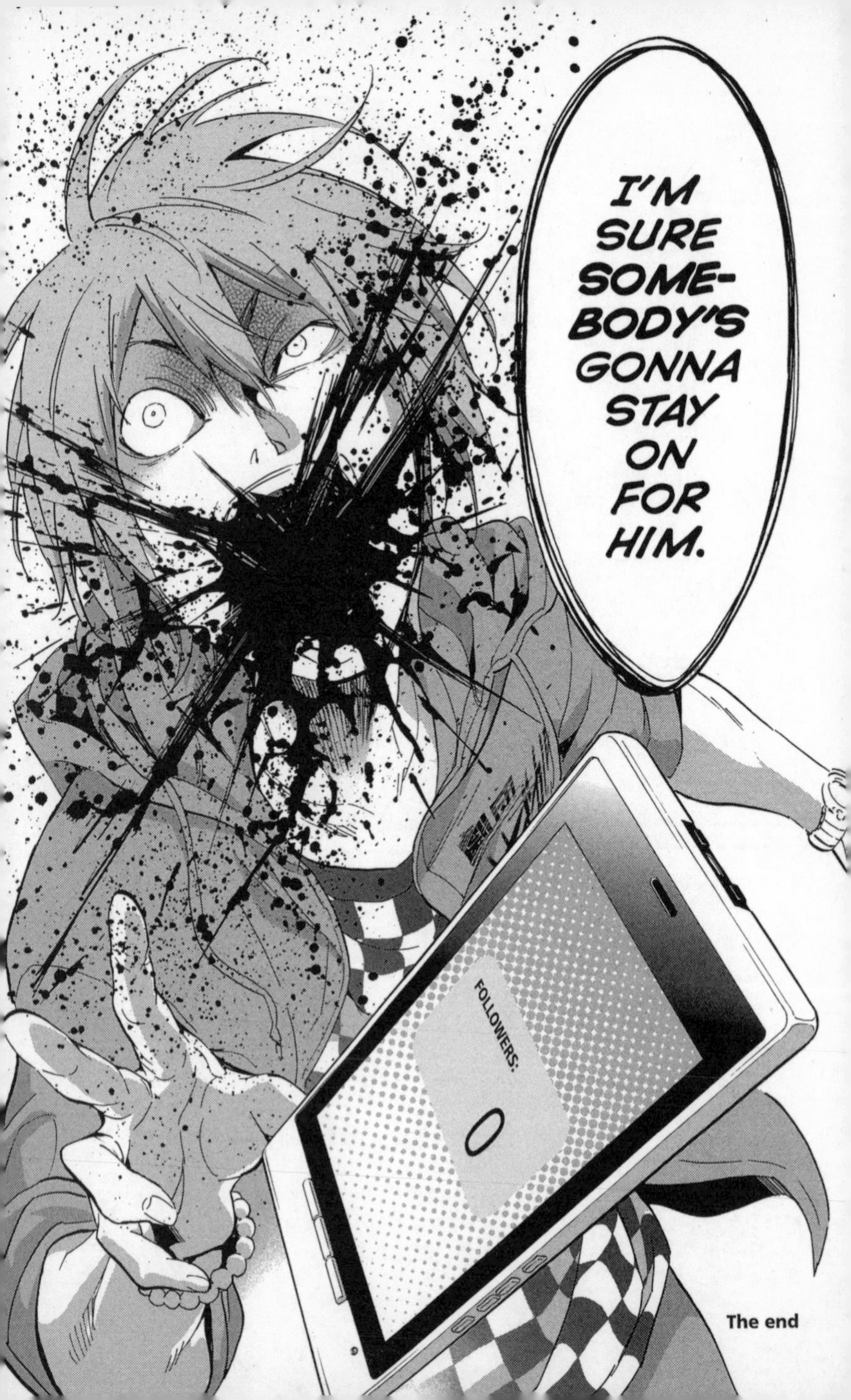
I'M SURE SOMEBODY'S GONNA STAY ON FOR HIM.
FOLLOWERS:
0
The end

Artist:
SHIZUMU WATANABE
Twitter account: @shizumukun
While drawing this manga and studying how things are with social media these days, I've found it odd how I feel both sad and tremendously relieved that the networks I used as a student aren't around anymore. Weird, isn't it?

Author:
OKUSHOU
Twitter account: @okushou
I got my first cell phone when I entered high school and immediately joined the social networks that were popular at the time. Now, nearly half of them are offline for good… I suppose someday the end will come for whatever social networks are popular today too. Although, personally, I have more bad memories about my high-school social network years than good…

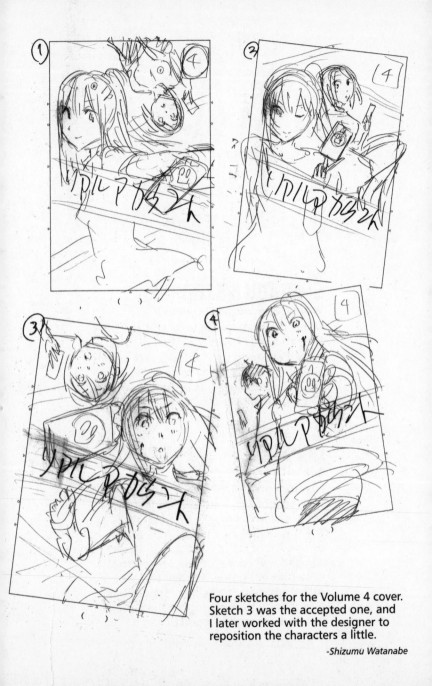

Four sketches for the Volume 4 cover.
Sketch 3 was the accepted one, and
I later worked with the designer to
reposition the characters a little.

-Shizumu Watanabe

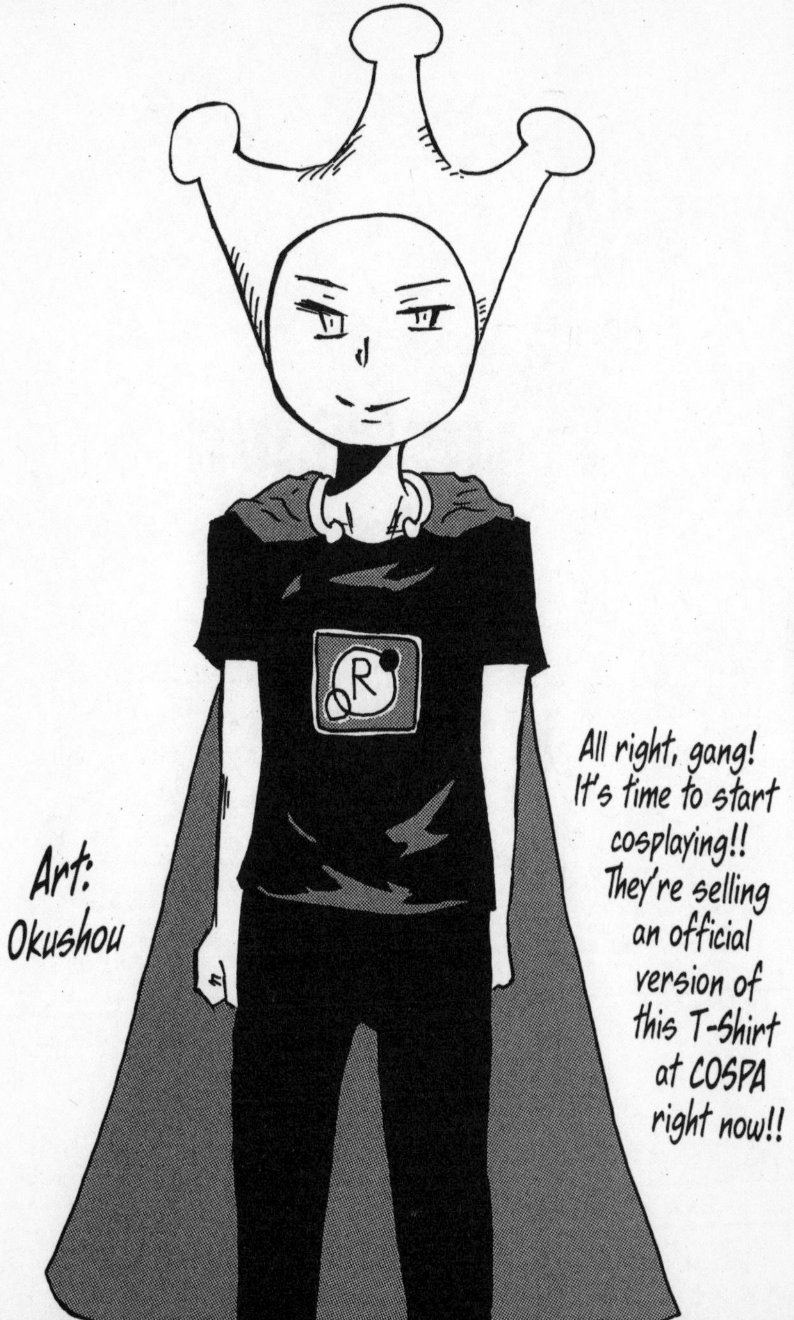
All right, gang! It's time to start cosplaying!! They're selling an official version of this T-Shirt at COSPA right now!!
Art: Okushou

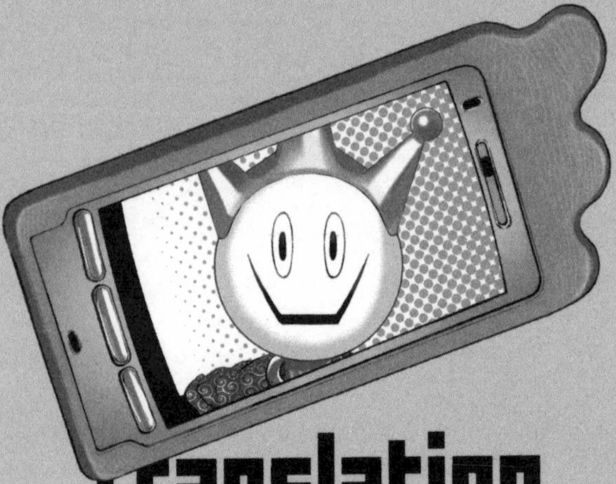

Translation Notes

PAGE 6

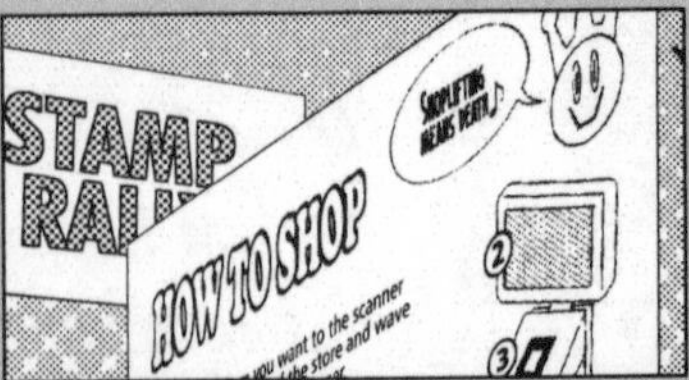
STAMP
SHOPLIFTING MEANS DEATH♪
HOW TO SHOP

STAMP RALLY
A "stamp rally" is a common sight at fairs or along train lines in Japan. Participants are given a blank sheet of paper to fill in with stamps available at each stop along the rally and can usually get an extra reward for getting all of the stamps on one sheet.

PAGE 4

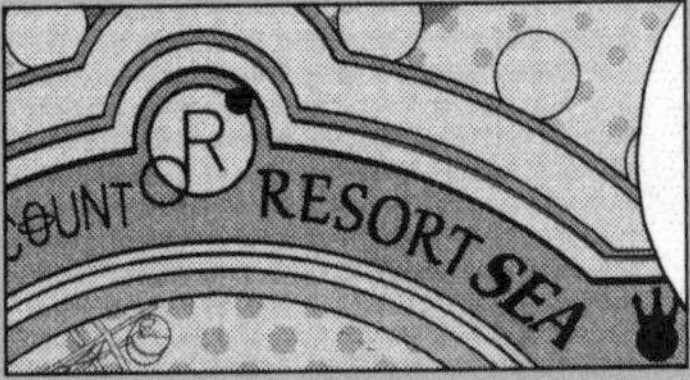
R
RESORT SEA

REAL ACCOUNT RESORT SEA
Many people outside of Japan may not think much about the fact that there is both a Real Account Resort and a Sea version of the resort. However, anyone familiar with Tokyo Disney would see the connection to Tokyo DisneySea, the second sea-themed park contained within the Tokyo Disney Resort.

PAGE 67

NAME:
SEX: Female
DATE OF BIRTH: Feb. 27
AFFILIATION: Part-timer
RELATIONSHIP STATUS: Single
FOLLOWING: 152
FOLLOWERS: 1
ABOUT ME:
no face pics! ✩ sorry! i guess people say i look kinda like Kyary tho

KYARY PAMYU PAMYU

Kyary Pamyu Pamyu is a Japanese fashion model, singer, blogger, and TV personality. Her debut single was the song "PonPonPon" and she is known for a bright, saccharine sweet image that takes Japanese cute fashion culture or "kawaii" to its extreme. Her producer is Yasutaka Nakata, a famous Japanese DJ and member of the electronica band CAPSULE. In addition to Kyary Pamyu Pamyu, he also produced Perfume.

PAGE 39

Kirika
sigh...
i'm so fat...凹

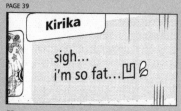

凹

This symbol is actually a Chinese character that represents the word "depression" in the sense of a hole or sunken area. If you look closely, it actually resembles exactly that. The word is also a homonym for depression as an affliction, and in this case, it's being used to express that Kirika is down in the dumps on account of her weight issues.

PAGE 84

R&A
MATOME
NEWS

MATOME SITES

"Matome sites" are round-up or aggregator sites that collect the best or most interesting threads on 2ch, twitter, and other websites to gather them in a single convenient spot. In some ways, this may be similar to /r/bestof on Reddit. The most famous matome site is Naver Matome (the same Naver that made Line), but these sites are usually administrated by individuals on their own sites with advertisements on them, leading to friction with some 2ch users who claim they're unethically profiting from their posts.

PAGE 75

YOU'RE A CROSS-TEXTER!

CROSS-TEXTER

"Cross-texter" is our take on *nekama*, a Japanese term for a man who poses as a women in online games or on social networks. It's a combination of the words "net" and "okama," a slang term for a homosexual man who is effeminate and may choose to dress as a woman.

PAGE 125

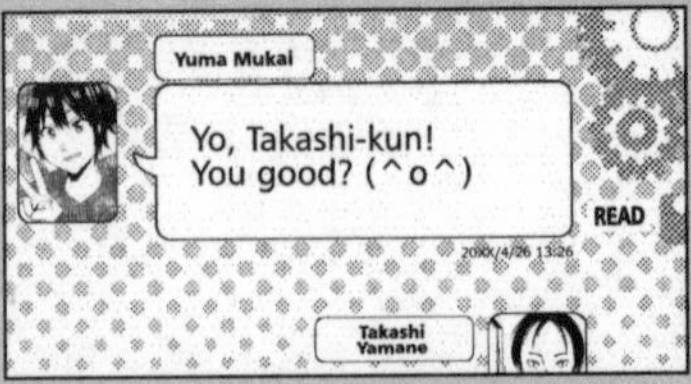
Yuma Mukai
Yo, Takashi-kun!
You good? (^o^)
READ
Takashi Yamane

HISTORY OF LINE AND "READ" STATUS

Line is a mobile chat application originally produced by the Korean online-search company, Naver. The application was originally created in response to the Great Tohoku Earthquake of 2011 and its key feature, read receipts, allows the sender of a message to see if the recipient has read their message. This was meant to allow people to see if victims of the disaster were still alive.

PAGE 92

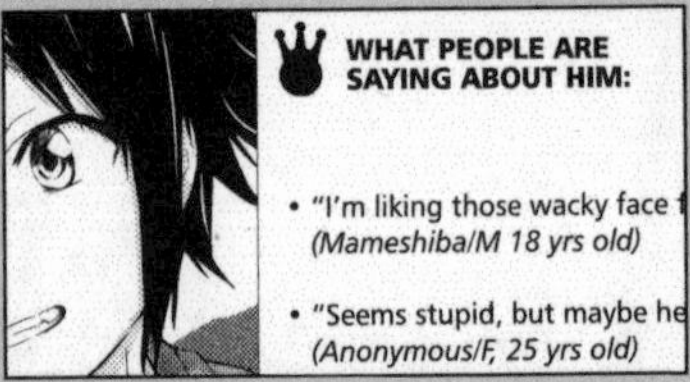
WHAT PEOPLE ARE SAYING ABOUT HIM:
• "I'm liking those wacky face
(Mameshiba/M 18 yrs old)
• "Seems stupid, but maybe he
(Anonymous/F, 25 yrs old)

MAMESHIBA

Mameshiba is a Japanese merchandising franchise that stars a family of beans with doglike characteristics. In Japanese *mame* means "bean" and *shiba* comes from the Shiba Inu breed of dog that is common in Japan. The Mameshiba franchise first debuted in 2008 and its commercials featured animations of a person who, as he or she was about to eat, would encounter one of these mameshiba in their food. The mameshiba would then speak to the person and give them a piece of trivia much to the bewilderment of the person. The trivia part of all this comes from a pun of the Japanese phrase *mamechishiki* which literally means "bean knowledge" but is typically translated as "trivia." Therefore, the joke is that the Mameshiba are trivia-spouting beans that look like dogs.

PAGE 165

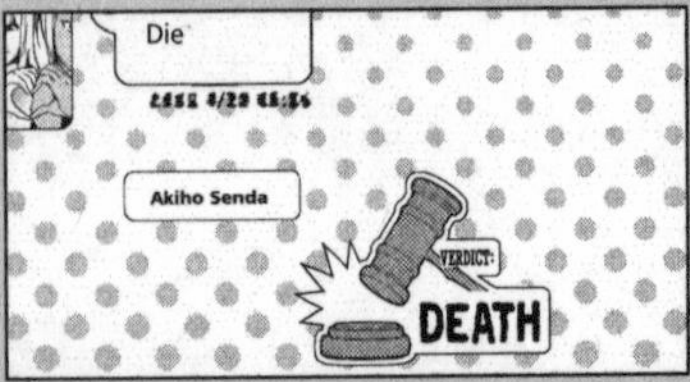
Die
Akiho Senda
VERDICT:
DEATH

LINE BULLYING AND CRIME

In Japan, Line is currently one of the most popular chat applications, but with its popularity comes many instances of abuse, crime, and bullying. Since becoming publicly available, there have been a number of cases where people have been harassed or bullied for "kidoku suruu" a term used to describe not replying to messages despite having seen or read them. This bullying has sometimes led to terrible things like suicide or murder. Line has also been used for various crimes, including prostitution. One of the most famous cases is the 2013 lynch-mob murder of a 16-year-old girl in Hiroshima. In this case, one 16-year-old girl, a 16-year-old boy, and 21-year-old man were charged with various crimes, including robbery, murder, confinement, and the abandonment of a corpse. All together, there were seven people involved in the murder, but the three other 16-year-old girls and additional 16-year-old boy were charged as accessories to the crimes and sent to juvenile detention. The motive for the murder stems from an argument over the distribution of profits for a prostitution ring conducted over Line by one of the 16-year-old girls.

PAGE 134

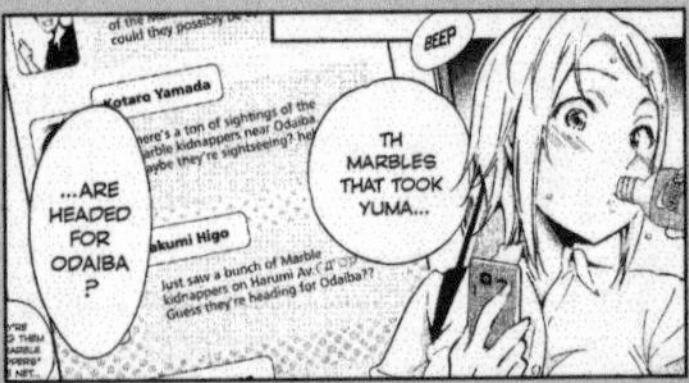
BEEP
TH MARBLES THAT TOOK YUMA...
...ARE HEADED FOR ODAIBA ?
Kotaro Yamada
Just saw a bunch of Marble kidnappers on Harumi Av.!
Guess they're heading for Odaiba??

ODAIBA

Odaiba is an artificial island in Tokyo Bay known as a popular residential and entertainment area, especially for couples out on a date. It is connected to Tokyo itself by the Rainbow Bridge, a large suspension bridge. Harumi Avenue stretches from the Imperial Palace in the center of Tokyo to an area a short distance from Odaiba.

PAGE 193

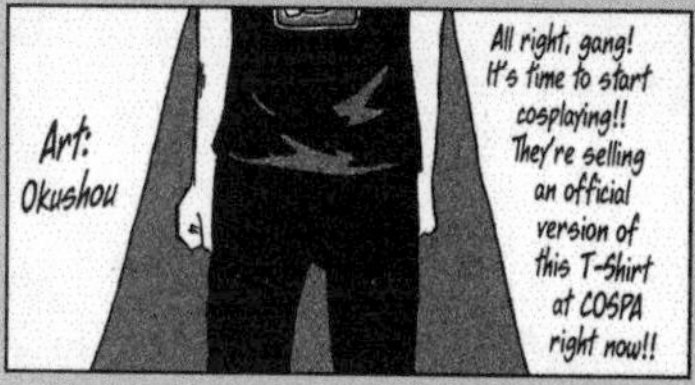
All right, gang! It's time to start cosplaying!! They're selling an official version of this T-Shirt at COSPA right now!!
Art: Okushou

COSPA
A famous Japanese apparel company. The name originates from an acronym for "Contents Communication Service Partner" and they are known for carrying cosplay costumes and officially branded clothing from various anime and manga.

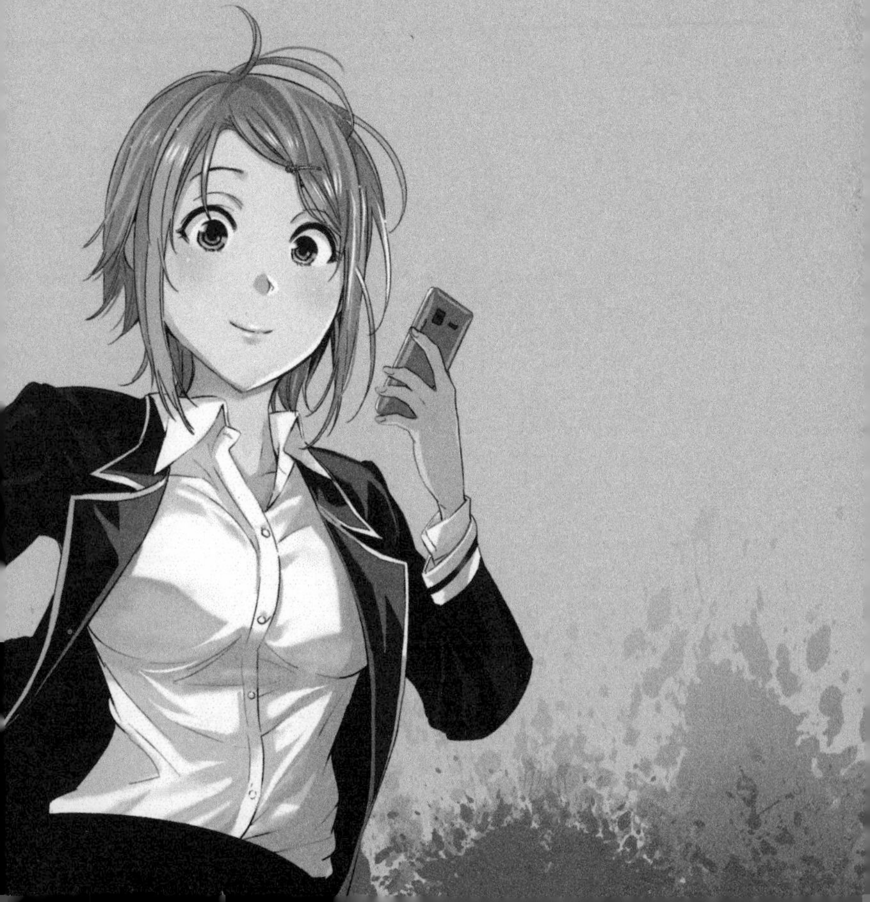

Fairy Tail takes place in a world filled with magic. 17-year-old Lucy is a wizard-in-training who wants to join a magic guild so that she can become a full-fledged wizard. She dreams of joining the most famous guild, known as Fairy Tail. One day she meets Natsu, a boy raised by a dragon which vanished when he was young. Natsu has devoted his life to finding his dragon father. When Natsu helps Lucy out of a tricky situation, she discovers that he is a member of Fairy Tail, and our heroes' adventure together begins.

FAIRY TAIL

MASTER'S EDITION

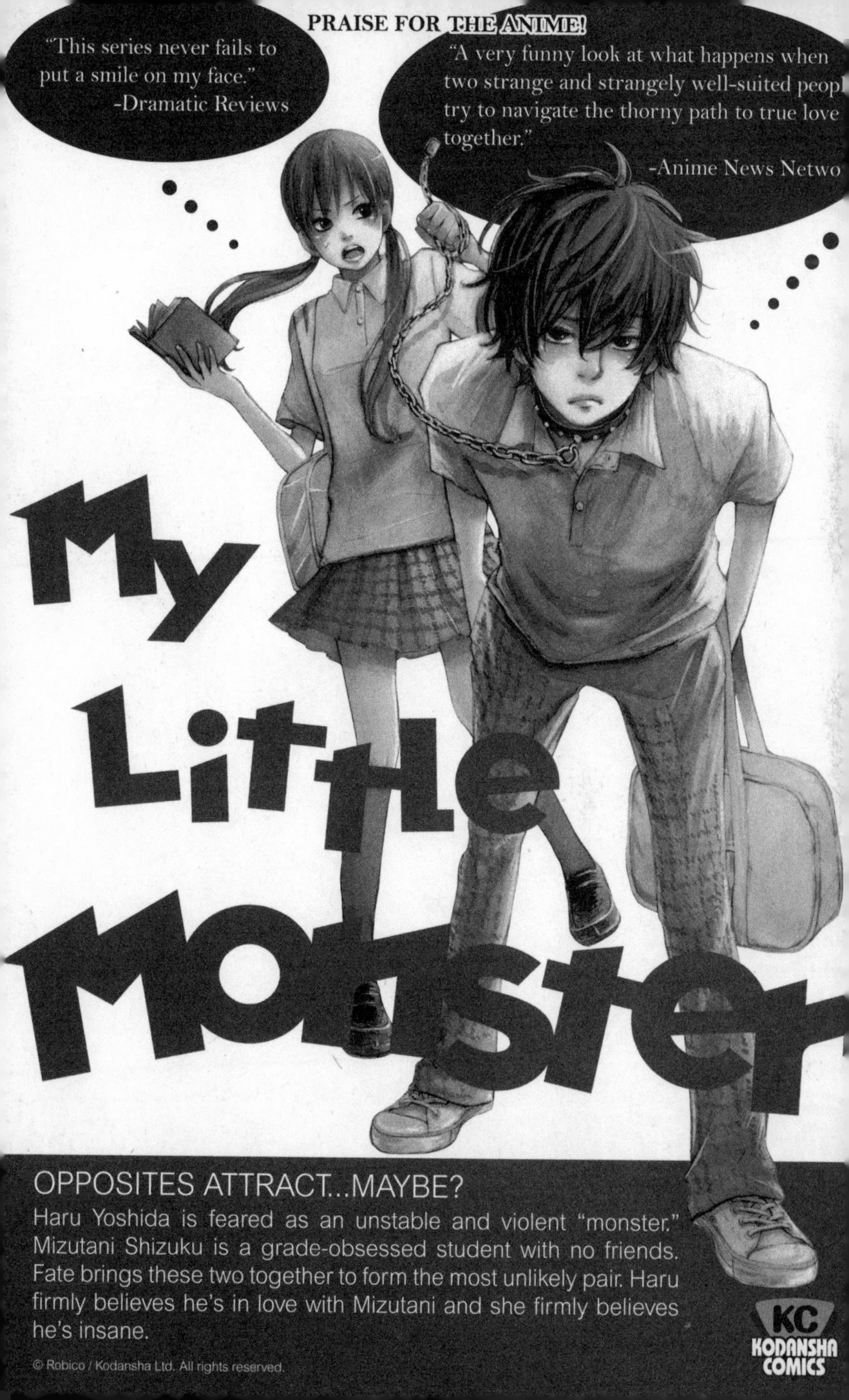
PRAISE FOR THE ANIME!
"This series never fails to put a smile on my face."
-Dramatic Reviews
"A very funny look at what happens when two strange and strangely well-suited peopl try to navigate the thorny path to true love together."
-Anime News Netwo
My Little Monster
OPPOSITES ATTRACT...MAYBE?
Haru Yoshida is feared as an unstable and violent "monster." Mizutani Shizuku is a grade-obsessed student with no friends. Fate brings these two together to form the most unlikely pair. Haru firmly believes he's in love with Mizutani and she firmly believes he's insane.
© Robico / Kodansha Ltd. All rights reserved.
KC
KODANSHA COMICS

Say I Love You.

KC
KODANSHA
COMICS

Mei Tachibana has no friends — and says she doesn't need them!

But everything changes when she accidentally roundhouse kicks the most popular boy in school! However, Yamato Kurosawa isn't angry in the slightest—in fact, he thinks his ordinary life could use an unusual girl like Mei. But winning Mei's trust will be a tough task. How long will she refuse to say, "I love you"?

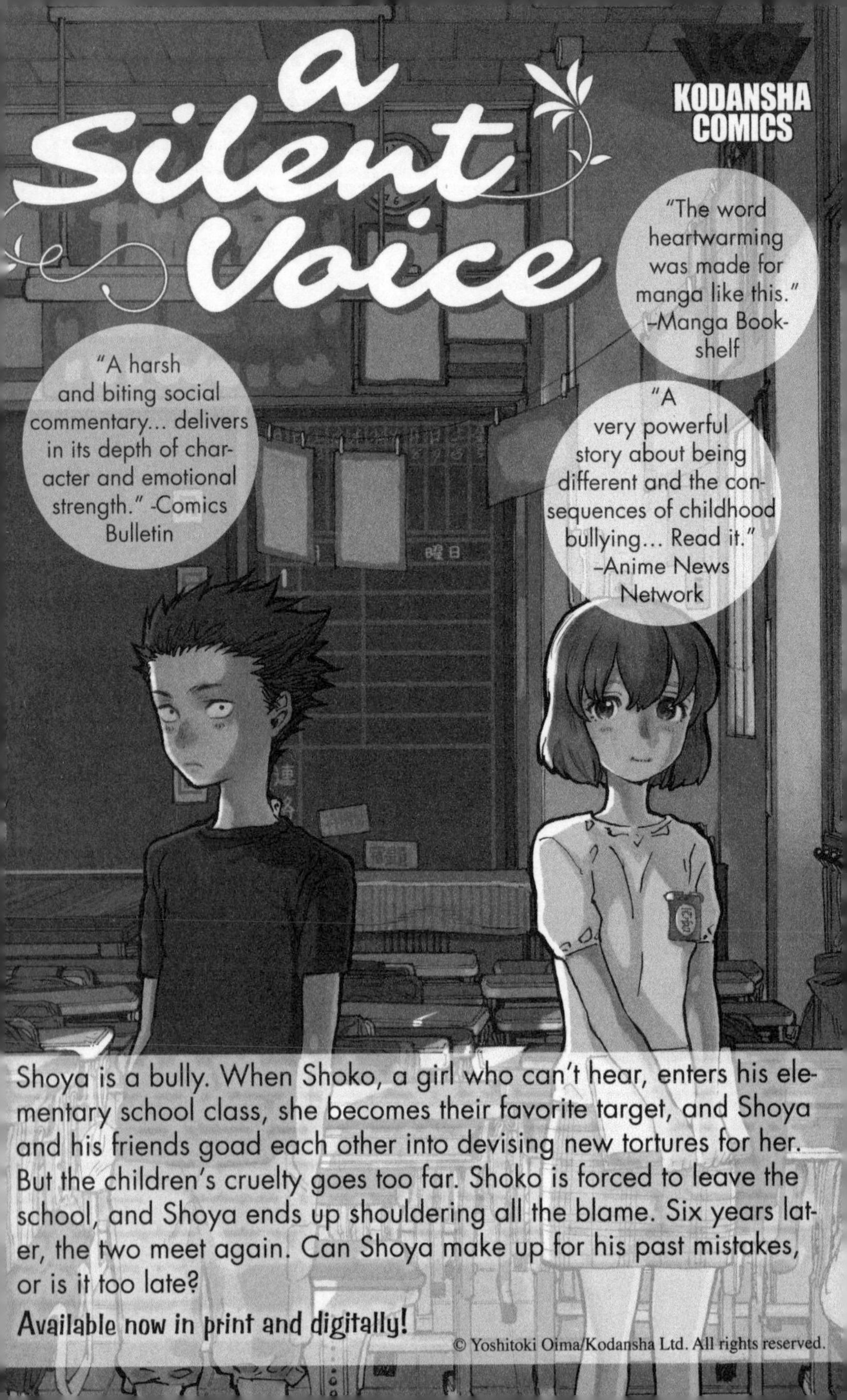
a Silent Voice
KODANSHA COMICS
"The word heartwarming was made for manga like this." –Manga Bookshelf
"A harsh and biting social commentary... delivers in its depth of character and emotional strength." -Comics Bulletin
"A very powerful story about being different and the consequences of childhood bullying... Read it." –Anime News Network
Shoya is a bully. When Shoko, a girl who can't hear, enters his elementary school class, she becomes their favorite target, and Shoya and his friends goad each other into devising new tortures for her. But the children's cruelty goes too far. Shoko is forced to leave the school, and Shoya ends up shouldering all the blame. Six years later, the two meet again. Can Shoya make up for his past mistakes, or is it too late?
Available now in print and digitally!
© Yoshitoki Oima/Kodansha Ltd. All rights reserved.

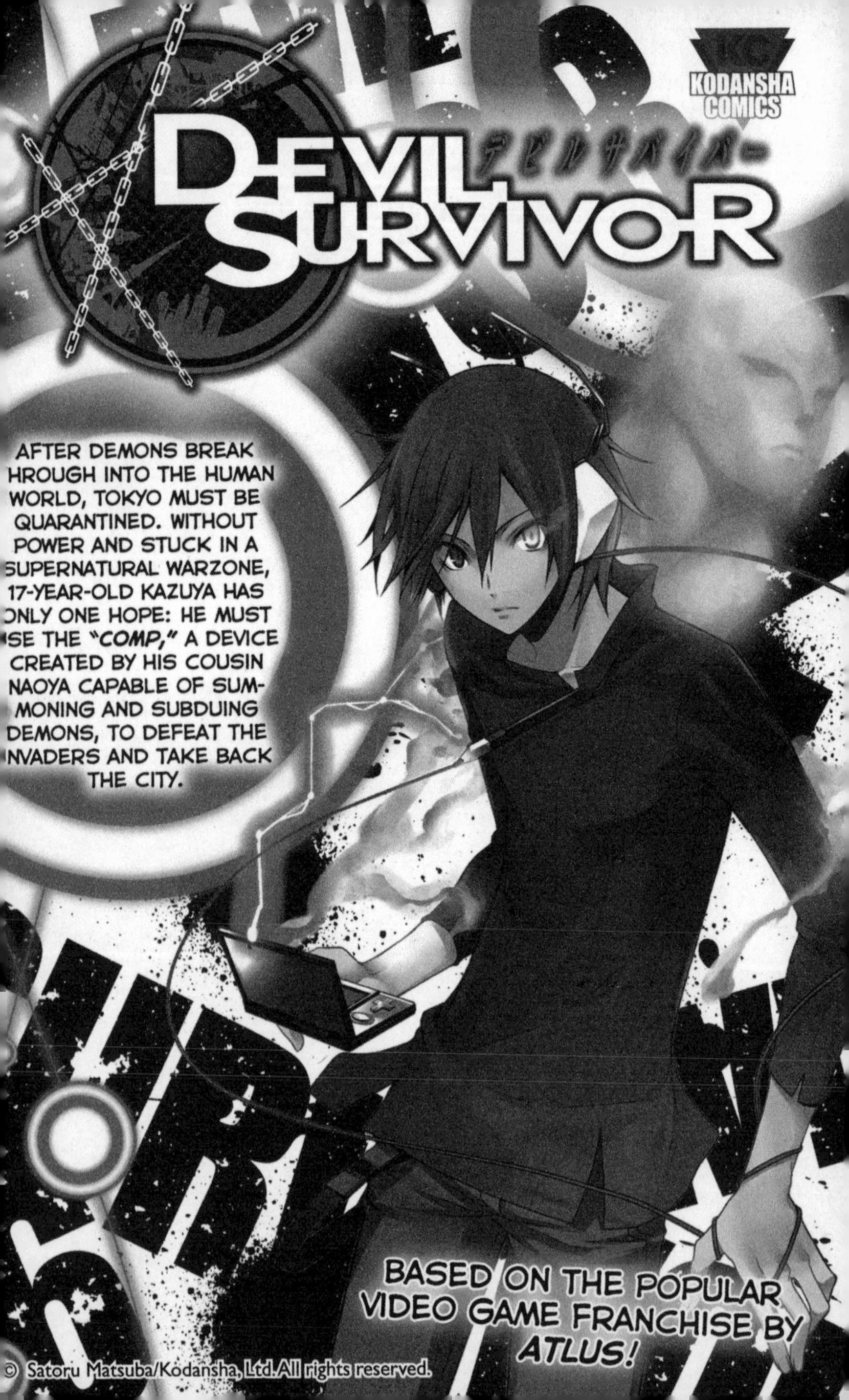
KODANSHA COMICS
DEVIL SURVIVOR
AFTER DEMONS BREAK HROUGH INTO THE HUMAN WORLD, TOKYO MUST BE QUARANTINED. WITHOUT POWER AND STUCK IN A SUPERNATURAL WARZONE, 17-YEAR-OLD KAZUYA HAS NLY ONE HOPE: HE MUST SE THE "COMP," A DEVICE CREATED BY HIS COUSIN NAOYA CAPABLE OF SUMMONING AND SUBDUING DEMONS, TO DEFEAT THE NVADERS AND TAKE BACK THE CITY.
BASED ON THE POPULAR VIDEO GAME FRANCHISE BY ATLUS!
© Satoru Matsuba/Kodansha, Ltd. All rights reserved.

INUYASHIKI

A superhero like none you've ever seen, from the creator of "Gantz"!

Ichiro Inuyashiki is down on his luck. He looks much older than his 58 years, his children despise him, and his wife thinks he's a useless coward. So when he's diagnosed with stomach cancer and given three months to live, it seems the only one who'll miss him is his dog.

Then a blinding light fills the sky, and the old man is killed… only to wake up later in a body he almost recognizes as his own. Can it be that Ichiro Inuyashiki is no longer human?

Comes in extra-large editions with color pages!

KODANSHA COMICS

Maria
THE VIRGIN WITCH

PURITY AND POWER

As a war to determine the rightful ruler of medieval France ravages the land, the witch Maria decides she will not stand idly by as men kill each other in the name of God and glory. Using her powerful magic, she summons various beasts and demons —even going as far as using a succubus to seduce soldiers into submission under the veil of night— all to stop the needless slaughter. However, after the Archangel Michael puts an end to her meddling, he curses her to lose her powers if she ever gives up her virginity. Will she forgo the forbidden fruit of adulthood in order to bring an end to the merciless machine of war?
Available now in print and digitally!

KC
KODANSHA
COMICS

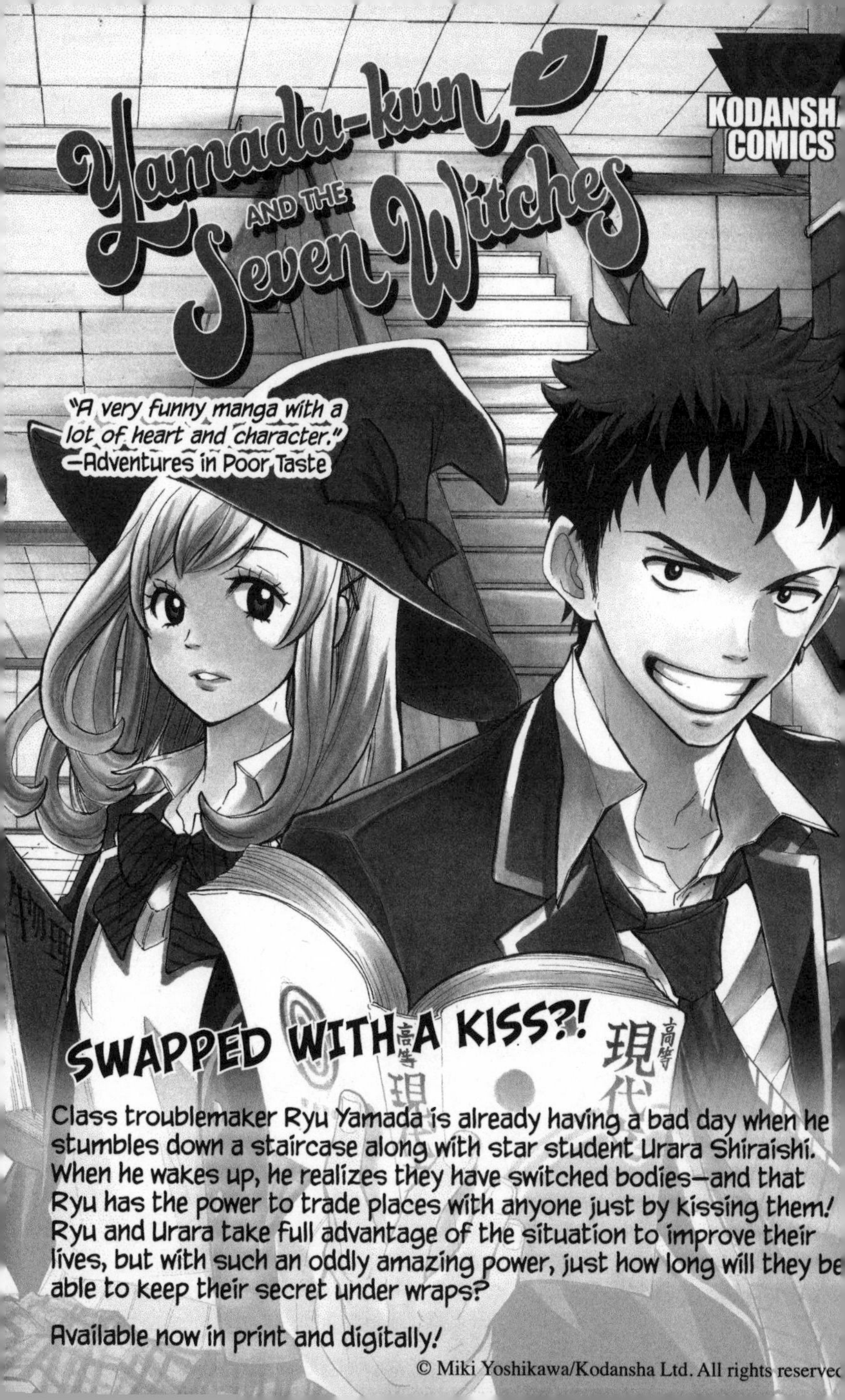
KODANSHA COMICS
Yamada-kun AND THE Seven Witches
"A very funny manga with a lot of heart and character."
—Adventures in Poor Taste
SWAPPED WITH A KISS?!
Class troublemaker Ryu Yamada is already having a bad day when he stumbles down a staircase along with star student Urara Shiraishi. When he wakes up, he realizes they have switched bodies—and that Ryu has the power to trade places with anyone just by kissing them! Ryu and Urara take full advantage of the situation to improve their lives, but with such an oddly amazing power, just how long will they be able to keep their secret under wraps?
Available now in print and digitally!
© Miki Yoshikawa/Kodansha Ltd. All rights reserved.

A Kodansha Comics Trade Paperback Original.

Real Account volume 4 copyright © 2015 Okushou/Shizumu Watanabe
English translation copyright © 2016 Okushou/Shizumu Watanabe

Published in the United States by Kodansha Comics,
an imprint of Kodansha USA Publishing, LLC, New York.

Publication rights for this English edition arranged through Kodansha Ltd.,
Tokyo.

First published in Japan in 2015 by Kodansha Ltd., Tokyo, as *Real
Account* volume 4.

ISBN 978-1-63236-237-7

Printed in the United States of America.

www.kodanshacomics.com

9 8 7 6 5 4 3 2 1

Translation: Kevin Gifford
Lettering: Evan Hayden
Editing: Ajani Oloye
Kodansha Comics edition cover design: Phil Balsman